Speaking, Reading, and Writing in Children With Language Learning Disabilities

New Paradigms in Research and Practice

Speaking, Reading, and Writing in Children With Language Learning Disabilities

New Paradigms in Research and Practice

Edited by

Katharine G. Butler
Elaine R. Silliman

LEA LAWRENCE ERLBAUM ASSOCIATES, PUBLISHERS
2002   Mahwah, New Jersey   London

Lawrence Erlbaum Associates, Inc., Publishers
10 Industrial Avenue
Mahwah, NJ 07430

Cover design by Kathryn Houghtaling Lacey

Library of Congress Cataloging-in-Publication Data

Speaking, reading, and writing in children with language learning
disabilities : new paradigms in research and practice / edited by
Katharine G. Butler, Elaine R. Silliman.
p. cm.
Includes bibliographical references and index.
ISBN 0-8058-3365-X (cloth : alk. paper)
ISBN 0-8058-3366-8 (pbk. : alk. paper)
1. Learning disabled children—Education—United States.
2. Language arts—United States. I. Butler, Katharine G.
II. Silliman, Elaine R.
LC4704.85 .S65 2002
371.9—dc21 2001040725
CIP

Books published by Lawrence Erlbaum Associates are printed on acid-
free paper, and their bindings are chosen for strength and durability.

Printed in the United States of America
10 9 8 7 6 5 4 3 2 1

To our spouses
Joe Butler   *Paul Silliman*
With them, nothing is impossible
Without them, nothing is possible

And to our grandchildren, who are the generational links
to the 21st century
Lilly, Mia,   *Lauren, Ryan, Julia,*
and Douglas   *Michael, and Jenna*

Contents

Preface

The 1990s produced a significant number of "evidence-based" accounts of research on literacy learning from a variety of sources. These sources included projects funded by the National Institute of Child Health and Human Development and the U.S. Department of Education, as well as basic and applied research studies conducted at universities in the United States, the United Kingdom, Western Europe, and Scandinavia, to name but a few. A major insight emerged from this massive investment in discovering the reasons why too many children develop difficulties with reading and writing. This broad-based research brought into sharp focus the essential role that oracy plays in reading and writing. Children's facility in explicitly managing the spoken language system—its sound structure, morphology, vocabulary, syntax, and discourse—for a wide variety of communicative purposes provides the oral language substrate onto which more literate language knowledge is constructed in both the spoken and print domains. Despite the torrent of evidence that disabilities in reading, writing, and spelling are primarily language-based, the translation of this research into everyday functional practices in-and-out of the classroom continues to move at a pace that, at best, can be described as tepid.

Speaking, Reading, and Writing in Children with Language Learning Disabilities was conceptualized many months ago following the convergence of separate, but related, events. In the late 1990s, the editors of this volume (Butler & Silliman) attended a national summit on research in learning disabilities in Washington, DC, one of the many summits being held by both governmental and association entities at that time. High-level conferences of this kind are designed to bring together researchers from a variety of disciplines. Nevertheless, noticeably absent were researchers whose work took them beyond phonological awareness and decoding to examine other spoken language–literacy relationships that might account for the literacy learning problems of so many students in our nation's schools.

To initiate a broadened dialogue about the language basis of learning disabilities, a transdisciplinary gathering, the West Coast Summit, was held in Monterey, California in December 1997. This conference was co-sponsored by The Center for Educational Research on Dyslexia, School of Education, San Jose State University through a grant from the Varian Family Foundation of Palo Alto, California and the Special Interest Division 1, Language Learning and Education, of the American Speech-Language Hearing Association (ASHA). Invitees to this 3-day conference were the presidents of a wide array of national associations, as well as researchers from public and private universities. National associations represented included: ASHA, the International Council for Exceptional Children (CEC; Division of Children's Communication Development and the Division of Learning Disabilities), the International Reading Association (IRA), the Learning Disabilities Association of America (LDA), the International Dyslexia Association (IDA), the International Society of Alternative and Augmentative Communication, the Association on Higher Education and Disability, and the National Association of School Psychologists. Many of these associations belong to the National Joint Committee on Learning Disabilities (NJCLD), a voluntary group that has been growing in size and importance since the 1970s.

Recommendations on oracy to literacy priorities for research, policy development, educational practice, and enhanced interdisciplinary collaboration were solicited from the attendees, who presided and presented on a number of presidential panels and small advisory focus groups. These recommendations were transmitted to the NJCLD and, of equal importance, were translated into an interdisciplinary core of topics for this volume. Readers will discover a meshing of perspectives on relationships between language and literacy learning in diverse children, new directions in clinical and educational practices grounded to classroom instruction, and current and emerging policy issues in special education and postsecondary education.

In completing a text that simultaneously serves as a 2002 status report and preview of what is to come, the Editors are indebted to many individuals. Foremost among these persons is Susan Milmoe of Lawrence Erlbaum Associates, who patiently and gently guided the editors and contributors through the book's completion. In addition, we are also grateful to our authors, dear colleagues who have been pivotal in this endeavor and retained their good humor despite the computer-based frenzy of writing, reviewing, editing, and re-reviewing literally thousands of manuscript pages. In terms of technical support, the considerable efforts of Lori Spurr and Steven Everling at the University of South Florida made possible the book's final completion.

The aim of this multidisciplinary volume is to offer an integrated perspective on the multiple factors involved in language and literacy learning

that must be considered in designing more effective instructional and intervention programs. Our anticipation is that readers will appreciate and benefit from the broader, language-based framework that motivated the
writing of this work.

—Katharine G. Butler
—Elaine R. Silliman

Part I

Perspectives On Language, Literacy, and Diversity

The Time Has Come to Talk
of Many Things

Elaine R. Silliman
University of South Florida

Katharine G. Butler
San Jose State University

Geraldine P. Wallach
California State University at Long Beach

"The Time Has Come to Talk of Many Things"

> *The time has come, the Walrus said,*
> *to talk of many things:*
> *Of shoes—and ships—and sealing wax—*
> *Of cabbages—and—kings—*
> *And why the sea is boiling hot—*
> *And whether pigs have wings*

—Lewis Carroll, 1832–1898 (1976, p. 186, stanza 11)

As Carroll figured out well over 100 years ago, and as readers of this volume will discover, time is of the essence. This is especially true when it comes to teaching all of America's children to be literate in the technological world of the 21st century, because all children, including those with disabilities, must now participate in the high-stakes assessment that states and school districts use to authenticate educational achievement. Standards-based educational reform efforts require that states and local school systems be held accountable for the learning of all children.

Federal legislation, including Goals 2000 of the Elementary and Secondary Education Act (ESEA) and the 1997 reauthorization of the Individuals with Disabilities Education Act (IDEA; see Osborne, chap. 13, this volume) require that all students participate in large-scale state and local assessment programs. The provision is that testing accommodations must be provided to those students with special needs who require such accommodations, including children with disabilities and those with limited English proficiency. For those children who are unable to take part in the general assessment, alternate assessments are proscribed (Thurlow, House, Scott, & Ysseldyke, 2000). Further, the performance of students on state and district assessments who receive special education and related services must now be separated from the scores of other students and reported publicly, as are the scores of students in general education. At the end of 1999, preliminary data from 12 states indicated that the majority of students in special education required accommodations for reading, writing, and math assessments (Thompson & Thurlow, 1999).

Also, during the 1990s, in combination with federal and state requirement for large-scale assessments, substantial amounts of state and federal dollars were invested to raise the academic achievement of children chronically struggling with literacy. In addition, the National Institutes of Health funded major research projects, as described in this volume, to achieve two purposes: One was directed to the identification of the cognitive and linguistic underpinnings of learning to read, and the other concerned in-depth study of evidence-based instructional practices that either prevented or ameliorated reading failure (Report of the National Reading Panel, 2000; Snow, Burns, & Griffin, 1998). As the new millenium begins, an important question is whether these efforts, grounded in standards-based educational reforms, resulted in positive changes in reading abilities across the diverse populations of American school children in general and special education.

OVER THE BRINK OF THE MILLENIUM:
THE STATE OF LITERACY LEARNING

Despite the concerted fiscal, research, and reform efforts of the 1990s, the 2000 National Assessment of Educational Progress (NAEP; National Center for Education Statistics [NCES], 2001) continues to paint a distressing portrait for grade 4 reading achievement for the children who are the primary focus of this volume. For example:

- 37% of all grade 4 students are reading below the basic level when a proficient level of achievement is the expected standard. Reading below a basic level means that not even partial mastery had been attained of the knowledge and skills essential for comprehending narrative and informational texts. Importantly, proficiency in reading comprehension is defined as students' ability to "demonstrate an overall understanding of the text, providing inferential as well as literal information ... drawing conclusions, and making connections to their own experience" (NCES, 2001, p. 14).

- 71% of Caucasian students and 78% of Asian American students read at or above the basic level, whereas 35% and 46% of these two groups, respectively, read at the proficient level.
- The reading performance for 63% of African American students and 58% of Hispanic students in grade 4 fell below the basic level. Moreover, 60% of those from poverty level homes and 47% of children attending inner city schools were reading below the basic level.
- Finally, 39% of students who required accommodations to take the NAEP (e.g., one-on-one testing, small group testing, extended time, or the oral reading of directions) performed below the basic level. Only 30% demonstrated basic knowledge and skills for reading comprehension.

Two cautions are warranted in interpreting these data (NCES, 2001). First, population comparisons found to be statistically significant, such as the selected comparisons for race, ethnicity, or both, cannot be interpreted as statements about the absolute practical significance, or educational relevance, of the differences among these subgroups. Instead, the NCES urges that findings on subgroup differences should be used to inform and extend meaningful dialogue among the many members of the educational constituency, from policy makers to educators and the public, about the scope of the problem and its possible solutions. Second, causal inferences cannot be made to how reading is taught in public schools because of the host of sociocultural and socioeconomic (SES) factors that are outside of teachers' control. These external factors also influence all aspects of learning to be literate. However, in regard to SES variables, recent longitudinal findings on home-school links between language and literacy development (Tabors, Snow, & Dickinson, 2001) showed that excellent pre-school experiences in language and literacy learning can counteract home experiences that "offer well below average access to language and literacy support" (p. 326).

Given these two qualifications, the 2000 report card shows a widening of the gap in reading abilities. Good readers improved their scores, whereas poor readers fell further behind. But there are other gaps that contribute in significant ways to the failure to meet adequately the literacy needs of all children. Among these gaps are the disciplinary and professional schisms that continue to exist among researchers and professionals, who, by virtue of their diverse training and interests, hold different views on, or have different levels of understanding about, the central role of language in learning. One outcome is the translation of these divergent views into practices that are often incompatible with conceptual frameworks and evidence about relationships between the multiple dimensions of language and literacy learning. As Lewis Carroll voiced through the Walrus, the time has come to talk across disciplines and professions, as this volume seeks to do, about the overarching importance of language in the educational lives of children. The central thesis of this text is that human communication underlies the ability to benefit from spoken and written discourse.

THE CENTRAL ROLE OF LANGUAGE
IN LITERACY LEARNING

Language is a tool for analyzing, synthesizing, and integrating what is heard or read in order to construct and express new interpretations. Early on, Halliday (1987) noted the absence of attention to spoken language processes in children's literacy:

> [Educational] investigators of the fifties and early sixties were not concerned with the particular place of spoken language in the learning process. It was assumed that students learnt by listening, but the expository aspects of teacher's language were given little attention, while the notion that a student might be using his own talk as a means of learning was nowhere part of the picture. (Halliday, 1987, pp. 55–56)

Unlike the picture that Halliday painted of earlier decades, a significant number of disciplines are now engaged in the study of language. These disciplines include, among others, education, developmental psychology, the neurosciences, bilingual language learning, linguistics (including psycholinguistics), language science (specifically, speech–language pathology), and special education (particularly learning disabilities). Each discipline or specialty approaches the study of language from its own perspective, which makes for enlivening commentary and, occasionally, valuable new insights.

One of the critical insights that emerged from the research conducted during the late 1980s and the 1990s, is the crucial role of phonological sensitivity and phonological processing in children's ability to master the alphabetic principle and develop automatic and fluent word recognition and spelling skills. *Phonological sensitivity* generally refers to the ability to consider the units of phonological structure at increasingly deeper levels of analysis, from the syllable level to the segmental (phonemic) level (Gottardo, Stanovich, & Siegel, 1996). *Phonological processing* pertains to those information processing capacities that are recruited by various tasks and require some level of more explicit analysis, such as segmentation, blending, or sound deletion (phonological awareness), the repetition of nonwords (phonological memory), or rapid naming (phonological retrieval). Letter name knowledge, knowledge of letter-sound names, and well-integrated phonemic awareness (sound-letter correspondences) are now well documented as the strongest kindergarten predictors of how adequately children will learn to read and spell in grade 1 (Report of the National Reading Panel, 2000; Snow et al., 1998). Phonological retrieval, as assessed by rapid naming tasks, may contribute more to individual differences in reading fluency at grade 4 rather than index the speed of accessing the segmental level in earlier grades (Torgesen et al., 2001).[1]

As shown in Fig. 1.1, contemporary models of reading disability from both the neuroscience and psychoeducational literature share the unitary view that a phonological core deficit is a primary cause of reading failure (e.g., Lyon, 1999; Scanlon & Vellutino, 1996, 1997; Shaywitz et al., 1996; Stanovich, 2000; Torgesen et al., 2001; Torgesen & Wagner, 1998; Torgesen, Wagner, & Rashotte, 1994; see Keogh, chap. 2, this volume, for a summary of these studies).

This view has also been described as a causal chain model (Scarborough, in press). Because the phonological route to recognize word meaning is not utilized efficiently, children do not have access to the meaning of print words, a situation that also affects their memory for spellings (Ehri, 2000). Subsequent problems with text comprehension and related consequences, such as the development of more literate vocabulary and syntactic constructions that are facilitated through reading, are then attributed to breakdowns at the level of phonological processing (Gottardo et al., 1996). Because of the strength and stability of this scientific evidence, new avenues have opened for the early identification of risk factors and the prevention, or reduction in the severity, of reading failure. Moreover, the current cross-disciplinary consensus is that the phonological core deficit represents a language-related impairment.

In spite of this basic consensus, a significant disparity exists among disciplines and their associated professions in the scope and meaning of "language-related." This discrepancy has enormous significance for the conduct of research, as well as for the implementation of instructional programs for struggling readers as a group, regardless of whether these readers receive general education, special education, or related services. Two perplexing questions are unresolved. One concerns whether the spoken language basis of the "critical component skills" (Lyon & Moats, 1997, p. 579) that comprise word recognition skills and that have been implicated in the failure to read and spell as the phonological core deficit is a first-order cause, or do other language subsystems make significant contributions to the picture of a phonological core deficit? The second question pertains to

---

[1]Of some interest, skilled adult readers whose word recognition is automatic and fluent no longer appear to retain the same level of phonological sensitivity. One reason for this reduction in sensitivity is related to the fact that orthographic strategies increasingly become the primary medium for representing words (Scarborough, Ehri, Olson, & Fowler, 1998).

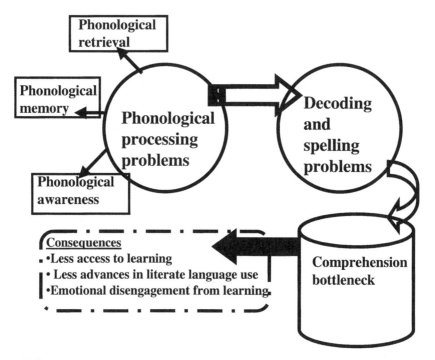

FIG. 1.1.   Unitary perspective: Unidirectional causality and related consequences.

the "fuzzy boundary" issue (Rumsey, 1996). Are a language disability and a
learning (reading) disability two sides of the same coin? Or do they represent separate and distinct conditions, which may co-occur, but are not identical (Lyon, 1996)? The fuzzy boundary issue is not trivial because the
recognition of a boundary has been codified in IDEA for over 25 years.

A language impairment and a learning disability are defined as two separate categories of disabilities. At the school level, this separation has resulted in the fragmentation of services for the very children who most need
instructional and related services that are coherent, integrated, and coordinated (Snow, Scarborough, & Burns, 1999). At the research level, dissimilar
disciplinary interests in the domains that influence literacy development,
such as "cognition, culture, socialization, instruction, and language" (Snow
et al., 1999, p. 49), have motivated a diverse set of research questions on the
causes and consequences of reading disabilities. An outcome of this extensive gap in research foci is a disconnection between what is known about
aspects of spoken language development, including atypical language de-

velopment, and how these same aspects may support or interfere with learning to read, write, and spell proficiently.

Bridging the Fuzzy Boundary Gap

On the surface, the notion that spoken and written language development and disabilities form a reciprocal relationship seems less a matter of speculation today than it was 10 years ago. To say that reading and writing are language-related skills (American Speech–Language-Hearing Association [ASHA], 2001a; Kamhi & Catts, 1999; van Kleeck, 1998) or that early language disorders become school-age learning and reading disabilities, as Bashir and colleagues (Bashir, Kuban, Kleinman, & Scavuzzo, 1984) speculated earlier, is to express concepts that drive aspects of current thinking in speech–language pathology. However, although it may seem obvious in practice to state that children with language disabilities, reading disabilities, and learning disabilities may not be children from distinct populations (Wallach & Butler, 1994), the evidence to date suggests caution in drawing this conclusion for two reasons.

First, apart from the extensive neuroscience and psychoeducational studies that have been conducted on phonological processing, other language-related abilities have not received sufficient empirical support for their contributions as primary risk factors in the failure to read and spell. However, a reason for equivocal findings on other language systems and processes may be due to the conceptual narrowness with which language is defined and assessed. Language systems are typically defined in terms of structural forms, which usually refer to the phonological, morphological, and syntactic systems (e.g., Moats, 2000; Moats & Lyon, 1996). Processes underlying spoken language comprehension, when addressed, are also evaluated narrowly, often with highly specific metalinguistic tasks that involve the existence of some level of syntactic awareness. Examples include measures of sentence grammaticality and sentence correction (Gottardo et al., 1996; Vellutino et al., 1996), both of which require mental comparisons of morphosyntactic structures (Vellutino et al; 1996; Vellutino, Scanlon, & Lyon, 2000; Vellutino, Scanlon, & Tanzman, 1994). Performance on these kinds of judgment tasks may be highly influenced by at least five variables that seldom have been considered in phonological processing studies. These factors include: (a) the amount and nature of practice that children are given, (b) the manner of verifying that children understand task requirements, (c) the method of elicitation, (d) the materials used, and (e) the extent of sentence parsing complexity that children must engage in to make a correct judgment (McDaniel & Cairns, 1996).

It should be pointed out that results from phonological processing studies do not deny the importance of these other language-related abilities in differentiating good readers from poor readers in kindergarten and grade 1. However, the predictive power of other measures, such as grammaticality judgments, is considerably less than is the predictive power of phonological processing skills, perhaps due to the lack of discriminative validity of the syntactic measures selected (Scarborough, 1991).

Catts, Fey, Zhang, & Tomblin (1999) crystallized the second issue. Most of the neuroscience and psychoeducational studies that argue for the phonological core deficit model of reading disabilities (e.g., Stanovich, 2000) have not included children with a full range of language abilities in proportion to the larger population of school-age children. A related methodological issue is that inclusion criteria for these studies often exclude children with reported histories of speech or language difficulties (e.g., Gottardo et al., 1996) or exclude those children whose IQs are below a standard score of 80 to 85. Catts et al. (1999) pointed out that IQ tests are highly correlated with verbal abilities, which may eliminate those children whose more severe language impairments place them most at risk for reading disabilities. A possible result of this exclusion is to reduce the variability between good and poor readers in other language-related abilities. Thus, the important question is not whether IQ should be an inclusion factor for sample selection, but the extent to which IQ becomes a significant predictor variable following collection of the data.

More data are now available from cross-sectional and longitudinal studies in communication sciences and disorders that provide potential insights into the nature of the language differences that may exist between children who are primarily language learning impaired and those whose primary problem is a pure reading disability. These studies tend to share a distributed causality perspective, as displayed in Fig. 1.2 in contrast to the unitary concept underlying the phonological core deficit model.

Cross-Sectional Studies.   In terms of more advanced vocabulary processes, derivational morphology appears to hold promise as an area that may potentially illuminate the fuzzy boundaries between aspects of a spoken language impairment and reading problems. Derivational morphology entails spelling–meaning relationships, rather than phoneme–meaning relationships (Bear, Invernizzi, Templeton, & Johnston, 2000; Nagy & Scott, 2000), and is intimately tied to new vocabulary learning beginning in grade 3 when children are expected to use reading and writing as major vehicles to learn and express new information (Anglin, 1993). Knowledge of root and affix forms allows children to work through the meanings of less familiar words that they hear, read, or spell and requires the ability to analyze the nature of changes in either pronunciation (phonology, including stress patterns and vowels), spelling (orthography), or both pronunciation and spelling. Examples of these translations might

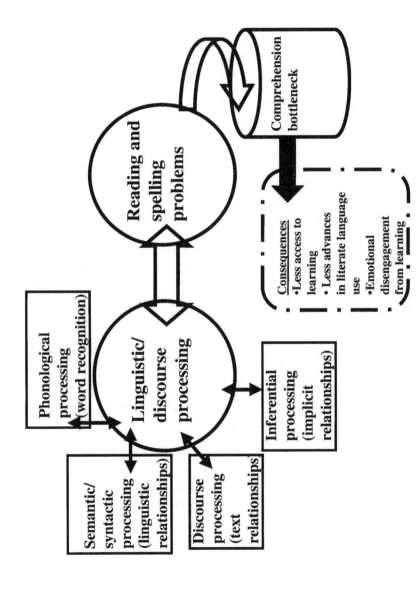

FIG. 1.2. Interactive perspective: Distributed causality and related consequences.

be: (a) no change in pronunciation or spelling (warm to warmth), (b) spelling change (begin–beginner), (c) change in pronunciation (equal–equality) and (d) changes in both spelling and pronunciation (decide–decision) (Carlisle, 1988).

In a study that refined Carlisle's (1987, 1988, 1995) framework, Windsor (2000) found that 10 to 12½-year-old children diagnosed with reading disabilities but who also scored below 1 standard deviation on a standardized measure of spoken language ability had significant problems with the accuracy of low-frequency derived forms presented orally. Specifically, decreased accuracy occurred when the derivation resulted from phonological changes. These children were significantly less accurate compared to same age peers, performing more similarly to children 2 years younger matched in terms of language age. Not surprisingly, performance on the oral derivation task also served as a predictor variable of both word recognition and passage comprehension.

Another promising avenue for investigating the overlap or distinctness of reading and language disabilities is the use of oral-writing contrasts within the same group of children. Two related studies (Scott & Windsor, 2000; Windsor, Scott, & Street, 2000), which are elaborated on in this volume (see Scott, chap. 9), examined the morphosyntactic complexity of narrative and expository discourse in the spoken versus written samples of 10-to-12½-year-old children who met the previous criteria in Windsor (2000) for both learning and language disabilities. Children were again matched with same-age and language-age peers. In the first study, 10 general language performance measures were compared for group, discourse genre, and modality (Scott & Windsor, 2000). Only the frequency of morphosyntactic errors per Terminable unit (T unit), a unit based on the clause, for the written narrative and expository summaries differentiated the children with language learning disabilities from both their chronologically age-matched and language-matched peers.

In the second study (Windsor et al., 2000), the most distinctive morphosyntactic violation that distinguished the group with language learning difficulties from the two other groups occurred only in the written discourse samples, particularly in the expository sample. This violation involved verb morphology, in this case selective omission of the regular past tense inflectional marker -ed, for example, "Paul and John walk (walked) home from school" and "He laugh (laughed) hard at the joke." (See Silliman, Bahr, Turner, & Wilkinson, chap. 5, this volume, for cautions regarding identical morphosyntactic patterns in children with dialect variations.) In writing, but less so in speaking, the consistent pattern of the preadolescents with language learning disabilities was omission of this past tense marker, "rather than misapplication of -ed to present tense contexts" (Windsor et al., 2000, p. 1331), a pattern that distinctly differed from younger typically developing children. This pattern suggests that, in preadolescence, the planning and organizational demands of writing, including the coordination of writing with spelling, may uncover persisting problems with clusters of less well-specified morphosyntactic representations that are not as evident as they are in the spoken language samples of younger children with specific language impairment (e.g., see Rice, 1999; Rice, Cleave, & Oetting, 2000).

Longitudinal Studies.   One important trend from longitudinal language research is that preschool language impairment, typically assessed in the semantic/syntactic and expressive phonology domains, remains associated with reading and spelling problems into at least late adolescence (Stothard, Snowling, Bishop, Chipchase, & Kaplan, 1998). Another strand of longitudinal language research has provided more direct information on the relationship between language disabilities and reading problems (Catts et al., 1999). A well-drawn sample identified in kindergarten before reading difficulties emerged has been followed through grade 4. Findings indicate that the percentage of those with a pure reading disability remains small in comparison to those with language learning disabilities who also have reading problems (for further discussion, see Kamhi & Catts, chap. 10, this volume). Those with a language learning disability evidence a broad spectrum of spoken language processing and production difficulties, not just problems with phonological processing.

There is increasing awareness across disciplines, which is particularly apparent in recent research on spelling (Apel & Masterson, 2001; Bourassa & Treiman, 2001; Ehri, 2000; Treiman, 1998a, 1998b; Treiman & Bourassa, 2000), that it is necessary to acknowledge the multilayered, dynamic, and reciprocal nature of the relationship between spoken and written language development and disorders. One issue for unraveling the complexity of this relationship is that causes are difficult to distinguish from consequences (Catts & Kamhi, 1999). In both the unitary and distributed causality models, the consequences are similar. Children with reading, writing, and spelling problems encounter reduced access to meaningful learning, which then limits the extent to which they can benefit from literacy activities as a means for advancing their own language knowledge. As a consequence, they have less experience with literate forms and functions, from vocabulary to text structures to the many and varied types of inferencing that characterize proficient reading comprehension (ASHA, 2001a; see Westby, chap. 4, this volume, for discussion of inferencing). When children are continuously confronted with failure as competent learners and communicators, they have reduced motivation to learn, which then leads to further cycles of failure and reduced self-esteem. An outcome for too many, which can begin as early as grade 4, is emotional disengagement from schooling and formal dropping out in high school (National Research Council, 1999). In comparison, children who demonstrate achievement early in their school careers have the foundation to capitalize on their educational experiences because success promotes engagement and the motivation to learn (Silliman & Diehl, in press; Stanovich, 2000; Wilkinson & Silliman, 2000).

A second issue pertains to the fuzzy boundary question. In the cross-sectional studies that found similar patterns of difficulty in older children with both language and learning disabilities, it becomes difficult to dissemble whether problems with derivations, which involve phonological change in the root form, or the omission of the past tense marker -ed in writing might stem from one of four possibilities. These include (a) less well-specified phonological representations (Stanovich, 2000; Torgesen et al., 2001), (b) broader information processing constraints (Miller, Kail, Leonard, & Tomblin, 2001; Windsor, Milbrath, Carney, & Rakowski, 2001), (c) variations in the quality of literacy instruction (Lyon & Moats, 1997), or (d) a combination of all three variables that make unique contributions to profiles of difficulty in the spoken and print domains. Furthermore, the cross-sectional studies included children already identified with word recognition and text comprehension problems; thus, the chronic effects of reading, writing, and spelling difficulties on other language domains becomes hard to untangle. Longitudinal research designs, such as Catts et al. (1999), offer the possibility to address more fully the fuzzy boundary question because children are identified with language learning problems prior to intensive reading instruction.

An Alternate View.   Related to the resolution of the fuzzy boundary issue, Scarborough (2001) urges that future longitudinal research should also rethink how changes over time in the patterns of language and reading impairment are measured. Both the unitary and distributed causality models currently tend to approach change as linear or cumulative advances when real development change proceeds continuously as a spiral, in spurts followed by plateaus.

For example, the often observed phenomenon that some children with preschool language delays appear to "catch up" only to have new symptoms emerge during the elementary years, which are now identified as a learning disability, has been called illusory recovery (Bashir et al., 1984; Leonard, 1998). This deceptive recovery may be one of the main reasons for the boundaries that have been built between a language and a learning disability. Scarborough (2001) posits that illusory recovery can be explained by the *ascendency hypothesis.* In this model, growth is viewed as nonlinear. Developmental differences will be most apparent between individual children when typically developing children are reaching a post-spurt plateau in particular language or reading skills and slower developing children are just beginning a spurt ("a catch-up phase"). Milder language delays will be manifested as lags in a particular domain, such as vocabulary knowledge, reflected in a smaller quantitative gap in development between typically developing children and those with a vocabulary delay. More severe language problems, including reading problems, will be characterized by persisting problems across multiple domains with a larger developmental gap appearing. According to Scarborough (2001), over time, a single underlying language impairment will be expressed differently, not as subtypes, but in degrees of severity depending on the domain being assessed and the method of assessment. The measurement challenge, therefore, is to employ tools of assessment capable of discerning individual differences when the skill of interest is ascending, not when it has plateaued (the "illusionary recovery" phase). Dynamic assessment methods, which are premised on concepts of scaffolded instruction, assess children's responsiveness to the construction of new understandings in a teaching situation (for elaboration, see Stone, chap. 7, this volume) and offer a means for determining children's potential to learn in a particular domain. If the "potential to learn with support" corresponds with the Scarborough (2001) notion of ascending skill, then dynamic assessment approaches may be valuable tools to employ in future longitudinal studies on the continuously evolving patterns of language development and reading disabilities.

Bridging the Research to Practice Gap

In the real world of schools, as the recent national assessment of grade 4 reading comprehension documents (NCES, 2001), the path toward literacy remains ill understood. For example, it is still unknown how decoding, or word recognition, skill specifically relates to reading comprehension (Report of the National Reading Panel, 2000). Because the path is not homogeneous for every child, a costly consequence is that services to both younger and older students from the preschool to postsecondary years tend to only partially address students' academic and social needs (see Donahue, chap. 10, and Prelock, chap. 11, this volume, for interactions between the social and academic domains). An often-cited reason for this reduced enlightenment is the quality of professional preparation in the language basis of literacy for teachers and speech language pathologists.

Preparation of Teachers in the Language Basis of Literacy.   In view of the strong empirical findings on connections between skills in phonological processing and mastery of the alphabetic principle, teacher education has been criticized on two grounds. One criticism is directed to the inadequate incorporation of these research findings into the undergraduate preparation of prospective teachers, as well as the inservice knowledge of experienced teachers.

Lyon (1999) and Moats (1999) argued that translation of the scientific research into relevant classroom practices would prepare teachers to select assessment and instruction protocols that would identify and reduce the number of children at risk for failure as readers, writers, and spellers. Moreover, it appears that few teachers in either general or special education systematically and explicitly integrate text comprehension strategies into children's literacy experiences despite the positive scientific evidence for their use (Pressley, 2000a; Report of the National Reading Panel, 2000; Vaughn, Gersten, & Chard, 2000). These include strategies for comprehension monitoring, organizing and connecting information, question answering, question generation, and summarization (see Blank, chap. 6, this volume). Similar concerns have been expressed about the need to incorporate explicit strategy instruction into text composition, beginning in kindergarten (see Graham & Harris, chap. 8, this volume, for discussion of explicit strategy instruction).

A second criticism is the failure of the teacher education curriculum, including special education preparation, to include sufficient academic experience with the components of language structure (phonology, morphology, and syntax) and content (semantics) (Moats, 2000; Pressley, 2000b). For example, Moats and Lyon (1996) cited the lack of a requirement for language study as a major factor responsible for the inadequate preparation of reading and learning disabilities specialists to teach reading, writing, and spelling. Scarborough et al. (1998) found that, in a sample of 46 well-educated adults enrolled in teacher education courses at two private colleges, only 28% could accurately map sound–letter correspondences. This low accuracy rate transpired despite the explicit instructions to "Determine which letter or letters correspond to sounds in the words" (Scarborough et al., 1998, p. 130). An outcome of insufficient professional preparation in language analysis is "insufficiently developed concepts about language and pervasive conceptual weaknesses in the very skills that are needed for direct, systematic, language-focused reading instruction, such as the ability to count phonemes and to identify phonic relationships" (Moats & Lyon, 1996, p. 79). An additional need is to support teachers in learning how to interpret errors in reading and spelling that indicate the level of analysis a particular child is using, such as the whole word, syllabic, onset-rime, or phonemic level (Scarborough et al., 1998). Moreover, for students to benefit appropriately from technology to support their literacy learning, such as computer-assisted instruction, teachers will need to understand the linkages among spoken language development, word recognition, and text comprehension (for discussion of technology, see Masterson, Apel, & Wood, chap. 12, this volume). Beyond these content knowledge needs for the more effective teaching of reading, a larger issue not yet resolved is how to restructure teacher education so that reading teachers are better prepared to manage the complexities and diversity of American classrooms (Anders, Hoffman, & Duffy, 2000).

Preparation of Speech-Language Pathologists in the Language Basis of Literacy. As Moats and Lyon (1996) noted, the undergraduate and graduate level preparation of speech language pathologists requires study of the components of spoken language. However, knowledge of the spoken language system does not readily translate into meaningful literacy assessment and intervention without equivalent knowledge of the language-based nature of the many forms of literacy. Two obstacles have contributed to less than full participation of speech language pathologists in literacy instruction.

One barrier for the development of more collaborative approaches to classroom-based services in language and literacy has been the long-standing confusion about the roles of speech-language pathologists in literacy instruction. The psychoeducational literature has seldom addressed this topic, but there is some acknowledgment that speech language pathologists have the professional qualifications for involvement in three areas, all of which are limited to the spoken language domain. These areas include:

- Administering diagnostic assessments of "reading-related language skills" (Snow et al., 1999, p. 56).
- Conducting language therapy for students with "language-based learning disorders" (Moats & Lyon, 1996, p. 83) that targets oral language skills germane for reading success, such as phoneme awareness, vocabulary development, and inflectional and morphological markers (Snow et al., 1999).
- Coordinating services with the classroom teacher and parents of children with speech and language problems who, as grade level demands increase, are at continued risk for problems with reading fluency and text comprehension (Moats & Lyon, 1996; Snow et al., 1999).

The position expressed is that, beyond these three areas, speech-language pathologists typically will not be responsible for basic reading instruction for children with either a language or a learning disability because this is the professional responsibility of the classroom teacher.

However, even when the service format in theory is one of collaborative teamwork, Giangreco (2000), from the perspective of a special educator, cautions that the clinical competencies of speech language pathologists, or the educational competencies of teachers, are not sufficient to ensure positive educational and social outcomes for individual students. Instead, beyond professional credentials, Giangreco makes the case that a clear team process for decision making must be in place. At a minimum, this process should include three components:

1. Developing a shared set of educational goals, which must incorporate the content areas of the general education curriculum in accord with the 1997 reauthorization of IDEA and be consistent with the educational standards and benchmarks established at the state and district levels (Silliman & Diehl, in press).

2. Team members accepting that "in some cases, people from other disciplines might be more necessary in the implementation of services than people from their own discipline" (Giangreco, 2000, p. 235). This acceptance might include the speech-language pathologist embedding language-related literacy activities into typical instructional activities, which the classroom teacher then implements, or the use of small group co-teaching practices, which the teacher and speech-language pathologist jointly implement in the classroom (Silliman, Ford, Beasman, & Evans, 1999).

3. Creating and maintaining a high level of involvement of family members and the general education teacher in order to problem solve the kind of specialist knowledge that might be most necessary at various points in time. As Giangreco (2000) pointed out, families and teachers have their own specialized knowledge about the children in their care, which, if utilized in meaningful ways, significantly contributes to the design of more appropriate classroom experiences and supports.

Ehren (2000) expressed a second barrier to the more intensive participation of speech language pathologists in literacy instruction. The concern is that, in assuming greater classroom responsibilities, their specific area of expertise in oral language will be lost. This attitude, if pervasive, may be a product of inadequate professional preparation in the language basis of literacy. The roles and responsibilities of speech-language pathologists in literacy learning for diverse groups of children, including those with language learning disabilities, has recently been delineated (ASHA, 2001a, 2001b). To some extent, this expanded position simultaneously agrees with and challenges prevailing views of other disciplines (e.g., Moats & Lyon, 1996; Snow et al., 1999). Consistent with the theme of this volume, two premises motivate an expanded concept of involvement, both of which require more immersion in academic and clinical preparation for prospective, and practicing, speech-language pathologists. First, reciprocal relationships exist for the effects of instruction in spoken language domains and their outcomes for promoting growth in written language (reading, writing, and spelling). Second, instruction in written language domains also has reciprocal effects on further advancing spoken language development. Five sets of roles and responsibilities are outlined within a collaborative framework (ASHA, 2001a):

1. Prevent literacy failure through fostering language acquisition and emergent literacy.
2. Identify children at risk for reading and writing problems in relation to early identification, as well as identify older students with literacy problems.
3. Assess reading and writing, particularly the language subsystems that relate to reading, writing, and spelling.
4. Implement intervention protocols that meet individual student's needs and documenting outcomes for literacy problems.
5. Assume other roles, such as assistance to general education teachers, parents, and students and advocate effective literacy practices.

A specific responsibility entails the provision of developmentally appropriate, comprehensive intervention programs in authentic learning activities. Speech-language pathologists are urged to design programs that center on promoting literate language use through a balanced focus on fluent word decoding/spelling and language comprehension/composition skills (ASHA, 2001b). Because the aim is to maintain children in the general education curriculum with appropriate supports, a strong position is taken. Evidence-based practices should be the core of intervention and "Important aspects cannot be omitted because an individual teacher may have an aversion to teaching certain elements or may particularly enjoy teaching another approach" (ASHA, 2001b, p. 44). In this era of standard-based reforms, successful achievement of these multiple aims will demand more collective responsibility for effects of instructional practices on children's learning, flexible teamwork, and the cooperative decision making structures that are essential ingredients of quality education (Elmore, 1999–2000; Giangreco, 2000).

• • • • • •

In summary, it might be said that, at the intersection of the language, learning, and literacy crossroads, researchers and professionals from diverse backgrounds have found some common ground. Research, clinical, and educational practices of the past 15 years have moved the knowledge bases in language and literacy well beyond the 1980s. Many language-based intervention and instructional approaches for school-age children and adolescents now meet standards for evidence-based practices (ASHA 2001a, 2001b; Report of the National Reading Panel, 2000; Snow et al., 1998). In addition, there is a greater understanding and acceptance of the long-term and pervasive nature of language and learning disabilities (Westby, 2000). Now attention is being directed to the postsecondary educational needs of young adults with language learning problems who continue to struggle with academic and social success (for a discussion of postsecondary issues, see Battle, chap. 14, this volume).

However, much of what is known about effective and balanced practices has yet to reach down into classrooms and intervention programs, as testified to by the NCES (2001) "report card" on grade 4 reading achievement. The reasons for children's literacy failures are complex. Causes and their consequences are intertwined with (a) SES and sociocultural variations in home socialization practices; (b) the relative absence of teacher education in linguistics; (c) the relative dearth of knowledge about the language basis of literacy in the professional preparation of speech-language pathologists; (d) the fragmentation of services that defines a school culture in which collaborative teamwork, the integration of children's educational goals, and shared decision-making are not valued; and (e) the tendency to allow "methods," rather than strategic teaching, to drive instructional and clinical practices. Strategic teaching is metacognitively demanding (Anders et al., 2000; Pressley, 2000b). It presumes that reading, writing, and spelling are well understood as language processes and requires the skills to explicitly monitor students as they are engaged in these activities in order to know how to assist and encourage them in appropriate ways.

By staying focused on the reciprocal nature of language–literacy relationships, researchers from different disciplines need to develop dialogues that will create more integrated research questions capable of addressing how underlying neurobiological mechanisms for spoken language affect literacy learning and how disrupted literacy learning may impact on subsequent language learning. Other integrated research questions should concern the ways in which instructional variations, including the instructional patterns of classrooms, resource rooms, and clinical settings, affect children's motivation to learn, as well as what they learn, as readers, writers, and spellers.

Specialists from different professions concerned with language and literacy, as well as school administrators, must be encouraged to create more collaborative programs that have clearly defined and coordinated decision-making processes in place. These problem-solving processes should empower teachers, reading specialists, speech-language pathologists, family members, and others to assume different roles and responsibilities in language and literacy teaching at different points in time, depending on a child's needs. Special education and related services should be directed to supporting children and teachers to the greatest possible extent within the general education curriculum.

The intent of this book is to create a cross-disciplinary and cross-professional dialogue on the central role of language in all learning. Contributors represent multiple disciplines. Although their perspectives and focuses may differ, all share the understanding that language and literacy learning are inseparable. All are also committed to the belief, expressed by Lewis Carroll's *Walrus*, that time is now of the essence when it comes to talking about why so many children are locked out of the multiple linguistic worlds that only literacy has the power to create.

REFERENCES

American Speech–Language-Hearing Association. (2001a). Position statement on the roles and responsibilities of speech-language pathologists with respect to reading and writing in children and adolescents (position statement, executive summary of guidelines, tech. rep.). *ASHA Supplement 21*, 17–27. Rockville, MD: Author.

American Speech–Language-Hearing Association. (2001b). Position statement on the roles and responsibilities of speech-language pathologists with respect to reading and writing in children and adolescents [On-line]. Available: http://professional.asha.org

Anders, P. L., Hoffman, J. V., & Duffy, G. G. (2000). Teaching teachers to teach reading: Paradigm shifts, persistent problems, and challenges. In M. L. Kamil, P. B. Mosenthal, P. D. Pearson, & R. Barr (Eds.), *Handbook on reading research* (Vol. 3, pp. 719–742). Mahwah, NJ: Lawrence Erlbaum Associates.

Anglin, J. M. (1993). Vocabulary development: A morphological analysis. *Monographs of the Society for Research in Child Development, 58* (No. 10).

Apel, K., & Masterson, J. J. (2001). Theory-guided spelling assessment and intervention: A case study. *Language, Speech, and Hearing Services in Schools, 32*, 182–195.

Bashir, A. S., Kuban, K. C., Kleinman, S., & Scavuzzo, A. (1984). Issues in language disorders: Considerations of cause, maintenance and change. In J. Miller & R. Schielfelbusch (Eds.), *ASHA Reports, 12*, 92–106.

Bear, D. R., Invernizzi, M., Templeton, S., & Johnston, F. (2000). *Words their way: Word study for phonics, vocabulary, and spelling instruction.* Upper Saddle River, NJ: Merrill.

Bourassa, D. C., & Treiman, R. (2001). Spelling development and disabilities: The importance of linguistic factors. *Language, Speech, and Hearing Services in Schools, 32*, 172–181.

Carlisle, J. F. (1987). The use of morphological knowledge in spelling derived forms by learning-disabled and normal students. *Annals of Dyslexia, 9*, 247–266.

Carlisle, J. F. (1988). Knowledge of derivational morphology & spelling ability in fourth, sixth, and eighth graders. *Applied Psycholinguistics, 9*, 247–266.

Carlisle, J. (1995). Morphological awareness and early reading achievement. In L. Feldman (Ed.), Morphological aspects of language processing (pp. 189–209). Hillsdale, NJ: Lawrence Erlbaum Associates.

Carroll, L. (1976). *The complete works of Lewis Carroll.* New York: Vintage Books.

Catts, H. W., Fey, M. E., Zhang, X., & Tomblin, J. B. (1999). Language basis of reading and reading disabilities: Evidence from a longitudinal investigation. *Scientific Studies of Reading, 3,* 331–361.

Catts, H. W., & Kamhi, A. G. (1999). Causes of reading disabilities. In H. W. Catts & A. G. Kamhi (Eds.), *Language and reading disabilities* (pp. 95–127). Boston, MA: Allyn & Bacon.

Ehren, B. J. (2000). Multiple perspectives for determining the roles of speech–language pathologists in inclusionary classrooms. *Language, Speech, and Hearing Services in Schools, 31,* 213–218.

Ehri, L. C. (2000). Learning to read and learning to spell: Two sides of a coin. *Topics in Language Disorders, 20* (3), 19–36.

Elmore, R. F. (1999–2000). Building a new structure for school leadership. *American Educator, 23*(4), 6–13, 42–44.

Giangreco, M. F. (2000). Related services research for students with low-incidence disabilities: Implications for speech–language pathologists in inclusive classrooms. *Language, Speech, and Hearing Services in Schools, 31,* 230–239.

Gottardo, A., Stanovich, K. E., & Siegel, L. S. (1996). The relationships between phonological sensitivity, syntactic processing, and verbal working memory in the reading performance of third-grade children. *Journal of Experimental Psychology, 63,* 563–582.

Halliday, M. A. K. (1987). Spoken and written modes of meaning. In R. Horowitz & S. J. Samuels (Eds.), *Comprehending oral and written language* (pp. 55–82). San Diego, CA: Academic Press.

Kamhi, A. G., & Catts, H. W. (1999). Language and reading: Convergences and divergences. In H. W. Catts & A. G. Kamhi (Eds.), *Language and reading disabilities* (pp. 1–24). Needham Heights, MA: Allyn & Bacon.

Leonard, L. B. (1998). *Children with specific language impairment.* Cambridge, MA: MIT Press.

Lyon, G. R. (1996, Spring). Learning disabilities. *The Future of Children, 6*(1), 54–76.

Lyon, G. R. (1999). Reading development, reading disorders, and reading instruction: Research-based findings. *Newsletter of the Special Interest Division 1, Language Learning and Education, of the American Speech-Language-Hearing Association, 6*(1), 8–16.

Lyon, G. R., & Moats, L. C. (1997). Critical conceptual and methodological considerations in reading intervention research. *Journal of Learning Disabilities, 30,* 578–588.

McDaniel, D., & Cairns, H. S. (1996). Eliciting judgements of grammaticality and reference. In D. McDaniel, C. McKee, & H. S. Cairns (Eds.), *Methods for assessing children's syntax* (pp. 233–254). Cambridge, MA: The MIT Press.

Miller, C. A., Kail, R., Leonard, L. B., & Tomblin, J. B. (2001). Speed of processing in children with specific language impairment. *Journal of Speech, Language, and Hearing Research, 44,* 416–433.

Moats, L. (1999). *Teaching reading is rocket science: What expert teachers of reading should know and be able to do.* Washington, DC: American Federation of Teachers.

Moats, L. C. (2000). *Speech to print: Language essentials for teachers.* Baltimore: Paul H. Brookes.

Moats, L. C., & Lyon, G. R. (1996). Wanted: Teachers with knowledge of language. *Topics in Language Disorders, 16*(2), 73–86.

Nagy, W. E., & Scott, J. A. (2000). Vocabulary processes. In M. L. Kamil, P. B. Mosenthal, P. D. Pearson, & R. Barr (Eds.), *Handbook of reading research* (Vol. 3, pp. 269–284). Mahwah, NJ: Lawrence Erlbaum Associates.

National Center for Education Statistics (2001). *The nation's report card: Fourth grade reading 2000.* U.S. Department of Education, Office of Educational Research and Improvement [On-line]. Available: http://www.ed.gov/pubs/edpubs.html

National Research Council (1999). *Improving student learning: A strategic plan for education research and its utilization.* Washington, DC: National Academy Press.

Pressley, M. (2000a). What should comprehension instruction be the instruction of? In M. L. Kamil, P. B. Mosenthal, P. D. Pearson, & R. Barr (Eds.), *Handbook on reading research* (Vol. 3, pp. 545–561). Mahwah, NJ: Lawrence Erlbaum Associates.

Pressley, M. (2000b). *Reading instruction that works: The case for balanced teaching.* New York: Guilford.

Report of the National Reading Panel. (2000). *Teaching children to read: An evidence-based assessment of the scientific research literature on reading and its implications for reading instruction.* Bethesda, MD: NICHD Clearinghouse.

Rice, M. L. (1999). Specific grammatical limitations in children with specific language impairment. In H. Tager-Flusberg (Ed.), *Neurodevelopmental disorders* (pp. 331–359). Cambridge, MA: MIT Press.

Rice, M. L., Cleave, P. L., & Oetting, J. B. (2000). The use of syntactic cues in lexical acquisition by children with SLI. *Journal of Speech, Language, and Hearing Research, 43,* 582–594.

Rumsey, J. M. (1996). Neuroimaging in developmental dyslexia: A review and conceptualization. In G. B. Lyon & J. M. Rumsey (Eds.), *Neuroimaging: A window to the neurological foundations of learning and behavior in children* (pp. 57–77). Baltimore, MD: Paul H. Brookes.

Scanlon, D. M., & Vellutino, F. R. (1996). Prerequisite skills, early instruction, and success in first-grade reading: Selected results from a longitudinal study. *Mental Retardation and Developmental Disabilities Research Reviews, 2,* 54–63.

Scanlon, D. M., & Vellutino, F. R. (1997). A comparison of the instructional backgrounds and cognitive profiles of poor, average, and good readers who were initially identified as at risk for reading failure. *Scientific Studies of Reading, 1,* 191–215.

Scarborough, H. S. (1991). Early syntactic development of dyslexic children. *Annals of Dyslexia, 41,* 207–220.

Scarborough, H. S. (2001). Connecting early language and literacy to later reading (dis)abilities: Theory and practice. In S. Neuman & D. Dickinson (Eds.), *Handbook for research in early literacy* (pp. 97–110). New York: Guilford Press.

Scarborough, H. S., Ehri, L. C., Olson, R. K., & Fowler, A. E. (1998). The fate of phonemic awareness beyond the elementary school years. *Scientific Studies of Reading, 2,* 115–142.

Scott, C. M., & Windsor, J. (2000). General language performance measures in spoken and written narrative and expository discourse of school-age children with language learning disabilities. *Journal of Speech, Language, and Hearing Research, 43,* 324–339.

Shaywitz, S. E., Shaywitz, B. A., Pugh, K. R., Skudlarski, P., Fulbright, R. K., Constable, R. T., Bronen, R. A., Fletcher, J. M., Liberman, A. M., Shankweiler, D. P., Katz, L., Lacadie, C., Marchione, K. E., & Gore, J. C. (1996). The neurobiology of developmental dyslexia as viewed through the lens of functional magnetic resonance imaging technology. In G. Reid Lyon & J. M. Rumsey (Eds.), *Neuroimaging: A window to the neurological foundations of learning and behavior in children* (pp. 79–94). Baltimore, MD: Paul H. Brookes.

Silliman, E. R., & Diehl, S. F. (in press). Assessing children with language learning disabilities. In D. K. Bernstein & E. Tiegerman-Farber (Eds.), *Language and communication disorders in children* (5th ed.). Needham Heights, MA: Allyn & Bacon.

Silliman, E. R., Ford, C. S., Beasman, J., & Evans, D. (1999). An inclusion model for children with language learning disabilities: Building classroom partnerships. *Topics in Language Disorders, 19*(3), 1–18.

Snow, C. E., Burns, M. S., & Griffin, P. (1998). *Preventing reading difficulties in young children.* Washington, DC: National Academy Press.

Snow, C. E., Scarborough, H. S., & Burns, M. S. (1999). What speech–language pathologists need to know about early reading. *Topics in Language Disorders, 21*(1), 48–58.

Stanovich, K. E. (2000). *Progress in understanding reading: Scientific Foundations and new frontiers.* New York: Guilford Press.

Stothard, S. E., Snowling, M. J., Bishop, D. V. M., Chipchase, B. B., & Kaplan, C. A. (1998). Language-impaired preschoolers: A follow-up into adolescence. *Journal of Speech, Language, and Hearing Research, 41,* 407–418.

Tabors, P. O., Snow, C. E., & Dickinson, D. K. (2001). Homes and schools together: Supporting language and literacy development. In D. K. Dickinson & P. O. Tabors (Eds.), *Beginning literacy with language* (pp. 313–334). Baltimore, MD: Paul H. Brookes.

Thompson, S., & Thurlow, M. (1999). *State special education outcomes: A report of state activities at the end of the century.* Minneapolis, MN: University of Minnesota, National Center on Education Outcomes [On-line]. Available: http://education.umn.edu/NCEO/OnlinePubs/99StateReport.htm/

Thurlow, M. L., House, A. L., Scott, D. L., & Ysseldyke, J. E. (2000). Students with disabilities in large-scale assessments: State participation and accommodation policies. *The Journal of Special Education, 34,* 154–163.

Torgesen, J. K., Alexander, A. W., Wagner, R. K., Rashotte, C. A., Voeller, K. K. S., & Conway, T. (2001). Intensive remedial instruction for children with severe reading disabilities: Immediate and long-term outcomes from two instructional approaches. *Journal of Learning Disabilities, 34,* 33–58, 78.

Torgesen, J. K., & Wagner, R. K. (1998). Alternative diagnostic approaches for specific developmental reading disabilities. *Learning Disabilities Research and Practice, 13,* 220–232.

Torgesen, J. K., Wagner, R. K., & Rashotte, C. A. (1994). Longitudinal studies of phonological processing and reading. *Journal of Learning Disabilities, 27,* 270–274.

Treiman, R. (1998a). Why spelling? The benefits of incorporating spelling into beginning reading instruction. In J. L. Metsala & L. C. Ehri (Eds.), *Word recognition in beginning reading* (pp. 289–313). Mahwah, NJ: Lawrence Erlbaum Associates.

Treiman, R. (1998b). Beginning to spell in English. In C. Hulme & R. M. Joshi (Eds.), *Reading and spelling: Development and disorders* (pp. 371–393). Mahwah, NJ: Lawrence Erlbaum Associates.

Treiman, R., & Bourassa, D. C. (2000). The development of spelling skill. *Topics in Language Disorders, 20*(3), 1–18.

van Kleeck, A. (1998). Preliteracy domains and stages: Laying the foundations for beginning reading. *Journal of Childhood Communication Development, 20*(1), 33–51.

Vaughn, S., Gersten, R., & Chard, D. J. (2000). The underlying message in LLD intervention research: Findings from research syntheses. *Exceptional Children, 67,* 99–114.

Vellutino, F. R., Scanlon, D. M., & Lyon, G. R. L. (2000). Differentiating between difficult to remediate and readily remediated poor readers: More evidence against the IQ-achievement discrepancy definition of reading disability. *Journal of Learning Disabilities, 33,* 223–238.

Vellutino, F. R., Scanlon, D. M., Sipay, E. R., Small, S. G., Pratt, A., Chen, R., & Denckla, M. B. (1996). Cognitive profiles of difficult-to-remediate and readily remediated poor readers: Early intervention as a vehicle for distinguishing between cognitive and experiential deficits as basic causes of specific reading disability. *Journal of Educational Psychology, 88,* 601–638.

Vellutino, F. R., Scanlon, D. M., & Tanzman, M. S. (1994). Components of reading ability: Issues and problems in operationalizing word identification, phonological coding, and orthographic coding. In G. R. Lyon (Ed.), *Frames of reference for the assessment of learning disabilities* (pp. 279–332). Baltimore, MD: Paul H. Brookes.

Wallach, G. P., & Butler, K. G. (1994). Creating communication, literacy, and academic success. In G. P. Wallach & K. G. Butler (Eds.), *Language learning disabilities in school-age children & adolescents: Some principles & applications* (pp. 2–26). Boston, MA: Allyn & Bacon.

Westby, C. (2000). Who are adults with learning disabilities and what do we do about them? *Topics in Language Disorders, 21*(1), 1–14.

Wilkinson, L. C., & Silliman, E. R. (2000). Classroom language and literacy learning. In M. L. Kamil, P. B. Mosenthal, P. D. Pearson, & R. Barr (Eds.), *Handbook on reading research* (Vol. 3, pp. 337–360). Mahwah, NJ: Lawrence Erlbaum Associates.

Windsor, J. (2000). The role of phonological opacity in reading achievement. *Journal of Speech, Language, and Hearing Research, 43,* 50–61.

Windsor, J., Milbrath, R. L., Carney, E. J., & Rakowski, S. E. (2001). General slowing in language impairment: Methodological considerations in testing the hypothesis. *Journal of Speech, Language, and Hearing Research, 44,* 446–461.

Windsor, J., Scott, C. M., & Street, C. K. (2000). Verb and noun morphology in the spoken and written language of children with language learning disabilities. *Journal of Speech, Language, and Hearing Research, 43,* 1322–1336.

2

Research on Reading and Reading Problems: Findings, Limitations, and Future Directions

Barbara K. Keogh
University of California, Los Angeles

Nearly 15 years ago, the National Institute of Child Health and Human Development (NICHD) and the Joint Committee on Learning Disabilities (JCLD) sponsored a major conference to determine the extent of our knowledge about learning disabilities (LD) and to identify needed research directions (Kavanagh & Truss, 1988). The conference led to an important publication that provided comprehensive "state of the art" reviews in disorder areas such as reading, writing, mathematics, and language, as well as social skills deficits, and hyperactivity/attention deficits (Kavanagh & Truss, Jr., 1988). The authors sketched a "road map" for needed research and underscored the limitations in intervention practices. The conference and publication were also important as they legitimized learning and reading disabilities as topics for scientific study and gave impetus to an explosion of studies focusing on various aspects of LD, especially problems in reading.

The concern for reading disorders is evidenced in the number of published articles found in both scientific and popular outlets in the preparation of this chapter. Over 10,000 citations in as many as 100 different journals in 10 different languages were identified through major computerized search systems. In addition to LD focused publications, such as the *Journal of Learning Disabilities* and *Learning Disabilities Research and Practice*, there are major journals addressing the issues involved in reading disorders. These included *Language, Speech, and Hearing Services in Schools, Exceptional Children,* the *Reading Research Quarterly,* the *Journal of Child Neurology,* and the *Journal of the American Academy of Child and Adolescent Medicine,* to name but a few. When the citations were organized according to problem subgroup, it was clear that the emphasis was on reading problems, specifically dyslexia. There is, obviously, increasing consensus that reading and language disabilities are core problems in children's development. The scope of the literature indicates that they are the concern of scientists from a range of disciplines and professional backgrounds, and that their study has moved beyond clinical and applied research to questions of etiology, developmental pathways, and genetic, biological, psychological, and social contributors. The research findings and their interpretation reflect both the strengths and weaknesses inherent in interdisciplinary efforts.

In this chapter, two major research approaches are briefly summarized and problems of potential importance for the years ahead are identified. The first approach involves research on neurobiological and neuropsychological processes and mechanisms that are assumed to underlie LD and reading disabilities. The second involves research on psychological and instructional processes, which are important in the acquisition of reading and contribute to reading disabilities and other educational problems. Both approaches are necessary for ultimate understanding. It is to be hoped that findings from both will be integrated in the service of more effective preventive and remedial programs for children with learning problems.

Much, although not all, of the research discussed, was supported by the National Institute of Child Health and Human Development (NICHD) (Lyon, 1995; 1999a). That agency is to be commended for its efforts.

NEUROSCIENCE RESEARCH

Researchers from the neuroscience perspective have studied a number of different processes that relate to problems in the areas of higher order cognition, language, and reading. This research is based on assumptions about the relationships between behavior and neurological functions, such that processing systems at one level are presumed to represent processing at the other level. This allows specification of the effects of particular neurological functions and conditions on overt behavior, that is, damage to the brain means impaired performance. Theoretically, at least, it also implies that neurological dysfunctions can be inferred from observable behavior.

Brain–Behavior Relationships: New Directions

Interest in brain–behavior relationships has a long history (Wiederholt, 1974), but the work of Hinshelwood (1917), a Scottish ophthalmologist, is of particular interest as he proposed a condition called "specific word blindness." His conclusion was based on a clinical study of an elementary school child who had good ability in mathematics and memory but who was completely unable to read, a condition Hinshelwood attributed to damage in a particular area of the brain. Orton (1937), Strauss and Lehtinen (1947), and Cruickshank and colleagues (Cruickshank, Bentzen, Ratzeburg, & Tannhauser, 1961) brought somewhat different theoretical orientations to the study of brain–behavior relationships, but also argued for the effects of underlying neural conditions on specific abilities and behaviors. Their work in total had a major impact on the direction of research and remedial strategies, directions that are now pursued by neuroscientists using sophisticated techniques to test brain–behavior models.

Current work in the neurosciences has obviously benefitted enormously from advances in neuroimaging techniques, which provide ways to view brain structures and functions. Until the 1980s, the relationships between brain development and actual observed behavior had to be inferred. Now neuroimaging techniques, such as positron emission tomography (PET), single photon emission computed tomography (SPECT), structural magnetic resonance imaging (MRI), and functional magnetic resonance imaging (fMRI) "… provide a window to the neurological bases of sensory, motor, attentional, perceptual, linguistic, and cognitive development" (Lyon & Rumsey, 1996, p.1). (See Krasuski, Horowitz, & Rumsey, 1996, for detailed reviews of these imaging techniques.) The techniques vary in their appropriateness for use with children as some involve the use of radioactive elements and invasive procedures. PET imaging, for example, exposes the individual to low doses of radiation, and therefore, must be used cautiously. The fMRI is particularly useful with children because it is not invasive and does not involve injections or radiation. The fMRI is a fast imaging technique that documents changes in blood flow and volume in tissues in areas of the brain under study. Thus, it allows identification of differences in individuals' brain activation patterns in response to different task demands. The uses, complexities, and limitations of fMRI are well described by Krasuski et al. (1996). As will be discussed, the fMRI is already a major technique in the study of reading problems in children.

Learning and Developmental Problems: Two Research Programs

It seems fair to say that neuroimaging techniques represent a quantum leap in our understanding of brain–behavior relationships, and hold great promise for the study of individuals with developmental and learning problems. Two examples of research from the neuroscience perspective are cited briefly. Both ongoing programs of research are extensive and address a number of important questions relative to LD and reading problems. The examples presented are illustrative only, and do not do justice to the richness and comprehensiveness of these research programs as a whole.

Yale Studies.   Researchers in the Yale Center for the Study of Learning and Attention (B. A. Shaywitz, S. E. Shaywitz, Fletcher, et al., 1997) conducted a program of research that addresses a number of aspects of learning and developmental problems. A major prospective study included follow-up of a large sample of unselected entering kindergarten children as they moved through the elementary and secondary school years. These data provided information about the prevalence and distribution of (a) learning disabilities (S. E. Shaywitz, Escobar, B. A. Shaywitz, Fletcher, & Makuch, 1992); (b) gender influences and sampling issues (S. E. Shaywitz, B. A. Shaywitz, Fletcher, & Escobar, 1990; B. A. Shaywitz, S. E. Shaywitz, Pugh, et al., 1995); (c) persistence and stability of problems (B. A. Shaywitz, Fletcher, & S. E. Shaywitz, 1995); and (d) the rate of neurobehavioral disorders in childhood (S. E. Shaywitz, Fletcher, & B. A. Shaywitz, 1994). Using advanced neuroimaging technology, this research group has mapped the neural organization involved in the reading task using fMRI techniques (S. E. Shaywitz, B. A. Shaywitz, Pugh, et al., 1998). Based on sets of carefully designed visual tasks, they have monitored neural activation patterns when individuals are presented stimuli with different linguistic and reading demands. Specifically, a subtraction process is used to study activation patterns in response to three component processes of reading: *orthographic coding* (letter identification), *phonological coding* (phoneme identification), and *lexical–semantic coding* (word meaning). The subtraction process employed involves a series of hierarchical visual tasks in which specific cognitive demands can be isolated by presenting a series of stimuli in which one demand is subtracted in each presentation. Individual responses are then monitored during the series of presentations using fMRI, and responses are compared to control presentations.

Findings confirm that different areas of the brain are activated by specific aspects of the reading task. Orthographic stimuli activate regions in the back of the brain; phonologic stimuli activate Broca's area; semantic stimuli activate regions in the midbrain. The Yale investigators documented that, during phonological tasks, brain activation in men is lateralized to the left inferior frontal gyrus regions; in women, activation is more diffuse, involving both the left and right inferior frontal gyrus. Thus, provisional evidence exists of a sex difference in the functional organization of the brain for language at the level of phonological processing. The findings from this ongoing program of research demonstrate that brain processing is linked to components of reading and therefore have implications for both instruction and remedial interventions.

Colorado Studies.   Researchers in the Colorado Learning Disabilities Research Center (DeFries et al., 1997) approached the study of reading disabilities and comorbid conditions from a number of different perspectives using a variety of research techniques. There are three components of this ongoing work. These include a family reading study involving children with reading disabilities and their parents (Gilger, Pennington, & DeFries, 1991), a longitudinal study of children with reading problems and comparison groups of nonproblem readers (DeFries, 1988), and a series of studies addressing reading and language processes and related conditions, such as attention deficit/hyperactivity and mathematics disability (Alarcon, DeFries, Light, & Pennington, 1997; Pennington et al., 1991). This program of research is of particular interest as many of the participants being followed are twins where one has reading problems and the other does not, thus allowing for systematic genetic analyses.

In related work, the Colorado investigators used neuroimaging methods to assess neural functions of children with reading disabilities and those with adequate reading skills, identifying gender effects, along with reading disability effects, and a reading disability by gender interaction on brain structures. Through their analytic techniques, they have documented heritable influences as contributors to deficits in reading (see Pennington, 1995, for a discussion). These investigators are continuing to use behavior–genetic and MRI techniques, as well as sophisticated statistical analyses to identify genetic contributions to specific reading and language skills, for example, phonemic and orthographic processes. They are also pursuing questions of gene–trait relationships, using multiple regression and laboratory techniques for localizing chromosomal regions and specific genes (Pennington & Smith, 1997).

In another component of Colorado research, researchers developed and tested a computer based instructional program targeted at deficits in phonological processing skills and reading comprehension (Olson & Wise, 1992; Olson, Wise, Johnson, & Ring, 1997; Wise & Olson, 1994, 1995). Called Reading with Orthographic and Speech Support (ROSS), this computer-assisted instruction uses synthetic speech to provide students with opportunities for reading in context at the same time providing immediate and meaningful feedback when students face difficult words. Findings to date demonstrate that this instructional intervention improves children's deficient phonological skills, facilitates learning letter–sound correspondences, and has a positive effect on reading in context. In sum, the Colorado work combines techniques from neuroscience, genetics, and computer based technology to test hypotheses about reading, mathematics, and attentional processes using the powerful sampling model of twins.

Despite the complexities and expense of many of the methods used by researchers in the neurosciences, the findings to date are promising, and converging evidence suggests that children with severe and persistent reading disorders, "… frequently show associated multifaceted language and other deficits … [which] … together with available neuropathological evidence, are compatible with the notion that subtle developmental anomalies ... may constitute the substrate of this disorder ...." (Rumsey, 1996, p. 73). However, part of the difficulty in linking neural functions to clinical syndromes is that the phenotypic, or behavioral expressions of clinically defined syndromes or conditions, are often not precisely conceptualized or described, and individuals captured in any diagnostic category vary on many dimensions and in the degree or severity of the problem. We are in the initial stages of this research, but the findings to date argue for the power and utility of the techniques used by neuroscientists to identify and isolate specific neural functions and to link them to the phenotypic expression of specific disorders.

PSYCHOLOGICAL/EDUCATIONAL RESEARCH

A second set of research programs directed at learning disabilities, and specifically at reading problems, have been conceptualized and implemented from a psychological–educational perspective. Current work is focused primarily on reading and language, particularly on the role of phonological processes in learning to read and in disorders in reading, a perspective argued early on by Liberman and associates (Liberman & Shankweiler, 1979). There is now consistent evidence from different investigative groups in different countries that underscores the critical importance of phonetic awareness and letter knowledge in the child's acquisition of reading (Bryant, MacLean, Bradley, & Crossland, 1990; Byrne & Fielding-Barnsley, 1989; Foorman, Francis, Novy, & Liberman, 1991; Lundberg, Olofsson, & Wall, 1980; Scanlon & Vellutino, 1996; Torgesen, Wagner, & Rashotte, 1997; Vellutino et al., 1996). These skills include, but are not limited to, phoneme segmentation and analysis, phonetic decoding, and encoding. It is interesting that some of the specific phonological tasks (e.g. rapid naming of digits and colors) came from the work of neuroscientists (Denckla & Rudel, 1976). In recent work, Wolf (1997, 1999), proposed a "double deficit" condition involving deficits in phonological awareness and naming speed, suggesting that children with severe reading problems may have dysfunctions in both. As Wolf proposes, clearly there are diagnostic and treatment implications if the two processes are independent or at least disassociated, as interventions aimed at one deficit (e.g., phonological abilities) would have little impact on the other.

Longitudinal Studies

Torgesen and associates (Torgesen, Wagner, Rashotte, Alexander, & Conway, 1997; Wagner, Torgesen, Rashotte, Hecht, Barker, Burgess, Donahue, & Garon, 1997) conducted a systematic program of research targeted at both the acquisition of reading and the remediation of reading difficulties. Their work is notable for its conceptual precision, methodological care, and for the careful analyses of measurement issues.

Based on study of kindergarten and grade 2 children, Wagner, Torgesen, Laughon, Simmons, and Rashotte (1993) determined that phonological awareness, phonological memory, and naming, although correlated, had some independence. For younger children, memory and phonological awareness were strongly associated, although they were clearly differentiated for second graders, suggesting the importance of considering age or developmental status in research designs. These researchers were also able to distinguish between analytic and synthetic aspects of awareness, as well as between naming tasks that required continuous or isolated responses. In a subsequent study of children kindergarten through grade 2, it was found that rates of development varied according to the specific phonological processes studied (Wagner, Torgesen, & Rashotte, 1994). This work as a whole underscores the importance of considering psychometric aspects of research tasks, and the need to exercise caution when drawing inferences about specific phonological abilities.

Findings from a longitudinal study (kindergarten through grade 4) by Wagner et al. (1997) confirmed high stability of phonological processing abilities over time. Coefficients were higher for phonological skills than for word level reading skills, suggesting a causal direction from phonological processing to reading. The causal direction inference receives support from statistical techniques of path analysis and structural equation modeling, and from studies of instructional effects (Bryant et al., 1990; Foorman, Francis, Beeler, Winikates, & Fletcher, 1997). Torgesen and Wagner (1995) concluded that their findings as a whole confirmed that phonological skills were proximal causes, not merely correlates of reading word difficulties, and that phonological measures provided a way of early identification for children at risk for reading failure (Torgesen & Wagner, 1998).

As part of a second long-standing program of longitudinal work, Vellutino and colleagues have assessed large samples of entering kindergarten children on a range of aptitudes and skills, including phonological processing (Scanlon & Vellutino, 1996; Vellutino, 1991; Vellutino et al., 1996; Vellutino, Scanlon, & Spearing, 1995). At the end of Grade 1, these investigators identified 190 children (125 boys and 65 girls) from an initial sample of over 1,000 children as having "great difficulty" in reading. Children were given a comprehensive battery of tests, which included cognitive, language, attentional, knowledge, and achievement measures. Approximately ½ of the target group received tutoring in a phonologically based intervention; the others were provided remediation in their home schools, the content and methods varying widely. At the end of Grade 2, the majority of children were reading at average or above average levels. Children who were difficult to remediate did not differ from their more successful peers in basic literacy concepts or in general knowledge or conceptual development, but had problems in number and counting skills which involved encoding and name retrieval. Comparisons of the adequate and poor readers on a series of phonological tasks confirmed differences favoring the good readers. These findings led to two conclusions: First, phonological coding deficits are a basic cause of reading disability and, second, these coding deficits are also related to the ability to profit from reading instruction.

In addition to characteristics of the children studied, Scanlon and Vellutino (1996) also examined characteristics of the kindergarten language arts programs the children experienced. The focus was assessing the amount of instructional time spent on drawing children's attention to the sound characteristics of words. Kindergarten children with poor language skills were frequently found to have problems reading in first grade, but there were differences in reading performance related to the nature of their kindergarten programs. Specifically, at-risk children profited from programs in which phonological skills were emphasized. These researchers concluded that, for some children, there are real and probably constitutionally based, phonological processing deficits that are the cause of their reading problems. However, the contributions of language experiences in the development of reading was also acknowledged.

WHAT DO WE KNOW?

The accumulating evidence from neuroscience and instructional and psychological research converges to identify phonological processing problems as causes of severe reading problems. The neuroscience work has demonstrated that specific neural functions are associated with problems or deficits, and heretability effects on reading disability and comorbid problems have been documented. Specific and targeted phonemic instructional interventions have, in varying degrees, been successful in improving children's basic word reading skills. The research programs cited are impressive in that there are coordinated efforts among component studies and investigators, careful attention has been paid to measurement, and the research questions have developed over time and in response to study findings. However, the volume and the variability of research reported in the large literature on LD as a whole and reading problems specifically make it important to consider some limitations before adopting phonological programs as the exclusive approach to reading instruction.

Limitations of Work to Date

In this section, five limitations of the phonological processing research are presented. First, variations in research designs and methods limit study findings and generalizations across studies. Investigators often use different criteria to identify participants, target different reading processes, and use different measures to assess outcomes. Troia (1999) identified a number of specific threats to internal and external validity in many studies of phonological interventions. These included, but were not limited to (a) design and analytic issues, such as nonrandom assignment of children to treatment groups; (b) confounds of settings and interventions; (c) measurement limitations; (d) failure to report on treatment fidelity; (e) and lack of control for possible effects of random or nonplanned conditions. Troia's findings were based on in-depth analyses of 39 studies selected from a data set of 68 published articles found in refereed journals. It is important to note that all of the 39 studies reviewed reported improvement in phonological measures as well as in reading and spelling when measured. However, only 18% of the studies reviewed (7 studies) met $\frac{2}{3}$ of accepted external and internal validity criteria. As a result, questions were raised about the interpretation and generalizability of findings.

Second, the outcome measures of reading used in much of the phonological instruction research have been narrow, for the most part limited to word level recognition. Few studies have included measures of comprehension or tapped higher order reading skills. Although there is clear support for the generalization that phonological skills are necessary for *adequate beginning reading*, which is defined as breaking the phonetic code and achieving word level recognition, there is less evidence to date that addresses other aspects of the phonology–reading comprehension relationship.

Third, and closely related, much of the research to date has been chronologically limited to short-term studies. *Longitudinal* is often defined as time between kindergarten and the end of grade 1 or grade 2. This is not surprising. The studies have, by design, focused on beginning readers, and longer follow-ups are in process. However, caution dictates conservative generalizations about "reading" when the outcome measures are narrow and the time frames are short. Phonological processing skills may be necessary, but not sufficient, to explain reading levels in older children and adults.

Fourth, an array of instructional methods focused on mastery of phonological skills has been tested and found effective relative to more global instructional approaches. However, to date, little evidence exists that argues for any one specific phonologically based method. Unfortunately, the larger discussion about instructional approaches has too often been framed as "either/or," specifically phonological instruction versus whole language instruction, leading to advocacy and occasional polemics. The recent work of Pressley and colleagues (Pressley et al., 2001) is relevant to this point. These investigators studied literacy instruction in first grade classrooms in five different states in the United States. They concluded that "effective-for-locale" classrooms were characterized by a balance of skills instruction and whole language and they argued for the importance of a rich instructional context.

Fifth, most comparisons of the effects of instructional programs quite logically are concerned with group level outcomes. For the most part, individual differences within groups are overlooked or viewed as "noise in the system." Yet, it is these very differences that may provide insight into the etiology of reading problems and/or provide the basis for the development of cohesive and defensible subgroups. We know that children enter school bringing a wide range of individual differences on many personal, cultural, and experiential dimensions (Adams, 1990; Juel, 1988), yet we have only limited knowledge about how these individual differences interact with instructional programs. Torgesen and Davis (1996), for example, found that children's pre-intervention abilities were differentially related to growth in specific phonological skills and Scanlon and Vellutino (1996) found both child and instructional program effects on reading skill. Phonological awareness skills are necessary in learning to read. However, they are not the only variables that contribute to skilled reading, and, likely, are not independent of other characteristics that may serve as compensating influences. This suggests the need for alternative strategies to reading (Byrne, Freebody, & Gates, 1992; Juel, 1988). This view also argues for a model of reading that includes multiple contributors to risk. Risk models are used by researchers in other disciplines, such as developmental psychopathology (Sameroff, 1994).

Some Generalizations and Needed Research

As a research community, we continue to struggle with issues of conceptualization, definition, and operationalization of clinical conditions, such as dyslexia and learning disabilities. Yet these decisions are critical in our research and clinical efforts, regardless of the sophistication and power of our technology. Controversial definitions and operational criteria in the selection of study samples have resulted in a heterogeneous and sometimes confused set of findings that challenge the viability and utility of specific syndromes. Stanovitch (1994) raised the question "Does Dyslexia Exist?" arguing that the term "carries with it … many empirically unverified connotations and assumptions" (p. 579), including the belief that reading disabilities associated with an average or above IQ represent a unique condition or syndrome, which is different from other reading problems. His view is consistent with that of S. E. Shaywitz et al. (1992), who argued that reading disability represents the extreme cases in a normal distribution of reading achievement. This view has led to a call for a redefinition of dyslexia and to preliminary efforts to clarify the critical features of dyslexia (B. A. Shaywitz et al., 1995). Issues to be addressed, then, are the definitional parameters of reading problems, as well as the language of research and clinical practice.

On a positive note, the advances in technology and in the sophisticated techniques available to neuroscientists and behavioral geneticists offer ways to address some of the questions limiting our insights to date. These techniques may provide a way to demonstrate the current missing links between underlying neural processes and the phenotypic, or observable, expression of specific subgroups of reading disabilities. An obvious caveat follows. Subject selection and the specification of subprocesses involved in research on reading and reading problems become critical considerations in research designs. Who we study is a fundamental question.

I have already referred to the importance of considering individual differences within research samples, and suggest that these differences may influence responses to instruction. Thus, they become important in evaluating and interpreting training effects. In almost all training studies, there are children who do not need specific training and there are those who do not respond positively to particular instructional programs. Summarizing findings from a number of studies of training effects, it appears that approximately 2% to 5% of children with reading problems are relatively unresponsive to intervention (Scanlon & Vellutino, 1996; Torgesen & Davis, 1996). These children may represent the "true dyslexic" whose problems are related to underlying neural dysfunctions (V. Brineger, personal communication, April 17, 1999). Alternatively, they may be victims of inadequate and/or inappropriate training procedures. Questions of appropriate instruction become especially important as many children with special needs are now being taught in general education classrooms. A challenge and a possible threat both to children and teachers is responding to an increasingly wide range of individual differences in instructional needs. We have learned a great deal about effective instruction from reading research to date. The task now is to transfer confirmed and replicated research findings to classroom practice.

There are still many unanswered questions relating to the content, intensity, and the length of training programs necessary in order to be effective with problem readers. Lovett and Steinbach (1997) instructed children in 35, 60-minute sessions four times weekly. Vellutino et al., 1996) provided daily 30 minute one-to-one tutoring for 70 to 80 sessions. Olson and Wise's (1992) initial computer study involved children for 30-minute sessions, 3 or 4 times per week for one semester, about 10 to 14 hours of computer reading. In the Torgesen et al. (1997) remedial intervention study, children were assigned to one of four instructional conditions; children in each condition received 20 min. of one-to-one tutoring 4 days per week for 2½ years, a total of about 80 hours. Clearly, intervention programs vary on a number of dimensions. How much time and in what format are questions that have practical, as well as research implications, as the feasibility and utility of general applications must be considered. It may be that a subset of poor readers essentially needs more time and more intense instruction; alternatively, they might profit from different types of instruction as specific outcomes have been found to be to related to program differences. For example, in a study by Lovett, Borden, DeLuca, Benson, and Brackstone (1994), students with severe reading disabilities responded positively to two interventions, one focused on direct instruction of phonological skills, the other focused on the acquisition and application of metacognitive decoding strategies. Both programs led to improved phonological processing skills and to reading gains. However, the transfer results varied according to program: The direct instruction children showed more gains in word identification skills and in reading unfamiliar words. The strategy trained children improved in word identification and in transfer to real words.

Blachman (1997) summarized many basic issues relating to phonological awareness and early intervention in a "cautionary tale." Blachman's questions have to do with children's age and developmental readiness, the appropriateness of content included in instructional programs, measurement, duration and intensity of interventions, needed follow-on efforts, treatment resistors, and long-term outcomes. Blachman wisely concluded that "The challenge remains to translate the research on phonological awareness into appropriate educational practices that remain grounded in theory and that are flexible enough to absorb new research as it becomes available" (p. 425). The empirical research reviewed in this chapter suggests that Blachman's admonition is being responded to, and that there are systematic research efforts directed at determining instructional effectiveness.

Based on the evidence gathered by a number of independent research groups, it is clear that mastery of the alphabetic code is requisite for word identification, and that adequate phonemic skills are critical in acquiring the alphabetic code. This is especially relevant for beginning readers and for children with reading problems. Less is known about the relationships of phonological processes and reading comprehension and fluency. To accept the importance of phonological skills in reading does not minimize the importance of other contributors to reading competence. It also does not imply that the only approach to reading is training in phonics. Rather, it seems reasonable to consider adequate phonemic awareness necessary for the acquisition of specific basic reading skills. Thus, the first instructional goal is to ensure that beginning readers and children with reading problems are provided with those necessary skills.

• • • • • •

Examination of ongoing research from both neuroscience and educational perspectives holds bright promise for resolving many of the issues related to reading problems and reading intervention programs. However, there are still unanswered questions that require attention. These include: (a) identification of the processes involved in comprehension and the relationship of underlying processes to more complex reading; (b) specification of individual differences that affect responses to instruction; and (c) analysis of the effects of the content and duration of instructional programs, including issues concerned with the fidelity of implementation. Still uncertain are issues of time, intensity, and specific instructional techniques necessary for program success. Closely related are questions of long-term outcomes, including what defines success in reading. Such questions necessarily require studies that go beyond the short term and assess reading competence across a broad age range and in different contexts. Despite the difficulties in conducting longitudinal research (Keogh & Bernheimer, 1998), it is likely that many of the fundamental questions in reading research will be answered only through longitudinal designs. It is important to note that these questions are being addressed in a multifaceted program of research sponsored by the NICHD (Lyon, 1999 a, 1999b).

The critical importance of reading and the recognition that many children have problems in learning to read has prompted reading reform initiatives at both local and national levels. The urgency of the problem led the U.S. Department of Education and the U.S. Department of Health and Human Services to request that the National Academy of Sciences (NAS) study the prevention of reading difficulties in young children. In 1996, the National Research Council (NRC) of the NAS convened a working group to consider this topic. Chaired by Professor Catherine Snow from Harvard University, the Committee on the Prevention of Reading Difficulties in Young Children was made up of 17 experts on language, reading, and development, and three NRC staff members. Over a 2-year period, the committee addressed both broad and specific aspects of early reading and reading problems, including comprehensive reviews of research on typical reading development, risk factors associated with failure to learn to read, and instructional approaches, prevention, and interventions leading to successful reading (Snow, Burns, & Griffin, 1998). In a final report, edited by Snow et al. (1998), the committee concluded that

Effective reading instruction is built on a foundation that recognizes that reading outcomes are determined by complex and multifaceted factors. On the assumption that understanding can move public discussion beyond the polemics of the past, we have made it an important goal to make the complexities known: many factors that correlate with reading fail to explain it;

many experiences contribute to reading development without being pre-requisite to it; and although there are many prerequisites, none by itself appears to be sufficient. (pp. 313–314)

Researchers and clinicians would be well advised to heed this sage observation. It is time to put an end to the "reading wars" that, too often, have characterized discussions to date. This requires replacing advocacy with evidence, and substituting reason for rhetoric.

REFERENCES

Adams, M. (1990). *Beginning to read.* MA: MIT Press.

Alarcon, M., DeFries, J. C., Light, J. G., & Pennington, B. F. (1997). A twin study of mathematics disability. *Journal of Learning Disabilities, 30,* 617–623.

Blachman, B. A. (1997). Early intervention and phonological awareness: A cautionary tale. In B. A. Blachman (Ed.), *Foundations of reading acquisition and dyslexia: Implications for early intervention* (pp. 409–430). Mahwah, NJ: Lawrence Erlbaum Associates.

Bryant, P. E., MacLean, M., Bradley, L. L., & Crossland, J. (1990). Rhymes and alliteration, phonemic detection, and learning to read. *Developmental Psychology, 26,* 429–438.

Byrne, B., & Fielding-Barnsley, R. (1989). Phonemic awareness and letter knowledge in the child's acquisition of the alphabetic principle. *Journal of Educational Psychology, 81,* 313–321.

Byrne, B., Freebody, P., & Gates, A. (1992). Longitudinal data on the relations of word-reading strategies to comprehension, reading time, and phonemic awareness. *International Reading Association, 27,* 141–151.

Cruickshank, W. M., Bentzen, F. A., Ratzeburg, F. H., & Tannhauser, M. T. (1961). *A teaching method for brain-injured and hyperactive children.* Syracuse, NY: Syracuse University Press.

DeFries, J. C. (1988). Colorado reading project: Longitudinal analysis. *Annals of Dyslexia, 33,* 129–130.

DeFries, J. C., Filipek, P. A., Fulker, R. K., Olson. R. K., Pennington, B. F., Smith, S. D., & Wise, B. W. (1997). Colorado learning disabilities research center. *Learning Disabilities. A Multidisciplinary Journal, 8,* 7–19.

Denckla, M. B., & Rudel, R. (1976). Naming of object drawing by dyslexic and other learning disabled children. *Brain and Language, 3,* 1–16.

Foorman, B. R., Francis, D. J., Beeler, T., Winikates, D., & Fletcher, J. M. (1997). Early interventions for children with reading problems: Study designs and preliminary findings. *Learning Disabilities. A Multidisciplinary Journal, 8,* 63–71.

Foorman, B. R., Francis, D. J., Novy, D. M., & Liberman, D. (1991). How letter-sound instruction mediates progress in first-grade reading and spelling. *Journal of Educational Psychology, 83,* 456–469.

Gilger, J. W., Penningtion, B. F., & DeFries, J. C. (1991). Risk for reading disability as a function of parental history in three family studies. *Reading and Writing: An Interdisciplinary Journal, 3,* 205–217.

Hinshelwood, J. (1917). *Congenital word blindness.* London: H. K. Lewis

Juel, C. (1988). Learning to read and write: A longitudinal study of 54 children from first through fourth grades. *Journal of Educational Psychology, 4,* 437–447.

Kavanagh, J. F., & Truss, T. J., Jr. (Eds.). (1988). *Learning disabilities: Proceedings of the national conference.* Parkton, MD: York Press.

Keogh, B. K., & Bernheimer, L. P. (1998). Issues and dilemmas in longitudinal research: A tale of two studies. *Thalamus, 16,* 5–13.

Krasuski, J., Horowitz, B., & Rumsey, J. M. (1996). A survey of functional and anatomical neuroimaging techniques. In G. R. Lyon & J. M. Rumsey (Eds.), *Neuroimaging. A window to the neurological foundations of learning and behavior in children* (pp. 25–52). Baltimore: Paul Brookes Publishing Co.

Liberman, I. Y., & Shankweiler, D. (1979). Speech, the alphabet, and teaching to read. In L. Resnik & P. Weaver (Eds.), *Theory and practice of early reading* (Vol. 2, pp. 109–132). Hillsdale, NJ: Lawrence Erlbaum Associates.

Lovett, M. W., Borden, S. L., DeLuca, L. L., Benson, N. J., & Brackstone, D. (1994). Treating core deficits of developmental dyslexia: Evidence of transfer of learning after phonologically and strategy-based reading training programs. *Developmental Psychology, 30,* 805–822.

Lovett, M. W., & Steinbach, K. A. (1997, April). *The effectiveness of remedial programs for reading disabled children of different ages: Is there decreased benefit for older children?* Paper presented at the Society for Research in Child Development, Washington, DC.

Lundberg, I., Olofsson, A., & Wall, S. (1980). Reading and spelling skills in the first school years predicted from phonemic awareness skills in kindergarten. *Scandinavian Journal of Psychology, 21,* 159–173.

Lyon, G. R. (1995). Research initiatives in learning disabilities: Contributions from scientists supported by the National Institute of Child Health and Human Development. *Journal of Child Neurology, 10* (Suppl. No. 1) S120–S126.

Lyon, G. R. (1999a, April). *NICHD support for research and training in child and adolescent development, developmental psychology, and population research.* Symposium presented at the meeting of the Society for Research in Child Development, Albuquerque, NM.

Lyon, G. R. (1999b). Programmatic research in learning disabilities. In R. Gallimore, L. P. Bernheimer, D. L. Macmillan, D. L. Speece, & S. Vaughn (Eds.), *Developmental perspectives on children with high-incidence disabilities* (pp. 213–227). Mahwah, NJ: Lawrence Erlbaum Associates.

Lyon, G. R., & Rumsey, J. M. (Eds.). (1996). *Neuroimaging. A window to the neurological foundations of learning and behavior in children.* Baltimore, MD: Paul Brookes.

Olson, R. K., & Wise, B. W. (1992). Reading on the computer with orthographic and speech feedback. *Reading and Writing, 4,* 107–144.

Olson, R. K., Wise, B., Johnson, M. C., & Ring, J. (1997). The etiology and remediation of phonologically based word recognition and spelling disabilities: Are phonological deficits the "whole" story? In B. A. Blachman (Ed.), *Foundations of reading acquisition and dyslexia: Implications for early intervention* (pp. 305–326). Mahwah, NJ: Lawrence Erlbaum Associates.

Orton, S. T. (1937). *Reading, writing, and speech problems in children.* New York: Norton.

Pennington, B. F., Gilger, J., Pauls, D., Smith, S. A., Smith, S. D., & DeFries, J. C. (1991). Evidence for major gene transmission of developmental dyslexia. *Journal of the American Medical Association, 266*, 1527–1534.

Pennington B. F., & Smith, S. D. (1997). Genetic analysis of dyslexia and other complex behavioral phenotypes. *Current Opinion in Pediatrics, 9*, 636–641.

Pressley, M., Wharton-McDonald, R., Allington, R., Block, C. C., Morrow, L., Tracey, D., Baker, K., Brooks, G., Cronin, J., Nelson, E., & Woo, D. (2001). A study of effective first-grade literacy instruction. *Scientific Studies in Reading, 5*, 35–58.

Rumsey, J. M. (1996). Neuroimaging in developmental dyslexia: A review and conceptualization. In G. R. Lyon & J. M. Rumsey (Eds.), *Neuroimaging: A window to the neurological foundations of learning and behavior in children* (pp. 57–78). Baltimore, MD: Paul Brookes.

Sameroff, A. (1994). Ecological perspectives on longitudinal follow-up studies. In S. A. Friedman & H. C. Haywood (Eds.), *Developmental follow-up: Concepts, domains, and methods* (pp. 45–64). San Diego: Academic Press.

Scanlon, D. M., & Vellutino, F. R. (1996). Prerequisite skills, early instruction, and success in first grade reading: Selected results from a longitudinal study. *Mental Retardation and Developmental Disabilities Research Reviews, 2*, 54–63.

Shaywitz, B. A., Fletcher, J. M., & Shaywitz, S. M. (1995). Defining and classifying dyslexia and attention-deficit/hyperactivity disorder. *Journal of Child Neurology, 10*, (Suppl. No. 1), S50–S57.

Shaywitz, B. A., Shaywitz, S. E., Pugh, K. R., Constable, R. T., Skudlarski, P., Fulbright, R. K., Bronen, R. A., Fletcher, J. M., Shankweiler, D. P., Katz, L., & Gore, R. (1995). Sex-differences in the functional-organization of the brain for language. *Nature, 373*, 607–609.

Shaywitz, B. A., Shaywitz, S. E., Fletcher, J. M., Pugh, K. R., Gore, R., Constable, T., Fulbright, R. K., Skudlarski, P., Liberman, A. M., Shankweiler, D. P., Katz, L., Bronen, R. A., Marchione, K. E., Holahan, J. M., Francis, D. J., Klorman, R., Aram, D. M., Blachman, B., Stiebing, K. K., & Lacadie, C. (1997). *Learning Disabilities. A Multidisciplinary Journal, 8*, 21–29.

Shaywitz, S. E., Escobar, M. D., Shaywitz, B. A., Fletcher, J. M., & Makuch, R. (1992). Evidence that dyslexia may represent the lower tail of a normal distribution of reading ability. *New England Journal of Medicine, 326*, 145–150.

Shaywitz, S. E., Fletcher, J. M., & Shaywitz, B. A. (1994). Issues in the definition and classification of attention deficit disorders. *Topics in Language Disorder, 14*(4), 1–25.

Shaywitz, S. E., Shaywitz, B. A., Fletcher, J. M., & Escobar, M. D. (1990). Prevalence of reading disability in boys and girls: Results of the Connecticut Longitudinal Study. *Journal of the American Medical Association, 264*, 998–1002.

Shaywitz S. E., Shaywitz B. A., Pugh K. R., Fulbright R. K., Constable R. T., Mencl, W. E., Shankweiler, D. P., Liberman, A. M., Skudlarski, P., Fletcher, J. M., Katz, L., Marchione, K. E., Lacadie, C., Gatenby, C., & Gore, J. C. (1998). Functional disruption in the organization of the brain for reading in dyslexia. *Proceedings of the National Academy of Sciences, 95*, 2636–2641.

Snow, C. E., Burns, M. S., & Griffin, P. (1998). *Preventing reading difficulties in young children.* Washington, DC: National Academy Press.

Stanovitch, K. E. (1994). Does dyslexia exist? *Journal of Child Psychology and Psychiatry, 35*, 579–595.

Strauss, A. A., & Lehtinen, L. E. (1947). *Psychopathology and Education Of the Brain-Injured Child.* New York: Grune & Stratton.

Torgesen, J. K., & Davis, C. (1996). Individual difference variables that predict response to training in phonological awareness. *Journal of Experimental Child Psychology, 63,* 1–21.

Torgesen, J. K., & Wagner, R. K. (1995, May). *Alternative Diagnostic Approaches for specific developmental reading disabilities.* Presentation to the National Research Council's Board on Testing and Assessment Workshop on IQ Testing and Educational Decision Making, Washington, DC.

Torgesen, J. K., & Wagner, R. K. (1998). Alternative diagnostic approaches for specific developmental reading disabilities. *Learning Disabilities Research & Practice, 13,* 220–232.

Torgesen, J. K., Wagner, R. K., & Rashotte, C. A. (1997). The prevention and remediation of severe reading disabilities: Keeping mind the end. *Scientific Studies of Reading, 1,* 217–234.

Torgesen, J. K., Wagner, R. K., Rashotte, C. A., Alexander, A. W., & Conway, T. (1997). Preventive and remedial interventions for children with severe reading Difficulties. *Learning disabilities: A multidisciplinary journal, 8,* 51–61.

Troia, G. A. (1999). Phonological awareness intervention research: A critical review of the experimental methodology. *Reading Research Quarterly, 34,* 28–52.

Vellutino, F. R. (1991). Introduction to three studies on reading acquisition: Convergent findings on theoretical foundations of code-oriented versus whole language approaches to reading instruction. *Journal of Educational Psychology, 83,* 437–443.

Vellutino, F. R., Scanlon, D. M., Sipay, E. R., Small, S. G., Pratt, A., Chen, R. S., & Cenckla, M. B. (1996). Cognitive profiles of difficult-to-remediate and readily remediated poor readers: Early intervention as a vehicle for distinguishing between cognitive and experiential deficits as basic causes of specific reading disability. *Journal of Educational Psychology, 88,* 601–638.

Vellutino, F. R., Scanlon, D. M., & Spearing, D. (1995). Semantic and phonological coding in poor and normal readers. *Journal of Experimental Child Psychology, 59,* 76–123.

Wagner, R. K., Torgesen, J. K., Laughon, P., Simmons, K., & Rashotte, C. (1993). The development of young readers phonological processing abilities. *Journal of Educational Psychology, 85,* 83–103.

Wagner, R. K., Torgesen, J. K., & Rashotte, C. A. (1994). Development of phonological abilities: New evidence of bi-directional causality from a latent variable longitudinal study. *Developmental Psychology, 30,* 73–87.

Wagner, R. K., Torgesen, J. K., Rashotte, C. A., Hecht, S. A., Barker, T. A., Burgess, S. R., Donahue, J., & Garon, T. (1997). Changing causal relations between phonological processing abilities and word-level reading as children develop from beginning to fluent reading: A five-year longitudinal study. *Developmental Psychology, 33,* 468–479.

Wiederholt, J. L. (1974). Historical perspectives on the education of the learning disabled. In L. Mann & D. A. Sabatino (Eds.), *The Second Review of Special Education* (pp. 103–152). Austin, TX: Pro-Ed.

Wise, B. W., & Olson, R. K. (1994). Computer speech and the remediation of reading and spelling problems. *Journal of Special Education Technology, 12,* 207–220.

Wise, B. W., & Olson, R. K. (1995). Computer-based phonological awareness and reading instruction. *Annals of Dyslexia, 45,* 99–122.

Wolf, M. (1997). A provisional integrative account of phonological and naming-speed deficits: Implications for diagnosis and treatment. In B. A. Blachman (Ed.), *Foundations of reading acquisition and dyslexia: Implications for early intervention* (pp. 67–92). Mahwah, NJ: Lawrence Erlbaum Associates.

Wolf, M. (1999, March). *The double deficit hypothesis.* Paper presented at the Newgrange Educational Outreach Center Conference: Implications of Brain Research on Reading and Learning Disabilities, Princeton, NJ.

The Language Basis of Reading: Implications for Classification and Treatment of Children With Reading Disabilities[1]

Alan G. Kamhi
University of Oregon

Hugh W. Catts
University of Kansas

It is now well accepted that reading consists of two components, decoding and comprehension (Aaron, Joshi, & Williams, 1999; Gough & Tunmer, 1986; Hoover & Gough, 1990). *Decoding* is the word recognition process that transforms print to words, whereas *comprehension* assigns meaning to words, sentences, and texts. It is also now widely accepted that reading is a language-based skill (see Catts & Kamhi, 1999). Word recognition relies heavily on phonological and lexical knowledge, whereas comprehension of larger discourse units requires syntactic, morphologic, semantic, and discourse knowledge. A logical consequence of the language bases of reading is that children who have deficiencies in one or more aspects of language will experience difficulty learning to read. Considerable evidence has accumulated over the last 25 years documenting the strong relationship between phonological knowledge and word recognition skills and the importance of semantic, structural, and discourse knowledge for reading comprehension. Nonlanguage factors, such as emergent literacy experiences, nature of instruction, naming speed, motivation, attention, perceptual, conceptual, and reasoning skills also affect reading ability. Al-

---

[1]Portions of this chapter were adapted from H. Catts & A. Kamhi (1999), *Language and Reading Disabilities,* Boston: Allyn & Bacon. Reprinted by permission.

though the focus of this chapter is on the language bases of reading, some of the nonlanguage factors are also discussed. The chapter is divided into four sections: word recognition, comprehension, classifying reading disabilities, and educational implications.

WORD RECOGNITION

In order to recognize or assign meaning to a word, it is necessary to associate the phonological or visual features with a word stored in the individual's mental lexicon. The stored concepts in the mental lexicon represent one's vocabulary. In reading, there are two ways to access the mental lexicon and a word's meaning: indirectly, by way of a phonological representation, or directly, by way of a visual representation. Use of a visual representation to access the lexicon is variously referred to as the direct, visual, look-and-say, or whole word approach. In accessing the lexicon in this way, a match is made between the perceived visual configuration and a visual representation that is part of the mental lexicon for the particular word.

Word meaning can also be accessed through a phonological representation. With this indirect or phonetic approach, the reader uses knowledge of phoneme–grapheme correspondence rules to recode the visually perceived letters into their corresponding phonemes. Individual phonemes are then blended together to form a phonological sequence that is matched to a similar sequence in the lexicon. The phonetic approach is particularly important in the development of reading. Most current theories of reading development (e.g., Share & Stanovich, 1995) emphasize the necessity of phonological decoding in learning to read. The ability to decode printed words phonetically allows children to read words they know but have never seen in print. Reading by the phonetic approach also causes the child to attend to letter sequences within words. The knowledge gained about letter sequences makes the child's visual representations more precise and leads to children being able to use analogies to recognize other words with similar letter sequences (cf. Goswami, 1988). Reading by the phonetic route is thus similar to speech recognition in that a word is recognized by way of its phonological representation.

There is one important difference, however, in using phonological representations to access meaning in comprehending spoken and written language. To successfully use the phonetic route in reading, one must have explicit awareness of the phonological structure of words, specifically the knowledge that words consist of discrete phonemic segments. These segments are not readily apparent to young children because the sound segments of speech are blended together in the acoustic signal. Although preschool children might show some phonological awareness, several years of explicit instruction and practice is usually required for a child to become efficient in using the phonetic approach.

Phonological Processes

It should be apparent from this discussion of the phonetic route of reading why phonological processes and, particularly, phonological awareness, are so important. Over the last 25 years, no variable has proven to be as consistently related to early reading ability as phonological awareness. The more young children are aware of the sounds of speech, the more quickly they will learn the sound–letter correspondences necessary to decode printed words. Evidence of a relationship between phonological awareness and reading has been demonstrated across a wide range of ages (Calfee, & Lindamood, 1973; Torgesen, Wagner, Rashotte, Burgess, & Hecht, 1997), experimental tasks (Catts, Wilcox, Wood-Jackson, Larrivee, & Scott, 1997), and languages (e.g., Hu & Catts, 1998; Lundberg, Olofsson, & Wall, 1980). In addition, children who have difficulty learning to read perform more poorly on measures of phonological awareness than typical readers (e.g., Bradley & Bryant, 1978, 1985; Fletcher et al., 1994). In one of the earliest studies in the area, Bradley and Bryant (1978) found that 10-year-old poor readers have poorer phonological awareness abilities than reading-matched peers who were 3½ years younger.

It is possible that the deficits in phonological awareness observed in poor readers are due, at least in part, to their reading problems (Morais, 1991). Because of the abstract nature of phonology, children are often unaware of some phonological aspects of language until their attention is directly drawn to these features of language. The knowledge that words are composed of individual phonemes does not become apparent to most language users until these units are explicitly highlighted through instruction and practice. Preschoolers as well as illiterate adults are generally unable to perform tasks that require the explicit segmentation of words into individual phonemes (Lundberg & Hoien, 1991; Morais, Bertelson, Cary, & Alegria, 1986).

The best evidence of the causal role of phonological awareness in reading comes from training studies (Ball & Blachman, 1988; Hatcher, Hulme, & Ellis, 1994; Lundberg, Frost, & Peterson, 1988; Torgesen, Morgan, & Davis, 1992; Wise & Olsen, 1995). These studies have shown that phonological awareness training significantly improved reading achievement. The best gains in reading were seen, however, when phonological awareness training was combined with explicit instruction in sound–letter correspondence and real reading.

Explaining Differences in Phonological Processing.   What would cause some children to perform poorly on phonological awareness tasks? One obvious factor is how much children are exposed to literacy artifacts and events. Children raised in low-literacy families with little exposure to books may enter school with little knowledge about the alphabet, letter names, and sounds. Explicit awareness of the phonological structure of words requires someone calling attention to the sounds in words. Most children require some formal instruction to learn to read. Children who are raised in low-literacy families are particularly at risk for reading difficulties. Instruction that emphasizes phonological knowledge is particularly important for these children.

In addition to the environmental and instructional factors that impact on phonological awareness, researchers have attempted to identify the basic processing limitation that underlies phonological awareness deficiencies. It is generally agreed that many of the children who experience these difficulties have difficulty constructing accurate phonological representations. Inaccurate or fuzzy phonological representations would clearly lead to problems in reflecting on the phonological structure of words. Supporting this view is a large body of literature documenting phonological memory deficits in poor readers (Mann & Ditunno, 1990; Rapala & Brady, 1990; Stone & Brady, 1995; Shankweiler, Liberman, Mark, Fowler, & Fischer, 1979). For example, Shankweiler et al. (1979), in a classic study, found that good readers often had more difficulty remembering lists of rhyming stimuli than nonrhyming stimuli. This difficulty is caused by interference or confusion caused in using phonological memory codes in the rhyming condition. Poor readers, on the other hand, did not show this performance difference because they did not use phonological memory codes in the ryhming condition.

Good and poor readers have also been compared on tasks involving memory of single items rather than strings of items (Catts, 1986; Kamhi, Catts, Mauer, Apel, & Gentry, 1988; Snowling, 1981; Snowling, Goulandris, Bowlby, & Howell, 1986; Stone & Brady, 1995). These tasks have usually required participants to repeat multisyllablic nonwords spoken by the examiner. Because repeating single words is less influenced by attentional factors and rehearsal strategies than repeating lists of words, it may be a more direct measure of the ability to use phonological codes in memory. In an early investigation, Snowling (1981) reported that children with dyslexia made more errors than reading-age matched control children in the repetition of nonwords such as "bagmivishent." Subsequent studies have confirmed these findings (Catts, 1986; Kamhi et al., 1988; Stone & Brady, 1995).

Deficits in phonological memory are not simply a consequence of reading problems because performance on memory tasks in kindergarten is predictive of reading achievement in the primary grades (N. Ellis & Large, 1987; Mann & Liberman, 1984; Wagner, Torgesen, & Rashotte, 1994). However, tasks measuring phonological memory do not account for variability in reading development independent of measures of phonological awareness (Torgesen, Wagner, & Rashotte, 1994; Wagner et al., 1994), thus suggesting that some common factor may underlie phonological memory and phonological awareness. Some of the likely candidates are difficulties in speech perception (Brady, Shankweiler, & Mann, 1983; McBride-Chang, Wagner, & Chang, 1997), temporal processing (Tallal, 1980), or speed of processing (Bowers & Wolf, 1993; Wolf, Bowers, & Biddle, 2000). A number of researchers have also considered the genetic and neurological bases of phonological processing deficits (e.g., Light & DeFries, 1995; Paulesu et al., 1995). In the next section, some of the recent research on naming speed is discussed.

Naming Speed

The ability to retrieve information about sounds, letters, and words is clearly necessary to become a proficient reader. Differences between good and poor readers have been consistently found on tasks that require rapid retrieval of names for common, serially presented letters, numbers, colors, and simple objects (e.g., Denckla & Rudel, 1976; Wolf, 1991). The difficulty poor readers have on these tasks cannot be attributed to differences in articulation rate, short-term memory difficulties, or visual scanning problems (cf. Wolf et al., 2000). Performance on these tasks during the preschool years has been found to be an excellent predictor of reading achievement during the school years (Badian, 1994; Catts, 1993; Felton, 1992; Wolf, Bally, & Morris, 1986). A growing body of literature has found that when children have phonological awareness and naming speed deficits, they are more impaired in reading than children with only a single deficit (e.g., Wolf et al., in press).

Wolf et al. (2000) argued that naming speed deficits should no longer be subsumed under phonological processing deficits because rapid serial naming not only involves accessing a phonological code; it also involves a demanding array of attentional, perceptual, conceptual memory, lexical, and articulatory processes. With its combination of rapid serial processing and the integration of cognitive, linguistic, and motoric processes, serial naming speed provides an early, simpler approximation of the reading process.

In support of the differentiation between naming speed and phonological processes are studies that find only modest correlations between phonological measures and rapid naming tasks (e.g., Blachman, 1984; Bowers, 1995). These studies have also shown that naming speed and phoneme awareness predict unique, independent variance in every reading measure in addition to significant common variance (Bowers, 1995; Catts, Fey, Zhang, & Tomblin, 1999a; Manis & Doi, in press). Manis and Doi, for example, found that naming speed accounted for more variance in the purer orthographic tasks than phoneme awareness and a similar amount of variance in tasks that included both orthographic and phonological components (e.g., word identification). Bowers (1995) found that only naming speed contributed to speed on reading measures. Based on this evidence, Wolf et al. (2000) concluded that there appears to be strong relationships between naming speed and word and text fluency and between phonological awareness and word attack (real and nonword). For children with severe reading problems, naming speed is a powerful and sometimes the strongest predictor of later reading well into grade 8 (also see Scarborough, 1998).

Orthographic Knowledge and Proficient Word Recognition

The discussion of the independent contribution rapid serial naming makes toward reading points out that reading involves more than learning sound–letter correspondences and reading novel words. Theories of reading development all acknowledge that at some point, word recognition becomes effortless and essentially automatic. Proficient word recognition involves the use of letter sequences and spelling patterns to recognize words visually without phonological conversion. As children accumulate sufficient knowledge of spelling patterns, they become able to recognize words visually without phonological conversion. Orthographic knowledge accumulates as children phonetically decode different words that share similar letter sequences, recognize these similarities, and store this information in memory (Ehri, 1991, Goswami, 1988). Children are most likely to learn the orthographic patterns that occur frequently. Morphemes (-*ing*, -*ed*, -*able*) with their consistent spelling and function, are one place children can begin to focus on orthographic rather than phonological sequences. The other place to look for orthographic regularities is in words that share letter sequences. Words can be thought of as belonging to a particular word family or orthographic neighborhood. For example, *light*, *right*, *might*, and *fight* all have the common stem—*ight*.

The ability to use a direct visual route with minimal phonological mediation to access semantic memory and word meaning is crucial for developing automatic word recognition skills. Without orthographic knowledge, readers would continue to have to sound out long multisyllabic words and rely on the more inefficient and time-consuming indirect phonological route to access semantic memory. Although orthographic knowledge is necessary to become a proficient reader, phonological knowledge is thought to be the means by which children acquire knowledge of specific orthographic patterns. This is the central claim of Share and Stanovich's (1995) self-teaching hypothesis, their popular view of how children learn to read. According to this view, phonological decoding (print-to-sound translation) functions as the primary self-teaching mechanism that enables the learner to acquire the detailed orthographic representations necessary for fast and accurate visual word recognition and for proficient spelling.

Direct instruction and contextual guessing may play some role in developing orthographic knowledge, but only phonological decoding offers a viable means for the development of fast, efficient visual word recognition. The problem with direct instruction is that children encounter too many unfamiliar words. There is no way teachers, parents, or peers can help children with all the unfamiliar words they encounter. The problem with contextual guessing is that the primary purpose of text is to convey nonredundant information, not redundant information. Gough (1983) referred to context as a false friend because it helps you when you least need it. It works best for high-frequency function words, but not very well for content words.

The self-teaching hypothesis attempts to explain one of the long-standing puzzles of how children learn to read. There are four features of the self-teaching role of phonological decoding: (a) item- or word-based decoding as opposed to stage-based decoding, (b) progressive "lexi- calization" of word recognition, (c) early onset, and (d) an asymmetric relationship between primary phonological and secondary orthographic components in the self-teaching process. We briefly discuss the first two factors. A more complete discussion of the other two can be found in Share and Stanovich (1995) or Kamhi and Catts (1999).

Item-Based Decoding.   The process of word recognition depends on how often a child has been exposed to a particular word and the nature and success of decoding that particular word. Familiar high-frequency words are recognized visually with minimal phonetic decoding, whereas novel or low-frequency words for which the child has yet to develop orthographic representations will be more dependent on phonetic decoding. The frequency of phonetic decoding will thus vary according to the children's familiarity with words in particular texts. If the reading is at the child's reading level or a little above, "a majority of the words will be recognized visually, while the smaller number of low-frequency unfamiliar words will provide opportunities for self-teaching with minimal disruption of ongoing comprehension processes" (Share, 1995, p. 155). Importantly, the self-teaching opportunities with these unfamiliar words represent the "cutting edge" of reading development not merely for the beginner, but for readers throughout the ability range (Share, 1995, p. 156).

Progressive Lexicalization.   The lexicalization of phonological recoding is a central aspect of the self-teaching hypothesis. Early decoding skill is based on simple one-to-one correspondences between sounds and letters. There is little sensitivity to orthographic and morphemic context. Share and

Stanovich (1995) suggested that with print exposure, these early sound-letter correspondences become "lexicalized" (p. 23); that is, they come to be associated with particular words. As the child becomes more attuned to spelling regularities beyond the level of simple one-to-one phoneme–grapheme correspondences, this orthographic information is used to modify the initial lexicalizations children develop. The outcome of this process of lexicalization according to Share and Stanovich (1995) "is a skilled reader whose knowledge of the relationships between print and sound has evolved to a degree that makes it indistinguishable from a purely whole-word mechanism that maintains no spelling–sound correspondence rules at the level of individual letters and digraphs" (pp. 23–24).

The notion of lexicalization resolves one of the classic enigmas of decoding—that the rules required for proficient decoding are very different from the simplistic and sometimes incorrect rules (e.g., /b/ = "buh") taught to beginning readers. Basic knowledge of simple sound–letter correspondences are a logical starting point for the beginning reader, but it is impossible to become a proficient reader using these rules. These simple rules are used as a bootstrap or scaffold for developing the "complex lexically-constrained knowledge of spelling–sound relationships that characterize the expert reader" (Share & Stanovich, 1995, p. 25).

Importantly, phonological decoding can occur on different size units of speech, such as phonemes, syllables, rimes/onsets, and morphemes. The most straightforward type of phonological decoding involves identifying and blending together the individual sounds in words. Because simple one-to-one sound blending is a very inefficient way to decode long words and words with irregular spellings, children will necessarily be looking for larger size units to phonetically decode. One of these ways involves dividing words into onsets and rimes. It is much easier to phonetically decode *fight* as f-ight and *bought* as b-ought than it is to sound out individual letters. As children begin to notice common morphemes in different words, they will use these language-based units to decode unfamiliar words. Once they get to this point, they should also be able to decode novel words by making analogies to other words that they already know (e.g., *mountain/fountain*). As novel words become familiar, children will be able to visually recognize the whole word without having to phonetically decode any part of the word.

Caveats. It is important to recognize that phonological decoding skill is no guarantee of self-teaching. According to Share and Stanovich (1995), "it only provides the opportunities for self-teaching. Other factors such as the quantity and quality of exposure to print together with the ability and/or inclination to attend to and remember orthographic detail will determine the extent to which these opportunities are exploited" (p. 25). Naming speed may also play an important role in how easily children learn to read. Wolf et al. (2000) speculated that when the speed and quality of visual information is deficient, letter identification proceeds too slowly both for making high-quality letter representations and also for constructing the links between letter sequences to store them as patterns. The consequences for reading are poor quality orthographic representations, fewer common orthographic patterns learned, and more exposure (practice) required for word identification.

In short, there is a lot of room for individual differences in word recognition ability due to variations in quality of exposure to print, the nature of instruction, phonological knowledge, and serial naming speed. If we add to this the individual variability in language and conceptual processes that underlie comprehension abilities, we begin to have a sense of how complex reading actually is.

COMPREHENSION

As discussed in the last section, phonological processes play a very important role in how readily children learn the correspondences between sounds and letters and develop proficient decoding skills. Phonological processes are also involved in processing speech, although in this case, phonological awareness is not as important as storing and retrieving phonological and orthographic information. Once we get to the point where meaning needs to be assigned to these phonological or orthographic codes, speakers and readers need to access lexical knowledge stored in their mental lexicons. Lexical knowledge is then used to process longer discourse units, such as sentences, conversations, lectures, stories, and expository texts. In addition, comprehension of these larger discourse units depends on structural, propositional, and situation knowledge as well as the ability to make inferences and integrate the information in these larger discourse units. The following sections briefly describe the knowledge required to construct interpretations of text-level discourses.

Lexical Knowledge

The stored concepts in the mental lexicon represent one's vocabulary. Importantly, the content and structure of the mental lexicon is essentially the same for reading and spoken language. The content of the lexicon includes information about the word's phonological or visual form as well as information about the word's meaning and how the word relates to other words. Just and Carpenter (1987) provided an example of what kind of conceptual information would appear in the mental lexicon for the word pencil: "It refers to an instrument used for writing or drawing; it is a man-made physical object, usually cylindrical in shape; and it functions by leaving a trail of graphite along a writing surface. ... A pencil is one of a class of writing instruments and a close relative of the pen, eraser, and sharpener" (p. 62). The mental lexicon also includes syntactic and semantic information that indicates part of speech (e.g., noun, verb, or adjective) and possible syntactic and semantic roles. For example, the syntactic information about pencil might indicate that it is a noun that functions semantically as an instrument ("She wrote the letter with a pencil") or as an object or patient ("Peggy bought a pencil").

Structural Knowledge

A variety of structural cues are used by listeners and readers to comprehend speech and text. These cues include word order, grammatical morphemes, and function words such as relative pronouns, conjunctions, and modals. Listeners and readers often use syntactic and morphologic cues to figure out the meaning of unknown words. Grammatical morphemes, for example, provide information about word classes. Adverbs are signaled by the inflections -ly and -y, whereas adjectives are marked by the suffixes -able and -al. Verbs are signaled by the inflections -ed, -ing, and -en. Nouns are marked by definite and indefinite articles, plural and possessive markers, and suffixes such as -ment and -ness. The reason why readers are able to make any sense at all out of a sentence like "Twas brillig and the slithy toves did gyre and gimble in the wabe" is that inflections (y and s) and syntactic markers (the and did) provide cues about grammatical form class.

Propositional Knowledge

Although structural knowledge may play an important role in understanding sentences, memory for extended discourse rarely maintains structural information. The fact that we generally store and remember the gist of what we hear or read suggests that processing resources must be devoted primarily to constructing meaningful propositions. A *proposition* is an idea-unit that consists of a predicate and its related arguments. It is generally agreed that listeners and readers use their knowledge of predicates and their inherent arguments to construct propositions. The predicate *give*, for example, requires three noun phrases or arguments, an agent to do the giving, an object to be given, and a recipient of the object. When listeners hear a sentence like *Alison gave the doll to Franne*, they look for the three arguments entailed by the predicate *give*.

A simple semantic strategy suggested years ago by Bever (1970) is that listeners and readers might use content words alone to build propositions that make sense. For example, if the words *pile, raked, girl, leaves,* were presented without any other syntactic information, it would be apparent that two propositions were involved: *the girl raked the leaves* and *the leaves were in a pile*. To show that listeners used content words to build propositions, researchers (e.g., Stolz, 1967) showed that semantically constrained sentences (example 1) were much easier to paraphrase than semantically unconstrained sentences (example 2).

1. The vase that the maid that the agency hired dropped broke on the floor.
2. The dog that the cat that the girl fought scolded approached the colt.

It has also been shown that propositional complexity influences processing time. Kintsch and Keenan (1973), for example, showed that sentence (example 3), which contains eight propositions, took significantly more time to read than sentence (example 4), which contains only four propositions. Note that the two sentences have about the same number of words.

3. Cleopatra's downfall lay in her foolish trust in the fickle political figures of the Roman world.
4. Romulus, the legendary founder of Rome, took the women of the Sabine by force.

Subsequent studies have examined the hierarchical networks of propositions that listeners and readers construct to link propositions within spoken discourse and text. Not surprisingly, researchers have found that many factors influence the propositions listeners and readers construct, including individual differences in knowledge of the world, processing capacity, and interest level as well as text factors, such as genre, level of vocabulary, and structural complexity.

Situation Knowledge and Inference Generation

It would be misleading to assume that comprehension is based solely on language knowledge. Phonological, structural, and propositional knowledge are crucial for constructing meaning, but an individual's knowledge of the world also plays an important role in comprehension as does the ability to generate inferences. Consider, for example, how world knowledge makes the sentence *Jake put the key in the box on the shelf* ambiguous, while a similar sentence *Jake put the key in the street on the shelf* is unambiguous. The first could mean either that the key in the box was put on the shelf or that the key was put in the box on the shelf. In the second sentence, there is only one meaning because it is not possible to put a street on a shelf. Such information is not specific to language; instead, it reflects general knowledge about the properties of boxes and streets.

World knowledge can be divided into knowledge of specific content domains and knowledge of interpersonal relations. Specific content domains would include academic subjects, such as history, geography, mathematics, and English literature; procedural knowledge such as how to fix a car, tie a shoelace, and play tennis; and scriptlike knowledge of familiar events. Interpersonal knowledge involves such things as knowledge of human needs, motivations, attitudes, emotions, values, behavior, personality traits, and relationships. All of these types of world knowledge play an important role in processing spoken and written language.

What might not be evident is that the ability to construct meaning requires more than interpreting explicit propositions. It involves accessing relevant world knowledge and generating inferences that are needed to make sentences cohere (local coherence) and to relate text to world knowledge (global coherence). Two main types of inferences have been identified (Just & Carpenter, 1987): backward and forward inferences. *Backward inferences* are variously referred to as bridging assumptions (H. Clark & E. Clark, 1977), integrative inferences, or connective inferences. Consider the sentences *He walked into the classroom* and *The chalk was gone*. To make sense of these sentences, one must infer that the classroom should have chalk in it. Forward inferencing, in contrast, embellishes or elaborates the representation of the currently spoken or read text. For example, for the sentence, *The two-year-old was eating ice cream*, a forward inference is that the child's face is smeared with ice cream.

It should be apparent that an accurate model of comprehension must contain not only language-based processes but conceptual and reasoning ones as well. Phonological, lexical, syntactic, morphologic, and semantic knowledge are all important in comprehending texts. But world knowledge and the ability to make inferences is necessary to integrate information across propositions and construct coherent representations of meaning.

LANGUAGE IMPAIRMENTS AND READING DISABILITIES

Given the importance of lexical, structural, propositional, and discourse knowledge for comprehension, one would expect that children who have difficulty learning to talk and understanding would be at high risk for reading difficulties. Similarly, children with reading disabilities would be expected to have deficiencies in one or more of these language domains. This is, in fact, the case. Numerous studies now show a link between preschool problems in spoken language and reading disabilities in the school years (e.g., Bishop & Adams, 1990; Catts, 1993; Tallal, Curtiss, & Kaplan, 1989). In the most comprehensive study to date, Catts, Fey, Zhang, and

Tomblin (1999a) followed a large group of children from kindergarten through grade 4. These children are a subsample of children who participated in an epidemiological study on the prevalence of language impairment (Tomblin et al., 1997). Based on a large battery of language and preliteracy tests, 225 kindergarten children were identified as having a language impairment. Measures of reading comprehension and word recognition were administered in the second and fourth grades. Children with language impairments performed significantly worse than their age peers on these reading measures and were 4 to 5 times more likely to have reading problems than the normal language children. The children with the most severe language impairments had the greatest likelihood of having reading problems.

Language Problems in Poor Readers

Evidence of an association between reading disabilities and language impairments also comes from investigations of the language abilities of poor readers. Generally, this work has involved selecting school-age children identified as reading disabled (or in some case learning disabled) and studying their performance on traditional measures of language development. This work has shown that children with reading disabilities often have deficiencies in vocabulary, morphology, and syntax (Doehring, Trites, Patel & Fiederowicz, 1981; Fry, Johnson, & Muehl, 1970; Stanovich & Siegel, 1994; Vogel, 1974; Wiig & Semel, 1975). Deficits have also been reported in the production and/or comprehension of text-level language (Donahue, 1984; Roth & Spekman, 1989; Stothard & Hulme, 1992; Yuill & Oakhill, 1991).

In a more recent study, Catts et al. (1999b) investigated the kindergarten language abilities of 183 children who performed at least one standard deviation (SD) below the mean on a composite measure of reading comprehension in the second grade. In comparison to age-matched peers, the poor readers had significantly lower scores on kindergarten measures of vocabulary, grammar, and narration. More than half of the poor readers (59%) had a language composite score in kindergarten that was at least one SD below the mean of the normative sample. These findings show that in addition to problems in phonological processing, many poor readers have more widespread deficiencies in basic language abilities.

Language Deficits: Causes or Consequences

There is little question about the close link between reading and language. Skilled word recognition depends largely on phonological knowledge and reading comprehension relies heavily on lexical, structural, propositional, and discourse knowledge. Children with problems in any of these areas of language or the processes that underlie them are clearly at high risk for reading difficulties. Although language deficits often are causally linked to reading problems, reading difficulties can also contribute to language problems. Poor readers do not read as much as good readers, and thus have less opportunity to improve their vocabulary, grammar, and text-level processing abilities.

The fact that language deficits are both a cause and consequence of reading disabilities ensures that language problems will be a major component of almost all cases of reading disabilities. Now we discuss our language-based classification system and the educational implications of this system.

CLASSIFYING READING DISABILITIES

The literature just reviewed not only supports a language-based view of reading disabilities, but also suggests that the simple view of reading can be used to divide children with reading disabilities into different subgroups on the basis of reading (decoding) and language (comprehension) abilities (Aaron et al., 1999; Catts, 1996; Catts & Kamhi, 1999). According to this scheme, one subgroup, typically referred to as *dyslexic*, has poor word recognition abilities (and problems in phonological processing) with at least average listening comprehension. Another subgroup has poor word recognition abilities and poor listening comprehension abilities. We refer to this group as *language learning disabled*. The other subgroup has problems primarily in listening comprehension, but with normal or above normal word recognition abilities. This reading/language profile has sometimes been referred to as *hyperlexia* (Aram & Healy, 1988). All three of these subgroups have reading comprehension difficulties, but for different reasons. Children with dyslexia exhibit poor reading comprehension because of their inaccurate and/or slow decoding skills. Children with hyperlexia have poor reading comprehension because of their language and cognitive deficiencies. Children with language learning disabilities have deficits in both word recognition and listening comprehension.

There is growing support for a subtyping system based on word recognition and/or comprehension deficits. Most research, however, has examined these subgroups individually. Considerable attention has been devoted to the dyslexic group, whose primary problems are in word recognition (e.g., D. B. Clark & Uhry, 1995; Thomson, 1984). The problems children with dyslexia have in word recognition are well documented (Bruck, 1988; Rack, Snowling, & Olson, 1992; Snowling, 1981; Stanovich & Siegel, 1994). Consistent with this research, most recent definitions of dyslexia specify word recognition deficits as the primary symptom of the disorder. Most definitions also state that children with dyslexia have at least normal intelligence.

Because intelligence is generally measured by verbally loaded tests, most children meeting the latter criterion would be expected to have normal listening comprehension abilities. Indeed, research confirms that, as a group, dyslexic children have listening comprehension abilities that are within the normal range (Aaron, 1989; Ellis, McDougall, & Monk, 1996; Fletcher et al., 1994; Shankweiler et al., 1995).

Children who have problems in both word recognition and listening comprehension have also received a lot of research attention. These children are the poor readers who often fail to meet the IQ-achievement discrepancy criterion for dyslexia. In the literature, they are variously referred to as backward readers (Jorm, Share, Maclean, & Matthews, 1986), low achievers (Fletcher et al., 1994), or garden-variety poor readers (Gough & Tunmer, 1986). We prefer to call these children language learning disabled (LLD) because this term focuses attention on the central role that language learning difficulties play in these children's reading problems.

Studies comparing children with dyslexia and LLD (defined on the basis of low IQ) have found that both groups have similar phonological processing deficits and word recognition problems (e.g., Ellis et al., 1996; Stanovich & Siegel, 1994). In contrast to children with dyslexia, children with LLD have significant deficits in listening comprehension that may be associated with global cognitive deficits or a specific language impairment. Those children with a specific language impairment will have deficits in vocabulary, morphosyntax, and text-level processing, but have normal nonverbal abilities.

Less is known about children with hyperlexia who exhibit problems in listening comprehension, but normal or above normal word recognition abilities. In a recent review of research on hyperlexia, Aram (1997) confirmed that there is a small number of children who have exceptional phonetic decoding skills and good sight-word reading abilities but correspondingly poor listening comprehension abilities. In its extreme case, hyperlexia has been found to be associated with one or more developmental disabilities such as mental retardation, autism, and schizophrenia (see Aram & Healy, 1988). In some cases, it co-occurs with other splinter skills such as exceptional music talent or memory for names and dates. Not all children who demonstrate primarily listening comprehension deficits fit this description of hyperlexia. For example, Stothard & Hulme (1992) identified a group of poor readers who had better word recognition than reading comprehension. These children did not demonstrate precocious or exceptional decoding ability or a history of autism or mental retardation. They did, however, have significant problems in listening comprehension and adequate or better word recognition abilities. Other studies have also described children with this profile (Nation, Adams, Bowyer-Crane, & Snowling, 1999; Yuill & Oakhill, 1991). Although these latter children do not fit the clinical profile of hyperlexia as it was originally conceived (e.g., precocious word recognition, autism), the term hyperlexia still seems to be an appropriate one to characterize these children.

EDUCATIONAL IMPLICATIONS

The classification system just presented has some important clinical and educational implications. By considering children's strengths and weaknesses in listening comprehension and word recognition, practitioners may be better able to describe reading problems, plan intervention, monitor progress, and determine prognosis (Aaron, 1991). In order to determine whether children most closely approximate the dyslexic, LLD, or hyperlexic profile, their word recognition, listening comprehension, and related cognitive processes need to be assessed. Word recognition abilities can be evaluated by standardized tests such as the Woodcock Reading Mastery Tests-Revised (WRMT-R; Woodcock, 1987) or the Wide Range Achievement Test–3 (Wilkinson, 1995). These tests provide an assessment of children's word reading accuracy. The Word Attack subtest of the WRMT-R assesses children's ability to read nonwords and thus provides an estimate of phonological decoding ability. Rate of word recognition is also important for reading comprehension and can be assessed by the Test of Word Reading Efficiency (Torgesen, Wagner, & Rashotte, 1998). In some cases, it will also be informative to measure phonological processing abilities that underlie word recognition. The most complete measure available for this assessment is the Comprehensive Test of Phonological Processing (Wagner, Torgesen, & Rashotte, 1999).

Our classification system also requires an assessment of listening comprehension abilities in order to differentiate the three subgroups. Assessment of listening comprehension can include traditional measures of receptive vocabulary and grammatical knowledge (Bishop, 1989; Carrow-Woolfolk, 1985; DiSimoni, 1978; Dunn & Dunn, 1997), as well as measures of the comprehension of extended spoken texts. Although standardized measures involving extended spoken texts are currently available (Newcomer, 1990; Wechsler, 1991, Wiig, Semel, & Secord, 1995; Woodcock, 1991), it may be better to use an alternate form of a reading comprehension test to evaluate listening comprehension. For example, Aaron (1991) used Form G of the Passage Comprehension subtest of the Woodcock Reading Mastery Tests (Woodcock, 1987) to measure reading comprehension and Form H to assess listening comprehension. In assessing listening comprehension, the passages and accompanying questions are read aloud to the child.

Improving Word Recognition Abilities

The proposed classification system should also help plan intervention programs. This system suggests that children with dyslexia and LLD share the need for intervention directed at word recognition abilities. The nature of this intervention may vary, however, depending on the specific problems a poor reader has in word recognition. For those poor readers who are primarily rate-disabled, intervention will need to provide opportunities to increase the automaticity of word recognition, which comes mainly from practice and repetition in reading. Repeated readings of the same passage can be helpful in this regard (Rashotte & Torgesen, 1985; Samuels, 1977). There are several other effective techniques to improve reading rate and fluency such as paired reading, reading with audio support, and imitative reading (Clark & Uhry, 1995; Rashotte & Torgesen, 1985; Samuels, 1977). With paired reading, students alternate turns reading the same passage. Reading with audio support involves the student reading along with an audio recording of the passage. For imitative reading, the teacher reads a passage aloud and then the student reads the same passage. Each of these activities are designed to give the poor reader a sense of success and appreciation for fluent reading.

Many children with dyslexia and LLD have problems with word recognition accuracy. For most of these children, difficulties in phonological decoding underlie these word recognition problems. Most will benefit from systematic instruction in phonological awareness and phonetic decoding, and there are numerous programs available to poor readers. Specifically, programs by C. H. Lindamood and P. C. Lindamood (1998) and Blachman, Ball, Black, and Tangel (2000) have been shown to be effective. The Lindamood program, for example, improves phonological awareness by helping children discover the articulatory positions and movements associated with different phonemes. Children learn to label sounds represented by letters. For example, /p/ and /b/ are lip poppers because of the way the lips pop open and air pops out when they are pronounced. After learning the articulatory gestures associated with each phoneme, children learn to "feel" the identify, sequence, and number of sounds in words. The program also provides explicit instruction in letter–sound correspondences and in decoding words. Torgesen (1997) found that this program led to significant gains in the accuracy of children's phonetic decoding skills. One-year follow-up data on 24 children found that they moved from below the second percentile on measures of phonetic reading to the average range.

It is generally recognized that for phonological awareness training to be most effective, it must also be combined with explicit, intensive, and supportive training in the use of the alphabetic principle and word recognition (Clark & Uhry, 1995; Torgesen, 1999). In other words, phonological awareness training should not occur in isolation. Adams (1990), in her seminal book on learning to read, captured the essence of what early reading programs need to focus on: "Phonological awareness, letter recognition facility, familiarity with spelling patterns, spelling–sound relations, and individual words must be developed in concert with real reading and real writing and with deliberate reflection on the forms, functions, and meanings of texts" (p. 422).

Improving Comprehension Abilities

Intervention for children with LLD and hyperlexia will need to focus on comprehension skills as well as word recognition abilities. Increasing vocabulary should be a primary focus of intervention to improve comprehension. Measures of vocabulary have been found to be highly correlated to spoken and written language comprehension (e.g., Maria, 1990). Another area to focus on is comprehension monitoring. The use of these monitoring strategies to improve reading comprehension has a long history, beginning with Brown's work more than 20 years ago (Brown, 1978; Palincsar & Brown, 1984). For example, Palincsar and Brown (1984) developed an approach called the *reciprocal teaching method*, in which students were taught four comprehension strategies—predicting, questioning, clarification, and summarization—using a reciprocal teaching method in which the teacher and student roles are gradually changed. Importantly, students were also taught to assume the responsibility for the use of the strategies.

There is now a rich literature on the use of strategy instruction to improve reading, and Pressley summarizes much of this in his recent books (Pressley, 1998; Pressley & Woloshyn (1995). Pressley recommends that students produce summaries while they read, and this has been shown to improve children's recall (Pressley & Woloshyn, 1995). The four rules for producing summaries are: (1) identify main information, (2) delete trivial information, (3) delete redundant information, and (4) relate main and supporting information. Many techniques are available to improve summarization abilities, including the use of mental imagery, mnemonic imagery, question generation and answering of self-generated questions, and activating prior knowledge (cf. Pressley & Woloshyn, 1995).

Educators are also combining various approaches to improve reading comprehension. Klingner and Vaughn (1999) described an approach called Collaborative Strategic Reading (CSR) that combines strategy instruction and cooperative learning. In CSR, students of mixed reading and achievement levels work in small, cooperative groups, using four reading strategies to facilitate comprehension of content area texts: (1) preview—note what they know about the topic and predict what the passage might be about; (2) click and clunk—monitor comprehension during reading by identifying difficult words and using fix-up strategies; (3) get the gist; and

(4) summarize. Klingner and Vaughn (1999) cited numerous studies demonstrating the effectiveness of this approach in improving reading comprehension in diverse populations of readers.

Kamhi (1997) discussed other ways to improve comprehension abilities that considered how meaning can be processed at different levels. In some instances, it may be sufficient for students just to get the gist of a text, whereas in other cases, it is necessary to read at a deeper, more analytic level. Teaching students to shift between different levels of reading thus should be a central objective in improving reading comprehension.

In the same article, Kamhi (1997) also talked how current theories view reading as a transaction between the reader and the text. *Comprehension* is an active process of constructing meaning that is influenced by social and cultural attitudes, previous knowledge, personal likes and dislikes, as well as the text, and the individual's reading ability. Consistent with this view, comprehension training needs to encourage active interpretive reading. *Transactional strategies instruction* is an approach that has been shown to be effective in achieving this (Anderson, 1992). The principle underlying this instruction is to use the text as a starting point for the construction of meaning and to expose students to different interpretations from the group of readers. Wollman-Bonilla and Werchadlo (1999) showed how even first-grade children could learn to write responses of texts that were reflective and interpretive. Through teacher modeling, instruction and feedback, and peer sharing, children's responses to texts became more personal, inferential, and interpretive.

Kamhi (1997) discussed some of the specific questions teachers might ask children to facilitate active responses to texts. Examples of these questions are listed.

1. What made the book interesting?
2. Did you like the book? Why or why not?
3. Are there characters in the book you would like to have as friends?
4. What other things would you like to see happen in the book?
5. If you were the main character, what would you have done differently in the story?
6. If you could meet the author of the book, what would you say?
7. What things would you change in the story?
8. Have you ever experienced some of the events or feelings that the characters in the book experienced?

These questions are very different than the questions students are usually asked by teachers or in standardized tests that have one correct answer. By showing students that there is more than one correct answer to these questions, student responses to texts will become more personal, inferential, and interpretive, thus making reading more enjoyable for students and perhaps improving their performance on more traditional measures of reading comprehension.

There are a number of excellent sources for specific intervention techniques to improve various aspects of the comprehension process (e.g., Carnine, Silbert, & Kameenui, 1997; Maria, 1990; Westby, 1999). These authors provide numerous suggestions of activities to improve vocabulary, schema knowledge, and grammatical understanding. There are also a number of excellent computer programs and websites worth visiting (see Appendix).

• • • • • •

In this chapter, we attempted to provide a relatively brief synopsis of the knowledge and processes involved in word recognition and comprehension, the two basic components of reading according to the simple view of reading (Gough & Tunmer, 1986). The importance of language was emphasized. Phonological knowledge plays a central role in word recognition, whereas lexical, syntactic, propositional, and discourse knowledge play important roles in understanding texts. The influence of some nonlanguage factors, such as naming speed and inferencing skills, were also discussed. A classification system was then presented that used the simple view of reading to subgroup children with reading disabilities according to their word recognition and comprehension abilities. The educational implications of the classification system were also discussed.

It all seems so straightforward. The simple view of reading leads to a discussion of word recognition and comprehension, which leads to a classification system and educational implications based on that system. If it were only that simple. One might imagine Gough and Tunmer, the researchers who came up with the term *classification system,* chuckling to themselves as the rest of us grapple with the complexities of the simple view of reading. Imagine how ludicrous it would be to have a simple view of other complex cognitive activities, such as language, memory, or reasoning. Gough and Tunmer (1986), of course, were merely attempting to provide a simple framework to understand the major processes involved in reading, and they fully recognized that reading is anything but simple. Indeed, if we have learned anything about reading in the last 25 years, it is that it is more complex than anyone thought.

It is generally accepted now that reading is a language-based skill, but this does not mean that it is a simple derivative of learning to talk. The language knowledge required to learn to read goes well beyond the knowledge required to be a competent user of spoken language. This is one reason many children can talk well and still have problems learning to read. We are beginning to understand how children learn to read. In addition to basic language and cognitive abilities, many other factors impact on reading, such as early literacy experiences, quality of instruction, motivation, and so forth. We are also only now beginning to understand the many factors that underlie difficulties in learning to read, how best to classify children with reading disabilities, and the best ways to treat these children. It is crucial for everyone involved in studying or teaching reading to understand that reading is arguably one of the most complex cognitive activities that most humans learn. Failure to understand the complexity of reading will inevitably lead to overly simplistic views of reading development, reading disabilities, and procedures to improve reading. Only by understanding the complexity of reading will those involved in teaching be able to develop and implement the type of instruction that has an impact on the many children who have difficulty learning to read.

APPENDIX

Computer Programs

1. Jumpstart For Reading (ages 4-11) www.jumpstart.com
2. Reading Blaster (ages 4-12) www.learningco.com
3. Disney's Reading Quest with Alladin (6-9)
4. Games for Kids (5-8)
5. Vtech—www.vtechkids.com

Websites Worth Visiting

1. Muskingum College Center for Advancement of Learning. www.muskingum.edu/~cal/database/reading.html
2. ERIC (do a search and type in ERIC and try the AskERIC site).
3. www.learninglink.net
4. LinguaLinks Library: Literacy Bookshelf. www.sil.org/lingualinks/library/literacy/Ltrctitl.gif
5. Learning to Read: www.toread.com
6. LD online: www.ldonline.org/index/html
7. CIERA: Center for the improvement of early reading achievement: www.ciera.org.index.html
8. www.creativewonders.com

REFERENCES

Aaron, P. G. (1989). Qualitative and quantitative differences among dyslexic, normal, and nondyslexic poor readers. *Reading and Writing: An Interdisciplinary Journal, 1,* 291–308.

Aaron, P. G. (1991). Can reading disabilities be diagnosed without using intelligence tests? *Journal of Learning Disabilities, 24,* 178–186.

Aaron, P. G., Joshi, M., & Williams, K. A. (1999). Not all reading disabilities are alike. *Journal of Learning Disabilities, 32,* 120–137.

Adams, M. (1990). *Beginning to read: Thinking and learning about print.* Cambridge, MA: MIT Press.

Anderson, V. (1992). A teacher development project in transactional strategy instruction for teachers of severely reading-disabled adolescents. *Teaching and Teacher Education, 8,* 391–403.

Aram, D. (1997). Hyperlexia: Reading without meaning in young children. *Topics in Language Disorders, 17,* 1–13.

Aram, D., & Healy, J. (Eds.). (1988). *Hyperlexia: A review of extraordinary word recognition.* New York: Guilford Press.

Badian, N. A. (1994). Preschool prediction: Orthographic and phonological skills, and reading. *Annals of Dyslexia, 44,* 3–25.

Ball, E., & Blachman, B. (1988). Phoneme segmentation training: Effect on reading readiness. *Annals of Dyslexia, 38,* 218–235.

Bever, T. (1970). The cognitive basis for linguistic structures. In J. R. Hayes (Ed.), *Cognition and the development of language* (pp. 279–352). New York: John Wiley & Sons.

Bishop, D. (1989). *Test of reception of grammar* (2nd ed.). Manchester, England: University of Manchester, Department of Psychology.

Bishop, D., & Adams, C. (1990). A prospective study of the relationship between specific language impairment, phonological disorders and reading retardation. *Journal of Child Psychology and Psychiatry, 31,* 1027–1050.

Blachman, B. (1984). Relationship of rapid naming ability and language analysis skills to kindergarten and first-grade reading achievement. *Journal of Educational Psychology, 76,* 610–622.

Blachman, B., Ball, W., Black, R., & Tangel, D. (2000). *Road to the code.* Baltimore, MD: Brookes Publishing.

Bowers, P. G. (1995, April). *Re-examining selected reading research from the viewpoint of the "Double-Deficit Hypothesis."* Paper presented at the Society for Research in Child Development. Indianapolis, IN.

Bowers, P. G., & Wolf, M. (1993). Theoretical links among naming speed, precise timing mechanisms and orthographic skill in dyslexia. *Reading and Writing: An Interdisciplinary Journal, 5*(1), 69–85.

Bradley, L., & Bryant, P. (1978). Difficulties in auditory organization as a possible cause of reading backwardness. *Nature, 301,* 419–421.

Bradley, L., & Bryant, P. (1985). *Rhyme and reason in reading and spelling.* Ann Arbor: University of Michigan Press.

Brady, S., Shankweiler, D., & Mann, V. (1983). Speech perception and memory coding in relation to reading ability. *Journal of Experimental Psychology, 35,* 345–367.

Brown, A. (1978). Knowing when, where, and how to remember: A problem of metacognition. In R. Glaser (Ed.), *Advances in instructional psychology* (pp. 293–319). Hillsdale, NJ: Lawrence Erlbaum Associates.

Bruck, M. (1988). The word recognition and spelling of dyslexic children. *Reading Research Quarterly, 23,* 52–69.

Calfee, R. C., & Lindamood, P. (1973). Acoustic-phonetic skills and reading—kindergarten through twelfth grade. *Journal of Educational Psychology, 64,* 293–298.

Carnine, D., Silbert, J., & Kameenui, E. (1997). *Direct instruction reading* (3rd ed.). Columbus, OH: Merrill.

Carrow-Woolfolk, E. (1985). *Test for Auditory Comprehension of Language-Revised.* Allen, TX: DLM Teaching Resources.

Catts, H. (1986). Speech production/phonological deficits in reading-disordered children. *Journal of Learning Disabilities, 19,* 504–508.

Catts, H. (1993). The relationship between speech–language impairments and reading disabilities. *Journal of Speech and Hearing Research, 36,* 948–958.

Catts, H. (1996). Defining dyslexia as a developmental language disorder: An expanded view. *Topics in Language Disorders, 16,* 14–29.

Catts, H. W., Fey, M., Zhang, X., & Tomblin, J. B. (1999a, November). *Reading outcomes in children with language impairments.* Paper presented at the Annual Conference of the American Speech-Language-Hearing Association, San Francisco, CA.

Catts, H. W., Fey, M., Zhang, X., & Tomblin, J. B. (1999b). Language basis of reading and reading disabilities: Evidence from a longitudinal investigation. *Scientific Studies of Reading, 3,* 331–361.

Catts, H. W., & Kamhi, A. G. (Eds.). (1999). *Language and reading disabilities.* Needham Hts., MA: Allyn & Bacon.

Catts, H. W., Wilcox, K. A., Wood-Jackson, C., Larrivee, L., & Scott, V. G. (1997). Toward an understanding of phonological awareness. In C. K. Leong & R. M. Joshi (Eds.), *Cross-language studies of learning to read and spell: Phonologic and othographic processing.* (pp. 31–52). Dordrecht, The Netherlands: Kluwer.

Clark, D. B., & Uhry, J. K. (1995). *Dyslexia: Theory and practice of remedial instruction.* Timonium, MD: York Press.

Clark, H., & Clark, E. (1977). *Psychology and language.* New York: Harcourt Brace Jovanovich.

Denckla, M. B., & Rudel, R. G. (1976). Rapid automatized naming (RAN): Dyslexia differentiated from other learning disabilities. *Neuropsychologia, 14,* 471–479.

DiSimoni, F. (1978). *Token Test for Children.* Chicago: Riverside.

Doehring, D., Trites, R., Patel, P., & Fiedorowicz, C. (1981). *Reading disabilities: The interaction of reading, language, and neuropsychological deficits.* New York: Academic Press.

Donahue, M. (1984). Learning disabled children's comprehension and production of syntactic devices for marking given versus new information. *Applied Psycholinguistics, 5,* 101–116.

Dunn, L., & Dunn, L. (1997). *Peabody Picture Vocabulary Test–III.* Circle Pines, MN: American Guidance.

Ehri, L. (1991). Development of the ability to read words. In R. Barr, M. Kamil, P. Mosenthal, & P. Pearson (Eds.), *Handbook of reading research* (Vol. 2, pp. 383–417). New York: Longman.

Ellis, A. W., McDougall, S., & Monk, A. F. (1996). Are dyslexics different? II. A comparison between dyslexics, reading age controls, poor readers, and precocious readers. *Dyslexia, 2,* 59–68.

Ellis, N., & Large, B. (1987). The development of reading: As you seek so shall you find. *British Journal of Psychology, 78,* 1–28.

Felton, R. H. (1992). Early identification of children at risk for reading disabilities. *Topics in Early Childhood and Special Education, 12,* 212–229.

Fletcher, J. M., Shaywitz, S. E., Shankweiler, D. P., Katz, L., Liberman, I. Y., Stuebing, K. K., Francis, D. J., Fowler, A. E., & Shaywitz, B. A. (1994). Cognitive profiles of reading disability: Comparisons of discrepancy and low achievement definitions. *Journal of Educational Psychology, 86,* 6–23.

Fry, M. A., Johnson, C. S., & Muehl, S. (1970). Oral language production in relation to reading achievement among select second graders. In D. Baker & P. Satz (Eds.), *Specific reading disability: Advances in theory and method* (pp. 123–159). Rotterdam, The Netherlands: Rotterdam University Press.

Goswami, U. (1988). Children's use of analogy in learning to spell. *British Journal of Developmental Psychology, 6,* 1–22.

Gough, P. (1983). Context, form, and interaction. In K. Rayner (Ed.), *Eye movements in reading* (pp. 203–211). New York: Academic Press.

Gough, P., & Tunmer, W. (1986). Decoding, reading, and reading disability. *Remedial and Special Education, 7,* 6–10.

Hatcher, P., Hulme, C., & Ellis, A. (1994). Ameliorating early reading failure by integrating the teaching of reading and phonological skills: A phonological linkage hypothesis. *Child Development, 65,* 41–57.

Hoover, W., & Gough, P. (1990). The simple view of reading. *Reading and Writing: An Interdisciplinary Journal, 2,* 127–160.

Hu, C., & Catts, H. (1998). The role of phonological processing in early reading ability: What we can learn from Chinese. *Scientific Studies in Reading, 2,* 55–79.

Jorm, A. F., Share, D. L., Maclean, R., & Matthews, R. (1986). Cognitive factors at school entry predictive of specific reading retardation and general reading backwardness: A research note. *Journal Child Psychology and Psychiatry, 27,* 45–54.

Just, M., & Carpenter, P. (1987). *The psychology of reading and language comprehension.* Boston: Allyn & Bacon.

Kamhi, A. (1997). Three perspectives on comprehension: Implications for assessing and treating comprehension problems. *Topics in Language Disorders, 17*(3), 62–74.

Kamhi, A., & Catts, H. (1999). Reading development. In H. Catts & A. Kamhi (Eds.), *Language and reading disabilities* (pp. 25–49). Needham Heights, MA: Allyn & Bacon.

Kamhi, A., Catts, H., Mauer, D., Apel, K., & Gentry, B. (1988). Phonological and spatial processing abilities in language and reading impaired children. *Journal of Hearing and Speech Disorders, 53,* 316–327.

Kintsch, W., & Keenan, J. (1973). Reading rate as a function of the number of propositions in the base structure of sentences. *Cognitive Psychology, 5,* 257–274.

Klingner, J., & Vaughn, S. (1999). Promoting reading comprehension, content learning, and English acquisition through Collaborative Strategic Reading (CSR). *The Reading Teacher, 52,* 738–747.

Light, J. G., & DeFries, J. C. (1995). Comorbidity of reading and mathematics disabilities: Genetic and environmental etiologies. *Journal of Learning Disabilities, 28,* 96–106.

Lindamood, C. H., & Lindamood, P. C. (1998). *Lindamood phoneme sequencing program for reading, spelling, and speech.* Austin, TX: Pro-Ed.

Lundberg, I., Frost, J., & Peterson, O. (1988). Effects of an extensive program for stimulating phonological awareness in young children. *Reading Research Quarterly, 23,* 263–284.

Lundberg, I., & Hoien, T. (1991). Initial enabling knowledge and skills in reading acquisition: Print awareness and phonological segmentation. In D. Sawyer & B. Fox (Eds.), *Phonological awareness in reading: The evolution of current perspectives* (pp. 74–95). New York: Springer-Verlag.

Lundberg, I., Olofsson, A., & Wall, S. (1980). Reading and spelling skills in the first school years predicted from phonemic awareness skills in kindergarten. *Scandinavian Journal of Psychology, 21,* 159–173.

Manis, F., & Doi, L. (in press). Naming speed, phonological awareness, and orthographic knowledge in second graders. *Journal of Learning Disabilities.*

Mann, V., & Ditunno, P. (1990). Phonological deficiencies: Effective predictors of future reading. In G. T. Pavlidis (Ed.), *Perspectives on dyslexia: Cognition, language and treatment* (Vol. 2, pp. 105–131). New York: John Wiley & Sons.

Mann, V. A., & Liberman, I. Y. (1984). Phonological awareness and verbal short-term memory. *Journal of Learning Disabilities, 17,* 592–599.

Maria, K. (1990). *Reading comprehension instruction: Issues and strategies.* Parkton, MD: York Press.

McBride-Chang, C., Wagner, R. K., & Chang, L. (1997). Growth modeling of phonological awareness. *Journal of Educational Psychology, 89,* 621–630.

Morais, J. (1991). Phonological awareness: A bridge between language and literacy. In D. Sawyer & B. Fox (Eds.), *Phonological awareness in reading: The evolution of current perspectives* (pp. 31–71). New York: Springer-Verlag.

Morais, J., Bertelson, P., Cary, L., & Alegria, J. (1986). Literacy training and speech segmentation. *Cognition, 24,* 45–64.

Nation, K., Adams, J. W., Bowyer-Crane, C. A., Snowling, M. J. (1999). Working memory deficits in poor comprehenders reflect underlying language impairments. *Journal of Experimental Child Psychology, 73,*139–158.

Newcomer, P. (1990). *Diagnostic Achievement Battery.* Austin, TX: Pro-Ed.

Palincsar, A., & Brown, A. (1984). Reciprocal teaching of comprehension fostering and comprehension-monitoring activities. *Cognition and Instruction, 1,* 117–175.

Paulesu, E., Connelly, A., Frith, D. C., Friston, K. J., Heather, J., & Myers, R. (1995). Functional MRI correlations with positron emission tomography: Initial experience using a cognitive activation paradigm on verbal working memory. *Neuroimaging and Clinical Neurophysiology Abstract, 5,* 207–212.

Pressley, M. (1998). *Reading instruction that words: The case for balanced teaching.* New York: Guilford Press.

Pressley, M., & Woloshyn, V. (1995) *Cognitive strategy instruction that really improves children's academic performance* (2nd ed.). Cambridge, MA: Brookline Books.

Rack, J. P., Snowling, M. J., & Olson, R. K. (1992). The nonword reading deficit in developmental dyslexia: A review. *Reading Research Quarterly, 27,* 28–53.

Rapala, M., & Brady, S. (1990). Reading ability and short-term memory: The role of phonological processing. *Reading and Writing, 2*, 1–25.

Rashotte, C. A., & Torgesen, J. K. (1985). Repeated reading and reading fluency in reading disabled children. *Reading Research Quarterly, 20*, 180–188.

Roth, F., & Spekman, N. (1989). Higher-order language processes and reading disabilities. In A. Kamhi & H. Catts (Eds.), *Reading disabilities: A developmental language perspective* (pp. 159–197). Boston: Allyn & Bacon.

Samuels, S. J. (1977). The method of reacted reading. *The Reading Teacher, 32*, 403–408.

Scarborough, H. (1998). Predicting future achievement of second graders with reading disabilities: Contributions of phonemic awareness, verbal memory, rapid naming, and IQ. *Annals of Dyslexia, 48*, 115–136.

Shankweiler, D., Crain, S., Katz, L. Fowler, A. E., Liberman, A. M., Brady, S. A., Thornton, R., Lundquist, E., Dreyer, L., Fletcher, J. M., Stuebing, K. K., Shaywitz, S. E., & Shaywitz, B. A. (1995). Cognitive profiles of reading-disabled children: Comparison of language skills in phonology, morphology, and syntax. *Psychological Science, 6*, 149–156.

Shankweiler, D., Liberman, I. Y., Mark, L. S., Fowler, C. A., & Fischer, F. W. (1979). The speech code and learning to read. *Journal of Experimental Psychology: Human Learning and Memory, 5*, 531–545.

Share, D. (1995). Phonological recoding and self-teaching: *sine qua non* of reading acquisition. *Cognition, 55*, 151–218.

Share, D., & Stanovich, K. (1995). Cognitive processes in early reading development: Accommodating individual differences into a model of acquisition. *Issues in Education, 1*, 1–57.

Snowling, M. J. (1981). Phonemic deficits in developmental dyslexia. *Psychological Research, 43*, 219–234.

Snowling, M. J., Goulandris, N., Bowlby, M., & Howell, P. (1986). Segmentation and speech perception in relation to reading skill: A developmental analysis. *Journal of Experimental Child Psychology, 41*, 489–507.

Stanovich, K., & Siegel, L. (1994). The phenotypic performance profile of reading-disabled children: A regression-based test of the phonological-core variable-difference model. *Journal of Educational Psychology, 86*, 24–53.

Stolz, W. (1967). A study of the ability to decode grammatically novel sentences. *Journal of Verbal Learning and Verbal Behavior, 6*, 867–873.

Stone, B., & Brady, S. (1995). Evidence for phonological processing deficits in less-skilled readers. *Annals of Dyslexia, 95*, 51–78.

Stothard, S., & Hulme, C. (1992). Reading comprehension difficulties in children: The role of language comprehension and working memory skills. *Reading and Writing: An Interdisciplinary Journal, 4*, 245–256.

Tallal, P. (1980). Auditory temporal perception, phonics, and reading disabilities in children. *Brain and Language, 9*, 182–198.

Tallal, P., Curtiss, S., & Kaplan, R. (1989). *The San Diego longitudinal study: Evaluating the outcomes of preschool impairment in language development.* Washington, DC: NINCDS.

Thomson, M. (1984). *Developmental dyslexia: Its nature, assessment, and remediation.* Baltimore: Edward Arnold.

Tomblin, J. B., Records, N. L., Buckwalter, P., Zhang, X., Smith, E., & O'Brien, M. (1997). The prevalence of specific language impairment in kindergarten children. *Journal of Speech, Language, and Hearing Research, 40,* 1245–1260.

Torgesen, J. (1997). The prevention and remediation of reading disabilities: Evaluating what we know from research. *Journal of Academic Language Therapy, 1,* 11–47.

Torgesen, J. (1999). Assessment and instruction for phonemic awareness and word recognition skills. In H. Catts & A. Kamhi (Eds.), *Language and reading disabilities* (pp. 128–153). Needham Heights, MA: Allyn & Bacon.

Torgesen, J., Morgan, S., & Davis, C. (1992). Effects of two types of phonological awareness training on word learning in kindergarten children. *Journal of Educational Psychology, 84,* 364–370.

Torgesen, J. K., Wagner, R. K., & Rashotte, C. A. (1994). Longitudinal studies of phonological processing and reading. *Journal of Learning Disabilities, 27,* 276–286.

Torgesen, J. K., Wagner, R. K., & Rashotte, C. A. (1998). *Test of Word Reading Efficiency.* Austin, TX: Pro-Ed.

Torgesen, J. K., Wagner, R. K., Rashotte, C. A., Burgess, S., & Hecht, S. (1997). Contributions of phonological awareness and rapid naming to the growth of word-reading skills in second-and fifth-grade children. *Scientific Studies in Reading, 1,* 161–185.

Vogel, S. A. (1974). Syntactic abilities in normal and dyslexic children. *Journal of Learning Disabilities, 7*(2), 47–53.

Wagner, R. K., Torgesen, J. K., & Rashotte, C. A. (1994). Development of reading-related phonological processing abilities: New evidence of bidirectional causality from a latent variable longitudinal study. *Developmental Psychology, 30,* 73–87

Wagner, R. K., Torgesen, J. K., & Rashotte, C. A. (1999). *Comprehensive Test of Phonological Processing.* Austin, TX: Pro-Ed.

Wechsler, D. (1991). *Wechsler Individual Achievement Test.* San Antonio, TX: The Psychological Corporation.

Westby, C. (1999). Assessing and facilitating text comprehension problems. In H. Catts & A. Kamhi (Eds.), *Language and reading disabilities* (pp. 154–223). Needham Heights, MA: Allyn & Bacon.

Wiig, E., & Semel, E. (1975). Productive language abilities in learning disabled adolescents. *Journal of Learning Disabilities, 8,* 578–586.

Wiig, E., Semel, E., & Secord, W. (1995). *Clinical Evaluation of Language Fundamentals* (3rd ed.). San Antonio, TX: Psychological Corporation.

Wilkinson, T. (1995). *Wide Range Achievement Test–3.* Wilmington, DE: Guidance Associates.

Wise, B. W., & Olson, R. K. (1995). Computer-based phonological awareness and reading instruction. *Annals of Dyslexia, 45,* 99–122.

Wolf, M. (1991). Naming speed and reading: The contribution of the cognitive neurosciences. *Reading Research Quarterly, 26,* 123–141.

Wolf, M., Bally, H., & Morris, R. (1986). Automaticity, retrieval processes, and reading: A longitudinal investigation. *Child Development, 57,* 988–1000.

Wolf, M., Bowers, P., & Biddle, K. (2000). Naming-speed processes, timing, and reading: A conceptual review. *Journal of Learning Disabilities, 33,* 387–407.

Wollman-Bonilla, J., & Werchadlo, B. (1999). Teacher and peer roles in scaffolding first graders' responses to literature. *The Reading Teacher, 52,* 598–607.

Woodcock, R. (1987). *Woodcock Reading Mastery Tests–Revised.* Circle Pines, MN: American Guidance Service.

Woodcock, R. (1991). *Woodcock Language Proficiency Battery–Revised.* Chicago, IL: Riverside.

Yuill, N., & Oakhill, J. (1991). *Children's problems in text comprehension: An experimental investigation.* New York: Cambridge University Press.

4

Beyond Decoding: Critical and Dynamic Literacy for Students With Dyslexia, Language Learning Disabilities (LLD), or Attention Deficit–Hyperactivity Disorder (ADHD)

Carol Westby
Wichita State University

WHAT IS LITERACY?

Literacy is an extension of language learning to print which involves more than decoding. Research in recent years sponsored by the National Institutes of Health has suggested that the riddle of reading disabilities has been solved. Brain anomalies and the location of a gene associated with dyslexia have been identified. Numerous studies have documented the significant role of *phonemic awareness,* which is the explicit awareness that is needed to segment, identify, or manipulate the phonemes in words, as well as rapid phonemic decoding skills in the reading process (Adams, 1990; Blachman, 1997; Kamhi & Catts, chap. 3, this volume; Keogh, chap. 2, this volume; Lyon, 1999). In response to these findings, there has been a plethora of assessment tools and intervention programs published to train phonemic awareness. Researchers, speech–language pathologists, and educators should not, however, assume that the cure for all reading disabilities has been identified. Reading problems manifest in a variety of ways, and although language difficulties are implicated in most reading problems, the specific nature of the language problems varies.

This chapter describes current functions of literacy and presents a framework for understanding the nature of reading comprehension. *Reading disabilities* are viewed as language-based disabilities involving several types

73

of linguistic deficits (phonological, syntactic, and semantic), inferencing deficits, and metacognitive monitoring deficits. Based on this language-disabilities approach, patterns of reading comprehension problems are described in students typically referred to as having dyslexia, language-learning disabilities (LLD), and attention deficit-hyperactivity disorder (ADHD).

The Role of Decoding

To be fluent readers, children must decode rapidly. They must be able to integrate their phonemic awareness skills into phonic principles (sound–symbol relationships) and must practice reading so that they develop efficient orthographic word recognition that is rapid, accurate, and eventually automatic (Catts, 1999; Kamhi, 1999; Lyon, 1999). With orthographic awareness, readers are able to use letter sequences and spelling patterns to recognize words visually and automatically without phonological conversion. For example, students learn that the letter sequence, "ight," in *right, light, bright, fight, might,* is always read the same. Phonemic awareness sets the stage for the development of fluent word recognition. Each time children successfully decode a word, they gain word specific orthographic information. The act of decoding serves as a self-teaching mechanism that enables children to develop knowledge of specific word spellings and orthographic conventions (Share & Stanovich, 1995).

In the past, once children had mastered phonemic code breaking and acquired orthographic knowledge that permitted them to read words on a page fluently, they were considered literate. The ability to break the print code and fluently recognize words orthographically is essential, but does not assure the high-order comprehension skills paramount for learning. Relatively little research has addressed the issue of students who are good at word recognition, but who have difficulty in comprehending and remembering text. In general, there is evidence to show that slow, inefficient decoders are poor comprehenders (Perfetti, 1985). Although there is a tendency for fast decoding and good comprehension to go together, there is no evidence for a direct causal link between the two (Coles, 2000). For example, training poor readers to recognize words as rapidly as a control group of readers did not improve comprehension (Fleischer, Jenkins, & Pany, 1979). Comprehension involves building a mental representation of a text. Mental representations are constructed from present perceptions or information in print and from a store of knowledge in long-term memory based on past experiences (Lahey & Bloom, 1994). This construction of mental representations requires that lexical processes, syntactic processes, and inference processes all interact with nonlinguistic world knowledge (Perfetti, 1994, 1997).

Types of Literacy

There is increasing concern about the literacy skills of students in the United States. The definition of what it means to be literate—and comprehend what one has read—has changed over the last century (Morris & Tchudi, 1996). Figure 4.1 shows the building blocks essential for literacy in the new millennium. These building blocks consist of three types of literacy—basic, critical, and dynamic. Each type, or level of literacy, has its own requirements and functions that incorporates and builds on the preceding level.

Basic Literacy.   When the United States was colonized in the 17th through the 19th centuries, being literate meant the ability to decode and encode, to say the words on a printed page, and to say what the words meant. This basic literacy is what has been associated with the 3Rs; it requires knowledge of phoneme/grapheme relationships, familiar words, and simple syntactic patterns. With basic literacy, persons can write notes to reinforce memory and read to memorize or follow instructions. Basic literacy was sufficient for the majority of jobs available through the first half of the 20th century.

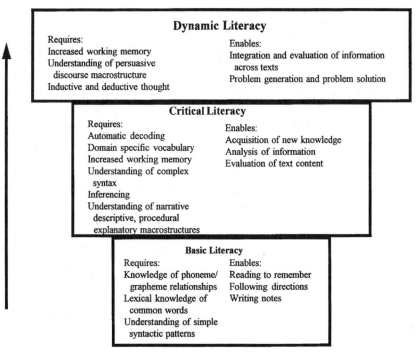

FIG. 4.1.   Literacy building blocks.

Critical Literacy.   By the second half of the 20th century, basic literacy was not sufficient for success. Increasingly, persons were required to have critical literacy. To engage in critical literacy, persons must decode text automatically, understand more specific vocabulary and complex syntax associated with print, and recognize a variety of text macrostructures or overall organization. They must, then, read between the lines. For critical literacy, persons must be able to move beyond literal meanings, to interpret texts, and to use writing not simply to record, but to interpret, analyze, synthesize, and explain.

Students must be able to do more than retell the events of a story or the steps in an experiment. They must be able to determine story theme, interpret characters' motivations, and perceive interrelationships among themes in different stories; they must be able to hypothesize what will happen in a science experiment and explain their observations. All these activities require critical literacy.

Dynamic Literacy.   Even critical literacy, however, is not sufficient to meet the literacy demands in the technological, global economy of the 21st century. Persons must now possess dynamic literacy (Morris & Tchudi, 1996). Dynamic literacy involves cumulative acquisition and use of knowledge over time. Adequate comprehension of narratives can be achieved by applying critical literacy to individual stories. Comprehension of scientific and social studies texts, however, generally requires that students go beyond individual texts; they must be able to compare and contrast the information provided in multiple texts on the same and similar topics, noting how the texts support or contradict one another. They must integrate and act on the content gained from multiple texts for problem-raising and problem-solving matters.

The experiences of students in Minnesota in 1995 who discovered many deformed frogs on a field trip represents an example of the use of dynamic literacy. The students and the scientists they informed of their findings asked why the frogs were deformed and what the significance of the deformed frogs might be to people. They had to integrate information about frog DNA, frog biology, ecology, toxicology, and parasitology to determine the cause or causes of the deformities. In the spring of 1999, California researchers reported that deformed Pacific coast tree frogs were infected with trematode parasites, which disrupted the metamorphosis of tadpoles into frogs (Milius, 1999). The media suggested that the cause for deformed frogs had been found and that further investigation was not warranted. Minnesota researchers, however, reported that their deformed frogs were not infected with the parasites (www.pca.state.mn.us/hot/frogs.html). Instead, the deformities in the Minnesota frogs appeared to be related to chemicals in the water that affected the frogs' thyroid glands. Clearly, the puzzle of the deformed frogs is still not solved. This example demonstrates that the reading a single text or research report can not provide a complete understanding of why the frogs are deformed and what can be done to halt the proliferation of deformed frogs. In fact, basing a conclusion about cause and designing an intervention on a single report could result in increased problems.

MENTAL MODELING FOR CRITICAL / DYNAMIC LITERACY

The Brazilian educator, Freire, was one of the first to introduce the concept of critical literacy (Freire, 1982). According to Freire, through literacy, persons come to develop "their power to perceive critically the way they exist in the world with which and in which they find themselves; they come to see the world not as a static reality, but as a reality in process, in transformation" (p. 71). Dynamic literacy can develop as critical literacy is applied to an increasing number of texts of different types (Morris & Tchudi, 1996). Critical and dynamic literacy give individuals the tools to change the structures of society. Such literacy is as important in the technological Western world as it has been in oppressed Third World countries. How does one acquire critical/dynamic literacy? A first step, of course, is being able to break the print code and recognize words orthographically with a reasonable degree of fluency. But what is needed beyond decoding to process and comprehend written texts? The concept of *mental modeling* offers a framework for understanding reading comprehension

What is Mental Modeling?

As technologies for measuring reading time and eye movements became more sophisticated, studies of text processing, as well as memory and comprehension for what was processed, began to emerge. Many of these studies support the conclusion that multiple levels of mental representation are involved in making meaning from oral and written discourse. These mental models change from moment to moment in response to changes in context, what is recalled from memory, and attitudes, beliefs, and feelings about the representations (Lahey & Bloom, 1994). Critical and dynamic literacy require that readers build a *mental model* or representation of what is described in a text (Perfetti, 1997; Yuill & Oakhill, 1991). To do so, readers must be able to recognize individual words, understand grammatical and semantic relations between words, and integrate ideas in the text, making inferences to aid integration and filling in implicit information. Each skill builds on the preceding skills. Without the ability to decode, one cannot understand grammatical and semantic relationships in the text; and without understanding of semantic relationships, one cannot integrate ideas in a text.

Components of Mental Models. To build mental models, readers must build a model of the text and a model of the situation reflected in the text. Figure 4.2 shows the components for building mental models for texts. To build the textbase model, readers must understand both the text microstructure and the text macrostructure (van Dijk & Kintsch, 1983). The *microstructure* is the local structure of the text—the words and syntax that form the sentence-by-sentence information. The *macrostructure* is the global organization of the text and the hierarchically ordered set of propositions representing a broad theme or gist that is derived from the microstructure. The macrostructure may be explicit in the text, but, more often than not, it must be inferred by the comprehender. As students read the microstructures and macrostructures, they form a textbase model that captures the meaning relations among elements within a sentence and across sentences in the text. This textbase reflects very minimal impact of prior knowledge. If the textbase is extremely explicit (incorporating every detail), then it also forms a situation or scenario-mapping model (Kintsch, 1998; Sanford & Garrod, 1998). Situation or scenario-mapping models capture the full referential meaning of the text, that is, the real or imaginary situation in the world that the text describes. If the text is not extremely

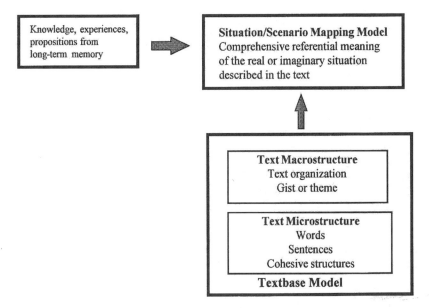

FIG. 4.2.   Mental modeling for individual texts.

explicit, then readers must supplement the information provided by the text with knowledge and experiences stored in their long-term memories. The complete situation mental model of the text that is produced is composed of both text-derived propositions (the textbase) and propositions (this includes imagery and actions) contributed from long-term memory. The situation model is, by its nature, inferential.

Situation mental models require sufficient world knowledge that includes knowledge of interpersonal relations and domain knowledge about specific topics or fields. For example, the following paragraph from the newspaper is readily understandable only to someone who has sufficient domain knowledge in the area of basketball:

> The rookie from Mississippi began the season on a tear, scoring 19, 21, and 18 points in the New Mexico Slam's first three games, including shooting 10 of 18 from behind the 3-point line. But in an eight-team league, word gets around fast, and Carter has been a marked man on the perimeter of late.

Readers with high domain knowledge tend to understand texts better and remember them better than readers with low domain knowledge. Readers who are knowledgeable about basketball understand that a rookie is a young, new player and that "the season" refers to the beginning of a long series of games the team will play (not to the seasons of summer, fall, winter, spring). They recognize that the rookie is doing very well for the team. Knowledgeable readers have a mental model for where the rookie stands on the basketball court when he throws the ball to earn three points, and they realize that players on the other teams know that the rookie will position himself to throw the ball from a location where he can earn 3 points. Consequently, they will be watching the rookie carefully and doing all they can to keep him from throwing the ball from these locations. Domain knowledge may even compensate for other facts, such as low IQ and low verbal ability (Recht & Leslie, 1988; Walker, 1987). One's knowledge base of a particular concept (schema) becomes better organized with general experience and with schooling, it becomes more easily accessible in encounters with texts. The result is improved comprehension.

Developing a situation mental model for a single text is sufficient for some degree of critical literacy for individual texts, but not for dynamic literacy. Dynamic literacy involves integration of information from multiple texts. Integration of this information requires what has been termed a documents model (Perfetti, 1997; Perfetti, Rouet, & Britt, 1999). Figure 4.3 represents a simplified version of a documents model. A documents model integrates situation models from several texts through an intertext model. The intertext model links the situation models from several texts in terms of their rhetorical relations through predicate relationships such as supports versus opposes, agrees with versus disagrees with, gives evidence for ver-

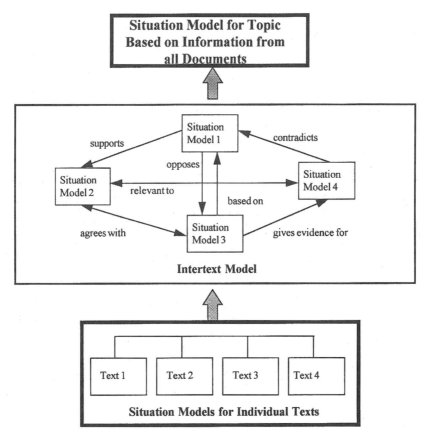

FIG. 4.3.   Example documents model.

sus gives evidence against, relevant to, based on, and so forth. That is, in the intertext model, the situation mental models developed for each of the texts are compared and contrasted. How are the models alike; how are they different; does one situation model provide support or evidence for another situation model or contradict it? Using dynamic literacy, the reader must analyze and synthesize the mental models for diverse, individual texts, or documents, into a mental model that represents the content of the various documents as a whole.

Mental Modeling for Critical Literacy.   A review of test items on the National Assessment of Educational Progress in Reading reflects the need for the formulation of mental models in reading comprehension and the expectation for critical literacy skills. For example, fourth grade students read a story about a turtle and a spider. Turtle visits Spider. Spider will not let Turtle eat until he washes his feet in the pond. Turtle trudges to the pond, but, by the time he returns to Spider's house, his feet are dirty again. Spider again tells him to wash his feet. By the time Turtle returns, spider has eaten all the food. The following are two multiple choice questions about the story:

> When Turtle remains quiet about his mistreatment by Spider, the author wants you to: (a) believe Turtle is afraid, (b) have sympathy for Turtle, (c) feel dislike for Turtle, (d) think Turtle deserved no dinner.
>
>   and
>
> Spider's behavior during the first part of the story is most like that of: (a) mothers protecting their children, (b) thieves robbing banks, (c) runners losing races, (d) people not sharing their wealth.

In addition to answering multiple choice questions, students must discuss how the statement, "Don't get mad, get even," applies to this story and explain how someone they know or have seen in movies or on television is like Turtle or Spider.

These questions cannot be answered by simply reading the words. The first question requires reading between the lines and making inferences. To answer the question, students must understand turtle's emotional response to the situation and the reason for his behavior in response to the spider's treatment. The second question requires that students have formulated a situation model to relate the information in the text to wider world knowledge and other experiences. The open-ended questions require that students analyze and evaluate the information in the story and synthesize it with knowledge from other sources.

Documents Modeling for Dynamic Literacy.   Formal testing seldom requires use of a documents model, but, as students progress through school, they must increasingly use a documents model in science and social studies activities to achieve dynamic literacy. Figure 4.4 shows the development of a documents model (a mental model) for a weather unit taught in the upper elementary grades. The teacher's goal is to have students develop an understanding of the effects of the water cycle and weather patterns on people and the environment. In the process, she exposes her students to an array of texts to acquaint them with the necessary vocabulary, concepts, and discourse styles from a variety of perspectives. She may begin the unit by reading the Cherokee myth, *How Thunder and Lightning Came to Be* (Harrel & Roth, 1995). She has the students read a sci-

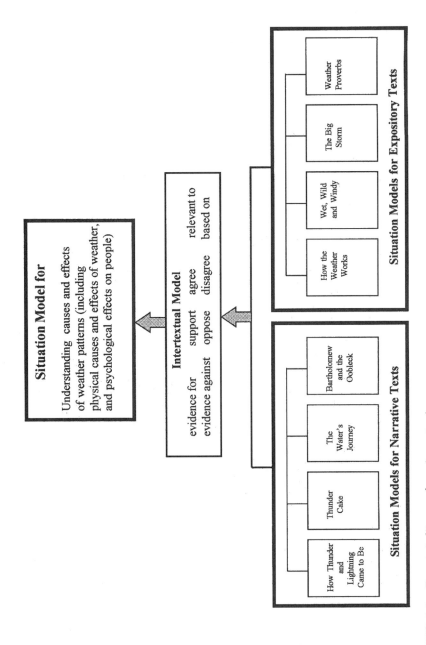

FIG. 4.4.   Dynamic literacy for science topic.

entific explanation of these events in *Wet, Wild, and Windy* (Llewellyn, 1997). Then, using activities from *How the Weather Works* (Allaby, 1995), she has the students conduct simulation experiments on the water cycle, lightning, and thunder. Following the water cycle simulation, the students read, *The Water's Journey* (Schmid, 1989), a narrative presentation of the water cycle beginning with snow falling in the mountains and melting to water flowing into streams to the water evaporating from the ocean and beginning the cycle again. The students compare the explanation for thunder and lightning given in the Cherokee story with what they have learned from their experiments and reading scientific texts.

Next the students read the story, *Thunder Cake* (Polacco, 1990), about how a grandmother and her granddaughter prepare to bake a cake before an approaching storm arrives. They discuss how the characters use the lightning and thunder to judge the distance of the approaching storm and their feelings about the storm. Following this story, they read and discuss, *The Big Storm* (Hiscock, 1993), which is a factual account of a devastating storm that crossed the United States in 1982. The book provides explanations for the blizzards, hail, avalanches and tornadoes that were spawned by the storm and pictures of the results. Students discuss predictions about the storm, relate what they have learned from the theoretical explanations of the water cycle and weather in *Wet, Wild, and Windy* (Llewellyn, 1997) and their simulation activities, and then discuss results of the storm in terms of devastation of property and people's experiences and feelings.

The teacher next introduces *Weather Proverbs* (Freier, 1992), and the students and teacher discuss the reasons why people have developed proverbs to predict and explain weather and how the proverbs are related to scientific fact. The teacher then raises the question of what would happen if something other than water, sleet, snow, or hail fell from the sky. The students read *Bartholomew and the Oobleck* (Dr. Seuss, 1949). They make oobleck (a colloid made of corn starch and water), explore its properties, predict the consequences of oobleck falling in their own community, and design solutions for cleaning up the oobleck.

These examples illustrate that each activity builds on what has come before. The students must employ a documents model to develop a broad perspective on the understanding of weather patterns, their causes and effects. In employing a documents model, students are using and developing dynamic literacy. They can raise further questions to explore about weather. For example, they can pursue how tornadoes and hurricanes differ, why different types of storms occur in different locations in the world, and what would happen if these weather patterns did not exist. They also can engage in problem solving strategies (how people might protect themselves against different types of storms).

Underpinnings for Mental Modeling.   If readers are to develop mental models, they must monitor the coherence and cohesiveness of the textbases they are reading. *Coherence* refers to how well the text makes sense. It depends on students being able to connect incoming information either with the representation of the previous information in the text, with prior knowledge, or with both. Coherence is not a property of the text per se, but rather, a property of the mental representation or interpretation that readers generate for the text (Sanford & Garrod, 1994). Coherence occurs in the mind of the reader.

Cohesiveness of a text is dependent on linguistic devices that represent connections between sentences. These devices hold a text together and can add to its coherence. Cohesive elements include pronominal reference (Spider decided to serve lunch. *He* invited Turtle), temporal and causal connectives (*then, when, while, because, so*), and use of related nouns and noun phrases (The *burglars* stole all the computers from the office. The police tracked the *criminals* down). Attention to cohesive elements maintains text coherence by activating antecedents in a text. Readers must be able to recognize and track anaphoric pronominal references; that is, they must be able to retrieve the original noun or noun phrase to which a pronoun refers. They must recognize related words (burglars are criminals), and they must comprehend a variety of temporal and causal relationships that contribute to textual coherence. Consider the following passage from the book, *Stellaluna* (Cannon, 1993):

> One night, as Mother Bat followed the heavy scent of ripe fruit, an *owl* spied her. On silent wings the *powerful bird* swooped down upon the bats. Dodging and shrieking, Mother Bat tried to escape but the owl struck again and again, knocking *Stellaluna* into the air. *Her baby wings* were as limp and useless as wet paper. Down, down, down she went, faster and faster, into the forest below.

The reader must recognize that the referent for "powerful bird" is "owl" and that "her baby wings" refers back to Stellaluna's wings, not the mother bat's wings. The reader must also recognize the causal relationship between Stellaluna's falling and the owl's attack, even though this is not explicitly stated. Interpreting the cause of Stellaluna's falling reflects the use of a *bridging inference,* a backward inference that links a present element (the fall—an effect) in the text with its cause (owl swooping), which occurred earlier in the text.

The ability to employ inferencing is essential for the generation of appropriate mental models; and mental models make possible the inferencing essential for "reading between the lines" when comprehending texts. Consider the following passage:

Once there was a king who had three lovely daughters. A dragon kidnapped the daughters. As they were being dragged off, they cried for help. Three heros heard their cries and set off to rescue them.

Knowledgeable readers are likely to construct a mental model for this text as a fairy tale. They will imagine the appearance of the dragon—most likely large, fire-breathing, with claws and a tail. They will envision the heros as strong, brave, clever men who will have some means for fighting the dragon such as with swords, potions, or magic. With this mental model for the text, additional text inferences are facilitated. For example, on encountering the sentence, "The heros fought the dragon and rescued the maidens," the readers will use their situational model for fairy tales about kings, beautiful maidens, dragons, and heros to infer that the heros wanted to free the maidens, that the dragon breathed fire on the heros, that the heros threw their spears or used their swords, and that the dragon died.

As just described, readers must make a variety of bridging inferences as they develop the mental models essential for establishing the coherence of texts. *Inferences* are text-based arguments and propositions that were not explicitly mentioned in a message (Singer, 1994). Readers must make the inferences that are necessary for comprehension, but to avoid overloading the system, they must not make all inferences that are possible during the reading process. Readers make several types of inferences. *Logical inferences* are one type of inference that are based on formal rules for induction and deduction. As a result, logical inferences are 100% certain. For example: *All mammals nurse their young. A whale is a mammal.* A logical inference requires the conclusion that a whale will nurse its young. *Pragmatic inferences* are a second type of inference. These are based on people's common knowledge and, although they are often probable, they are not certain. The statement, *The burglar was arrested*, pragmatically implies that a police officer performed the arrest, but it is possible that a law-abiding citizen performed a "citizen's arrest."

Some of these logical and pragmatic inferences must be made if the text is to be understood, whereas some are not essential. Logical or pragmatic inferences that function as *elaborative inferences* can assist in building a mental model, but not all possible elaborative inferences need to be made. If one reads, *Jeffrey was furious with his brother Mark. He threw Mark's Gameboy as hard as he could at the wall. It cost him four weeks allowance to replace it,* for the text to be coherent, the pragmatic bridging inference must be made that the Gameboy broke. In contrast, if one reads, *Jeffrey was furious with his brother Mark. He threw Mark's Gameboy as hard as he could at the wall. He had been angry with Mark for weeks ever since he teased him about liking Jennifer,* the elaborative inference can be made that the Gameboy broke, but this inference is not essential to maintain text coherence.

Another support for mental modeling is working memory. Studies have implicated the role of working memory deficits in difficulties with the development of mental modeling and comprehension monitoring (Kintsch, 1998; Pennington, Bennetto, McAleer, & Roberts, 1996; Perfetti, Marron, & Foltz, 1996) . *Working memory* is responsible for storing and processing incoming information while simultaneously retrieving and integrating information from long-term memory (Just & Carpenter, 1992). An efficient working memory is essential for formulating mental models because the reader must process the information in the textbase and simultaneously search and retrieve relevant knowledge and experiences from long-term memory to develop a situation mental model. The demands on working memory are even greater for developing a mental representation for a documents model, because readers must formulate a mental model for each text, hold all of these models in mind while analyzing, evaluating, and synthesizing them to produce a mental representation that captures a summary interpretation of ideas from all the texts. The nature of mental models and the types of inferences that must be made for comprehension vary in different types of texts, which are now discussed.

Narrative Text Mental Models

The understanding of mental models is best understood for narrative texts. Considerable work in story grammar has documented the components of stories (setting, initiating event, reaction, goal/plan, attempts, consequence, resolution). Labels for story components, however, do not convey the conceptualizations that underlie these narrative components. In many stories, the plot is determined by the characters' motivations and goals. Recognizing motivations and goals requires an understanding of time relationships. Goals are set in the present (Turtle decides to get even) in response to something that happened in the past (Spider's trick on Turtle), to make a difference in the future (teach Spider a lesson so he will not trick others). Characters in stories cannot develop plans and attempts unless they are able to make links between past events, present motivations, and future goals (Benson, 1997).

Recognizing motivations also requires an understanding of psychological causality. Readers must identify the ways that events trigger emotional responses in characters and the ways that characters' emotional responses trigger events. Understanding psychological causality influencing characters requires perspective taking that is dependent on a developing *theory of mind*. Theory of mind is a system for inferring the full range of mental states from behavior (Baron-Cohen, 1995). It involves the sociocognitive ability to represent the mental states of others. It is not sufficient to associate an event with an emotion (being chased by a big dog results in fear; losing a favorite pet results in sadness). One must also appreciate a character's desire, beliefs and thinking/problem-solving strategies to generate a mental model of the text from the characters' viewpoint. Students must have a well-integrated theory of mind if they are to form mental models for narrative texts in which they recognize and interpret characters' emotions. When reading about Spider and Turtle, students must recognize Spider's intentions to trick Turtle. Spider is not really worried about Turtle having clean feet; he just does not want Turtle to have any food. Readers must recognize how Turtle feels about this treatment (although his feelings are never explicitly stated in the text). They must understand how Turtle's feelings trigger his plan to get even. Being able to "read" story characters' minds is essential if students are to understand the plots and themes of stories.

The ability to infer and interpret emotions, such as happy, sad, mad, and scared, does not assure that students will be able to comprehend more complex emotions in more complex situations. Emotions, such as guilt, embarrassment, and pride require that children have internalized sociocultural rules and expectations and that they recognize the types of emotions triggered as a result of adherence to or violations of these rules (Lewis & Michalson, 1983). Some situations entail a series of emotions evolving over time (excited to have a friend visit, then irritated with the friend grabbing toys, then relieved when the friend goes home). Other situations involve several emotions occurring simultaneously (excited and proud to have been selected to give a valedictorian speech, but scared to have to do it; Harter, 1983). These multiple aspects of emotions place more demands on working memory because they require coordinating several emotions with events over time or resolving apparently conflicting emotions in response to a particular event. Many of the inferences that are made in situation models for narratives texts are pragmatic; readers must draw from their own social experiences to infer characters' emotions and reasons for their behaviors. Such inferences are probable, but not certain. Consequently, there can be more than one interpretation or mental model for narrative texts.

Science Text Mental Models

Science texts present more demands on students for formulating mental models of texts. Students are generally familiar with the situations presented in narratives; they are much less likely to be familiar with situations in science. Development of mental models for science texts require more logical inferences compared to narrative texts, which rely more on pragmatic inferences. Science presents students with unfamiliar entities (germs, atoms, convection currents, refraction) that must be brought into existence through complex syntactic and cohesive structures (Ogborn,

Kress, Martins, & McGillicuddy, 1996). Consider the construction of the concept of refraction:

> Light *travels more slowly* through glass or water than it does through air. If light hits glass or air at an angle *this slowing down* makes it *change direction*. *The bending of light* is called *refraction*.

The words in italics are linked cohesively. *Travels more slowly* is the referent for *this slowing down*; *change direction* is the referent for *bending of light*; and all of the italicized words are referents for *refraction*. Tracking referents in science texts requires more than tracking pronominal referents.

Moreover, scientific literacy involves several types of explanations, such as:

- Empirical, which provide an answer to *What has happened to cause ... ?*
- Intentional, which provide an answer *For what purpose ... ?*
- Deductive, which provide an answer to *How do you know that ... ?*
- Procedural, which provide an answer to *How do you do ... ?*

Explanations can be empirical or deductive and refer to physical, psychological, or theoretical relationships (Donaldson, 1986). For example:

Empirical physical: The window broke because the ball hit it.

Empirical psychological: Mary hit John because he pulled her hair.

Deductive physical: (We can tell that) the window broke because there is glass on the ground.

Deductive psychological: (We can tell that) the clown is sad because he is crying.

Deductive theoretical: (We can tell that) half of nine is not four because four and four make eight.

The ability to comprehend and produce explanations requires the understanding of temporal and cause–effect relationships, the linguistic connectives that are used to mark these relationships (e.g., *because, so, for, if-then, while, when, before, after, therefore, etc.*), and the structure of clauses used to express the concepts (Donaldson, 1986). Each of these connectives has complex cognitive unpinnings. For example, the connectives *because* and *so* convey information about causal direction, temporal order, and direction of deductions as the following examples show:

- Information about causal direction and temporal order
  Because introduces a cause, which is the event that happened first.

The ice melted *because* the temperature became too warm.

Joel was embarrassed *because* he forgot his lines in the play.

So introduces an effect, which is the event that happened next.

The temperature became too warm, *so* the ice melted.

Joel forgot his lines in the play, *so* he was embarrassed.

- Information about direction of deduction

  Because introduces evidence

    We know the snow will melt *because* snow melts at 32°F and it is now 40°F.

  So introduces a conclusion

    Snow melts at 32°F and it is now 40°F *so* we know the snow will melt.

The need for understanding syntactic relationships and bridging logical inferences can be seen in the science activity about blood types presented to a group of fourth grade students:

Dracula complains of experiencing terrible reactions after biting certain victims. He needs to learn about universal donors and universal recipients to avoid mixing his blood with that of mismatched donors.

The students are given beakers with clear (type O blood), red (type A blood), blue (type B blood), and purple (type AB blood) water and a number of test tubes in which they can mix the different "bloods." The teacher may identify several "Draculas." One group of students is told that the clear blood is from Dracula 1; a second group is told that the red blood is from Dracula 2, and so forth. The students systematically combine each of the blood types. A change in color of the recipient's blood (Dracula's blood), when donor blood (victim's blood) is added to it, indicates that the blood is incompatible and will make the recipient (Dracula) sick. After completing the experiment, students use the evidence or hypotheses to draw conclusions (or logical inferences), for example,

Dracula can take blood from everybody (evidence), so he is type AB (conclusion).

Dracula is type O (conclusion) because he gets sick when he takes blood from type A, type AB, and type B victims (evidence).

When Dracula takes blood from a type B victim he does not get sick (evidence), therefore he must be type B or type AB (conclusion).

If Dracula is type O and takes blood from a type O victim, he will not get sick.

If Dracula is type A, he can take blood from victims with type A and type O blood.

Evidence or hypotheses that give rise to conclusions in science experiments or social studies are dependent on *diachronic thinking*. This type of thinking is a particular conceptualization of time that involves the capacity to represent changes over time and to relate a current state to its past or future states (Montangero, 1996). Plants and animals grow over time; weather patterns move over time; matter changes states from solid, to liquid, to gas (and back) over time, and so forth. Consider the nature of diachronic thinking necessary for fourth grade activities involving the water cycle. As part of a water cycle unit, students learn that matter has three states and that these states are affected by changes in temperature. Children must understand the durative nature of both cause and effect in activities related to changing states of matter. They must understand that the cause of melting (warm temperature) occurs over time and results in an effect (melting) that also occurs over time. Although the speed with which this occurs may vary (depending on the specific temperature and the amount of ice to be melted), the process is always the same. Twelve-year-olds will generally comprehend the durative aspects of cause–effect involving the water cycle. Seven-year-olds have difficulty with the durative aspects of cause–effect; they tend to expect immediate relationships between cause and effect (e.g., ice should melt as soon as the sun shines on it). They also assume that the process is different if the ice melts quickly as opposed to slowly.

Forming mental models for science texts is challenging for both children and adults. This task is difficult enough for individual texts because of the abstractness of the vocabulary, the complexity of the syntax, and the inductive and deductive thought essential to comprehend the temporal and causal relationships presented. Readers must not only form complex mental models for individual science texts, but they must also compare and contrast the mental models for individual texts, integrating the information from all of the models into a comprehensive documents mental model.

LANGUAGE DEFICITS AFFECTING CRITICAL
AND DYNAMIC LITERACY

Poor comprehenders have difficulty building mental models, but the specific bases for their difficulties can vary. Comprehension requires that readers:

- Decode the print automatically;
- Interpret the syntactic and semantic information in the text;
- Inference appropriately to "read between the lines";
- Use metacognitive skills to monitor comprehension and remedy comprehension failure.

Deficits in any of these areas will affect students' ability to build mental models and, consequently, to comprehend what they read. Figure 4.5 shows the components of reading comprehension and their relationship to decoding skills.

Students who lack automatic decoding skills are likely to be poor comprehenders of written texts because so much of their efforts are devoted to decoding that they are unable to attend to the meaning of the texts (Perfetti, 1985). Some of these students who are inefficient decoders have adequate listening comprehension skills, whereas other inefficient decoders experience comprehension difficulties even when listening to texts read to them. Students who have poor listening comprehension or poor reading comprehension despite fluent decoding may have deficits in one or more of the following areas: (a) interpreting syntactic and semantic information and integrating information from different parts of the text; (b) making relevant inferences; and (c) using metacognitive skills to notice inconsistencies in texts, recognize when they do not comprehend, and remedy comprehension failure. These components of comprehension build on one another. Readers will experience difficulty inferencing if their semantic/syntactic skills are inadequate; and they will fail to monitor their comprehension well if they are not making the essential inferences.

Linguistic/Language Deficits

Numerous studies show that listening and reading comprehension are closely related and are dependent on similar, if not identical, underlying processes (Kamhi & Catts, 1999, chap. 3, this volume; Stothard & Hulme, 1996). The low level of comprehension exhibited by many poor comprehenders is consistent with their other verbal skills and should be considered part of a more global verbal/semantic deficit. On tests of language comprehension, the performance of poor comprehenders tends to be similar to that of younger children matched for reading comprehension. In contrast to their impaired general language skills, poor comprehenders may exhibit normal phonological and decoding skills (Stothard & Hulme, 1992).

Poor comprehenders exhibit poorer use of linguistic devices that foster cohesion, such as anaphora and causal relationships. When 7- and 8-year-olds were asked to retell stories that had limited use of temporal and causal connectives, 75% of skilled comprehenders added a variety of temporal and causal connectives, whereas only 25% of less skilled comprehenders added any connectives and none of those were causal. Poor comprehenders also used more ambiguous pronouns and were more likely than good comprehenders to tell stories from pictures in present rather than past tense (Yuill & Oakhill, 1991). These differences were less marked in 9-year-olds, but were still present.

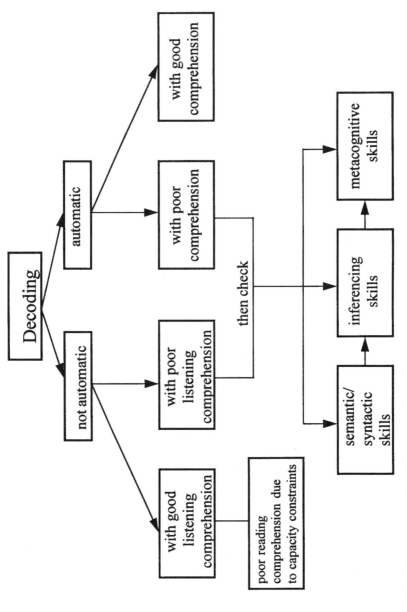

FIG. 4.5. Components of reading comprehension.

Yuill and Oakhill (1991) also investigated children's ability to give empirical and deductive explanations using Donaldson's (1986) explanation categories (discussed earlier). Good and poor comprehenders performed similarly in giving empirical explanations (e.g., Mary finds a mouse in her bed. Mary is hiding in the corner. Why is Mary scared?), but the poor comprehenders were significantly poorer than the good comprehenders on deductive explanations (e.g., Mary gets soaked. Mary is sneezing. How do you know that Mary has a cold?). Poor comprehenders tended to interpret *because* as empirical rather than deductive. Consequently, when asked to complete a sentence such as "We can tell that Mary has a cold because ... , they were likely to respond with "because she got soaked" instead of "... because she is sneezing." Such a misinterpretation would result in inadequate mental models for texts that code deductive relationships and suggests that poor comprehenders would be more likely to give pragmatic inferences when logical inferences would be required.

The problems poor comprehenders exhibit in their oral language are also reflected in their reading comprehension errors, particularly in their difficulties in taking advantage of the cohesive links in a text. Poor comprehenders exhibit greater difficulty in identifying pronominal references, particularly when the pronoun and its referent are not adjacent. They are more dependent upon explicit causal links. Causal relationships are central components of mental models for both narrative and expository texts (Ogborn et al., 1996; Schank & Abelson, 1977; Trabasso & van den Broek, 1985). Recall of a text unit is a function of the number of causal links connecting it with other text units (Trabasso & van den Broek, 1985). Poor comprehenders are less likely than good comprehenders to draw causal inferences when the causal relationships are not marked linguistically. For example, when reading

Diego wanted a new bike. He worked as a waiter at Garduños. He often had to work late at the restaurant. Diego had trouble staying awake in class.

Poor comprehenders are less likely to draw the causal inferences that Diego is working as a waiter so he can earn money to buy a new bike, and that he is falling asleep in class because he is working very late and not getting enough sleep at night. Poor readers would comprehend the passage more easily if it were written as

Diego wanted a new bike so he took a job as a waiter at Garduños to earn money. Diego had trouble staying awake in class because he often had to work late at the restaurant.

Poor readers employ their causal knowledge in a compensatory manner. The more causal relations there are in a text, the faster poor readers can read it. In contrast, the number of causal relations has no effect on reading times for good readers (Bisanz, Das, Varnhagen, & Henderson, 1992).

Inferencing Deficits

Poor comprehenders exhibit significantly greater difficulties in making inferences about texts, and with reduced inferencing, they experience greater difficulties in formulating mental models that are essential for comprehension. Part of this difficulty may be related to their inefficient use of linguistic devices that signal cohesion within texts. They may also experience difficulty inferencing because they (a) lack general knowledge, (b) have difficulty accessing relevant knowledge and integrating it with what is in the text because of processing limitation, or (c) may not realize that inferences are necessary or even permissible (Oakhill & Yuill, 1996). Although all reasons are possible, it is most likely that the problems lie in recognizing the need for inferences and accessing the relevant information. Poor comprehenders fail to make inferences even when the content should be obvious. For example,

> John got up early to learn his spelling. He was very tired and decided to take a break. When he opened his eyes again the first thing he noticed was the clock on the chair. It was an hour later and nearly time for school. He picked up his two books and put them in a bag. He started pedalling to school as fast as he could. However, John ran over some broken bottles and had to walk the rest of the way. By the time he had crossed the bridge and arrived at class, the test was over (Yuill & Oakhill, 1991, p. 71).

All students should be familiar with the idea of pedalling a bicycle to school and should understand that running over glass could result in a flat tire. Poor comprehenders, however, had significantly greater difficulty than good comprehenders when asked "How did John travel to school? Why did John have to walk some of the way to school? How do you know that John was late?"

Deficits in working memory capacity could also contribute to inferencing difficulties (Perfetti et al., 1996). Generally, poor readers are not significantly different from good readers on immediate short-term memory tasks that require them to repeat numbers, words, or sentences. They are more likely to exhibit greater difficulties on working memory tasks that require them to hold onto what has already been processed while simultaneously integrating new incoming information with earlier information (Swanson & Berninger, 1995). Working memory has a limited capacity, but the capacity does gradually increase during the school years (Case, 1985). Deficits in working memory capacity may inhibit students' abilities to process and manipulate a sufficient amount of text simultaneously. If they cannot remember and simultaneously relate a variety of ideas in the text, readers will not recognize the need to inference.

Inefficient decoding and linguistic skills can also affect the use of working memory for inferencing. As previously mentioned, working memory is a limited capacity system. If considerable space in working memory is being occupied with decoding or interpreting syntactic, semantic, or cohesive relationships, sufficient space will not be available for inferencing.

Metacognitive/Executive Deficits

As students form their mental models, they must constantly be updating or readjusting the model as they obtain additional information from the text. This requires efficient working memory (Lahey & Bloom, 1994). In fact, verbal and nonverbal working memory are viewed as major components to an executive processing system (Barkley, 1997; Pennington et al., 1996). *Nonverbal working memory* is the capacity to hold events and information in mind that will be used to control subsequent behavior. The use of nonverbal working memory activates past sensory events allowing for hindsight and forethought. The retention of a sequence of events in working memory provides the basis for the human sense of time. All of these elements of nonverbal working memory are essential for developing appropriate situation mental models that will form the background for comprehension monitoring.

The internalization of speech and language knowledge results in verbal working memory that enables one to talk with oneself to provide reflection, description, instruction, and questioning which, in turn, facilitates monitoring of comprehension, problem solving, the development of rules about rules, and moral reasoning. Verbal working memory enables the comprehension monitoring essential in reading. If students have developed inadequate mental models of text, they cannot be expected to make adequate judgments of their comprehension. Adequate mental models, however, do not assure adequate monitoring of comprehension.

Poor comprehenders exhibit a variety of metacognitive monitoring deficits (Ehrlich, 1996). They are less aware of the purpose of reading and may not even realize that they are not comprehending (Yuill & Oakhill, 1991). Compared to good comprehenders, they are less likely to notice or identify contradictory information in texts when such information is not in adjacent sentences. For example, in the following text, they may fail to notice that the statement "gorillas sleep in trees" contradicts the earlier statement, "gorillas sleep on the ground."

> Gorillas are clever animals that live together in groups in Africa. *Gorillas sleep on the ground on a bed of leaves* and they like to eat different types of fruit.

They are shy and gentle and they hardly ever fight with each other. Gorillas have flat noses and a very poor sense of smell, but their eyesight is good. They move about the ground on their hands and feet. *Gorillas sleep in trees and they often build a shelter out of leaves* about them to keep the rain out (Oakhill & Yuill, 1996, p. 79).

Poor comprehenders have greater difficulty in judging the most important information, main points, and theme in a text, and, as a result, they will devote less attention to comprehending and learning the important information.

Metacognitive/executive function skills are essential for successful dynamic literacy. In addition to verbal and nonverbal working memory, executive function also includes *reconstitution,* which involves the analysis and synthesis of behavior and generation of goal-directed flexibility and creativity for the resolution of a problem or attainment of a future goal. Without the executive skills associated with reconstitution, readers will not be able to build the mental representations essential for a documents model and dynamic literacy. As a consequence, they will not be able to raise new questions and seek solutions to new problems.

TYPES OF READING DIFFICULTIES

Many students experience language-based reading difficulties. The nature of their difficulties can vary, however. A typical approach to classification considers reading in terms of students' word recognition (decoding related to phonological processing) and listening comprehension (related to broader language abilities—syntactic, semantic, pragmatic; Catts & Kamhi, 1999; Kamhi & Catts, chap. 3, this volume). Critical and dynamic literacy requires good word recognition and listening comprehension, plus metacognitive skills. Figure 4.6 shows the components essential for developing the mental models underlying reading comprehension—decoding, linguistic skills, and metacognitive skills—and the types of disabilities associated with each component. Some students will experience deficits at all these levels, whereas other students may exhibit deficits primarily in one area. There is, however, a hierarchical nature to these components. Linguistic knowledge cannot be employed unless a reader has been able to decode the words, and a reader will not effectively monitor text if syntactic and semantic knowledge has not been used to build a representation of the text. If students with reading disabilities are to achieve critical and dynamic literacy, it is necessary that educators and researchers understand the variety of factors that contribute to reading difficulties and that specific intervention programs be designed to address the specific nature of a student's reading disability. Three types of conditions associated with reading problems are presented next.

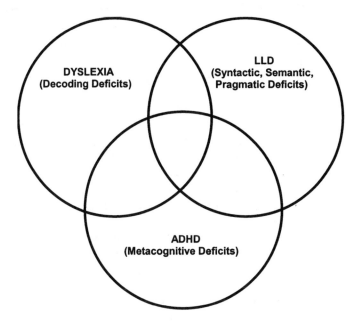

FIG. 4.6.   Types of reading disabilities.

Dyslexia

Students who are diagnosed as dyslexic exhibit primary deficits in decoding print due to problems in phonological processing and phonological awareness (Torgesen, Wagner, & Rashotte, 1994; Vellutino & Scanlan, 1987). They fail to break the alphabetic code. There are several possible levels or components to this code breaking. The student (a) must be able to match graphemes and phonemes, (b) must have the visual memory skills to remember orthographic configurations, and (c) must be able to retrieve the sound-symbol and orthographic representations quickly and automatically. Deficits in any of these areas will result in slow, halting reading, and with so much working memory devoted to decoding/retrieval, few resources are left for comprehension.

Traditionally, students with dyslexia have been viewed as students who can comprehend what is read to them, and who, once they break the code, are able to comprehend what they read. This may indeed be true for many students with dyslexia, but neither researchers nor practitioners should automatically assume that, once these students break the code, they will comprehend the text. A number of students with dyslexia exhibit more broad-based language delays and disorders. About 50% of readers with poor phonological processing have additional language processing deficits that affect their reading comprehension (Catts, Fey, Zhang, & Tomblin, 1999).

Language Learning Disabilities, Language Differences, and Reading

Specific Language Impairment. Considerable evidence shows that a high percentage of students who exhibit specific language impairment (SLI) in the preschool years are at risk for difficulties in literacy acquisition (Bashir & Scavuzzo, 1992; Bishop & Adams, 1990; Catts, 1993). A number of these students are slow to develop phonemic awareness skills, but many do break the print code eventually. Once they break the code, however, their difficulties are not over. They exhibit difficulties at the text microstructure level (involving semantics, syntax, and cohesion) and at the text macrostructure level (involving overall organization and gist). At the microstructure level, they fail to comprehend words and concepts, they have difficulty tracking cohesive elements, and they fail to understand and use more complex syntactic structures involving dependent clauses and modifiers, such as adjectives, adverbs, and prepositional and participial phrases. At the macrostructure level, they fail to recognize that different types of texts have different types of components, and they fail to integrate information across one or more texts to develop the overall gist of texts (Westby, 1999; Westby & Clauser, 1999).

Some children appear to develop language normally during the preschool years. They master the alphabetic print code when they enter school, but exhibit reading comprehension problems as they move through school (Oakhill & Yuill, 1996; Stothard, 1994). These children may have had subtle language delays or differences that were not obvious during the preschool years, or their language skills may have been adequate for oral interactions but not for the literacy tasks of "reading to learn." The literate language demands of reading to learn that emerge in middle elementary school involve more abstract vocabulary, more complex syntax, more inferencing, and extended organized texts with a variety of macrostructures.

Cultural/Linguistic Diversity. Children who enter school not speaking English are also at risk for reading comprehension difficulties in later elementary or middle school if educators assume that the students' oral language skills represent language proficiency (Chamot & O'Malley, 1994; Cummins, 1984). Although the majority of these students do not have intrinsic language learning disabilities, they often do not have the higher level vocabulary and syntactic language skills required for reading to learn. In addition, students with limited English proficiency may have a limited knowledge base, particularly in culturally specific areas, that makes it difficult to draw information from long-term memory to assist them in building mental models.

For example, children unfamiliar with the American celebration of Thanksgiving may have difficulty understanding the stories, *Turkey for Thanksgiving* (Bunting, 1991) or *Gracias, the Thanksgiving Turkey* (Cowley, 1996). If they do not know that a turkey is usually the food centerpiece of a Thanksgiving meal, in the Bunting book they will not understand why Turkey is frightened when Mr. and Mrs. Moose invite Turkey for dinner. Furthermore, they will not appreciate the humor of Turkey's hosts wanting him as a guest at the table, not on it. In the Cowley book, they will not recognize that Miguel's father is sending a turkey as an animal to be fattened for a meal, not as a pet for Miguel. As a consequence, they may not recognize the significance of the turkey following Miguel to church, which saves the turkey's life.

Children from culturally/linguistically diverse backgrounds may also have difficulty interpreting texts when the values and beliefs presented differ from their own. For example, a group of Vietnamese students expressed confusion understanding a story about a donkey that was advised to "take time to smell the roses." The confusion was generated because these students maintained that it was the donkey's job to work to help others, not to use his time for his own enjoyment.

Hyperlexia. There are some children who quickly develop fluent decoding but have significant problems with comprehension. These children may be referred to as hyperlexic (Aram, 1997; Kamhi & Catts, chap. 3, this volume). They are able to read the words of any text, yet their comprehension of what they read is, at best, limited to very literal interpretations.

Increasing numbers of children diagnosed with a semantic–pragmatic disorder, high-functioning autism, or Asperger syndrome fall into this category. They frequently exhibit severe deficits in theory of mind, which affects their ability to make social–pragmatic inferences. Consequently, they are unable to interpret characters' thoughts and feelings in response to situations, and they are unable to identify characters' motivations and goals (Happe, 1994; Tager-Flusberg & Sullivan, 1995). They may appear to do somewhat better with descriptive or procedural texts that require minimal inferencing, but they have difficulty predicting or reasoning about all texts. Although their syntax may be error free, they tend to have difficulty comprehending complex syntax involving embedded clauses, such as "Turtle believes *that Spider cannot be trusted*" (Tager-Flusberg, 1997).

Children with language learning disabilities affecting their reading comprehension are also quite likely to exhibit deficits in metacognition necessary for text monitoring. If they have not processed information adequately at the sentence level, they cannot be expected to monitor their comprehension well over the course of the text.

Attention Deficit-Hyperactivity Disorder

Some students who exhibit reading comprehension difficulties have deficits only at the metacognitive level. These students are fluent decoders and have relatively good linguistic skills that they employ adequately on short texts. Their comprehension difficulties arise because they fail to monitor the coherence of what they are reading. They exhibit deficits in executive functioning, which involves the ability to inhibit inappropriate behaviors, plan, and develop and maintain mental representation of tasks and goals (Pennington et al., 1996). Good comprehenders must understand the goal or purpose for their reading and must be able to evaluate how well they are achieving that goal.

Some students with attention deficit hyperactivity disorder (ADHD) are particularly likely to exhibit reading comprehension problems related to executive dysfunctions. Children with dyslexia and specific language impairment may also have ADHD. In fact, in some clinical studies, more than half of children identified initially with specific language impairment were later also diagnosed with ADHD (Cantwell, Baker, & Mattison, 1979, 1981). Many studies find that children identified with ADHD to be somewhat more delayed in the onset of talking than normal children (6% to 35% vs. 2% to 25% of normal children; Hartsough & Lambert, 1985; Szatmari, Offord, & Boyle, 1989) and to have a frequent diagnosis of language disorder (Cantwell et al., 1979, 1981; Love & Thompson, 1988; Trautman, Giddan, & Jurs, 1990). By elementary school, however, the language problems of some students with ADHD may not be obvious. Their articulation and syntax are well within normal limits, as may be their semantic skills. This does not, however, mean that language problems are not present.

Our understanding of the nature of ADHD is changing. The conceptualizations of ADHD as a primary problem of attention or impulsivity are losing their explanatory and prescriptive power and are being replaced with constructs of poor self-regulation, particularly behavioral inhibition. Converging evidence from clinical, neurobiological, and neuropsychological studies suggests that the surface behavioral manifestations in ADHD reflect an underlying problem in executive function (Barkley, 1997; Pennington & Ozonoff, 1996). Students with ADHD may have decoding and syntactic/semantic language problems unrelated to their ADHD that affect their reading abilities. A number of students with ADHD, however, may exhibit deficits only at the executive function/metacognitive level that affect their reading comprehension (Purvis & Tannock, 1997). For these students, their associated reading problems are a result of their executive function deficits.

Such students with ADHD exhibit difficulties with pragmatic aspects of language and using language to plan, monitor, and evaluate behavior that reflect metacognitive or executive function deficits (Landau & Milich, 1988; Tannock, & Schachar, 1996; Westby & Cutler, 1994; Whalen, Henker, Collins, McAuliffe, & Vaux, 1979). They exhibit metacognitive deficits involving failure to monitor and evaluate their behavior in a variety of domains. This lack of monitoring and evaluation occurs when they read, as well as in social interactions. They may fail to monitor their comprehension, and as a consequence, fail to notice inconsistencies in texts, particularly when the inconsistent pieces of information are separated in the texts. Such students may be distracted by detail when reading, failing to understand the main ideas of the text (Brock & Knapp, 1996; Cherkes-Julkowski & Stolenberg, 1991; Tannock & Schachar, 1996). When students with ADHD do recognize their failure to comprehend, they may not possess, or use, appropriate strategies to repair their comprehension failure. The nature of the reading difficulties in students with ADHD may be misinterpreted as due to attention or motivational issues. As a consequence, the students do not receive the appropriate interventions.

• • • • • •

Children with dyslexia, language-learning disabilities, and ADHD are all at risk for difficulties in acquiring critical and dynamic literacy. Research from a number of projects funded by the National Institutes of Health has shown that, for many children, the teaching of phonological awareness and related sound–symbol relationships are essential if children are to learn to read. Exposure to high quality literature alone is not sufficient to develop literacy. Neither, however, are phonological awareness and sound–symbol knowledge sufficient. If educators are to facilitate the development of literacy in students, they must understand what is required, not only for basic literacy, but also what is required for critical and dynamic literacy, and they must develop specific intervention strategies to address children's individual needs. Some children exhibit difficulty in one aspect of language skills—decoding, syntactic/semantic linguistic skills and inferencing skills, or metacognitive monitoring skills. Other children exhibit multiple disabilities—they may have attentional/hyperactivity issues and associated metacognitive deficits, they may have difficulty breaking the print code, and they may exhibit a variety of linguistic deficits affecting their syntactic, semantic, and pragmatic language skills.

Current whole-language approaches to reading instruction frequently use a relatively unstructured constructivist orientation. The belief is that children construct their knowledge about the alphabetic code, syntax, and text organization by being exposed to high-quality texts. Teachers facilitate the constructive process by providing students with interesting reading materials and encouraging them to discuss what they read. Many students with reading disabilities, however, are not prepared to take advantage of such instruction because they lack comprehension monitoring and have a passive approach to tasks, inefficient text-scanning strategies, and insensitivity to text structure (Williams, 1998). Without such foundational skills in place, a constructivist, whole language curricula is not likely to be effective. Just as research has shown the importance of incorporating direct instruction in phonemic awareness into reading instruction, consideration needs to be given to incorporating more explicit instruction in comprehension. This explicit instruction should emphasize attending to language, inferencing, and metacognitive skills in meaningful literacy activities that encourage critical and dynamic literacy (Hancock, 1999; Pressley, 1998).

Many students are left guessing regarding what they have to do to be successful readers either because teachers do not know what students must do to learn or because they do not see any reason for explicit teaching. Persons working with students with reading disabilities should determine the specific nature of a student's reading difficulties and provide explicit instruction to build the skills needed to promote the development of mental modeling necessary for reading comprehension. For some students, the focus will be on the development of phonological awareness skills to facilitate their decoding abilities. For others, the emphasis will be on expansion of syntactic/semantic knowledge and use of this knowledge in inferencing. For still others, attention will be on the development of metacognitive skills for monitoring comprehension and engaging in dynamic literacy. Many students will require some combination of all these interventions.

Since the late 1970s, research has documented the usefulness of comprehension strategy instruction. At the heart of this instruction is the process of teachers demonstrating skills and strategies to students and how to apply the skills and strategies by thinking aloud (Duffy & Roehler, 1989). The likelihood of long-term appropriate use of all taught skills and strategies is facilitated by metacognitive training that makes students aware of the usefulness or purpose of the strategies they are learning. In this rapidly changing world, educators cannot teach students all the facts and ideas they will need in the future. A recent SONY advertisement in a magazine shows one boy pushing another boy in a homemade soap box. The caption says,

50 years ago, it was: "Who can build the best soap box?"

Now it's: "Who can build the best Web site?"

What will they build tomorrow?

Educators must prepare students to build what neither they nor their students can even conceptualize at the present time. If students are to be future builders, they must learn how to learn—they must achieve dynamic literacy. They must not only be able to employ phonological, syntactic, semantic, and pragmatic skills and knowledge relatively automatically in both oral and written contexts, but they must also be able to develop purposes for using these skills and knowledge. Finally, they must be able to use metacognitive skills to monitor consciously the degree to which they are achieving their purposes—adapting and modifying their behaviors as necessary to achieve goals for themselves and society.

REFERENCES

Adams, M. (1990). *Beginning to read: Thinking and learning about print.* Cambridge, MA: MIT Press.

Allaby, M. (1995). *How the weather works.* Pleasantville, NY: Reader's Digest.

Aram, D. (1997). Hyperlexia: Reading without meaning in young children. *Topics in Language Disorders, 17*(3), 1–13.

Barkley, R. A. (1997). *ADHD and the nature of self-control.* New York: Guilford Press.

Baron-Cohen, S. (1995). *Mindblindness.* Cambridge, MA: MIT Press.

Bashir, A., & Scavuzzo, A. (1992). Children with language disorders: Natural history and academic success. *Journal of Learning Disabilities, 21*(1), 53–65.

Benson, J. (1997). The development of planning: It's about time. In S. L. Friedman & E. K. Scholnick (Eds.), *The developmental psychology of planning* (pp. 43–75). Mahwah, NJ: Lawrence Erlbaum Associates.

Bisanz, G. L., Das, J. P., Varnhagen, C. K., & Henderson, H. K. (1992). Structure and components of reading times and recall for sentences in narratives: Exploring changes with age and reading ability. *Journal of Educational Psychology, 84,* 102–114.

Bishop, D. V. M., & Adams, C. (1990). A prospective study of the relationship between specific language impairment, phonological disorders and reading retardation. *Journal of Child Psychology and Psychiatry, 31,* 1027–1050.

Blachman, B. A. (Ed.). (1997). *Foundations of reading acquisition and dyslexia: Implications for early intervention.* Mahwah, NJ: Lawrence Erlbaum Associates.

Brock, S. W., & Knapp, P. K. (1996). Reading comprehension abilities of children with attention-deficit/hyperactivity disorder. *Journal of Attention Disorders, 1,* 173–186.

Bunting, E. (1991). *Turkey for Thanksgiving.* New York: Clarion Books.

Cannon, J. (1993). *Stellaluna.* San Diego: Harcourt Brace.

Cantwell, D. P., Baker, L., & Mattison, R. E. (1979). The prevalence of psychiatric disorder in children with speech and language disorder: An epidemiological study. *Journal of the American Academy of Child Psychiatry, 18,* 450–459.

Cantwell, D. P., Baker, L., & Mattison, R. (1981). Prevalence, type and correlates of psychiatric diagnosis in 200 children with communication disorder. *Developmental and Behavioral Pediatrics, 2,* 131–136.

Case, R. (1985). *Intellectual development: Birth to adulthood.* New York: Academic Press.

Catts, H. W. (1993). The relationship between speech-language impairments and reading disabilities. *Journal of Speech and Hearing Research, 36,* 948–958.

Catts, H. W. (1999). Phonological awareness: Putting research into practice. *Language Learning and Education, 6*(1), 17–19.

Catts, H. W., & Kamhi, A. (1999). Classification of reading disabilities. In H. Catts & A. Kamhi (Eds.), *Language and reading disabilities* (pp. 73–94). Needham, MA: Allyn & Bacon.

Catts, H. W., Fey, M. E., Zhang, X., & Tomblin, J. B. (1999). Language basis of reading and reading disabilities: Evidence from a longitudinal investigation. *Scientific Studies of Reading, 3,* 331–361.

Chamot, A. U., & O'Malley, J. M. (1994). *The CALLA handbook: Implementing the cognitive academic language learning approach.* Reading, MA: Addison-Wesley.

Cherkes-Julkowski, M., & Stolenberg, J. (1991). Reading comprehension, extended processing and attention dysfunction. (ERIC Document Reproduction No. ED 340 194).

Coles, G. (2000). *Misreading reading: The bad science that hurts children.* Portsmouth, NH: Heinemann.

Cowley, J. (1996). *Gracias, the Thanksgiving turkey.* New York: Scholastic.

Cummins, J. (1984). *Bilingualism and special education: Issues in assessment and pedagogy.* San Diego: College-Hill.

Donaldson, M. L. (1986). *Children's explanations.* New York: Cambridge University Press.

Dr. Seuss. (1949). *Bartholomew and the oobleck.* New York: Random House.

Duffy, G. G., & Roehler, L. R. (1989). Why strategy instruction is so difficult and what we need to do about it. In C. B. McCormick, G. Miller, & M. Pressley (Eds.), *Cognitive strategy research: From basic research to educational applications* (pp. 133–154). New York: Springer-Verlag.

Ehrlich, M.-F. (1996). Metacognitive monitoring in the processing of anaphoric devices in skilled and less skill comprehenders. In C. Cornoldi & J. Oakhill (Eds.), *Reading comprehension difficulties: Processes and intervention* (pp. 221–249). Mahwah, NJ: Lawrence Erlbaum Associates.

Fleisher, L. S., Jenkins, J. R., & Pany, D. (1979). Effects on poor readers' comprehension of training in rapid decoding. *Reading Research Quarterly, 15,* 30–48.

Freier, G. D. (1992). *Weather proverbs.* Tucson, AZ: Fisher Books.

Freire, P. (1982). *Pedagogy of the oppressed.* New York: Continuum.

Hancock, J. (1999). *The explicit teaching of reading.* Newark, DE: The International Reading Association.

Happe, F. G. E. (1994). An advanced test of theory of mind: understanding of story characters' thoughts and feelings by able autistic, mentally handicapped, and normal children and adults. *Journal of Autism and Developmental Disorders, 24,* 129–154.

Harrel, B. O., & Roth, S. L. (1995). *How thunder and lightning came to be: A Choctaw legend.* New York: Dial Books.

Harter, S. (1983). Children's understanding of multiple emotions: A cognitive-developmental approach. In W. F. Overton (Ed.), *The relationship between social and cognitive development* (pp. 147–194). Hillsdale, NJ: Lawrence Erlbaum Associates.

Hartsough, C. S., & Lambert, N. M. (1985). Medical factors in hyperactive and normal children: Prenatal, developmental, and health history findings. *American Journal of Orthopsychiatry, 55,* 190–210.

Hiscock, B. (1993). *The big storm.* New York: Atheneum.

Just, M., & Carpenter, P. A. (1992) A capacity theory of comprehension: Individual differences in working-memory. *Psychological Review, 99,* 122–149.

Kamhi, A. (1999). The path to proficient word recognition. *Newsletter of Division 1, Language Learning and Education, American Speech-Language-Hearing Association, 6*(1), 4–7.

Kamhi, A., & Catts, H. (1999). Language and reading: Convergence and divergence. In H. Catts & A. Kamhi (Eds.), *Language and reading disabilities* (pp. 1–24). Boston: Allyn & Bacon.

Kintsch, W. (1998). *Comprehension: A paradigm for cognition.* New York: Cambridge University Press.

Lahey, M., & Bloom, L. (1994). Variability and language learning disabilities. In G. P. Wallach & K. G. Butler (Eds.), *Language learning disabilities in school-age children and adolescents* (pp. 354–372). New York: Merrill.

Landau, S., & Milch, R. (1988). Social communication patterns of attention deficit-disordered boys. *Journal of Abnormal Child Psychology, 16*, 69–81.

Lewis, M., & Michalson, L. (1983). *Children's emotions and moods.* New York: Plenum.

Llewellyn, C. (1997). *Wild, wet, and windy.* Cambridge, MA: Candlewick Press.

Love, A. J., & Thompson, M. G. G. (1988). Language disorders and attention deficit disorder in young children referred for psychiatric services. *American Journal of Orthopsychiatry, 24*, 52–63.

Lyon, G. R. (1999). Reading development, reading disorders, and reading instruction: Research-based findings. *Newsletter of Division 1 Language Learning and Education, American Speech-Language-Hearing Association 6*(1), 8–16.

Milius, S. (1999). Parasites make frogs grow extra legs. *Science News, 155*(18), 277.

Montangero, J. (1996). *Understanding changes in time: The development of diachronic thinking in 7– to 12–year-old children.* Bristol, PA: Taylor & Francis.

Morris, P. J., & Tchudi, S. (1996). *The new literacy: Moving beyond the 3Rs.* San Francisco: Jossey-Bass.

Oakhill, J., & Yuill, N. (1996). Higher order factors in comprehension disability: Processes and remediation. In C. Cornoldi & J. Oakhill (Eds.), *Reading comprehension difficulties: Processes and intervention* (pp. 69–92). Mahwah, NJ: Lawrence Erlbaum Associates.

Ogborn, J. Kress, G., Martins, I., & McGillicuddy, K. (1996). *Explaining science in the classroom.* Bristol, PA: Open University Press.

Pennington, B., Bennetto, L., McAleer, O., & Roberts, R. J. (1996). Executive functions and working memory: Theoretical and measurement issues. In G. Reid Lyon & N. A. Krasnegor (Eds.), *Attention, memory, and executive function* (pp. 327–348). Baltimore: Paul Brookes.

Pennington, B., & Ozonoff, S. (1996). Executive functions and developmental psychopathology. *Journal of Child Psychology and Psychiatry, 37*, 51–87.

Perfetti, C. (1985). *Reading ability.* Oxford: Oxford University Press.

Perfetti, C. (1994). Psycholinguistics and reading ability. In M. A. Gernsbacher (Ed.), *Handbook of psycholinguistics* (pp. 849–894). San Diego: Academic Press.

Perfetti, C. (1997). Sentences, individual differences, and multiple texts: Three issues in text comprehension. *Discourse Processes, 23*, 337–355.

Perfetti, C., Marron, M. A., & Foltz, P. W. (1996). Sources of comprehension failure: Theoretical perspectives and case studies. In C. Cornoldi & J. Oakhill (Eds.), *Reading comprehension difficulties: Processes and intervention* (pp. 137–165). Mahwah, NJ: Lawrence Erlbaum Associates.

Perfetti, C., Rouet, J.-F., & Britt, M. A. (1999). Toward a theory of documents representation. In H. v. Oostendorp (Eds.), *The construction of mental representation during reading* (pp. 99–122). Mahwah, NJ: Lawrence Erlbaum Associates.

Polacco, P. (1990). *Thunder cake.* New York: Putnum & Grosset.

Pressley, M. (1998). *Reading instruction that works: The case for balanced teaching.* New York: Guilford Press.

Purvis, K. L., & Tannock, R. (1997). Language abilities in children with attention deficit hyperactivity disorder, reading disabilities, and normal controls. *Journal of Abnormal Child Psychology, 25,* 133–144.

Recht, L. M., & Leslie, L. (1988). Effect of prior knowledge on good and poor readers. *Journal of Educational Psychology, 80,* 16–20.

Sanford, A. J., & Garrod, S. M. (1994). Selective process in text understanding. In M. A. Gernsbacher (Ed.), *Handbook of psycholinguistics* (pp. 669–719). San Diego: Academic Press.

Sanford, A. J., & Garrod, S. M. (1998). The role of scenario mapping in text comprehension. *Discourse Processes, 26* (2–3), 159–190.

Schank, R. C., & Abelson, R. (1977). *Scripts, plans, and goals.* Hillsdale, NJ: Lawrence Erlbaum Associates.

Schmid, E. (1989). *The water's journey.* New York: North-South Books.

Share, D., & Stanovich, K. (1995). Cognitive processes in early reading development: Accommodating individual differences into a model of acquisition. *Issues in Education, 1,* 1–57.

Singer, M. (1994). Discourse inference processes. In M. A. Gernsbacher (Ed.), *Handbook of psycholinguistics* (pp. 479–515). San Diego: Academic Press.

Stothard, S. E. (1994). The nature and treatment of reading comprehension difficulties in children. In C. Hulme & M. Snowling (Eds.), *Reading development and dyslexia* (pp. 200–238). San Diego: Singular.

Stothard, S. E., & Hulme, C. (1992). Reading comprehension difficulties in children: The role of language comprehension and working memory skills. *Reading and Writing, 4,* 245–256.

Stothard, S. E., & Hulme, C. (1996). A comparison of reading comprehension and decoding difficulties in children. In C. Cornoldi & J. Oakhill (Eds.), *Reading comprehension difficulties: Processes and intervention* (pp. 93–112). Mahwah, NJ: Lawrence Erlbaum Associates.

Swanson, H. L., & Berninger, V. (1995). The role of working memory in skilled and less skilled reader's comprehension. *Intelligence, 21,* 83–108.

Szatmari, P. Offord, D. R., & Boyle, M. H. (1989). Correlates, associated impairments, and patterns of service utilization of children with attention deficit disorder: Findings from the Ontario Child Health Study. *Journal of Child Psychology and Psychiatry, 30,* 205–217.

Tager-Flusberg, H. (1997). Language acquisition and theory of mind: Contributions from the study of autism. In L. B. Adamson & M. A. Romski (Eds.), *Communication and language acquisition* (pp. 135–160). Baltimore: Paul Brookes.

Tager-Flusberg, H., & Sullivan, K. (1995). Attributing states to story characters: A comparison of narratives produced by autistic and mentally retarded individuals. *Applied Psycholinguistics, 16,* 241–256

Tannock, R., & Schachar, R. (1996). Executive dysfunction as an underlying mechanisms of behavior and language problems in attention deficit hyperactivity disorder. In J. H. Beitchman, N. J. Cohen, M. M. Konstantareas, & R. Tannock (Eds.), *Language, learning, and behavior disorders: Developmental, biological, and clinical perspectives*. New York: Cambridge University Press.

Torgesen, J. K., Wagner, R. K., & Rashotte, C. A. (1994). Longitudinal studies of phonological processing and reading. *Journal of Learning Disabilities, 27*, 276–286.

Trabasso, T., & van den Broek, P. W. (1985). Causal thinking and the representation of narratives events. *Journal of Memory and Language, 24*, 612–630.

Trautman, R. C., Giddan, J. J., & Jurs, S. G. (1990). Language risk factor in emotionally disturbed children within a school and day treatment program. *Journal of Childhood Communication Disorders, 13*, 123–133.

van Dijk, T. A., & Kintsch, W. (1983). *Strategies of discourse comprehension*. New York: Academic Press.

Vellutino, F. R., & Scanlon, D. (1987). Phonological coding, phonological awareness, and reading ability: Evidence from a longitudinal and experimental study. *Merrill-Palmer Quarterly, 33*, 321–363.

Walker, C. H. (1987). Relative importance of domain knowledge and overall aptitude on acquisition of domain-related knowledge. *Cognition and Instruction, 4*, 25–42.

Westby, C. E. (1999). Assessing and remediating text comprehension problems. In H. Catts & A. Kamhi (Eds.), *Language and reading disabilities* (pp. 154–219). Boston: Allyn & Bacon.

Westby, C. E., & Clauser, P. (1999). The right stuff for writing: Assessing and facilitating written language. In H. Catts & A. Kamhi (Eds.), *Language and reading disabilities* (pp. 259–324). Boston: Allyn & Bacon.

Westby, C. E., & Cutler, S. (1994). Language and ADHD: Understanding the bases and treatment of self-regulatory behaviors. *Topics in Language Disorders, 14*(4), 58–76.

Whalen, C. K., Henker, B., Collins, B. E., McAuliffe, S., & Vaux, A. (1979). Peer interaction in structured communication tasks: Comparisons of normal and hyperactive boys and of methylphenidate (Ritalin) and placebo effects. *Child Development, 50*, 388–401.

Williams, J. P. (1998). Improving the comprehension of disabled readers. *Annals of Dyslexia, 48*, 213–238.

Yuill, N., & Oakhill, J. (1991). *Children's problems in text comprehension: An experimental investigation*. New York: Cambridge University Press.

Language Variation and Struggling Readers: Finding Patterns in Diversity

Elaine R. Silliman
Ruth Huntley Bahr
University of South Florida

Louise C. Wilkinson
Rutgers, The State University of New Jersey

Candida R. Turner
University of South Florida

> Information about dialect differences is important no matter what approach is being used to teach reading. ... First, general knowledge about the nature of language diversity is required. Without understanding the systematic and patterned nature of differences, it is difficult to appreciate dialects for what they are—natural subgroupings in a language. Second, knowledge of particular structures in the dialects [that students speak] ... is essential to understanding why certain forms occur, where they occur, and how they should be viewed in the context of assessing reading skills
>
> —Wolfram, Adger, & Christian, 1999, pp. 144–145

This chapter examines language variation in the context of those African-American children who are struggling to read. The first section speaks to language variation within the changing standards for academic success in American classrooms. Next, struggling readers who are African American are approached through a social dialect framework. The challenges that dialect variation present are discussed and then examined in the context of studies conducted over the past 27 years on the development of African-American Vernacular English (AAVE) and possible linguistic markers of a spoken language impairment. In the final section, some promising avenues are offered for considering possible relationships among the nature of phonological representations, dialect variation, and instructional practices that may be responsive to the language variation needs of struggling readers with and without a spoken language impairment.

LANGUAGE VARIATION AND SOCIAL DIALECT DIVERSITY

Language variation refers to ordinary differences in the ways a language is used for a variety of complex communicative purposes. All speakers of a language produce variations. Some of these variants are the product of how individuals define their group identities through the integration of such variables as gender, occupation, socioeconomic status, geographic region, or ethnic identification. For example, regardless of cultural or ethnic heritage, all speakers have a dialect, defined by Wolfram & Schilling-Estes (1998) as "a neutral label that refers to a variety of a language, which is shared by a group of speakers" (p. 2). This broad definition encompasses Standard American English (SAE) as a type of social dialect that represents language variety, as well as other dialect variations, such as AAVE. In this context, a vernacular is the form and style of speaking used in everyday routine social interactions (Labov, 1995). The valuation of SAE as a preferred mode for speaking is a social judgment, however, governed by larger societal beliefs that this way of talking is the "right way."

Other within-language variations are situational. All speakers, regardless of the dialect they speak, tailor their discourse and linguistic choices to meet social conventions for interactional and linguistic appropriateness within a particular social system. A powerful social system in the lives of children is school. Learning to be literate entails acquiring new ways of thinking and talking. For many children the expectations for literate language use may challenge existing beliefs about their collective and individual identities because of how they talk. Thus, the obstacles that social dialect variation can produce for diagnostic and educational decision making has resulted in an intensive search for linguistic markers and culturally less biased measures of language processing that might differentiate a language difference from a language impairment in African-American children (e.g., Campbell, Dollaghan, Needleman, & Janosky, 1997; Craig & Washington, 2000; Seymour, Bland-Stewart, & Green, 1998; Weismer et al., 2000).

Although social dialect diversity is an expected type of language variation, language and learning disabilities also reflect variations that are not primarily attributed to sociocultural experience. The issue is whether children with one or both of these conditions process information differently. In other words, the language learning of these children does not adhere to the expected blueprint (Leonard, 1998). However, identifying the boundaries of the expected blueprint increases in complexity when dealing with language communities whose practices for language and literacy socialization may differ in some important respects from the "standard" blueprint. To date, the evidence suggests two important trends (Bates, 1997). First, individual variation in many aspects of language development is the rule and not the exception in most language communities; second, language variation is patterned and predictable. The challenge for research, as well as for clinical and educational practices, is to reveal these patterns of diversity.

THE NEW STANDARDS FOR LANGUAGE AND LITERACY LEARNING

During the past 10 years, the United States has undertaken major educational reform to lead to an improved system of K–12 education for all children. The goal is to attain equality of opportunity in all areas, for all Americans. To achieve equal opportunity in education, high standards of achievement are expected for all students.

Implementation of New Standards: Benchmarks

How these national standards translate into particular curricular and instructional decisions is determined at both the state and local levels (e.g., districts, schools, and classrooms). For example, the Florida Sunshine State Standards for Language Arts (Florida Department of Education, 1996) established expectations, or benchmarks, for achievement from kindergarten through high school. One expectation is that, by the end of kindergarten, students will have achieved knowledge of the alphabetic principle and be able to apply appropriate reading and spelling strategies for decoding unfamiliar words. It is also expected that kindergarten age students will possess the necessary prerequisite skills for text comprehension. These skills include recalling story events in their appropriate order, knowing how to identify the main themes of informational text, and being able to make inferences based on the text and their own world knowledge about story characters' motivations and actions. By grade 5, it is expected that students will have a sufficiently rich linguistic repertoire to understand how spelling–meaning patterns are influenced by variations in inflectional and derivational morphology (Templeton & Morris, 2000). Examples of these patterns include syllable juncture (where syllables join within printed words), such as *hoping* vs. *hopping*, attending to prefixes and suffixes, vowel selection in unstressed syllables (*confide* vs. *confidence*), and consonant alternation, which changes how related word meanings are spelled (*confident* vs. *confidence*; Bear, Invernizzi, Templeton, & Johnston, 2000).

Implications for Learning to Read

These benchmarks are consistent with three findings from the scientific literature on learning to read and the prevention of reading failure. First, based on predictive and longitudinal research, the ability to apply phonological strategies systematically for word analysis at the segmental level, rather than discrepancies between IQ and achievement level, is a strong predictor at kindergarten and first grade of who will become a good "decoder" (Blachman, 2000; Catts, Fey, Zhang, & Tomblin, 1999, 2001; Fletcher et al., 1997; Gottardo, Stanovich, & Siegel, 1996; Juel, 1988; Scanlon & Vellutino, 1996, 1997; Scarborough, 1998; Stanovich, 2000; Torgesen, Wagner, & Rashotte, 1994; Torgesen et al., 2001; Vellutino & Scanlon, 1987; Vellutino et al., 1996; Vellutino, Scanlon, & Lyon, 2000; Wagner et al., 1997).

Second, research evidence supports the interdependence between learning to read and spell because both derive from similar linguistic processes (Ehri, 1997, 1998, 2000; Treiman, 1998a, 1998b; Treiman & Bourassa, 2000). These sources of shared knowledge include phonological, lexical, orthographic, and morphological knowledge.

Third, in terms of prevention and the design of instructional programs for beginning readers and spellers, recent reports, which evaluated a broad range of studies, affirm the necessity for a balanced instructional curriculum. *Balanced instruction* means explicit instruction that optimally facilitates children's insight into the alphabetic principle and the development of strategies for comprehending a variety of texts (Snow, Burns, & Griffin, 1998). Moreover, balanced instruction should begin in the preschool years by promoting children's enthusiasm for the functions and forms of print and their motivation to read, write, and spell (Snow, Scarborough, & Burns, 1999). Most critically, the kind of reading program selected to achieve the goals of balanced instruction is less important than are the components now known to be essential for advancing language and literacy skills (National Institute of Child Health and Human Development [NICHD], 2000).

Although one goal of the standards-based reform movement in the United States is to improve education for all students, achieving this goal has proven to be somewhat elusive thus far for two reasons. One issue is the naive assumption that teachers can simply focus on students' learning of content and ignore all that students bring to the classroom, such as their affective, emotional, sociocultural, ethnic, and linguistic differences. A second roadblock is how the movement at state and local levels toward uniform educational standards will mesh with the inclusion trend and the significant number of struggling readers already present in American classrooms. The special education population continues to increase, as do parental demands for the least restrictive environment, such as an inclusion placement in the general education classroom (Rueda, Gallego, & Moll,

2000). Also, the 1997 reauthorization of the Individual With Disabilities Education Act (IDEA) now requires that individualized educational programs (IEPs) be connected with the general education curriculum to support content learning (see Osborne, chap. 13, this volume, for further discussion).

In addition, Snow et al. (1998) reported that, in 1996, "Among black and Hispanic students, the percentages of fourth graders reading below the basic level are 69 and 64 percent, respectively—this translates into about 4.5 million black and 3.3 million Hispanic children reading very poorly in fourth grade" (p. 97). Other data submitted to the United States Senate (Lyon, 1999) documented that, as recently as 1994, regardless of socioeconomic status, 44% of Caucasian students in fourth grade in California lacked basic reading skills. Such percentages represent an epidemic of reading failure among segments of the child population and offer a considerable challenge to general and special educators who are expected to deal effectively with the multiple dimensions of language variation.

DIALECT VARIATIONS IN AFRICAN AMERICAN STUDENTS AND PHONOLOGICAL PROCESSING

The Role of Dialect Variations in Beginning Reading and Spelling: The Controversy

The recent controversy on Ebonics showcases the emotions and suppositions associated with AAVE and whether it is a significant factor accounting for the struggles that many African-American children encounter in beginning to read and spell. Clearly, social and economic factors play a role in children's early literacy failures. Rickford (1999a) cited some of these factors, such as insufficient school resources and facilities, inadequate teacher preparation, students' socioeconomic backgrounds, lower teacher expectations for academic performance, and students' eventual "disidentification" (p. 8) with academic achievement. Rickford attributes this disengagement to the reduced self-esteem often associated with lowered academic expectations.

The degree to which variations in the use of AAVE might function as a possible obstacle to mastering the alphabetic principle has not been systematically explored. In the absence of empirical evidence, the assumption that "it does not matter much" has prevailed for decades. For example, over 30 years ago, Labov (1970) offered the cultural conflict hypothesis. The reading failure of many African-American students, it was argued, did not reside in the linguistic aspects of their dialect, but in the ways in which the beliefs and values of their vernacular culture conflicted with the beliefs and values of the dominant culture classroom. Despite the body of evidence that children's level of phonological sensitivity is a major predictor of success with beginning reading and spelling, a more recent view still tends to de-emphasize connections between acquiring the Standard American English (SAE) code and developing skill with print word recognition. For example, Wolfram, Adger, and Christian (1999) argued that "… there is no clear-cut evidence that learning Standard English will, in itself, increase the ease of learning to read … the acquisition of a spoken Standard English dialect requires different skills from those involved in the acquisition of word recognition skills" (pp. 157–158). In a somewhat different version of Wolfram et al.'s position, Delpit (1998) viewed the problems faced by children who are AAVE speakers in learning to read primarily as an instructional issue. In other words, AAVE use is not a barrier; instead, the major factor is that many children frequently enter school with insufficient knowledge of letter names and sound–letter correspondences.

These perspectives have merit as hypotheses; however, because successful performance on phonological processing tasks are based on SAE forms, an important question concerns the nature of the phonological representations that children who are AAVE speakers bring to these tasks. It may be the case that typically developing African American children who have less experience with analyzing the distinctive phonological features of SAE structures may be less responsive to explicit instruction in phonological awareness and decoding. In turn, this reduced sensitivity may then increase their risk of being identified with a language or a learning disability.

For example, recent findings on the scope of the letter–sound knowledge that children initially bring to kindergarten support the contributions of intrinsic factors for success with letter–sound learning (Treiman, Tincoff, Rodriguez, Mouzaki, & Francis, 1998). Moreover, the influential Report of the National Reading Panel (NICHD, 2000) acknowledged that intervention studies on phonological processing have not considered dialect, including the impact of regional dialect variations, as a "moderator variable" (pp. 2–31) in study designs. In fact, a review of the literature found that only nine studies conducted over the past 23 years explicitly described the inclusion of African-American students, including some statement about their socioeconomic status (SES; Catts et al, 1999; Foorman, Fletcher, Mehta, Francis, & Schatscheider, 1998; Juel, 1988, 1996; Juel & Minden-Cupp, 1998; Treiman et al., 1998; Wagner et al, 1997; Wallach, Wallach, Dozier, & Kaplan, 1977; Yopp, 1988). However, only the approximate percentages of African American students in the total sample are provided in eight of the nine studies, making it difficult to determine whether representative samples have been studied (Craig, 1996). Also, other studies might have included African-American students, but do not describe the demographic characteristics of their sample adequately. Some studies referred only to "inner city" participants (e.g., Blachman, Tangel, Ball, Black, & McGraw, 1999; Brady,

Fowler, Stone, & Winbury, 1994) or only generally described sample selection procedures that were presumed to reflect "the larger population from which the sample was selected" (Torgesen et al., 2001, p. 37). Most importantly, none of these studies addressed dialect issues, even indirectly, or considered variations in the frequency of the AAVE feature use as an inclusion criterion. To address the question of whether AAVE dialect use plays a facilitating or neutral role in the development of phonological sensitivity for SAE forms, a first step is obtaining consensus on what dialect forms are most characteristic of AAVE and when they emerge as productive forms.

THE OVERLAP BETWEEN SAE VARIETIES AND AAVE

On linguistic grounds, the determination of who is an AAVE dialect speaker is a complicated issue. One factor contributing to this complexity is the fact that "Although AAVE is a dialect of English and differs with SAE in many linguistic features, the majority of features that make up the English language are no different between the two dialects" (Seymour et al., 1998, p. 97). In other words, within any AAVE dialect speaker, the two dialect systems co-exist with one other but how they interact differs (Labov, 1998). Labov's work, among others, has led researchers to examine the nature of overlaps between these parallel dialect systems and how interactions are further influenced by sociocultural, socioeconomic, and geographic variables.

Types of Overlap

More Overlap.   AAVE syntax shares many elements in common with Southern White American English (SWAE), such as negative inversion (*Didn't nobody like that mess*); the absence of inversion in embedded questions (*What he do that for?*); and double modals (*They might could do it*; Labov, 1998; Martin & Wolfram, 1998; Oetting, Cantrell, & Horohov, 1999). In their verb systems, both SWAE and AAVE mark aspect, or the duration of activity, as ongoing or completed. They also share the same mood categories (indicative, imperative, and subjective), modal elements (*can, do, would, might, ought*), and voice (active, passive), with some variations in the forms of expression.

Less Overlap.   When particular types of linguistic categories are examined, the frequency of overlap between the two dialect systems decreases (Labov, 1998). In other words, certain forms, which often involve the verb system, appear more often in AAVE than in other dialects.

1. *Linguistic zeros*—One category distinguished by a higher frequency of occurrence in AAVE involves the linguistic zeros. This category is characterized by "the complete absence of linguistic material" (Labov, 1995, p. 29) when the anticipation is for the elements to be present. Examples include the zero marking of regular third person (*He see himself in the mirror*); the plural (*They got four dollar*); regular past (*And the boy kiss me*); the irregular past (*They bring it yesterday*); the possessive (*That the girl doll*); and the copula (*He a fast runner*). As Labov (1995) commented, the zero copula tends to occur where the finite form of *to be* (*is, are, am, was, were*) would be employed as a main verb in other dialects. However, the zero copula may also occur where other dialects use *to be* as a finite auxiliary with the progressive (e.g., "*Boot always comin' over my house to eat,*" Labov, 1995, p. 31).

Moreover, as with many AAVE forms, the zero copula can be variably applied within and across individuals. Contracted and full forms both appear, for example, in the first person (*I'm sleepy*), tag questions (*Is that a surprise or is it not?*) and in embedded *Wh*-clauses (*That's what she is a sister*). These patterned variations in the inclusion or deletion of the copula are attributed to the nature of the phonetic context, including interactions between stress patterns and the phonological shape of syllables, and the interactions of the phonetic context with the preceding and following syntactic contexts. For example, the zero copula is a preferred form when contraction is possible (Labov, 1995; Wolfram et al., 1999). Wyatt (1996) also discussed effects of the discourse context on variable inclusion of the copula by 3- to 5-year-old children who are AAVE speakers. In Labov's (1995) analysis, variable inclusion is also strong evidence that knowledge of the copula form (or any SAE form) is present in underlying grammatical schemas.

2. *Auxiliary verbs*—A second category where less overlap exists between SAE and AAVE entails a specialized set of auxiliary verbs: *be, done, been done, been*, and *come*. Comparable to the zero copula, these auxiliary verbs can function as camouflaged forms because their meanings differ from the same SAE form. One example is stressed, or remote time, *béen* as in "The man *béen married*" (Martin & Wolfram, 1998, p. 14). Stressed *béen* serves as an aspectual marker of remote past time; that is, an action or a state is not recent but may still be relevant. Wolfram & Schilling-Estes (1998) cited a second example, the motion verb, *come*, in structures with an *-ing* verb, such as "She *come* acting like she was real mad" (p. 173). However, the meaning is not equivalent to "She came running." Instead, in this linguistic context, "come" also functions as a specialized auxiliary verb, in this situation to express indignation. Also, there is some suggestion that AAVE may utilize aspect more so than SAE, where the duration of activity tends to be represented through

tense marking of verbs (Seymour & Roeper, 1999). Furthermore, Seymour & Roeper (1999) questioned whether the specialized use of auxiliary verbs actually represents a category that is separate from the main verb *be*, which is often referred to as *habitual be*. This form expresses that an event or activity is not ongoing, but occurs sporadically over time or space, for example "My ears *be* itching" (Wolfram et al., 1999, p. 211).

3. *Phonological features*—Less overlap, or more variable use, is found for certain phonological features as a function of positional constraints (Rickford, 1999b; Stockman, 1996; Wolfram et al., 1999). The medial and final consonantal positions are more salient locations for variants than the initial position. Examples include such substitutions as *baftub/bathtub* and *baf/bath* [but less often *fum* for *thumb*] (Stockman, 1996), stopping of fricatives (*sebm/seven*), and segment deletion in word-final consonant clusters (*pos/post, des/desk, guess/guessed*). Certain changes are further influenced by syllable structure and stress patterns, for example, postvocalic /l/ may be absent when it follows a weak neutral vowel (*hep/help*; Rickford, 1999b; Wolfram et al., 1999).

However, Bailey and Thomas (1998) argued that many of these "less overlap" examples, in fact, can also be found in varieties of English other than AAVE, such as SWAE; thus, their status as true variants is suspect. The untangling of these issues is complicated further by the dynamic nature of language change. For example, the direction of vowel shift alterations in SWAE appears to differ from vowel shifts occurring in northern dialects (Wolfram, 1991). A final point is that more information is available about AAVE consonantal differences in children (e.g., Cole & Taylor, 1990; Moran, 1993). Few studies have directly studied vowel variants associated with AAVE as a function of sociocultural, SES, and regional differences (Stockman, 1996).

Sociocultural, SES, and Regional Influences

As just mentioned, sociocultural and regional variations affect AAVE findings in both the morphosyntactic and phonological domains. Wolfram and Schilling-Estes (1998) highlighted the dimensions of this issue just in terms of regional variation: "... some of the Northern metropolitan versions of AAVE are distinguishable from some of the Southern rural versions, and South Atlantic coastal varieties are different from those found in the Gulf region" (p. 174). These authors also acknowledge that the task confronting child language researchers and language specialists alike is to discover the shared core of AAVE features that transcend region, sociocultural membership, and SES. Wolfram & Schilling-Estes (1998) argued that a germane research strategy for distinguishing the common core is to investigate the SWAE of rural Caucasian speakers with similar SES status. Two reasons are offered for this approach: first, the sociohistorical roots of AAVE are grounded to low SES southern rural contexts; second, the long history of segregation in the south, and elsewhere, significantly limited opportunities for African Americans to engage in the broader language contact that fosters dialect change.

One study has applied the "southern strategy" as a method for investigating how a social dialect variation, SWAE, might also co-exist with a language impairment. Oetting et al. (1999) studied 31 Caucasian children who lived and attended school in the same rural Louisiana county (parish). Children's SES ranged from low-to-middle class strata. Of the total 31 participants, 9 were diagnosed as language impaired (Mean chronological age [CA] = 6:3 [yrs:mon]), 11 age-matched children had typically developing language abilities, and an additional 11 were also typically developing language users (Mean CA = 4:1), matched by mean length utterance (MLU) to the children with language impairment. Play interactions served as the method for obtaining production data on morphosyntactic development in the context of dialect variations. The interesting findings from this study concern the variants of SWAE produced by all three groups. These variations, which constituted approximately 20% of the total utterances, also overlapped with AAVE forms in a number of cases. Examples included the nonmarking of the copula (e.g., *He happy*; *He walking*) and subject–verb agreement in which the verb choice, typically the auxiliary *do*, disagreed in number (*Sometimes he don't play on it*).

This preliminary study demonstrated three valuable points consistent with the Wolfram and Schilling-Estes (1998) framework. First, evidence materialized for system overlaps between SAE and SWAE, as well as overlaps between SWAE and AAE, in children's production of certain morphosyntactic categories. Second, even among 4- to 6-year-old Caucasian children, the amount of dialect variation as assessed in this study was relatively low. This may indicate that either SWAE feature development was still emerging for some children or that high-density feature use actually involved a relatively limited subset of SWAE forms that focused on aspects of the verb system (Wolfram, 1991). Finally, child studies that examine known regional dialect variations, in this case rural SWAE, are a relevant strategy for disambiguating boundaries among cultural, SES, and regional memberships.

In summary, both linguistic and sociocultural factors characterize the overlap issue. In Labov's (1995, 1998) analysis, the current evidence is that AAVE consists of two distinct components, a general English component similar to the morphosyntax of SAE and an AAVE component. Each component is neither strongly integrated with nor totally independent from the other. The general English component provides an access route to the lexical, syntactic, and phonological systems of SAE, whereas the AAVE component allows speakers to construct forms for expressing meanings and intents that are not as readily available in SAE. In turn, these constructions generated through the AAVE component serve as a mechanism for maintaining individual cultural identity and social solidarity with the larger cultural group. Thus, from research and practice perspectives, distinguishing between the morphosyntactic and phonological features of certain American English vernacular dialects, such as SWAE (Oetting et al., 1999), and features more specific to AAVE dialect, continues to be a challenging task. Moreover, it is currently unknown whether variable inclusion of the linguistic zeros and auxiliary verbs in children's everyday speaking is also associated with performance on measures of phonological processing and morphosyntactic knowledge, both of which are constructed in SAE. The metacognitive and metalinguistic demands of tasks comprising these measures require some level of phonological or morphosyntactic sensitivity, which then allows children to analyze SAE phonological and syntactic structures in linguistic contexts where the these forms are obligatory.

CHILDREN'S DEVELOPMENT OF AAVE

Because critical information is unavailable on spoken language correlates of emerging literacy in African-American children who are AAVE speakers, by default, SAE developmental and normative frameworks have served as the basis for clinical and educational decisions about who is language impaired or reading disabled. For example, the overreferral of children who are AAVE speakers for special education and speech-language services is often attributed to the inappropriate application of SAE frames of reference, such as performance on tests that assess SAE knowledge of phonological and morphosyntactic structures (Tomblin et al., 1997; Wyatt, 1996).

At the same time, children might be underreferred for necessary services because educational staff or researchers have insufficient understanding about how a language impairment can co-exist with AAVE dialect patterns (Seymour et al., 1998). The limited instructional research on phonological processing that has included sufficient numbers of African-American children provides indirect evidence that this misunderstanding may be operating for children described as "hard-to-remediate" (e.g., Foorman et al., 1998; Juel, 1988, 1996, Wagner et al., 1997). One reason for this misunderstanding may be due to that fact that studies on the development of AAVE and SAE only began to gain momentum in the mid-1990s.

Approaches to the AAVE and SAE Overlap

Table 5.1 displays a summary of the 12 cross-sectional studies that have been conducted with African-American children on the morphosyntactic development of AAVE in the past 27 years. Three points are pertinent. None of the 12 studies investigated children's emerging literacy skills; therefore, longitudinal control group studies remain to be conducted that might reveal possible interactions between AAVE development and the phonological sensitivity that predicts success with achieving insight into the alphabetical principle. Furthermore, the morphosyntactic domain has been the focus of these studies; thus, comparable developmental information remains to be gathered on other components of the spoken language system and how these components interact with morphosyntactic development. In addition, the majority of this research has been conducted in an urban area of the middle west. In practice, regional variations, with one exception (Oetting & McDonald, 2001), have not been considered as a variable that might significantly affect outcomes. Given these caveats, three types of frameworks distinguish research on children's development of AAVE for the purpose of discovering morphosyntactic markers that also might be specific to a spoken language impairment. These frameworks, which overlap to some extent, are the age-referenced approach, the noncontrastive analysis approach, and the contrastive dialect analysis approach.

The Age-Referenced Approach.   As apparent from Table 5.1, the largest data base on AAVE development derives from the work of Craig, Washington, and colleagues (Craig & Washington, 1994, 1995, 2000; Craig, Washington, & Thompson-Porter, 1998a, 1998b; Washington & Craig, 1994, 1998; Washington, Craig, & Kushmaul, 1998). All of these studies, except one (Craig et al., 1998b), concentrated on spoken language production.

Three purposes motivated this research. One aim was to gather age-referenced data on the morphosyntactic development of 4- to 6-year old children who were AAVE speakers and primarily from low SES families. *Age referencing* means that children's levels of spoken language production are compared only to an age standard, not to the adult standard. To maximize achievement of this aim, only examiners who were African American (all females) and also spoke AAVE elicited language samples from the participating children. A second objective involved the examination of variables that might influence variability in the type and frequency of AAVE feature use, including the measurement of feature density. The third purpose was a longer term clinical objective, to apply the data on typical development in the 4- to 6-year-old age range to the construction of a culturally appropriate assessment battery for identifying child AAVE speakers with a spoken language impairment. It did not appear, however, that a goal was to define a common core of AAVE features that differentiated AAVE from SAE. Instead, the aim was to gather data on children's development of AAVE as a language system in its own right. Six significant outcomes of this research are summarized next.

TABLE 5.1
12 Studies on AAVE Morphosyntactic Development, 1973–2000

Study	Participant Characteristics	State/Region	Assess Degree of AAE Feature Use?
Ramer & Rees (1973)	*90 children	New York City	No
	*Preschool, 12 (CA 4: to 5:5); kdg., 25 (CA 5:6 to 6:4); grade 1, 27 (CA 6:6 to 7:4), grade 5, 11 (CA 11:4 to 12:7); grade 8, 15 (CA 14:2 to 15:7)		
	*Gender—NS		
	*SES—Low		
Craig & Washington (1994)	*45 children, CA 4:0 to 5:6, in "at-risk" preschool	Metropolitan Detroit	Yes
	*21 males, 24 females *SES—Low		
Washington & Craig (1994)	*45 children, CA 4:0 to 5:5 (same sample)	Metropolitan Detroit	Yes
Craig & Washington (1995)	*45 children, CA 4:0 to 5:6 (same sample)	Metropolitan Detroit	Yes
Issacs (1996)	*114 African-American children, 57 Caucasian children in grades 3, 5, 7;	Charlotte, NC	No
	*40 males, 74 females *SES—Middle		
Craig, Washington, & Thompson-Porter (1998a)	*95 children, CA 4 to 6:6 (younger children enrolled in preschool program for "at-risk");	Metropolitan Detroit	Yes
	*45 males, 50 females *SES—Low		
Craig et al. (1998b)	*63 children, CA 4:0 to 7:2	Metropolitan Detroit	Yes
	*31 males, 32 females		
	*Preschool, 12; kdg., 32; grade 1, 19		
	*Primarily middle SES		
Washington & Craig (1998)	*66 children, CA 5:2 to 6:3, all in kdg	Metropolitan Detroit	Yes
	*30 males, 36 females		
	*SES—33 low, 33 middle		

continued on next page

Study	Participant Characteristics	State/Region	Assess Degree of AAE Feature Use?
Washington, Craig, & Kushmaul (1998)	*65 children, CA 4:4 to 6:3 *32 males, 33 females *SES—Low	Metropolitan Detroit	Yes
Seymour, Bland-Steward, & Green (1998)	*7 with LI; mean CA = 7.1; 5 males, 2 females *7 without LI; mean CA = 6.9; 4 males, 2 females *SES—NS	NS	No
Craig & Washington, (2000)	*24 with LI (mean CA = 6:9, 18 males; 6 females) *24 typically developing, matched for CA (mean CA = 6:9, 19 males, 8 females) *24 typically developing matched for MLCUw (16 males, 8 females) *Relatively equal SES distribution (low and middle) across the three groups	Metropolitan Detroit	Yes
Oetting & McDonald (2001)	*31 with LI; n = 16 African American, 9 males, 7 females, mean CA = 6:4; n = 15 Caucasian, 12 males, 3 females, mean CA 6:3 *31 typically developing, age-matched; n = 12 African American, 5 males, 7 females, mean CA = 6:2; n = 19 Caucasian, 13 males, 6 females, mean CA = 6:3 *31 typically developing, matched by MLUw and MLUm; n = 12 African American, 5 males, 7 females, mean CA = 4:7; n = 19 Caucasian, 12 males, 7 females; mean CA = 4.0 *SES—Low to middle	Rural area, southeastern Louisiana	Yea

Note. Kdg. = Kindergarten; CA = Chronological age; SES = Socioeconomic status; NS = Not specified; LI = Language impairment; MLCUw = Mean length communication unit in words; MLUw = Mean length utterance in words; MLUm = Mean length utterance in morphemes.

122

1. *Morphological and syntactic development*—The first series of studies identified 17 morphological and syntactic features of AAVE and documented more complex syntactic development (Craig & Washington, 1994, 1995; Washington & Craig, 1994). An important finding was that children who spoke AAVE produced the same types of complex syntactic forms as SAE speakers of comparable ages. Examples of more complex syntax included basic subordination devices, such as the simple infinitive with the same subject (He don't need *to stand up"*); infinitive with a different subject (The bus driver told the kids *to stop"*; and Wh-infinitive clauses (She know *how to do a flip"*; Craig & Washington, 1994).

2. *Type and frequency of feature use*—Frequency of feature use was initially defined as the proportion of utterances containing at least one AAVE form. This definition led to the differentiation of three distinct groups of children who varied in their frequency of AAVE features, from a maximum of 39% of utterances produced to a minimum of 0% (Washington & Craig, 1994). A second important finding concerned the linguistic zero forms (e.g., zero possessive, past tense, plural, and copula/auxiliary), which tended to be used variably within and across children (Craig & Washington, 1995). Frequency of AAVE use was unrelated to age or the types of forms produced, but distributions of types across the three groups did differ in that the zero copula, zero auxiliary, and subject–verb agreement were the types produced the most often. However, fine distinctions in classification can affect how patterns are identified and interpreted. For example, across these studies, unlike other definitions (e.g., Labov, 1995; Martin & Wolfram, 1998), auxiliary verbs were classified as modals (e.g., *will, can, do*), with remote past *been* defined as a separate type (Craig & Washington, 1994, 1995; Craig et al., 1998a; Washington & Craig, 1994).

3. *Measurement of AAVE feature use*—The existence of the linguistic zeros combined with their variable inclusion also effects the general measurement of clausal length and complexity and can create significant measurement error if not addressed from within an AAVE framework. For example, different results may be obtained when morphemes versus words are selected as the unit of analysis. A subsequent study with the same 4- to 6-year-old sample sought to establish the validity of two units for assessing morphosyntactic growth in terms of the length of clauses produced. These units were mean length of communication units in words (MLCUw) and mean length communication unit (C-unit) in morphemes (MLCUm; Craig et al., 1998a). The major question concerned whether these two units were dialect sensitive or independent of the degree of dialect usage. Neither MLCUw nor MLCUm were correlated with dialect use in the 4- to 6-year-old age range, perhaps, due to the previous finding that the frequency of AAVE forms was relatively modest in this

sample as a whole (0 to 21% for the majority of the sample). A positive relationship emerged, however, between the amount of complex syntax that children used and the MLCUw measure.

Using a school-age sample matched for SES and gender, Craig and Washington (2000) subsequently developed a dialect density measure (DDM). This metric is derived by "dividing the frequencies (tokens) of AAE by the number of words (tokens) in standard length 50 C-unit samples" (p. 368). The resulting ratio for typically developing children with a mean age of 6:9 was relatively low (.06, SD = .03). In general, then, it appeared that AAVE dialect density was either low in the various groups of urban midwestern children included in the samples across a 6-year period or that frequency of feature use decreased from ages 4 years to 6½ years.

4. *Other variables affecting frequency of feature use*—Unlike the negative findings for linguistic variables, such as MLCUw and the DDM, frequency of feature use appears sensitive to differences in gender, SES, and the nature of the discourse (sampling) task. Regarding SES, at kindergarten age, children from low SES generated more AAVE forms than did children from middle-class SES, whereas boys produced more AAVE forms than did girls (Washington & Craig, 1998). The SES results were tempered by the acknowledgment that SES is a global indicator only of complex familial conditions, resources, values, and beliefs. In comparison, gender findings were interpreted as consistent with Issacs (1996; see Table 5.1), who examined social dialect variations in older children. By grade 5, females were found to be better at code switching into SAE than were males. However, Issacs did not specify the particular "nonstandard" dialects examined or the numbers of children speaking each nonstandard dialect. In general, minimal data are available on the often subtle linguistic and sociocultural variables that affect the nature and degree of code switching or the acquisition of bidilectalism (Craig, 1996; Seymour & Roeper, 1999; Wolfram et al., 1999).

With regard to discourse task effects, AAVE feature use was greater in a narrative (picture description) task than in child structured play with toys (Washington et al., 1998). The narrative task resulted in four distinct groups of AAVE speakers, from a very high user group (19.6% to 17.6% feature use) to a low group (4.1% to 3.1% feature use). In contrast, the child structured play task yielded only two groups of AAVE speakers, a high group (16.1% to 8.2 % of AAVE production) and a low group (7.3% to 8.2%). These findings suggest that the nature of the task, when considered within the patterns of interaction for play contrasted with narration, influenced children's feature selection.

5. *Frequency of feature use and syntactic comprehension.* In the only comprehension study conducted (Craig et al., 1998b), the question

asked again concerned whether the degree of dialect use and performance on the comprehension of certain syntactic constructions were related, this time in typically developing children from middle-SES backgrounds. Frequency of AAVE use was not correlated with performance on the comprehension of *Wh*-questions and reversible (active/passive) sentences. The *Wh*-question task was presented using AAVE constructions, primarily the zero copula, e.g., *Who this?*, *Why he shovelin' here?* Again, these findings were interpreted as indicating that performance on comprehension tasks that required the processing of syntactic relationships encoded in *both* SAE and AAVE did not correlate with the degree of dialect use in children of preschool, kindergarten, and grade 1 ages.

6. *Linguistic markers of a spoken language impairment.* The ultimate goal of this extensive body of age-referenced research was the development of an assessment battery for the identification of a spoken language impairment in African-American children that also included components independent of a child's degree of AAVE use (Craig & Washington, 2000). In other words, the premise is that a diagnostically accurate measure grounded to principles of least biased assessment must provide evidence that its proposed components are sensitive to a language impairment only. An essential first step for this claim would be the demonstration that the DDM (a measure of dialect density), SES, or gender do not differentiate children with known language impairment from their chronological age peers or younger children matched on MLCUw. Preliminary results supported this premise (Craig & Washington, 2000). A second source of evidence resides in the potential power of traditional, and rather global, measures of sentence comprehension and complex syntax to identify a language impairment. Although the Craig and Washington findings indicate that these two components of their battery have the potential to attain this goal, what is left unclear is how either component reveals specific linguistic markers of a language impairment. One such marker might be reduced phonological sensitivity to the segmental properties of spoken words, an area not explored in these studies.

In conclusion, this body of work has yielded at least five significant contributions to the understanding of first language development in children who are AAVE speakers.

- First, the evidence is that AAVE and SAE develop together in terms of the morphosyntax component, including complex syntax. Moreover, this research explicitly documents the overlap of this component in the two dialect systems from a developmental perspective.

- Second, both the types of morphosyntactic development, as well as overall rate of development, appear to parallel comparable development in SAE speaking children.
- Third, the research was conducted without reference to SAE as the standard for language development.
- Fourth, depending on how it was measured, the degree of dialect use did not appear to be associated with clausal length and complexity in children with and without language impairment whose mean ages were 4 to 6 years. However, the extent to which the amount of dialect use is independent of demographic and contextual variables, such as gender, SES, and the type of discourse task, awaits more refined research (Horton-Ikard & Miller, 2000; Weismer et al., 2000).
- A final major contribution is the dialect density measure (DDM), which allows differentiation among degrees of AAVE use. It should be kept in mind, however, that the DDM is a global index only, which does not illuminate potentially important differences in types of patterns.

Given these significant contributions, many unanswered questions remain. One critical problem concerns accounting for the variable inclusion of even high-frequency AAVE forms, such as the zero copulas and other linguistic zero markers. Both Labov (1995) and Wyatt (1996) underscored the necessity to examine the phonetic, semantic, syntactic, pragmatic, and discourse contexts and their interactions that all regulate whether the inclusion of a linguistic zero is permissible. For example, differences in frequency of feature use as a function of the speaking task may actually index qualitatively different linguistic and discourse contexts that influence how speaking is formulated and produced. As one illustration of the complex interactions between context and structure, Wolfram et al. (1999) mentioned that, in many vernacular dialects, certain types of co-occurrence relations hold between verbs and other sentential constituents as a function of the meaning to be expressed. Semantic reference may be broadened, narrowed, or shifted for particular verb forms, as in "He *carried* her to the movies"; or shifts take place in the transitive status of verbs, whether or not the verb is required to have an object, such as "If we *beat*, we'll be champs." Because of the diversity of these variable inclusions, these types of meaning changes and co-occurrence relations must be individually examined. A complicating matter with children is that in-depth analyses of the linguistic and discourse contexts that frame speaking are difficult to conduct when AAVE forms may still be emerging. The absence of a form, much less its variable inclusion, may represent a developmental issue, or even a spoken language impairment, rather than simply be a frequency-of-use issue.

A second critical issue is grounded to the current debate about the efficacy of knowledge-dependent versus processing-dependent measures in the construction of language assessment batteries. Craig and Washington (2000) built a case for the incorporation of traditional knowledge-dependent measures into an assessment battery, such as tasks that access the comprehension of *Wh*-questions or vocabulary and syntactic knowledge. Others (Campbell et al., 1997; Weismer et al., 2000) argued that these tasks are more culturally biased in that the accuracy of responses, including how to respond, depends on the extent of children's world and situational knowledge, both of which are subject to sociocultural variations in experience (see Westby, chap. 4, this volume). An alternate speculation is that processing-dependent measures, such as nonword repetition tasks, draw more on culturally independent cognitive processes, like the ability to translate novel words into their phonological representations via phonological memory and other aspects of verbal working memory. Weismer et al. (2000) found that African-American children in grade 2 in Iowa performed more poorly on traditional knowledge-dependent measures, although they performed similarly to Caucasian peers, matched for age and the level of maternal education, on a nonword repetition task. Variations in dialect use could not be ruled out as a factor accounting for the less adequate performance of the African-American children on the traditional language measures. However, Weismer et al. (2000) did not specifically assess dialect density.

A third critical question awaiting resolution from the Craig and Washington (2000) research concerns the generalization of findings to other populations. Because their studies were conducted in one urban area, how results apply to AAVE child speakers in other regions, such as the south, remain tentative.

Stockman (2000) articulated a final question with substantial implications for clinical and educational practice. Is it realistic to pursue the development of culturally unbiased assessment batteries? In Stockman's opinion, the degree to which any measure can demonstrate an absence of bias is relative, rather than absolute, because some degree of bias is unavoidable for any standardized measure. Simply stated, outcomes cannot be separated from the specific groups studied and the standards employed to evaluate a test's unbiased status. As a result, any claims for "nonbiased" should be tempered with the awareness that no single measure or assessment battery can ever meet sufficiency criteria for evaluating what children know or are capable of doing.

The Noncontrastive Analysis Approach.   Because of the overlap between AAVE and SAE, Seymour et al. (1998) took the position that valid clinical distinctions do not exist yet for differentiating AAVE feature use from patterns of feature use that co-exist with a language impairment. Because of this conundrum, the temporary solution offered is that "the diagnostic focus should be on those features that do not contrast between AAE and SAE" (p. 96). In other words, *noncontrastive features* are those that function similarly in both dialects (Seymour & Roeper, 1999). These include articles (*a, the*), conjunctions (*and, but, so, because*), prepositional phrases, pronouns, and the basic subordinated constructions that both AAVE and SAE child speakers typically acquire by kindergarten age (Craig & Washington, 1994, 1995; Washington & Craig, 1994). In comparison, *contrastive features* are those that occur more frequently in AAVE, such as the linguistic zeros and camouflaged auxiliary verb forms, as well as the "invisible agreement" (Seymour & Roeper, 1999, p. 127) of third person with the verb, for example, "*She go.*"

However, Seymour et al. (1998) also recognize that variable inclusion occurs for many of the contrastive features as a function of the linguistic context. A problem attenuating the selection of contrastive features most characteristic of AAVE is that their linguistic constraints, with the exception of the copula (Labov, 1995; Wyatt, 1996), have not been sufficiently described in children. This is not the case for children speaking SAE where obligatory and optional contexts are well understood (Leonard, 1998). As a consequence, it is not possible to discern with any degree of certainty, for example, whether the absence of habitual *be* or the copula *be* in individual African-American children is due to emerging AAVE development or a language impairment. Seymour et al. (1998) proposed that, if a child has a language impairment, noncontrastive features should also be marked by similar absences of morphosyntactic forms.

In selecting shared (noncontrastive) features for analysis, the underlying assumption is that these features, which are similar to SAE, are obligated to occur in specific linguistic contexts. For example, children may or may not include the plural /s/ marker in all of their opportunities to do so, although this is obligatory in SAE. Like Ramer and Rees (1973), in one of the first studies that utilized obligatory SAE contexts in research with African American children (see Table 5.1), Seymour et al. (1998) based their approach on the concept of obligatory SAE contexts. Specifically, they concentrated on noncontrastive linguistic markers that might identify a spoken language impairment in 14 African-American children who spoke AAVE (mean age 6:9; 7 with and 7 without a spoken language impairment). Two Caucasian speech-language pathologists were selected to obtain language samples on the assumption that children would produce a fuller range of both SAE and AAVE features.

Results suggested that the noncontrastive feature analysis yielded more clinical information about the existence of spoken language impairment than did the contrastive feature analysis. For example, comparable to the Craig and Washington (2000) findings, the children without spoken language impairment produced more complex syntax than did the children with a language impairment. This outcome may be attributed, in part, to the small sample size, as well as the points that dialect density variations, as well as examiner ethnicity and SAE use, were not ruled out as possible confounding factors. Because of these three factors, the potential clinical relevance of the study is limited. The value of the noncontrastive analysis approach rests more on its theoretical claims that shared SAE and AAVE morphosyntactic features examined in obligatory contexts can identify specific linguistic markers of a language impairment in children who are AAVE speakers.

The Contrastive Dialect Analysis Approach. Only one study to date has specifically attempted to specify core features of AAVE as the outcome of intersections among regional, cultural, and SES memberships. Drawing on previous work with Caucasian children with and without spoken language impairment who spoke a rural variation of Southern White English (Oetting et al., 1999), Oetting & McDonald (2001) presented the case that contrastive morphosyntactic features can yield reliable clinical information. At the same time, they also question whether the notion of obligatory contexts is salient for distinguishing specific morphosyntactic patterns in children who are AAVE speakers. The basis of this argument is related to the existence of variable inclusions, which makes it untenable to determine what obligatory contexts might be. In addition, other patterns, such as the camouflaged auxiliary verbs and multiple negation, are more likely to occur in some linguistic contexts than in others.

Similar to the matching procedures of Craig and Washington (2000), Oetting and McDonald (2001) selected three groups of 31 children from a rural area of southeastern Louisiana, a typically developing group, a younger language-matched group, and a group with a previously diagnosed spoken language impairment. These groups of 31 children were further matched where possible by the mother's educational level and further subdivided by ethnicity (African American and Caucasian) and gender (see Table 5.1). Comparable to Seymour et al. (1998), Caucasian examiners elicited language samples (via children's narration of play with toys and three pictures). The analysis contrasted two dialect patterns, Southern White Vernacular English (SWVE) and Southern African-American Vernacular English (SAAVE). Five areas from this study are synthesized next.

1. *Measurement of dialect density*—A total of 35 different types of social dialect variations characteristic of SWVE and SAAVE were identified from the 20,171 utterances that comprised the language samples. As an index of dialect density and to control for differences in the size of language samples, the total number of each pattern (types of forms) was divided by the total number of complete and intelligible utterances in

each sample. Thus, if a child produced 26 instances of a dialect variation in a 200-utterance sample, the resulting dialect density proportion would be .13 (13%). J. B. Oetting (personal communication, June 2000) reports a substantial relationship between this index and three similar indices of dialect density (Craig & Washington, 2000; Oetting et al., 1999; Washington & Craig, 1994), suggesting that all four indices are measuring similar language behaviors. However, the stability of these indices across discourse activities other than play and simple picture narration is not yet known.

2. *Frequency of feature use*—Across the three SAAVE dialect groups, the mean rate of feature use was 34% (general range, 24% to 67%). This rate qualifies these children as *very high* to *high* users according to previous criteria for degree of feature use in urban midwestern children (Washington & Craig, 1994; Washington et al., 1998). By contrast, the mean rate of feature use for the three SWVE groups was 13% (general range, 5% to 25%), a rate comparable to a moderate user classification based on the same urban midwestern criteria; thus, the feature production of the combined SAAVE groups was nearly 2½ times greater than the feature production of the combined SWVE groups. Also, significant variability was found in the rate at which individual patterns were produced. For example, across groups, the copula was the most frequently occurring of the 35 patterns, while *I'ma* (*I'ma go peek*) occurred the least often, an indicator that this latter form was seldom used.

3. *Dialect category membership*—Table 5.2 presents a synopsis of findings on morphosyntactic development from eight of the studies previously discussed that included typically developing African-American children, ages 4- to 6-years old. Unlike Oetting and McDonald (2001), none of these studies factored regional dialect variation into their data analyses. A discriminate analysis of the 35 patterns that Oetting and McDonald identified from their language samples accurately classified 97% of the child speakers into the correct *dialect category,* that is, SWVE or SAAVE. A stepwise discriminant analysis revealed that a reduced model of four features, shown in Table 5.3 (zero marking of regular third, zero marking of copula, subject–verb agreement with *be,* and zero marking of irregular past) predicted the child speakers as users of SAAVE or SWVE with 94% accuracy. In other words, the first four features on Table 5.3 are those that most often correctly identified the SAAVE dialect users across the three groups and indicated less overlap with SWVE.

Inspection of the features listed in both Table 5.2 and Table 5.3 indicate similarity among them in AAVE feature use independent of regional variation. The general pattern that emerges focuses on the linguistic zeros and related marking of verb paradigms, including the auxiliary verb system (see also Wolfram, 1991). Table 5.3 also provides 10 additional features SAAVE speakers produced more often than SWVE speakers in the Oetting and McDonald (2001) study. With the exception of the subordinated clauses included in Table 5.2, correspondences are apparent once again in the types represented, but, for these 10 remaining types, more overlap occurred between SAAVE and SWVE.

4. *Diagnostic group membership*—A discriminate analysis applied to predict *diagnostic group membership* for the 35 patterns considered only two groups, the children with language impairment and their chronological age peers. It will be recalled that Craig and Washington (2000) were concerned with addressing the independence of dialect from the attributes of a spoken language impairment. Oetting and McDonald (2001), on the other hand, approached this relationship differently with a more comprehensive view of the language production process. The critical

TABLE 5.2

AAVE Morphosyntactic Features of Typically Developing Children, Ages 4 to 6 Years, Across Eight Studies in Which Regional Dialect Differences Were Not Considered

(Craig & Washington, 1994, 1995; Craig et al., 1998a; Ramer & Rees, 1973; Seymour et al., 1998; Washington & Craig, 1994, 1998; Washington et al., 1998)

Category	Examples
• Zero plural	Two dogs; Ghost are boys.
• Zero past tense	And this car crash.
• Zero possessive (singular and plural)	The dog hat; Both dog hat; She hit the lady car.
• Zero regular 3rd person	But when she poo on herself I don't change her.
• Zero irregular past	He fall down.
• Subject-verb agreement (3rd person, don't)	And she don't go to school.
• Habitual/durative be	My sister be sick.
• Zero copula/auxiliary	How you do this; Pokemon in the can.
• Had+past	Last week I had went to the ball game.
• Infinitive same subject	She don't want to sit down.
• Noninfinitive wh-clause	This where they live at.
• Relative clause	That's the noise that I like.
• Multiple negation	He don't want no people there.
• Indefinite article	It's a animal story.
• Zero of	He don't wanna tell too much the story.
• Demonstrative	She wrecked them dishes.

Note. The term, zero, means the particular feature is not explicitly marked in what is said.

TABLE 5.3
Morphosyntactic Features That More Often Identified Children,
Ages 4 to 6 Years, as Speakers of Southern African American
Vernacular English
(SAAVE; Oetting & McDonald, 2001)

Category	Example
1. Zero marking of regular third	But when she poo on herself I don't change her.
2. Zero marking of copula	Oscar in the can.
3. Subject verb agreement with be	When we was about to got to church.
4. Zero marking of irregular past	Cause I brung him up real fast.
5. Habitual/durative be	It be on the outside.
6. Subject verb agreement with don't	And she don't go to school.
7. Zero regular past	I dress them before.
8. Had + past	One day I had went to the beach.
9. Multiple negation	She don't want no people on the stairs.
10. Indefinite article	It's a animal story.
11. Zero plural	Six dollar and five cent.
12. Zero possessive	That Mary hat.
13. Zero of	I can't tell too much the story.
14. Demonstrative	He wrecked them back tires.

Note. The first four features were found to be most frequent in SAAVE child speakers.

questions asked whether the morphosyntactic attributes associated with spoken language impairment were similarly evident in the two dialects or whether they varied as an outcome of the dialects spoken. The provisional answers both concur and disagree with Craig and Washington (2000), and to, a greater extent, diverge from Seymour et al. (1998).

First, it appears that children with spoken language impairment are relatively adept at learning the dialect features to which they are exposed and that minimal overlap occurs between the patterns that identify dialect and diagnostic category memberships. This finding supports Craig and Washington (2000) in that identification of a spoken language impairment, relative to predictive accuracy, does not seem to be correlated with the degree of dialect use. Second and contrary to the Craig and Washington (2000) results, the type of dialect spoken can shape the attributes of a spoken language impairment. The strong implication is that the morphosyntactic dimensions of the dialect variation that children speak do influence the linguistic profile of a spoken language impairment. In effect, a spoken language impairment will "look" different depending on the type of features that are most characteristic of the particular dialect. For example, regardless of obligatory context opportunities, SWVE children with language impairment, as might be expected, produced more zero markings than did their age peers. On the other hand, the SAAVE children produced fewer tokens of zero markings in expected AAVE obligatory contexts compared to the use of this category by their age peers.

Oetting and McDonald (2001) conceded, however, that the diagnostic group results are qualified by the fact that effects of the narrative discourse genre on the morphosyntax forms formulated, as well as their manner of formulation, were not examined. This acknowledgment is consistent with recent recommendation (Perfetti, 1997; Silliman, Jimerson, & Wilkinson, 2000; Tager-Flusberg & Cooper, 1999) that, due to the interdependencies between the linguistic and discourse levels, approaches to both research and practice need to consider interactions among multiple domains across wide age ranges. In such a dynamic systems approach, analysis of interacting levels with a developmental framework allows the examination of the system in action and does not reduce the language system into isolated and discrete components, with each probed independently.

5. *Linguistic markers of spoken language impairment*—What might be a diagnostic indicator of language impairment in children whose dialect variation are either SAAVE or SWVE? Oetting and McDonald (2001) suggested that a possibility, which also emerged from earlier work with SWVE child speakers (Oetting et al., 1999), resides in the morphologically driven options children have available for tense marking, particularly for the zero copula, zero irregular past, and zero irregular third. For the SAAVE children, an implication is that those with language impairment less frequently produce obligatory contexts for these structures. A second, larger implication is that the sources of a spoken language impairment do not differ as a function of the dialect spoken. A continuing debate is whether these sources are best explained as limitations in (Leonard, 1998; Rice, Wexler, Marquis, & Hershberger, 2000): (a) the consolidation of underlying morphosyntactic representations, (b) the general capacity to process salient morphophonological input rapidly due to insufficiently encoded representations, (c) a specific breakdown in phonological memory strategies for the subsequent storage of linguistic information in long-term memory, or (d) interactions among all three sources.

The Next Steps

Although the three language variation approaches just reviewed addressed potential relationships between AAVE dialect patterns and linguistic markers of spoken language impairment, their aims did not incorporate any connections to literacy learning. One example of a connection would be the phonological sensitivity that serves as the bootstrap for children's eventual discovery of the alphabetic principle. Instead, the language variation approaches sought to narrow the expansive question continuously asked over the past 20 years. This broad question asked what are the meaningful properties of cultural differences in spoken language use and when is a difference also a language impairment. All three approaches clearly reinforce the obvious conclusion that certain categories of morphosyntactic differences, which characterize AAVE, are superficial differences only. What appear on the surface to be "qualitative differences," instead, manifest patterned regularities that, potentially, can be revealed through enhanced understanding of the linguistic and discourse constraints that govern a social dialect variation, including a regional variant. At a more substantive level, the three approaches are addressing either directly or indirectly the identification and assessment of patterns that index atypical language development in AAVE child speakers.

Longitudinal intervention studies of African-American children struggling to read generally focus on direct instruction in phonological awareness and grapheme–phoneme relations (e.g., Foorman et al., 1998; Juel, 1988, 1996, Torgesen et al., 2001; Wagner et al., 1997). The outcomes provide suggestive evidence that, approximately 85% of African-American children who are struggling readers do not have a spoken language impairment. In other words, as a group, these children profited from the instructional emphasis provided to them. The remaining 15% were described as "hard to remediate" or "treatment resisters" (Blachman, 1997), terms that describe those less responsive to instruction. These studies, conducted primarily from educational or cognitive psychology frameworks, did not address the role of dialect patterns or the existence of undetected spoken language impairments in explaining why children might be less responsive to explicit instruction.

An important next step would be to meld the phonological processing and language variation frameworks to confront two essential questions. First, what might some AAVE child speakers who are struggling readers share in common, including those with and without a spoken language impairment, which could reveal a possible source of difficulty that then culminates in significant problems with mastering the alphabetic principle? One likely candidate is the role of phonological representations in the struggle to read. Second, if the nature of the phonological representations inherent to certain patterns of AAVE do play a contributory role, what are some diagnostic and instructional implications for those children who are not responsive to phonological awareness and decoding interventions? These two issues are now discussed.

WHAT MIGHT BE THE ROLE OF PHONOLOGICAL REPRESENTATIONS IN THE STRUGGLE TO READ?

In the print domain, *phonological memory* refers to the conversion process by which orthographic information (letters and letter patterns) are recoded and temporarily stored in working memory for translation into phonological representations (Tunmer & Chapman, 1998). Phonological memory codes also serve as a process for storing linguistic information in long-term memory (Catts & Kamhi, 1999). Impaired phonological memory, or the inability to convert letters and letter patterns readily into their corresponding phonological representations, makes it difficult to perform phonemic blending (Torgesen & Wagner, 1998).

Phonological awareness is a concept that indexes phonological sensitivity about the segmental properties of words (Gottardo et al., 1996). This type of phonological sensitivity originates as a spoken language skill that, eventually, is transformed in a manner that allows children to analyze and manipulate the phonemic structure of words more consciously (Torgesen & Wagner, 1998), for example, by segmenting words into phonemes or blending phonemes to produce real words. As strategies, phoneme segmentation assists students to generate more complex spellings, while blending supports the decoding of words (NICHD, 2000).

Phonological retrieval is the ability to recall easily phonological information that is stored in long-term memory (Catts & Kamhi, 1999). This ability is commonly assessed by timed serial naming tasks, either printed letters, digits, colors, objects, or nonwords. The rationale is that "Theoretically, rapid-naming tasks are linked to reading because they are thought to index the speed of processes that are intrinsically related to the cognitive activities involved in word identification" (Torgesen & Wagner, 1998, p. 223).

These three components of phonological processing reflect the new ways in which the functions of phonological and lexical representations must be shifted from everyday listening and speaking to the translation of alphabetic information into meaning if children are to learn to read. Thus, the integrity of phonological representations may be a primary factor in the development of the phonological sensitivity necessary for rapid and effective uses of phonological recoding, awareness, and retrieval.

Three different theories, which overlap to some extent, attempt to explain the relationship between phonological representations and phonological sensitivity. Two of them are based in the speech perception literature. The other focuses on phonological retrieval. Each theory also offers a potential avenue for enhancing future research on the role of dialect variations in the development of the phonological sensitivity essential for learning to read. These theories, which emphasize either the size or the quality of the underlying phonological unit, include the segmentation hypothesis (Brady, 1997;

Fowler, 1991), the lexical restructuring deficit hypothesis (Metsala & Brown, 1998; Metsala & Walley, 1998), and the distinctness hypothesis (Elbro; 1996; Elbro, Borstrøm, & Petersen, 1998). Each describes prerequisites for learning to read words by "sight."

Segmentation Hypothesis

The *segmentation hypothesis* derived from research on speech perception that focused on phonetic differences between words. According to this hypothesis, phonemic access is not solely attributed to retrieval factors, such as those typically accessed by nonword reading and rapid naming tasks. Instead, difficulties may be related to subtle problems in formulating, retrieving, and maintaining phonological representations (Fowler, 1991). Fowler proposed that children's phonological representations became less syllabic and more segmental with growth. For example, young children may consider the phrases, *"can ya see," "come mere [come here],"* and *"need ta go"* as single multisyllabic "words." With maturity and increasing experiences with language, including emerging literacy experiences and the effects of instruction, children begin to realize that this phrase actually consists of two or three individual words. This process apparently occurs over the preschool years as children move from lexical representations that represent whole words to being able to analyze individual phonemic components of these words.

Brady (1997) further developed the segmentation hypothesis by proposing that "language weaknesses stem from deficits in a more basic phonological process—(the) ability to encode phonological representations" (p. 21), presenting a strong case for the role of speech perception in the development of reading ability. Specifically, Brady (1997) found that children with reading disabilities tended to have difficulties with making fine distinctions within a phoneme category (e.g., allophones of a particular phoneme), whereas, these same children were readily able to recognize differences between phoneme categories (e.g., /s/ vs. /f/). Brady attributed the ability to differentiate within phonemic categories to the integrity of the phonological representation. However, if the quality of phonetic input does not contain sufficiently sharp distinctions *within* phonemic categories, the result will be weakly defined, or insufficiently encoded, phonological representations. It should be noted that Brady did not consider the possible effects of social, linguistic, or instructional experiences on the ensuing quality of the phonological representation.

Lexical Restructuring Deficit Hypothesis

Metsala and Brown (1998) first proposed the *lexical restructuring deficit hypothesis* as the "phonemic restructuring of lexical items" (p. 254) or the process of moving from more holistic to segmental or analytic representations of lexical items. This hypothesis also stems from speech perception research, which, in this case, centers on the word level (e.g., using minimal pairs contrasts). The major premise is that the gradual restructuring of lexical representations throughout childhood is motivated by the cognitive demands that a rapidly growing vocabulary creates for memory storage.

According to Metsala and Walley (1998), lexical restructuring depends on such factors as vocabulary size and word and sound familiarity. Vocabulary size is distinguished by how many phonetically similar words are stored in long-term memory. This growth is characterized by the degree of *neighborhood density.* "Neighbors" are defined as words that differ from one another by one phoneme or whether phonemes are added, deleted, or substituted. For example, the words, *cap, can, tap,* and *cop* are all in the same neighborhood; therefore, as the number of neighbors increases, so does the neighborhood density. Hence, rapid vocabulary growth necessitates that new phonemic distinctions be made on a continuing basis.

If children persist with holistic strategies for lexical representations, phonological processing difficulties may occur because these representations "do not become segmentalized in a developmentally appropriate manner or time frame" (Metsala & Walley, 1998, p. 102). Therefore, if lexical restructuring does not take place in a timely fashion, then protracted development can result in (a) difficulties with phonemic access (phonological retrieval), (b) reduced ability to discover grapheme–phoneme relationships (phonological awareness), and (c) less skill in recognizing unfamiliar words (decode), all of which are key components in the development of initial reading skill. As a result, children will not gain insight into the alphabetic principle due to the absence of sufficient phonological sensitivity.

Distinctness Hypothesis

The *distinctness hypothesis* originates from speech production research and explains how "differences in *distinctness* of phonological representations of lexical items is a cause of many of the diverse differences in phonological processing associated with success or failure in reading development" (Elbro, 1996, p. 454). In using the term *distinctness,* Elbro is referring to the degree to which a lexical representation differs from its neighbors, mainly in terms of phonetic features.

Elbro (1996) proposed that poor readers "have *poorer access to the most distinct variants of spoken words* than other children" (p. 467). Some possible sources of differences in distinctness are optional phoneme omissions (e.g., *often* becomes *ofen*), reduction in vowel quality as linked to stress (e.g., *could have* becomes *could've*), and differences in distinctive features (e.g., the voiced–voiceless distinction for fricatives depending on the duration of the preceding vowel as in *eyes* versus *ice*). The result of these naturally occurring phonological processes is that the "preferred variant" of the target word is less distinct or there is a problem in associating word forms with different levels of distinctness. This relationship, which is essentially connectionist in nature, is depicted in Fig. 5.1. In this case, the phrase *that's mine* can be produced in several different ways, depending on various combinations of utterance stress, coarticulation, and dialect features. As Fig. 5.1 shows, children who lack distinctness of phonological representations will tend to have phoneme boundaries that overlap, making it difficult for them to select the appropriate form for the desired linguistic and discourse context. Conversely, children with distinct boundaries will have clear delineation (i.e., specifications) for phoneme selection. In regard to reading, Elbro (1996) also pointed out that the written forms of words "are always closest to the most distinct spoken variant" (p. 468). The question then becomes whether this form is also the most distinct variant for individual AAVE child speakers.

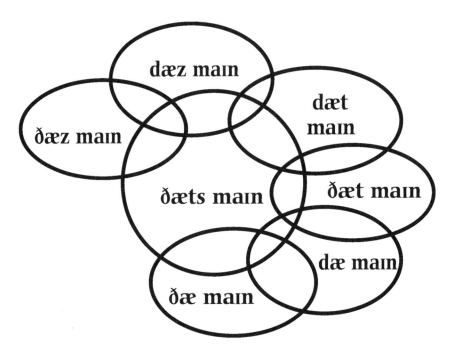

FIG. 5.1.   Fuzzy phonological boundaries for possible pronunciations of *"that's mine."* The circle represents the complete phonological form; the ovals depict possible variants of this phrase.

Similarities and Differences Among the Three Theories

These theories differ from one another in at least two important ways: the basic unit and form of phonological contrast and the impact of neighborhood density. Brief contrasts are now offered.

Both the lexical restructuring deficit hypothesis and the segmentation hypothesis support the notion that the word is the basic unit of phonological contrast in young children. Both propose that, during the course of development, children reorganize their more holistic lexical representations into a more segmental unit of word formation. However, the segmentation hypothesis also considers the quality of the phonological representation, which is not unlike the distinctness hypothesis. The latter theory targets the spoken phonological form of the word and focuses on the quality, or degree of specification, of that representation. The extent to which phonological representations are distinct then drives vocabulary growth. In contrast, the segmentation theory focuses on the role of phonemic distinctions in the development of intact phonological representations, which are then responsible for promoting vocabulary growth. The segmentation and distinctness hypotheses both suggest that insufficient sensitivity to subtle differences between similar phonetic productions can result in qualitatively underdeveloped phonological representations, which would then impede strategies for recoding, retrieval, and segmentation (see also Stanovich, 2000, for further applications to reading disabilities).

All three hypotheses predict that neighborhood density is critical for improving the quality of phonological representations. As previously defined, neighborhood density refers to the relative distance between a phonological representation and its possible variants (Elbro et al., 1998). The distinctness hypothesis purports that a dense neighborhood provides more information to assist the speaker/reader in producing a related target, whereas the segmentation and lexical restructuring deficit hypotheses state that a dense neighborhood lends itself to a more fine-grained segmental, or phonemic, analysis. The distinctness hypothesis, however, provides a much stronger account of how vocabulary words are learned, as well as a stronger account of connections between pronunciation patterns and the development of distinct phonological variants. The two other hypotheses better explain differences in phonological awareness. In other words, according to the distinctness hypothesis, it is not the ability to segment that interferes with word-level reading, but "fuzzy boundaries" among neighboring phonemic representations that impede lexical access.

The Possible Contributions of Dialect Variations in the Struggle to Read

Both the segmentation theory and the lexical restructuring deficit hypothesis can support the idea that dialect variations play a role in the development of phonological representations. Because AAVE child speakers are receiving input from both AAVE and SAE dialects, they have to incorporate this sometimes divergent information into their phonological system. For a child speaker of AAVE who also may have a higher frequency of certain patterns, such as the linguistic zeros that mark main and auxiliary verbs, subtle distinctions then have to be drawn between the lexical and phonological representations of words with superficially similar meanings. For example, if the child reads *He's done trying to please everyone,* the meaning of *done* as a present completed action is not the same as the AAVE meaning of *done* as a completed past action (Wolfram et al., 1999). Hence, the phonological form would be the same, but the semantic context determines the specific interpretation. At other times, these distinctions may be quite small, as in the phrase, *two dollar* for *two dollars.* In this case, the phonological form only differs by one morpheme (or one phoneme at the level of the phonological representation). However, the child AAVE speaker may not use the plural form because it provides redundant linguistic information.

As these examples show, it is likely that particular patterns of dialect variations increase the complexity of both the phonological and lexical neighborhoods that must be attended to in word-level analysis, making it more difficult for the child to identify critical distinctions. It is equally possible that necessary connections with the phonological neighborhood would not be adequately established due to the competing nature of AAVE and SAE productions. The result could be less robust lexical and phonological representations for SAE, depending on the nature of individual experiences with SAE. The scope of SAE phonological and lexical knowledge that children bring to school may originate in their home literacy experiences that enhance their motivation to read combined with opportunities for analyzing SAE as a written form in these naturally occurring, early, print experiences (Purcell-Gates, 2000).

In terms of relating the distinctness hypothesis to the study of dialect variations, it is easy to see how children may have difficulty linking variants with the SAE form because the dialect itself may create more variants to classify than would be typically encountered. As a consequence, in learning to read, some AAVE child speakers can face a complex task. They must learn all of the possible variations that SAE speakers would use and then incorporate into their mental lexicons any phonological variations that may interfere with their production of a target word. In short, if the phonological representation has many entries that lack sufficient distinction, child speakers/readers can find it challenging to select the appropriate entry.

• • • • • •

Research Implications.   The three theories just presented offer exploratory pathways for addressing further whether certain AAVE dialect patterns simply influence decoding skills in less consequential ways or, in certain child speakers, interfere with the acquisition of the alphabetic principle (Wolfram et al., 1999). The potential answer to this question may depend on whether the distinctness of phonological representations is another spoken language correlate that (a) plays a role in the ease or difficulty of learning to read in certain AAVE child speakers and (b) serves as a factor in the profile of a language impairment in some of these same children. Two research issues seem pertinent.

First, phonological representations are embedded in morphosyntax and directly influence the tense marking of verbs (Leonard, 1998; Rice et al., 2000), although in different ways for SAE and AAVE. It may be the case that children who are more bidialectal have a stronger sense of preferences for SAE targets and are more adept at managing obligatory contexts and variable inclusions in both dialects. Those who are less bidialectal, in comparison, may come to school not yet distinguishing fully between possible options for SAE targets because they have more fuzzy boundaries (less dense SAE neighborhoods). These children may be the ones who are less responsive to phonemic awareness instruction.

Second, recent studies with AAVE child speakers on linguistic markers of a language impairment (Craig & Washington, 2000; Oetting & McDonald, 2001; Seymour et al., 1998) suggested that, at least for some of these children, a common underlying source of difficulty may reside in less distinct phonological representations for certain SAE variants. One consequence is that they produce less obligatory AAVE contexts for tense marking of main verbs and the auxiliaries (Oetting & McDonald, 2001). It may also be the case, given the assumed relationship between neighborhood density and vocabulary, that some children will have less diverse vocabularies. A third consequence might be fewer instances of basic subordinated constructions, such as the simple infinitive (Craig & Washington, 2000). Based on these possibilities, it might also be anticipated that these children would be less responsive to phonemic awareness instruction.

Assessment Implications.   From an assessment perspective, an important clinical and educational issue is how to distinguish between these two groups of children in kindergarten and grade 1. This question is probably not fully answerable at this time. However, to reduce unwarranted referrals, classroom teachers, speech–language pathologists, teachers of specific learning disabilities, and reading teachers should have more than just a superficial understanding of AAVE dialect variation (see Wolfram et al., 1999, on the specific knowledge base professionals should possess about dialect differences).

In terms of specific assessment components and consistent with kindergarten benchmarks, all children should be evaluated for basic letter recognition and letter–sound knowledge (Treiman et al., 1998). Letter recognition is a strong predictor in kindergarten of who will become a successful reader by grade 3 (Catts et al., 2001). Additional components of assessment should include measures of phonological processing, such as phonological awareness, phonological memory, and phonological retrieval. To relate findings to possible spoken language correlates, at a minimum, representative samples of spoken language should be obtained and analyzed for dialect density, the morphosyntactic patterns that are more characteristic of AAVE use, and the number of different words as a general indicator of vocabulary diversity.

Instructional/Intervention Implications.   Instructional implications also emerge from the wedding of the phonological processing and language variation perspectives. A primary instructional goal is to convey respect for children's vernacular dialect. In doing so, engaging language and literacy experiences should be provided that systematically promote the distinctness of SAE phonological variants, which should also assist in the development of new lexical knowledge. At the same time, children should always explicitly understand the purpose of these activities and, most critically, be taught strategies for when and where to apply this knowledge. A qualification is warranted, however. Letter recognition, letter–sound knowledge, and the ability to employ a strategic orientation to the analysis of SAE grapheme–phoneme relations in order to understand how the alphabetic system works all represent foundational skills to be achieved, not a complete reading program (NICHD, 2000), much less a comprehensive language intervention program.

In our increasingly diverse society, language variation continues to present researchers and practitioners alike with bewildering challenges that, sometimes, make it difficult to see the larger picture because of a focus on the individual parts. If the bigger picture is considered, variation can provide the clues for discovering the underlying linguistic processes shared in common among AAVE child speakers. Understanding these patterns of diversity can then lead to more effective instructional approaches, which will benefit their language and literacy learning.

REFERENCES

Bailey, G., & Thomas, E. (1998). Some aspects of African-American vernacular English phonology. In S. S. Mufwene, J. R. Rickford, G. Bailey, & J. Baugh (Eds.), *African-American English: Structure, history and use* (pp. 85–109). New York: Routledge.

Bates, E. (1997). Origins of language disorders: A comparative approach. *Developmental Neuropsychology, 13,* 447–476.

Bear, D. R., Invernizzi, M., Templeton, S., & Johnston, F. (2000). *Words their way: Word study for phonics, vocabulary, and spelling instruction.* Upper Saddle River, NJ: Merrill.

Blachman, B. A. (1997). Early intervention and phonological awareness: A cautionary tale. In B. Blachman (Ed.), *Foundations of reading acquisition and dyslexia: Implications for early intervention* (pp. 409–430). Mahwah, NJ: Lawrence Erlbaum Associates.

Blachman, B. A. (2000). Phonological awareness. In M. L. Kamil, P. B. Mosenthal, P. D. Pearson, & R. Barr (Eds.), *Handbook of reading research* (Vol. 3, pp. 483–502). Mahwah, NJ: Lawrence Erlbaum Associates.

Blachman, B. A., Tangel, D. M., Ball, E. W., Black, R., & McGraw, C. K. (1999). Developing phonological awareness and word recognition skills: A two-year intervention with low-income, inner-city children. *Reading and Writing: An Interdisciplinary Journal, 11,* 239–273.

Brady, S. A. (1997). Ability to encode phonological representations: An underlying difficulty of poor readers. In B. Blachman (Ed.), *Foundations of reading acquisition and dyslexia: Implications for early intervention* (pp. 21–47). Mahwah, NJ: Lawrence Erlbaum Associates.

Brady, S., Fowler, A., Stone, B., & Winbury, N. (1994). Training phonological awareness: A study with inner-city kindergarten children. *Annals of Dyslexia, 44,* 28–59.

Campbell, T., Dollaghan, C., Needleman, H., & Janosky, J. (1997). Reducing bias in language assessment: Processing-dependent measures. *Journal of Speech, Language, and Hearing Research, 40,* 519–525.

Catts, H. W., Fey, M. E., Zhang, X., & Tomblin, J. B. (1999). Language basis of reading and reading disabilities: Evidence from a longitudinal investigation. *Scientific Studies of Reading, 3,* 331–361.

Catts, H. W., Fey, M. E., Zhang, X., & Tomblin, J. B. (2001). Estimating risk of future reading disabilities in kindergarten children: A research-based model and its clinical implications. *Language, Speech, and Hearing Services in Schools. 32,* 38–50.

Catts, H. W., & Kamhi, A. G. (1999). Causes of reading disabilities. In H. W. Catts & A. G. Kamhi (Eds.), *Language and reading disabilities* (pp. 95–127). Needham Heights, MA: Allyn & Bacon.

Cole, P. A., & Taylor, O. L. (1990). Performance of working class African-American children on three tests of articulation. *Language, Speech, and Hearing Services in Schools, 21,* 171–176.

Craig, H. K. (1996). The challenges of conducting language research with African American children. In A. G. Kamhi, K. E. Pollack, & J. L. Harris (Eds.), *Communication development and disorders in African American children: Research, assessment, and intervention* (pp. 1–17). Baltimore: Paul H. Brookes.

Craig, H. K., & Washington, J. A. (1994). The complex syntax skills of poor, urban, African-American preschoolers at school entry. *Language, Speech, and Hearing Services in Schools, 25,* 181–190.

Craig, H. K., & Washington, J. A. (1995). African-American English and linguistic complexity in preschool discourse: A second look. *Language, Speech, and Hearing Services in Schools, 26*, 87–93.

Craig, H. K., & Washington, J. A. (2000). An assessment battery for identifying language impairments in African American children. *Journal of Speech, Language, and Hearing Research, 43*, 366–379.

Craig, H. K., Washington, J. A., & Thompson-Porter, C. (1998a). Average C-unit lengths in the discourse of African American children from low-income, urban homes. *Journal of Speech, Language, and Hearing Research, 41*, 433–444.

Craig, H. K., Washington, J. A., & Thompson-Porter, C. (1998b). Performances of young African American Children on two comprehension tasks. *Journal of Speech, Language, and Hearing Research, 41*, 445–457.

Delpit, L. (1998). What should teachers do? Ebonics and culturally responsive instruction. In T. Perry & L. Delpit (Eds.), The real Ebonics debate: *Power, language, and the education of African-American children* (pp. 17–26). Boston: Beacon Press.

Ehri, L. C. (1997). Learning to read and learning to spell are one and the same, almost. In C. A. Perfetti, L. Rieben, & M. Fayol (Eds.), *Learning to spell: Research, theory, and practice across languages* (pp. 237–269). Mahwah, NJ: Lawrence Erlbaum Associates.

Ehri, L. C. (1998). Grapheme-phoneme knowledge is essential for learning to read words in English. In J. L. Metsala & L. C. Ehri (Eds.), *Word recognition in beginning literacy* (pp. 3–40). Mahwah, NJ: Lawrence Erlbaum Associates.

Ehri, L. C. (2000). Learning to read and learning to spell:Two sides of a coin. *Topics in Language Disorders, 20*(3), 19–36.

Elbro, C. (1996). Early linguistic abilities and reading development: A review and hypothesis about distinctiveness of phonological representations. *Reading and Writing: An Interdisciplinary Journal, 8*, 453–485.

Elbro, C., Borstrøm, I., & Petersen, D. K. (1998). Predicting dyslexia from kindergarten: The importance of distinctness of phonological representations of lexical items. *Reading Research Quarterly, 33*, 33–60.

Fletcher, J. M., Morris, R., Lyon, G. R., Stuebing, K. K., Shaywitz, S. E., Shankweiler, D. E. , Katz, L., & Shaywitz, B. A. (1997). Subtypes of dyslexia: An old problem revisited. In B. Blachman (Ed.), *Foundations of reading acquisition and dyslexia: Implications for early intervention* (pp. 95–114). Mahwah, NJ: Lawrence Erlbaum Associates.

Florida Department of Education. (1996). *Sunshine State Standards* [On-line]. Available: http://www.firn.edu/doe/curric/prek12/frame2.htm

Foorman, B. P., Fletcher, J. M., Mehta, P., Francis, D. J., & Schatschneider, C. (1998). The role of instruction in learning to read: Preventing reading failure in at-risk children. *Journal of Educational Psychology, 90*, 37–55.

Fowler, A. E. (1991). How early phonological development might set the stage for phoneme awareness. In S. A. Brady & D. P. Shankweiler (Eds.), *Phonological processes in literacy: A tribute to Isabelle Y. Liberman* (pp. 97–117). Hillsdale, NJ: Lawrence Erlbaum Associates.

Gottardo, A., Stanovich, K. E., & Siegel, L. S. (1996). The relationships between phonological sensitivity, syntactic processing, and verbal working memory in the reading performance of third-grade children. *Journal of Experimental Psychology, 63*, 563–582.

Horton-Ikard, R., & Miller, J. F. (2000, June). *Factors influencing African American English usage in school age children: A look at age, gender, and context.* Paper presented at the Fourth Biennial Memphis Research Symposium on Communication and Literacy in African-American Children and Youth, Memphis, TN.

Issacs, G. J. (1996). Persistence of non-standard dialect in school-age children. *Journal of Speech and Hearing Research, 39,* 434–441.

Juel, C. (1988). Learning to read and write: A longitudinal study of 54 children from first through fourth grades. *Journal of Educational Psychology, 80,* 437–447.

Juel, C. (1996). What makes literacy tutoring effective? *Reading Research Quarterly, 31,* 268–289.

Juel, C., & Minden-Cupp, C. (1998). *Learning to read words: Linguistic units and strategies* (CIERA Rep. No. 1-008). Ann Arbor, MI: University of Michigan Center for the Improvement of Early Reading Achievement.

Labov, W. (1970). *The educational implications of sociolinguistic study.* Urbana, IL: The National Council of Teachers of English.

Labov, W. (1995). The case of the missing copula: The interpretation of zeros in African-American English. In L. R. Gleitman & M. Liberman (Eds.), *Language: An invitation to cognitive science* (2nd ed., pp. 25–54). Cambridge, MA: MIT Press.

Labov, W. (1998). Co-existent systems in African-American Vernacular English. In S. S. Mufwene, J. R. Rickford, G. Bailey, & J. Baugh (Eds.), *African-American English: Structure, history and use* (pp. 110–153). New York: Routledge.

Leonard, L. B. (1998). *Children with specific language impairment.* Cambridge, MA: The MIT Press.

Lyon, G. R. (1999). Reading development, reading disorders, and reading instruction: Research-based findings. *Newsletter of the Special Interest Division 1, Language Learning and Education, American Speech-Language-Hearing Association, 6*(1), 8–16.

Martin, S., & Wolfram, W. (1998). The sentence in African-American vernacular English. In S. S. Mufwene, J. R. Rickford, G. Bailey, & J. Baugh (Eds.), *African-American English: Structure, history and use* (pp. 11–36). New York: Routledge.

Metsala, J. L., & Brown, G. D. A. (1998). Normal and dyslexic reading development: The role of formal models. In C. Hulme & R. M. Joshi (Eds.), *Reading and spelling: Development and disorders* (pp. 235–261). Mahwah, NJ: Lawrence Erlbaum Associates.

Metsala, J. L., & Walley, A. C. (1998). Spoken vocabulary growth and the segmental restructuring of lexical representations: Precursors to phonemic awareness and early reading ability. In J. L. Metsala & L. C. Ehri (Eds.), *Word recognition in beginning literacy* (pp. 89–120). Mahwah, NJ: Lawrence Erlbaum Associates.

Moran, M. (1993). Final consonant deletion in African American children speaking Black English: A closer look. *Language, Speech, and Hearing Services in Schools, 24,* 161–166.

National Institute of Child Health and Human Development. (2000). *Report of the national reading panel: An evidence-based assessment of the scientific literature on reading and its implications for reading instruction.* Bethesda, MD: NICHD Clearing House.

Oetting, J. B., Cantrell, J. P., & Horohov, J. E. (1999). A study of specific language impairment (SLI) in the context of non-standard dialect. *Clinical Linguistics and Phonetics, 13,* 25–44.

Oetting, J. B., & McDonald, J. L. (2001). Nonmainstream dialect and specific language impairment. *Journal of Speech, Language, and Hearing Research, 44,* 207–223.

Perfetti, C. A. (1997). Sentences, individual differences, and multiple texts: Three issues in text comprehension. *Discourse Processes, 23,* 337–355.

Purcell-Gates, V. (2000). Family literacy. In M. L. Kamil, P. B. Mosenthal, P. D. Pearson, & R. Barr (Eds.), *Handbook of reading research* (Vol. 3, pp. 853–870). Mahwah, NJ: Lawrence Erlbaum Associates.

Ramer, A., & Rees, N. (1973). Selected aspects of the development of English morphology in Black American children of low socioeconomic background. *Journal of Speech and Hearing Research, 16,* 569–577.

Rice, M. L., Wexler, K., Marquis, J., & Hershberger, S. (2000). Acquisition of regular past tense by children with specific language impairment. *Journal of Speech, Language, and Hearing Research, 43,* 1126–1145.

Rickford, J. R. (1999a). Language diversity and academic achievement in the education of African American students: An overview of the issues. In C. T. Adger, D. Christian, & O. Taylor (Eds.), *Making the connection: Language and academic achievement among African American students* (pp. 1–29). McHenry, IL: Center for Applied Linguistics and Delta Systems.

Rickford, J. R. (1999b). *African American vernacular English: Features, evolution, educational implications.* Malden, MA: Blackwell.

Rueda, R., Gallego, M. A., & Moll, L. C. (2000). The least restrictive environment: A place or a context? *Remedial and Special Education, 21,* 70–78.

Scanlon, D. M., & Vellutino, F. R. (1996). Prerequisite skills, early instruction, and success in first-grade reading: Selected results from a longitudinal study. *Mental Retardation and Developmental Disabilities Research Reviews, 2,* 54–63.

Scanlon, D. M., & Vellutino, F. R. (1997). A comparison of the instructional backgrounds and cognitive profiles of poor, average, and good readers who were initially identified as at risk for reading failure. *Scientific Studies of Reading, 1,* 191–215.

Scarborough, H. S. (1998). Early identification of children at risk for reading disabilities: Phonological awareness and some other promising predictors. In B. K. Shapiro, P. J. Accardo, & A. J. Capute (Eds.), *Specific reading disability: A view of the spectrum* (pp. 75–107). Baltimore: York Press.

Seymour, H. N., Bland-Stewart, L., & Green, L. J. (1998). Difference versus deficit in child African American English. *Language, Speech, and Hearing Services in Schools, 29,* 96–108.

Seymour, H. N., & Roeper, T. (1999). Grammatical acquisition of African American English. In O. L. Taylor & L. B. Leonard (Eds.), *Language acquisition across North America: Cross-cultural and cross-linguistic perspectives* (pp. 109–153). San Diego, CA: Singular Publishing.

Silliman, E. R., Jimerson, T. L., & Wilkinson, L. C. (2000). A dynamic systems approach to writing assessment in students with language learning problems. *Topics in Language Disorders, 20*(4), 45–64.

Snow, C. E., Burns, M. S., & Griffin, P. (Eds.). (1998). *Preventing reading difficulties in young children.* Washington, DC: National Academy Press.

Snow, C. E., Scarborough, H. S., & Burns, M. S. (1999). What speech-language pathologists need to know about early reading. *Topics in Language Disorders, 20*(1), 48–58.

Stanovich, K. E. (2000). *Progress in understanding reading: Scientific foundations and new frontiers.* New York: Guilford Press.

Stockman, I. J. (1996). Phonological development and disorders in African American children. In A. G. Kamhi, K. E. Pollack, & J. L. Harris (Eds.), *Communication development and disorders in African American children: Research, assessment, and intervention* (pp. 117–153). Baltimore: Paul H. Brookes.

Stockman, I. J. (2000). The new Peabody Picture Vocabulary Test—III: An illusion of unbiased assessment? *Language, Speech, and Hearing Services in Schools, 31,* 340–353.

Tager-Flusberg, H., & Cooper, J. (1999). Present & future possibilities for defining a phenotype for specific language impairment. *Journal of Speech, Language, and Hearing Research, 42,* 1275–1278.

Templeton, S., & Morris, D. (2000). Spelling. In M. L. Kamil, P. B. Mosenthal, P. D. Pearson, & R. Barr (Eds.), *Handbook of reading research* (Vol. 3, pp. 525–543). Mahwah, NJ: Lawrence Erlbaum Associates.

Tomblin, J. B., Records, N. L., Buckwalter, P., Zhang, X., Smith, E., & O'Brien, M. (1997). Prevalence of specific language impairment in kindergarten children. *Journal of Speech, Language, and Hearing Research, 40,* 1245–1260.

Torgesen, J. K., Alexander, A. W., Wagner, R. K., Rashotte, C. A., Voeller, K. K. S., & Conway, T. (2001). Intensive remedial instruction for children with severe reading disabilities: Immediate and long-term outcomes from two instructional approaches. *Journal of Learning Disabilities, 34,* 33–58, 78.

Torgesen, J. K., & Wagner, R. K. (1998). Alternative diagnostic approaches for specific developmental reading disabilities. *Learning Disabilities Research & Practice, 13,* 220–232.

Torgesen, J. K., Wagner, R. K., & Rashotte, C. A. (1994). Longitudinal studies of phonological processing and reading. *Journal of Learning Disabilities, 27,* 270–274.

Treiman, R. (1998a). Why spelling? The benefits of incorporating spelling into beginning reading instruction. In J. L. Metsala & L. C. Ehri (Eds.), *Word recognition in beginning reading* (pp. 289–313). Mahwah, NJ: Lawrence Erlbaum Associates.

Treiman, R. (1998b). Beginning to spell in English. In C. Hulme & R. M. Joshi (Eds.), *Reading and spelling: Development and disorders* (pp. 371–393). Mahwah, NJ: Lawrence Erlbaum Associates.

Treiman, R., & Bourassa, D. C. (2000). The development of spelling skill. *Topics in Language Disorders, 20*(3), 1–18.

Treiman, R., Tincoff, R., Rodriquez, K., Mouzaki, A., & Frances, D. J. (1998). The foundations of literacy: Learning the sounds of letters. *Child Development, 69,* 1524–1540.

Tunmer, W. E., & Chapman, J. W. (1998). Language prediction skill, phonological recoding ability, and beginning reading. In C. Hulme & R. M. Joshi (Eds.), *Reading and spelling: Development and disorders* (pp. 33–67). Mahwah, NJ: Lawrence Erlbaum Associates.

Vellutino, F. R., & Scanlon, D. M. (1987). Phonological coding, phonological awareness, and reading ability: Evidence from a longitudinal and experimental study. *Merrill-Palmer Quarterly, 33,* 321–363.

Vellutino, F. R., Scanlon, D. M., & Lyon, G. R. L. (2000). Differentiating between difficult to remediate and readily remediated poor readers: More evidence against the IQ-achievement discrepancy definition of reading disability. *Journal of Learning Disabilities, 33,* 223–238.

Vellutino, F. R., Scanlon, D. M., Sipay, E. R., Small, S. G., Pratt, A., Chen, R., & Denckla, M. B. (1996). Cognitive profiles of difficult-to-remediate and readily remediated poor readers: Early intervention as a vehicle for distinguishing between cognitive and experiential deficits as basic causes of specific reading disability. *Journal of Educational Psychology, 88,* 601–638.

Wagner, R. K., Torgesen, J. K., Rashotte, C. A., Hecht, S. A., Barker, T. A., Burgess, S. R., Donahue, J., & Garon, T. (1997). Changing relations between phonological processing abilities and word-level reading as children develop from beginning to skilled readers: A 5–year longitudinal study. *Developmental Psychology, 33,* 468–479.

Wallach, L., Wallach, M. A., Dozier, M. G., & Kaplan, N. E. (1977). Poor children learning to read do not have trouble with auditory discrimination but do have trouble with phoneme recognition. *Journal of Educational Psychology, 69,* 36–39.

Washington, J. A., & Craig, H. K. (1994). Dialectal forms during discourse of poor, urban, African-American preschoolers. *Journal of Speech and Hearing Research, 37,* 816–823.

Washington, J. A., & Craig, H. K. (1998). Socioeconomic status and gender influences on children's dialectal variations. *Journal of Speech, Language, and Hearing Research, 41,* 618–626.

Washington, J. A., Craig, H. K., & Kushmaul, A. J. (1998). Variable use of African American English across two language contexts. *Journal of Speech, Language, and Hearing Research, 41,* 1115–1124.

Weismer, S. E., Tomblin, J. B., Zhang, X., Buckwalter, P., Chynoweth, J. G., & Jones, M. (2000). Nonword repetition performance in school-age children with and without language impairment. *Journal of Speech, Language, and Hearing Research, 43,* 865–878.

Wolfram, W. (1991). *Dialects and American English.* Englewood, NJ: Prentice-Hall.

Wolfram, W., Adger, C. T., & Christian, D. (1999). *Dialects in schools and communities.* Mahwah, NJ: Lawrence Erlbaum Associates.

Wolfram, W., & Schilling-Estes, N. (1998). *American English.* Malden, MA: Blackwell.

Wyatt, T. A., (1996). Acquisition of the African American copula. In A. G. Kamhi, K. E. Pollack, & J. L. Harris (Eds.), *Communication development and disorders in African American children: Research, assessment, and intervention* (pp. 95–115). Baltimore: Paul H. Brookes.

Yopp, H. K. (1988). The validity and reliability of phonemic awareness tests. *Reading Research Quarterly, 23,* 159–177.

Part II

The Classroom as Context— New Instructional Directions

Classroom Discourse:
A Key to Literacy

Marion Blank
Columbia University

LITERACY, LANGUAGE, AND SCHOOL FAILURE

Across the nation, anxiety about education runs deep, none more powerful than the issue of literacy. Schools are the institution set up to teach reading and writing and the subjects rooted in these activities, including science, social studies, literature, and mathematics. Despite intense effort, schools are seen as failing to meet these obligations. Witness front page headlines such as the following:

- It's Official: OUR KIDS CAN'T READ (New York Post, 1999, story on the failure of the majority of New York State fourth graders on a new achievement test) and
- Students Taking Test Crucial to Schools "We've been gearing (up) to this for the entire year." (San Diego Union-Tribune, 1999, story on the massive effort in California's schools to raise achievement scores.)

Although the difficulties may have been overblown by the media, the statistics are dismaying. A comprehensive U.S. government report conducted by the National Institute for Literacy (State of Literacy Report, 1992) found that on a scale of I to V, over 45% of adults in our country fall into categories I and II—categories that reflect a "quite limited repertoire" of literacy skills, which render them unable to deal with many tasks considered essential for daily life.

This chapter addresses a component of the problem so overlooked that it may not even be perceived as pertinent. That component is the role of school discourse in the attainment of literacy. Although interest in school discourse has surged over the past several decades (Bernstein, 1975; Cazden, 1986; Christie & Martin, 1997; Delamont, 1983; Dillon, 1988; Donoahue, van Tassell, & Patterson, 1996; Eder, Evans, & Parker, 1995; Flanders, 1970; Hicks & Hicks, 1996; Kutz, 1997; Mehan, 1979; Stiller, 1998), little of the effort has been aimed at linking the language spoken between teachers and students with the students' mastery of written language.

The neglect is understandable. Although spoken language is deemed prerequisite for written language, the two language systems are markedly different and serve different purposes (Allwright, 1998; Blank & White, 1998; Brown, 1998; Halliday & Hasan, 1989; Horowitz & Samuels, 1987; Lemke, 1995; Sinclair, Hoey, & Fox, 1993). Paradoxically, the differences are precisely the reason why linkages between the two systems should be explored.

The disconnection between spoken and written language means that students who are not regularly exposed to written language experience it as foreign. The strangeness, of course, vanishes with steady use. For a high percentage of children, however, that steady use does not happen. Students, parents, and teachers, in a rare display of unanimity, agree that reading is a low priority activity that is avoided whenever possible. Despite efforts to change these patterns, our high tech, multimedia society makes a significant turnaround unlikely.

Within this context, school discourse occupies a unique role. Unlike most spoken language situations, the talk of the classroom does revolve around written language; specifically, the texts of the curriculum. This factor is responsible for so much of the school day—from first grade through college—being taken up with discussions about assigned readings. From the Pied Piper in a second grade literature unit, to the Revolutionary War in a fourth grade social studies unit, to concepts of ecology in a sixth grade science unit, to concepts of algebraic measurement in a ninth grade mathematics unit, classroom discourse is clearly deemed to be a handmaiden to literacy.

For students who are conversant with "book language," classroom discussion is an additional source for dealing with the curriculum. For students who are not conversant, class talk occupies a different position. It offers their only opportunity to learn how to translate the "alien" language of written text into something that is comprehensible; it represents the sole vehicle for "written language novices" to figure out what book language is all about.

It may be the case that classroom discussion, by itself, cannot fill the gap that exists between students' spoken language skills and the unfamiliar demands of written text. But we are far from having to reach such a disheartening conclusion. At this stage, our focus should be on exploring the potential of school talk to meet the challenge that exists. That is the purpose of this chapter, which targets the following three components of the "literacy-classroom discourse" constellation:

- identifying key features of books that render their language so difficult for many students;
- determining key patterns of classroom discourse and the role they play in complementing literacy;
- defining modifications in classroom discourse that might further the attainment of literacy.

SOME KEY FEATURES OF "BOOK LANGUAGE"

Years before they enter school, children develop a broad range of (oral) language skills. Prior to reading a word, they can produce long, complex sentences, convey ideas about their observations, relate events they have seen, and create imaginary scenarios. Their accomplishments are truly impressive, leading to the commonly held belief that the basis for mastery of book (written) language is in place. In other words, the children's oral skills are often seen as sufficient for literacy skills (see Blank, Marquis, & Klimovitch, 1994, 1995).

This assumption is called into question by examining the sorts of texts children are expected to read even in the early primary grades. The following segment, from a book on fossil formation designed for second to third grade students, represents one such example.

> For millions of years the bones lie under the ground. Rain falls. It seeps down through the ground, dissolving minerals in the rocks. The rainwater carries the minerals along as it trickles down, down to the bones.
>
> Like all bones, the Brontosaurus bones are filled with holes too small to see. The rainwater seeps into the holes. The water evaporates. But the minerals in the water stay and harden in the bones. Little by little what once was bone turns to stone. The bones are now stone fossils. Earthquakes rattle these fossil bones around. Volcanoes erupt and bury the bones under layers of lava. Glaciers drag tons of ice and snow over the bones. Oceans flow over the land. Their currents lay tons of sand and broken shells over the bones. The weight presses on the mud around the bones. Slowly the weight turns the mud around the bones to stone too. (McMullen, 1989, pp. 8–10)

Among the potential difficulties are limitations in decoding, or deciphering, the printed words; those, however, are not the problems of relevance here. Our concerns are with comprehension. Even when the text is read aloud (so that decoding demands are minimized), the language can still be overwhelming for many youngsters. Years of conversation leave them unprepared for sentences like: *The rainwater carries the minerals along as it trickles down, down to the bones* or *Like all bones, the Brontosaurus bones are filled with holes too small to see.* That is not how people talk to one another.

Many factors are behind the chasm separating the spoken language of everyday life from the written language of books. Everyday language is characterized by high-frequency words, short sentences, and the "here and now" topics of personal interest, whereas book language uses low-frequency words, longer sentences, and the "there and then" topics of the impersonal curriculum. To see how powerful the differences can be, two features of book (text) language are analyzed at length. They are

- the verbal concepts cascading through the material; and
- the implicit, invisible language that permeates the text.

The Verbal Concepts of Text

School texts are concerned with the exposition of knowledge-based topics—topics that are laden with complex verbal concepts (e.g., the settlement of the west, the development of scientific tools, the habitats of animals; Anderson, Spiro & Montague, 1977; Brown, 1998; Hirsch, 1988; Kintsch & Keenan, 1973; Vygotsky, 1962, 1978). Words critical to the meaning of the text pile on, one after the other—like an avalanche of information.

In the aforementioned segment on dinosaurs, for example, primary grade students are required, within a 1-min time span, to deal with such terms as *minerals, dissolve, trickle, evaporate, fossil, erupt,* and *currents,* and the way these terms link in the passage. It is one thing to know the word "rattle" in its common use. It is quite another to conjure up a reasonable meaning in connection with bones being thrust about by an earthquake. In addition, the concepts steadily intermesh with one another to create a coherent message. The process is then repeated page after page, resulting in a slew of concepts appearing at an incredibly rapid rate.

In offering these texts, educators assume that students know the concepts in question and are able to manipulate, combine, and apply them so as to glean a meaningful message. When the skill is not in place, however, the confusion can be overwhelming.

The following excerpt, from another primary school text, conveys a flavor of what the experience might be like. It does so by replacing seven of the original concepts with nonsense words, resulting in a modification of only 17 words, or 12% of the passage.

Smith had made a promise. But could Turboland keep it?

By 1961 some jabots had reached a few hundred kiloms up into the surrounding belt. But the glerf was almost a quarter of a million kiloms away!

A trip to the glerf and back would take eight yims. By 1961 only one Turbian had even been up in a jabot-and for only fifteen stashes!

Just aiming for the glerf was a problem in itself. A jabot couldn't be aimed at where the glerf was in the belt because the glerf moves about 50,000 kiloms each day. Scientists would have to aim at an empty spot in the belt where the glerf was going to be by the time the jabot got there. It would take some very careful figuring out. If there was a mistake, the jabot would go off into the belt forever!

The original text is:

Kennedy had made a promise. But could America keep it?

By 1961 some rockets had flown a few hundred miles up into space. But the moon was almost a quarter of a million miles away!

A trip to the moon and back would take eight days. By 1961 only one American had even been up in space-and for only fifteen minutes!

Just aiming for the moon was a problem in itself. A rocket couldn't be aimed at where the moon was in the sky because the moon moves about 50,000 miles each day. Scientists would have to aim at an empty spot in space where the moon was going to be by the time the spacecraft got there. It would take some very careful figuring out. If there was a mistake, the spacecraft would go off into space forever! (Donnelly, 1989, pp. 19–20)

Now it all makes sense—but only because you already knew the words that are critical to meaning. The consequences of a limited concept base are profound. A small percentage of unknown words can wreck the chances of effective comprehension.

The Implicit, Invisible Meaning in Text

Texts are composed not simply of words, but of "ensembles of sentences" (Scinto, 1986, p. 109), which combine to create a unified message. The discrete sentences can do their work only if the overall text is coherent (i.e., written so that the text can be interpreted as a whole, rather than as an unorganized collection of words; Blank, 1987; Goldberg, 1998; Halliday & Hasan, 1976, 1989; Schnotz, 1984; Schilperoord & Verhagen, 1998; Stiller, 1998; Tannen, 1984).

Coherence is, of course, dependent on the skill of the writer. Published writers fortunately demonstrate this skill; but a writer's production of coherence is not sufficient. The reader must know how to link the separate sentences so as to extract a unified message. For example, consider again the segment offered earlier on fossil creation.

For millions of years the bones lie under the ground. Rain falls. It seeps down through the ground, dissolving minerals in the rocks. The rainwater carries the minerals along as it trickles down, down to the bones.

The sentence, *Rain falls,* seems to come out of the blue. Why should an event connected to the weather suddenly appear in a discussion involving bones lying under the ground? Admittedly, it is one of the events that takes place while the bones are under the ground, but lots of events have taken place as well (e.g., other animals appeared in evolution, plants grew, many other forms of weather occurred, etc.) Further, once rain is mentioned, the topic of bones seems to disappear as the passage goes on to describe the action of the rain (seeping down and dissolving minerals). Then, just as suddenly, it re-emerges at the end of the paragraph.

For unskilled readers, the text is meandering in unpredictable directions, with concepts appearing and disappearing for no apparent reason. For skilled readers, the experience is totally different. They have learned to "see" the hidden logic connecting the sentences so that they know that the text's intended meaning is something to the effect:

> For millions of years the bones lie under the ground. *Although they are deep underground, they are affected by events that take place above ground. One such event is that* rain falls. *Although the rainwater first hits the surface, it does not stay there, on top of the ground. Instead,* it seeps down into the ground *and begins a process that will affect the bones. Gradually, after it goes underground,* it dissolves minerals *that it has contact with* in the rocks. *So now it is not simply rainwater, but rainwater with minerals in it. Next, that* rainwater, with the minerals, trickles down, down to the bones ...

The "invisible connections" (in italics) are often more extensive than the text itself. With the introduction of these connections, the text can be understood. Without it, there is bewilderment. For text to be comprehended, the reader must steadily bring in the invisible system that links the sentences together.

Readers have rarely been told that they must engage in this sort of "filling in" process, but it is what they are expected to do (see Beck, McKeown, Sinatra, & Loxterman, 1991). The creator of the text assumes that the reader possesses this ability and is able to introduce it throughout the text. Implicit messages are the invisible, essential support system for the language of the curriculum.

"Everyday language" generally does not impose demands for this type of implicit meaning. Serving different functions, it is permitted to jump from topic to topic. A conversation between friends can, without confusion, skip from a selecting a place to eat, to concern about the weather, to vacation plans for the summer, to chatting about a friend. Rarely is there the need to cope with the sort of coherence required by the language of literacy. Consequently, students whose experience is restricted to the nonliterate world have little understanding of the skills required for coherence. Here is another source for their experiencing school texts as a foreign language.

Given the vast differences between the language of everyday life and the language of classroom texts, the failure rate reported around the nation is not surprising. Indeed, it is to be expected. At the same time, it cannot be tolerated. What can be done to reverse the situation?

PATTERNS OF CURRENT CLASSROOM DISCOURSE

As noted, for many students, the spoken language of the classroom offers the sole opportunity for reviewing and evaluating the content of literacy and, in so doing, revealing the properties of written language. To determine the effectiveness with which classroom discourse meets its potential, it is worthwhile to examine instances of teacher–student exchanges. Consistent with the discussion just mentioned, the exchanges offered next will be analyzed for their handling of the twin issues of verbal concepts and implicit meaning.

Verbal Concepts: Their Role in Classroom Discourse

Segment 1: A Preschool Class
(the children are selecting and describing objects)

Teacher: Well, let's see Steven. Would you like to go into the box and pick out something.

Steven: (selects a multicolored ball)

Teacher: What's that? You just look at it. What's that?

Child: A ball

Teacher: (exclaims) A ball!

Teacher: What colors are in the ball, Pauline?

Pauline: Red.

Teacher: *Any other colors?*

Pauline: (shakes head)

Teacher: *Peter, could you tell Pauline what other colors are on the ball.*

Peter: Orange, yellow, and blue…

Segment 2: A first grade class learning early decoding skills
(the teacher has written the word "horse" on the board)

Teacher: *If you know what the word is, raise your hand.*

Ann: *Honey*

Teacher: *Who else wants to try?*

Michael: Horse

Teacher: (writes another word on the board) Who knows this one?

Segment 3:   A high school class on health
(the topic is the AIDS crisis)

Teacher: All right, why are we suddenly so conscious of AIDS ? Sabrina?

Sabrina: Because it's in the straight community now.

Teacher: Right. *Why is AIDS so scary? Shawn?*

Shawn: *It's fatal.*

Teacher: I see. *Does AIDS kill? Curtis?*

Curtis: *No. It breaks down the cells in your immune system to let other diseases kill you.*

Teacher: That's it. You die of opportunistic diseases. Now if we are going to have intercourse, what should we do to stop AIDS? Jenny?

Student: Use condoms.   (Davis, 1987, p. 40)

Segment 4:   A high school class in social studies
(the topic is international trade)

Teacher: *For instance, what were your 1934 Reciprocal Trade Agreements? How did they work? What were they designed to do? Ellen?*

Student: I don't know.

Teacher: *We studied that just last week when we were studying the New Deal. All right, Ron?*

Student: Well, we agreed, I think we agreed to lower the tariffs for import duty in our country. Then the other country would reciprocate by agreeing to lower theirs.

Teacher: Very good. (Bellack, Kliebard, Hyman, & Smith, 1966, p. 34)

Segment 5:   A high school class in literature
(the discussion is of Romeo and Juliet)

Teacher: (reads a segment from Act II) *What does she mean, Sylvia, when she says it is "too rash, too sudden"?*

Sylvia: *I don't know.*

Teacher: James, do you think she is talking about the marriage contract at the top of page 78 when she says, "It is too rash, too sudden."?

James: Yeah.

Teacher: So how does she feel about getting married, James?
                                          (Haroutunian-Gordon, 1991, p. 102).

This type of teaching is so predictable and pervasive that it is regularly found in almost any film depicting classroom scenes. The following excerpt from the film, *Hope and Glory* captures the process. In this exchange, a class at about the 4th grade level is "discussing" England's empire.

Teacher: (tapping on map of world) PINK! PINK! PINK! PINK! What are all the pink bits? Rowan!

Student: (stands up) They're ours, Miss.

Teacher: Yes, British Empire. Harper!

Student: (stands up)

Teacher: *What fraction of the Earth's surface is British?*

Student: *I don't know, Miss.*

Teacher: Anyone … (walks among rows) Jennifer Baker!

Student: Two-fifths.

Teacher: Yes. Two fifths. Ours! That's what this war is all about. Men are fighting and dying to save all the pink bits …

This exchange is nearly indistinguishable from the "real" ones offered because it contains the same simple, invariant patterns that have been the coin of the classroom realm since the start of mass education (see Blank & Klig, 1982; Blank & White, 1986; Dillon, 1988; Flanders, 1970). In all these excerpts, the language, like book language, abounds with verbal concepts. Indeed, the interactions are remarkable for the number of concepts raised in short periods of time. The process is ubiquitous, cutting across the developmental span—from asking a preschooler, *What colors are in the ball?* to asking a high school student to explain the meaning of *too rash, too sudden?*

At the same time, the exchanges are not structured in ways that will enable students to grasp the concepts that elude them. The questions come at too rapid a pace to permit an understanding of the unknown to emerge. Instead, the queries clearly presume that the students already possess the sought-for information (through assigned readings, discussions with peers and parents, etc.). As a result, classroom discourse serves largely as a test of the students' acquired knowledge rather than as a vehicle for teaching concepts not yet mastered (Blank & White, 1986).

Students who have the information may not be unhappy with the system. Although the inquiry may not represent a judicious use of time, the students themselves may be satisfied. Their effective responses earn them admiration and good grades. For students who do not have the information, the process is fraught with problems. It not only fails to teach what they need to learn, but it also regularly evokes failure (see Blank, 1972)—a process that can, and does, devastate many students. (Instances of "wrong response sequences" are in italics in the discourse segments just cited.) The following description summarizes the consequences on one scarred veteran of the experience:

> School had been unremitting torment for him. … The scars left by his school experiences reached down to his very soul. No amount of love or admiration … ever totally erased his low self-esteem or the conviction that he was unable to learn. (Schell, 1999, p. 36)

Implicit Meaning: Its Role in Classroom Discourse

The segments just cited illustrate not only the use of concepts in classroom discourse, but also the handling of implicit meaning (i.e., the extent to which students are helped to see the intricate, unstated mesh of connections present in an expository topic). Reconsider, for example, the Hope and Glory excerpt from the point of view of a student who has never been in that particular class. For such a individual, the words, *PINK! PINK! PINK! PINK! What are all the pink bits?* would almost certainly evoke bewilderment. No topic has been set forth. Only a few disconnected words have been blurted out.

What accounts for the teacher's behavior? Because her purpose is not to confuse the students, she must be working under the assumption that the question is legitimate. For her, the presence of the map and the lands pointed to make it "clear" that the topic is the "extent of the British empire" (Brown, 1998). It is as if she were saying,

> Here is a map of the whole world and on this map, there are countries and regions in every continent that are colored pink. That pink is not just arbitrary. It has a message and that message connects all these lands to Great Britain. What is the connection to Great Britain?

But she does not say any of those things. The teacher's language is even less "spelled out" than is the language of books. The following exchange from a junior high social studies class shows a similar instance in the "real" world of teaching.

Teacher: OK, current events. Glenn?

Student: Pablo Casals, the well known cellist died at age 96.

Teacher: OK, shush. Jim?

Student: The war in the Middle East is still going on.

Teacher: Is it going on in the same way? Frank?

Student: Egypt asked the Syria to intervene. They want a security meeting or a quick meeting of the U.N. Security Council.

Teacher: OK. For what reason? Do you know? Anyone know why Egypt has called a meeting of the Security Council of the U.N.? What has the Security Council just initiated?

Student: A cease fire.

Teacher: A cease fire. So what is Egypt claiming?

Student: Israel violated ...

Teacher: Israel violated the cease fire. And what is Israel claiming? (Peshkin, 1978, p. 102).

Just as the cinematic teacher assumed that everyone would understand the words, "Pink, pink, pink," this teacher assumes that everyone will understand the question, "Current events?" Were this question to be raised in a novel setting, its inappropriateness would be apparent. Someone interested in a meaningful discussion would not start off with a disconnected phrase such as "Current events?" but rather with a more expanded utterance such as "What do you think of the latest developments in the mid-East?" The topic would be explicitly stated.

The problems of overly implicit language can be seen by transforming the question–answer pattern into statement form so that the text mirrors the usual format for presenting expository text. The Middle East discussion in statement form would be:

The war in the Middle East is still going on. It's not going on in the same way. Egypt asked Syria to intervene. They want a security meeting or a quick meeting of the U.N. Security Council. There is a reason Egypt has called a meeting of the Security Council of the U.N. The Security Council has just initiated a cease fire. Egypt is claiming that Israel violated the cease fire.

The text is meaningful in that an experienced listener, or reader, could garner the main message. At the same time, the language is near telegraphic. Ideas that call for elaboration are stripped to bare essentials. It is as if the "connective tissue" is missing, leaving the message even more implicit than written text. Once again, students who have cracked the code of classroom discourse can figure out what is going on. For students in difficulty, however, the situation fails to offer them the redundancy and elaboration they must have to extract a meaningful message.

POSSIBLE MODIFICATIONS
IN CLASSROOM DISCOURSE

The patterns of classroom discourse are not arbitrary. Their ancestry can be traced to the forces operating on public education at its inception. The aim was to attain literacy at the lowest cost possible. Resources were minimal, with often only a single book to a class. Teachers, seeking assurance that the material has been read and retained, would test the students' knowledge of the book contents. The result was the emergence of the now familiar and ubiquitous memory-based question–answer format (see Blank & Klig, 1982). As so often happens with the first in a system, the technique took firm hold. Like the QWERTY keyboard, a form constructed to meet the constraints of one period has continued on, well past its point of usefulness.

If students are to have a better chance at success, change is essential. Clearly, a variety of options must be explored before determining the techniques that work best. The material that follows provides the outlines of one approach (see Blank et al., 1994, 1995). Consistent with the issues just raised, its focus is on providing a system that enables students to grasp the *verbal concepts* and *implicit meaning* of text. Among the principles governing this approach, four are central. These are:

1.   High levels of redundancy: New ideas cannot be mastered through one or two exchanges. Sustained examination of an idea is essential and it can be achieved through the use of redundancy, that is, repeating the essence of an idea over a prolonged set of exchanges. At the same time, the repetitions are never identical; rather they are structured to contain the variation (in wording, materials, etc.) needed to ensure attention and motivation.

2.   Extensive use of comments: The implicit must be made explicit. For this to occur, it is essential to present the "missing information." Questions, by their very nature, can rarely provide the implicit information students need to recognize. The only reasonable option is to impart the information in comment form. Accordingly, in a high percentage of the exchanges, elaborated comments should form the bulk of the teacher's utterances.

3.   Varied, but simple questions: Although they occupy a smaller percentage of the exchange than is usually the case, questions continue to serve a vital role in getting students to actively process the information being offered. At the same time, their failure-generating power is controlled by constraining the questions so that they (a) are simple enough to be easily answered, (b) are not based on the assumption of an already acquired knowledge base, and (c) require higher level processing (e.g., prediction, inferences) only about ideas that have been demonstrated within the lesson.

4.   Integration of physical (nonverbal) materials: Once past the preschool period, the teaching of concepts relies heavily on verbal explanation. This can be overwhelming, particularly for students with limited verbal mastery. The problem is dramatically eased by extensively inte-

grating physical materials into the scenario and by dissecting the analysis of the materials in the slow, detailed way needed to take in new information.

This constellation of principles is reflected throughout the sample lesson that follows. The content involves a second- to third-grade text on the gold rush in California. In the preceding lesson, it was established (via text and discussion) that a man [Marshall] has been laughed at for predicting that the land he was working on might contain gold. Then one day, on finding a sparkling nugget, he believes his wildest dream may have come true. So he "bursts" into his boss's office [Sutter] to show his find.

The text to be discussed is:

Sutter peered at the nugget. "Well," he said, "it *looks* like gold. Let's test it."

He got down an encyclopedia.

He read that gold is softer than any other metal. A piece of gold the size of a pea can be stretched into a wire that is two miles long. Gold can be pounded so thin that you can see a greenish light shining through it. Gold is eight times heavier than stones and sand. Gold is sturdy, yet soft. It will not rust or tarnish.

Sutter and Marshall tested the rock. They pounded it. It flattened easily-just like gold. They weighed it. It was heavier than a whole handful of silver coins. They rubbed acid on to see if it would rust or tarnish. Nothing happened!

Marshall got wild with excitement. He spun around the room. "Gold! Gold!" (McMorrow, 1996, pp. 7–10)

The lesson is divided into three columns (see Table 6.1). The column on the left, titled *Instructional Discourse,* presents the language the teacher actually uses. The column in the center, titled *The "Why" of What Is Taught,* offers the rationale for what the teacher is doing. The column on the right, titled *The "What" That Is Excluded* indicates patterns of current classroom practice that have been avoided.

The center column, The "Why" of What Is Taught, deals with queries commonly raised about the teacher's specific utterances. It is worthwhile to address other concerns that are not directly linked to the specific exchanges. One concerns the length of the lesson. It seems so long! In fact, this is not the case. Although it takes considerable space on a page to detail meaningful discourse, in real time, the exchange moves quickly and there is a steady give and take. Rarely do students have to listen for as long as 20 seconds before having to take an active role (through having to perform an action or answer a question).

TABLE 6.1
Classroom Discourse

Instructional Discourse	The "Why" of What Is Taught	The "What" That Is Taught	The "What" That Is Excluded
• Material in bold represents the actual content from the book. • Underlined material represent questions and commands which require student responses. • All other material generally represents "making the implicit explicit."	The (unstated) theme underlying this segment might be phrased "Using Rigorous Testing to Turn a Dream into Reality." Each exchange is tailored to develop and impart this idea ...		
At this point, the book says **Sutter peered at the nugget. "Well," he said, "it looks like gold. Let's test it."** Keep in mind that finding gold is something special. Many people, including the ones who laughed at Marshall, would not have believed that the nugget might really be gold. If they didn't believe it, what might they say?	The (unstated) concept of "potential" (implied via "looks like" and "let's test") is central. To help students recognize the significance of Sutter's response, they are provided—in comment form—with (hypothetical) alternative reactions.		Questions on knowledge of the topic (e.g., "Who knows what the gold rush in California was? When did the California Gold Rush take place?"). If this information is needed, it should be supplied.
That, of course, is not what Sutter said. What did he say?	They are then asked to use and extend those reactions to answer a series of questions focused on having them realize (a) the expression of possible alternative reactions and (b) the significance of what Sutter actually did say.		Analysis of vocabulary which is not central to the text (e.g., *peered*).
But still what he said does not mean that he believes it **is** gold. He said "looks like" which means that he believes it **might** be gold. So what he would like to do now is to figure out if it **really** is gold. So how does he propose to do that? What does he say he wants to do to see if it is gold?	Some complex questions (e.g., *how does he propose to do that?*) are not aimed at eliciting answers, but at helping students adjust to hearing difficult material. A simpler version of the question follows—that is the version be answered (*what does he say he wants to do to see if it is gold ... ?*)		Demands for major inferences (e.g., "Why do you think he wants to test it?")

Yes, he says: "Let's test it"" Now we've got to figure out just what he means by that. We can begin to figure it out by going to the next sentence. <u>What does it say?</u>

Right, it says, **He got down an encyclopedia.** That's the kind of book we've used a lot to look up information. Remember, we used this book (taking out encyclopedia that had been used by class). We used it when we were studying birds and we needed to find out ....

The question (*"what does it say?"*) aims to get the students to note the encyclopedia (in anticipation of the role it will play). It aims at helping students link (known) encounters with material in the text. (If they fail to see the link, there is still no interference with the flow of the discourse since no questions are asked about this noncentral point).

Questions concerning the students' opinions (e.g., *"Do you think it is ...?" "How would you feel ...?"*) are not relevant to the text at this point. The focus here is on making a determination, and not (yet) on the feelings associated with the determination.

But let's see what information Sutter is looking up. Remember, he wants to determine if the nugget IS gold. So what does he find out from the encyclopedia? It says: **He read that gold is softer than any other metal. A piece of gold the size of a pea can be stretched into a wire that is two miles long. Gold can be pounded so thin that you can see a greenish light shining through it. Gold is eight times heavier than stones and sand. Gold is sturdy, yet soft. It will not rust or tarnish.** The book is saying lots of different things, but all the different things relate to gold. It's giving a series of features, or attributes, of gold. Features or attributes refer to the way something looks, or feels, or sounds. For example, one feature the encyclopedia mentions is the softness of gold. You've had experience with soft things—like these marshmallows or this bubble gum. The softness of things like this allow them to be stretched or pulled. Here's the gum. <u>Try stretching it.</u>

Feature or attribute, though not explicitly mentioned in the text, is a central concept organizing the disparate facts and so, is introduced to help students cluster the information under discussion.

Questions relying on an assumed knowledge base (e.g., *"What kinds of tests could he be talking about?"*)

continued on next page

165

TABLE 6.1 (continued)

Instructional Discourse	The "Why" of What Is Taught	The "What" That Is Excluded
What happened to the gum? And the softness of these sorts of things also allows leads them to become very thin when they are pounded. Let's see how that works. Here (offering relevant tool) try this (on the marshmallow). What happened with the pounding?	The introduction of physical material, the command to perform an action ("try stretching it") and the subsequent question (on the result of the action) are aimed at focusing the students on one of the testing criteria for gold. A comparable sequence (to the one just mentioned) is repeated on other material (reflecting the concept of redundancy with variation).	Questions involving 'personal' (nonshared) information (e.g., "Do you have an encyclopedia? When do you use it?," etc.). Although intended to encourage recognition, these questions can draw attention away from the text.
What feature, what attribute do the gum and marshmallow have that caused them to react in the way they did to the stretching and pounding?	The question is designed to get the students to use one of the defining criteria (feature) just introduced.	Questions about the findings from previous encyclopedia searches (such questions will take the topic astray and lead to potential confusion).
Now what did the book say about the softness of gold? So if it is gold, what should happen to Marshall's nugget if they try to stretch it? And if they try to pound it?	This series of questions is aimed at having the students (a) refocus from the peripheral material (of gum and marshmallow) to the main material (of gold), and (b) use the information just observed (on the peripheral material) to predict the response of gold to the same tests.	Questions about noncentral characteristics (e.g., "What is the color of the light when it goes through gold? How much heavier is gold than rock?")
Softness is just one feature of gold that the encyclopedia mentions. It also talks about another feature, or attribute, of gold. What feature is mentioned next?	The discussion shifts from softness to weight. The comments and question are aimed at having students recognize this shift, within the overriding concept of feature.	Questions relying on an established knowledge base such as those comparing metals (e.g., "How do most metals feel? In what ways is gold different from other

Weight is how heavy something is. Which of the sentences that we read refers to the weight of gold? Let's see the kind of information they will get from weighing. Let's take another marshmallow. And now over there, are a group of stones. Find one that is about the same size as the marshmallow. Now let's weigh the marshmallow and the stone on this scale. They are about the same size but they are not the same weight. Which do you think will weigh more? Go ahead, let's weigh them and see if you're right.	The action sequence (on weight) and the one that follows (on rusting) are comparable to the one above on softness. (Again, the physical material plays a central role and there is extensive redundancy but at the same time, it contains major variation in wording.)	metals.") (These sorts of questions can be posed if all relevant materials are present. However, they require extensive preparation and may take so long as to interfere with the flow of the discussion.)
Gold, according to the encyclopedia, is very heavy—even heavier than the rock you just weighed. What sentence tells us that feature of gold?	The actual sentence in the text (i.e., *Gold is eight times heavier ...*) is markedly different from the phrasing used in the discourse. The rephrasing is aimed at helping the students realize the variety of ways in which the concept may be expressed.	Most questions that can be answered by a direct recitation of the text (e.g., *"What did Marshall and Sutter do to the gold?, What did Sutter read in the encyclopedia?"*).
And then there is a final feature that is mentioned. It says that gold will not rust or tarnish. Over there, I have some examples of something that has rusted. Here are two pieces of iron. This one has been inside a house but this one has been left outside in the rain. What's the difference between the two?	Again, demonstration via physical material is provided, followed by a question that highlights the effects of conditions that have been put forth.	Questions about the reasons responsible for a substance being heavy or light.
That reddish stuff is rust. Now the encyclopedia says that gold will not rust. So if we left a piece of pure gold outside in the rain, what would happen? Would it rust like this piece of iron did, or would it stay its original color?	With the knowledge base established, students are asked to apply the information to deal with higher level processes such as prediction.	Questions or discussions on the causes of rusting (although potentially demonstrable, the time constraints prevent a meaningful demonstration). *continued on next page*

167

TABLE 6.1 (continued)

Instructional Discourse	The "Why" of What Is Taught	The "What" That Is Excluded
So let's <u>summarize the features of gold</u> that the encyclopedia pointed out to Sutter and Marshall.	Here the students are being asked to consolidate the specific, varied, critical features of gold that have been outlined. (Consolidation, or the preservation of meaning, across a host of sentences is a critical process in the mastery of literacy.)	Questions which demand unguided consolidation (e.g., "What just took place between Marshall and Sutter?" "What was the main point in this section?")
Now Sutter looked in the encyclopedia not just to find out about the features of gold. He wanted to determine if the piece of rock that Marshall brought to him was gold. Remember, before he looked in the encyclopedia, he said, "Let's test it." <u>So how was he going to use the information about gold's features that he found in the encyclopedia?</u>	Because the knowledge base has been established, students are asked to apply the information to deal with higher level processes such as reasoning and rationalization.	
That's exactly what they did. **Sutter and Marshall tested the rock. They pounded it. It flattened easily—just like gold. They weighed it. It was heavier than a whole handful of silver coins. They rubbed acid on to see if it would rust or tarnish. Nothing happened!** Let's go over this point by point. First, Sutter and Marshall's first test was to pound the rock. And what was the result? What was the next test they carried out? <u>How well did gold meet that test?</u> <u>And what was the final test?</u> <u>And how well did gold meet that test?</u>	The questions in this section are marked by an absence of embellishing comments (the "implicit" need not be made "explicit") because the preceding discussion established the necessary connections. Instead, the discourse here is structured to present a cluster of questions. The questions, which call for a near-direct recitation of the text, are appropriate because the goal is to coalesce key details. The questions, though, are still varied enough to prevent simple, thoughtless recitation. For example, the final question, "*And how well did the gold meet that test?,*" is structured so that it cannot be answered appropriately by repeating the *Nothing happened* from the book. The absence of a response in that case is a significant, positive reaction and rewording is essential.	

Before the tests, Sutter thought the nugget might be gold. But now, since the nugget met all the tests for gold, <u>What do you think he now thought?</u>	This interchange is aimed at having the students (a) connect this part of the text to the original, critical point (on the difference between possibility [*might*] and actuality [*is*]), and (b) see the switch that has occurred in Sutter's judgment.
That's precisely the conclusion he reached. And that was precisely the conclusion that Marshall, the man who found the nugget, desperately wanted to hear. <u>Do you remember what Marshall had been predicting about the minerals in the land?</u> <u>So what do you think Marshall's reaction was to his nugget passing all the tests.</u>	In the next sentence, the written material is going to switch from the theme of testing to emotional reactions. This section is designed to have the students prepare for the switch by comments and questions that focus on (a) recalling information read prior to this segment, and (b) using that information to reinforce the intensity of his reaction.
That's right. It's not exactly in the same words, but it's the same idea. Here, read the next section. **Marshall got wild with excitement. He spun around the room. "Gold! Gold!"**	

This type of discourse moves more slowly than the discourse typical of school settings. That quality, however, is anything but a negative. The extensive comments (a) provide useful information and (b) block the fast pace of questions long recognized as a counterproductive force in classroom life.

Other questions of verbal length also arise. Although no examples are offered of the students' responses, it is nevertheless clear that the amount of teacher talk far exceeds the amount of student talk. In this respect, the proposed teaching does not differ markedly from current practice. This imbalance has regularly been found and generally condemned, with teachers being indicted for dominating the scene and causing boredom. The solution, from this perspective, is to have teachers reduce their speaking time while having students increase theirs.

From the vantage point of literacy, however, this suggestion seems off track. All books share a common characteristic. They represent an (absent) author "talking" at length to a silent reader who is expected to take in the lengthy exposition being put forth. In other words, the ability to attend to sustained verbal information from another person is key to literacy and not an undesirable attribute targeted for elimination. In structuring the discourse so that it mirrors this aspect of books, the chances for fostering for literacy are enhanced.

Needless to say, this is no justification for teachers imposing long, boring stretches of talk on students. Just as a book cannot afford to be boring, neither can a teacher. The key is not to reduce teacher talk, but to repackage it so that it evokes interest and facilitates comprehension.

Central to the repackaging is the type of text under consideration. In the lesson just offered, the text is from the curriculum area of science (see Halliday & Martin, 1993). Accordingly, the discussion is structured to help students see the type of analysis needed for this genre (e.g., critical components involve attention to specific details, sequencing, fine distinctions between concepts of certainty and probability, etc.). Texts from other areas require equally careful, but different patterns of analysis. Literature texts, for example, need to focus on issues on motivation and the role they play in human interaction, whereas social studies texts have to highlight key categories of group existence, such as economics, government, military, and art. Further, the discussions need not be confined to books. This type of analysis can be carried out on any material involving sequences of integrated, verbally based information, such as scientific experiments, newspaper articles, and films. (Illustrations of the varied discourse patterns for the range of school texts can be found in Blank et al., 1994, 1995.)

Finally, it is useful to return to the central issue raised at the start of the chapter where the study of classroom discourse was urged for its potential in enabling students to gain insight into the foreign language of written text. At the same time, it was accompanied by the caveat that *It may be the case that classroom discussion cannot, by itself, fill the gap that exists between students' skills and the unfamiliar demands of text.* That caveat still holds. Extensive forays into classroom discourse have to be carried out before a clear determination can be made of its power to foster literacy. Still, I feel confident in closing on an optimistic note. In my experience, the approach offered here has proven itself to be an invaluable tool in helping students gain mastery of the world of print. At a minimum, hopefully it will serve as a catalyst for exploring dramatically different, more productive modes of discourse.

• • • • • •

For many in our population, literacy is a vital, but elusive, achievement. Restricted largely to the language of everyday life, students are ill-prepared for written text that imposes such demands as (a) grasping ideas conveyed in densely distributed, unfamiliar concepts, and (b) extracting coherence from seemingly disparate statements whose links are invisible. For these students, classroom discourse is the major resource for uncovering the complexities of literacy. However, in its current form, school talk is often not packaged in ways that will alleviate the students' problems. In the realm of concepts, its structure is more characteristic of testing than teaching; and in the realm of connected text, it provides little of the elaboration and redundancy required for coherence. Productive change requires a dramatic transformation of classroom discourse. This chapter provides the outlines of an alternative approach.

REFERENCES

Allwright, D. (1998). Contextual factors in classroom language learning: An overview. In K. Malmkjaer & J. Williams (Eds.), *Context in language learning and language understanding* (pp. 115–134). Cambridge, England: Cambridge University Press.

Anderson, R. C., Spiro, R. J., & Montague, W. E. (1977). *Schooling and the acquisition of knowledge.* Hillsdale, NJ: Lawrence Erlbaum Associates.

Beck, I. L., McKeown, M. G., Sinatra, G. M., & Loxterman, J. A. (1991). Revising social studies texts from a text-processing perspective: Evidence of improved comprehensibility. *Reading Research Quarterly, 26,* 251–276.

Bellack, A. A., Kliebard, H. M., Hyman, R. T., & Smith, F. L., Jr. (1966). *The language of the classroom.* New York: Teachers College Press.

Bernstein, B. (1975). *Class, codes and social control.* New York: Schocken.

Blank, M. (1972). The wrong response: Is it to be ignored, prevented, or treated? In R. K. Parker (Ed.), *The preschool in action* (pp. 36–54). Boston: Allyn & Bacon.

Blank, M. (1987). Classroom text: The next stage of intervention. In R. L. Schiefelbusch & L. L. Lloyd (Eds.), *Language perspectives: Acquisition retardation and intervention* (2nd ed., pp. 367–392). Austin, TX: Pro-Ed Press.

Blank, M., & Klig, S. (1982). The child and the school experience. In C. B. Kopp & J. B. Krakow (Eds.), *The child: development in a social context* (pp. 456–513). Reading, MA: Addsion-Wesley.

Blank, M., Marquis, A. M., & Klimovitch, M. (1994). *Directing school discourse.* San Antonio, TX: Communication Skill Builders.

Blank, M., Marquis, A. M., & Klimovitch, M. (1995). *Directing early discourse.* San Antonio, TX: Communication Skill Builders.

Blank, M., & White, S. J. (1986). Questions: A powerful form of classroom exchange. *Topics in Language Disorders, 6*(2), 1–12.

Blank, M., & White, S. J. (1998). Activating the zone of proximal development in school: Obstacles and solutions. In P. Lloyd & C. Fernyhough (Eds.), *Lev Vygotsky: Critical Assessments, Volume 3: The Zone of Proximal Development* (pp. 331–350). London: Routledge.

Brown, G. (1998). Context creation in discourse understanding. In K. Malmkjaer & J. Williams (Eds.), *Context in language learning and language understanding* (pp. 171–192). Cambridge, England: Cambridge University Press.

Cazden, C. B. (1986). Classroom discourse. In M. C. Wittrock (Ed.), *Handbook of research on teaching* (pp. 432–463). New York: MacMillan.

Christie, F., & Martin, J. R. (1997). *Genre and institutions: Social processes in the workplace and school.* London: Cassell Academic.

Davis, P. (1987, May 31). Exploring the kingdom of AIDS. *New York Times Magazine,* 32–36, 38, 40.

Delamont, S. (1983). *Interaction in the classroom.* London: Methuen.

Dillon, J. T. (1988). *Questioning and teaching: A manual of practice.* New York: Teachers College Press.

Donnelly, J. (1989). *Moonwalk: The first trip to the moon.* New York: Random House.

Donoahue, Z., van Tassell, M. A., & Patterson, L. (1996). *Research in the classroom: Talk, texts, and inquiry.* Newark, DE: International Reading Association.

Eder, D., Evans, C. C., & Parker, S. (1995). *School talk: Gender and adolescent culture.* Piscataway, NJ: Rutgers University Press.

Flanders, N. (1970). *Analyzing teacher behavior.* Reading, MA: Addison-Wesley.

Goldberg, A. E. (1998). Semantic principles of predication. In J. P. Koenig (Ed.), *Discourse and cognition: Bridging the gap* (pp. 41–54). Stanford, CA: Center for the Study of Language and Cognition.

Halliday, M. A. K., & Hasan, R. (1976). *Cohesion in English.* New York: Longman.

Halliday, M. A. K., & Hasan, R. (1989). *Language, context, and text: Aspects of language in a social-semiotic perspective.* London: Oxford University Press.

Halliday, M. A. K., & Martin, J. R. (1993). *Writing science: Literacy and discursive power.* Pittsburgh, PA: University of Pittsburgh Press.

Haroutunian-Gordon, S. (1991). *Turning the soul: Teaching through conversation in the high school.* Chicago: University of Chicago Press.

Hicks, D., & Hicks, D. (Eds.). (1996). *Discourse, learning, and school.* Cambridge, England: Cambridge University Press.

Hirsch, E. D. (1988). *Cultural literacy: What every American needs to know.* Boston, MA: Houghton Mifflin.

Horowitz, R. H., & Samuels, S. J. (1987). *Comprehending oral and written language.* New York: Academic Press.

Its official: Our kids can't read. (1999, May 26). *New York Post,* p. 1.

Kintsch, W., & Keenan, J. (1973). Reading rate and retention as a function of the number of propositions in the base structure of sentences. *Cognitive Psychology, 5,* 257–274.

Kutz, E. (1997). *Language and literacy: Studying discourse in communities and classrooms.* Portsmouth, NH: Greenwood-Heinemann.

Lemke, J. L. (1995). *Textual politics: Discourse and social dynamics.* Bristol, PA: Taylor & Francis.

McMorrow, C. (1996). *Gold fever.* New York: Random House.

McMullen, K. (1989). *Dinosaur hunters.* New York: Random House.

Mehan, H. (1979). *Learning lessons.* Cambridge, MA: Harvard University Press.

Peshkin, A. (1978). *Growing up in America: Schooling and the survival of the community.* Chicago: University of Chicago Press.

Schell, M. (1999). *An encyclopedia of love.* New York: Picador.

Schilperoord, J., & Verhagen, A. (1998). Conceptual dependency and the clausal structure of discourse. In J. P Koenig (Ed.), *Discourse and cognition: Bridging the gap* (pp. 141–163). Stanford, CA: Center for the Study of Language and Cognition.

Schnotz, W. (1984). Comparative instructional text organization. In H. Mandl, N. L. Stein, & T. Trabasso (Eds.), *Learning and comprehension of text* (pp. 53–81). Hillsdale, NJ: Lawrence Erlbaum Associates.

Scinto, L. F. M. (1986). *Written language and psychological development.* New York: Academic Press.

Sinclair, J. M., Hoey, M., & Fox, G. (Eds.). (1993). *Techniques of description: Spoken and written discourse.* London: Routledge.

State of Literacy Report. (1992). Washington, DC: National Institute for Literacy.

Stiller, G. F. (1998). *Analyzing everyday texts: Discourse, rhetoric, and social perspectives.* Thousand Oaks, CA: Sage Publications.

Students taking test crucial to schools. (1999, April 20). *San Diego Union-Tribune,* p. 1.

Tannen, D. (Ed.). (1984). *Coherence in spoken and written discourse: Advances in discourse processes,* (Vol. 12), Norwood, NJ: Ablex.

Vygotsky, L. S. (1962). *Thought and language.* Cambridge, MA: MIT Press.

Vygotsky, L. S. (1978). *Mind and society: The development of higher psychological processes.* (M. Cole, V. John-Steiner, S. Scribner, & E. Souberman, Eds.). Cambridge, MA: Harvard University Press.

Promises and Pitfalls of Scaffolded Instruction for Students With Language Learning Disabilities

C. Addison Stone
University of Michigan

Over the last 15 years or more, the metaphor of scaffolding has played an important role in discussions of the teacher's activity during effective instructional exchanges in the classroom (Berk & Winsler, 1995; Cazden, 1988; Hogan & Pressley, 1997; Rosenshine & Meister, 1992; Wong, 1998). Central to the scaffolding metaphor are the two notions of support and relinquishment. Scaffolded instruction supports the child's construction of new understandings, but does so in a manner that allows for the eventual removal of that support. Such instruction has been seen as a powerful force in helping children to take ownership of new knowledge and procedures. In addition, scaffolded instruction is seen as having the potential to meet the needs of individual children during group activities, by accommodating learning style and knowledge gaps, and thereby, to level the "playing field" (Day & Cordon, 1993).

Indeed, under the right conditions, scaffolded instruction has enormous potential as a means of fostering genuine learning in a wide range of children. However, the conditions are not always right. Teachers are not always aware of each child's knowledge and special support needs, and are not always available in real time for tailored support. Children are not always ready for "uptake" of that support. Thus, the promise of scaffolded instruction is not always realized. This situation may be especially true for children with language/learning disabilities (LLD). The purpose of the present chapter is to examine the promises and pitfalls of scaffolded instruction for such children. The chapter will begin with a brief overview of the original scaffolding metaphor and its evolution. In this context, an analysis of the essential elements of scaffolded instruction is presented. One emphasis of this discussion is an argument that many recent applications of the metaphor have often stripped it of essential dynamics and reduced it to nothing more than a shorthand allusion to guidance. As this point is developed, the central role of communicational challenge in effective scaffolding is emphasized. Within the context of an enriched conception of scaffolded instruction, the special case of children with LLD is considered, with a particular emphasis on their readiness for engagement in such exchanges. The chapter ends with discussion of the implications of these arguments for the development of truly effective instruction for atypical children, both in the classroom and in the home.

ORIGINS AND EVOLUTION OF THE SCAFFOLDING METAPHOR

The earliest extensive discussion and application of the scaffolding metaphor to the analysis of instruction was provided by Wood, Bruner, and Ross (1976), in what is now a classic paper (see Wood, 1990, for an interesting discussion of the original impetus for the metaphor). The work presented by Wood et al. (1976) was focused on the instructional dynamics of parent–child interactions in early childhood, and many of the subsequent applications of the scaffolding metaphor also focused on parent–child interaction. However, the potential relevance of the metaphor for the analysis of instructional interactions in the classroom was not long ignored (Cazden, 1983, 1988). In the following paragraphs, this evolution is traced briefly, starting with the original presentation of the metaphor and dwelling at more length on recent applications to classroom instruction. (See Stone, 1998, for a more extensive treatment.)

The Original Metaphor

In their seminal application of the scaffolding metaphor to the analysis of instructional interactions, Wood et al. (1976) presented a case study of an adult assisting a preschool child in the assembly of a block tower containing complex interlocking pieces. Their characterization of the tutoring dynamics as scaffolding was presented as follows:

> [tutoring] involves a kind of "scaffolding" process that enables a child or novice to solve a problem, carry out a task or achieve a goal which would be beyond his unassisted efforts. This scaffolding consists essentially of the adult "controlling" those elements of the task that are initially beyond the learner's capacity, thus permitting him to concentrate upon and complete only those elements that are within his range of competence. (Wood, et al., 1976, p. 90)

The authors' list of key functions of scaffolding captured clearly the many types of assistance provided by the adult within the task setting:

- Recruitment—engaging student interest
- Reduction of degrees of freedom—constraining the task
- Direction maintenance—supporting goal-directedness and risk-taking
- Marking critical features—highlighting discrepancies between progress and goal
- Frustration control—mediating frustration and independence
- Demonstration—modeling solutions (Wood et al., 1976, p. 98)

However, it is important to emphasize that Wood et al. (1976) saw scaffolding as more than mere assistance with a difficult task. In making this point, they noted that, "The [scaffolding] process can potentially achieve much more for the learner than an assisted completion of the task" (p. 90). Instead, they argued, scaffolding maximizes the potential for genuine mastery of a new skill. The process by which this might happen is discussed in a later section.

Extensions to the Classroom

The original work of Bruner, Wood, and colleagues (Wood et al., 1976) led to a wealth of applications of the scaffolding metaphor to analyses of adult–child interactions. Without in any way intending to diminish the importance of this work and its continuing potential, it is important to note for our present purposes that later work continued to focus on informal instruction in dyadic contexts, most often using fairly constrained tasks.

We owe to Cazden (1986, 1988) the initial efforts to extend the scaffolding metaphor to the analysis of classroom instruction. One interesting point emphasized by Cazden is that classroom participation structures (i.e., predictable activity routines) serve as scaffolds for children's mastery of new ways of talking and thinking about their world. In making this argument, Cazden used an analogy to the early childhood game of peekaboo (Cazden, 1983), noting that, in playing peekaboo with their parents, children engage in a clear and repetitive structure, which has a restricted format. That format contains positions (and expectations) for appropriate vocalizations. In addition, it has reversible role relations; that is, the child is expected to take turns playing the parent's part of the game. By extension, classroom exchanges have a similar structure, and children are expected to take over key parts of the activity initially modeled by the teacher.

By far the most prominent application of the scaffolding metaphor to the development and analysis of effective classroom instructional activities is the case of *Reciprocal Teaching* (Palincsar, 1986; Palincsar & Brown, 1984). In its original form, Reciprocal Teaching was developed as a means of fostering active reading comprehension in children with adequate decoding skills but low reading comprehension scores. Small groups of students engaged with their teacher in the joint reading and discussion of expository texts. Working repetitively with natural segments of the text, teachers and students took turns implementing a set of four reading strategies (summarizing, questioning, clarifying, and predicting). As students took their turns, the teacher assisted them as necessary in carrying out the strategies.

Reciprocal Teaching embodies two levels of scaffolded instruction. At the broadest level, the recursive activity represented by the cyclical turn-taking within the group constitutes an example of assisted incorporation into a classroom participation structure (note the parallel to Cazden's, 1983, discussion of Peekaboo). At a more specific level, the teacher's graduated assistance for each child as s/he takes a turn at implementing a given strategy represents the type of guidance studied by Wood et al. (1976).

As the group work proceeds, the students are led to construct the meaning of the target text, but, as Wood et al. (1976) would have predicted, the students benefit far beyond the mere analysis of that one text. Indeed, Reciprocal Teaching represents one of the most powerful interventions for reading comprehension yet developed, with clear evidence of generalization to other reading texts and settings. In a reflection on the question of why Reciprocal Teaching appears to be so effective in improving children's reading skills, Palincsar (1986) pointed to the key role of student–teacher dialogue. She argued that the exchanges evident in transcripts of Reciprocal Teaching sessions are filled with examples of teacher guidance, feedback, and encouragement.

Many of the features of scaffolding as applied to the case of classroom instruction are captured effectively in a list provided by Meyer (1993):

- Teacher supports student efforts
- Student participation/choice
- Collaboration/nonevaluative
- Instruction at appropriate level
- Importance of dialogue
- Transfer of responsibility

In one guise or another, these elements are evident in numerous recent discussions of scaffolded instruction (e.g., Hogan & Pressley, 1997). Such discussions are useful in highlighting key features of scaffolding; however, they often stop short of providing an explicit analysis of the underlying dynamics. Such a discussion is not just an academic issue. Rather, a focus on the communicative process during scaffolded instruction serves to highlight the crucial prerequisites for effective learning.

HOW AND WHY DOES SCAFFOLDING WORK?

At the risk of some simplification, it is possible to argue that much of what is essential to the notion of scaffolding can be captured by the three terms, *context, contingency,* and *challenge* (see Table 7.1). To be effective at scaffolding new learning, the instructor must engage the child in a joint goal-directed activity, which provides a motivational context for the interaction. At the same time, it serves to maximize mutual understanding during ongoing communication because any ambiguous utterances can be interpreted in terms of the overarching context. In the initial applications of the metaphor, the contexts studied tended to be concrete activities with relatively clear end goals, such as a block-building activity or a model copy task. Later applications have often involved more abstract goals such as telling a good story. Regardless of the exact nature of the situation, a clear context is important, both for motivation and meaning-making.

The second key ingredient of effective scaffolding is contingency. During the interaction, the instructor must engage in ongoing assessment of the learner's current understanding and need for support. The support provided must be contingent on the learner's current understanding. Following the original example of Wood et al. (1976), contingency has often been operationalized (for the purposes of coding interactions or implementing an "ideal" scaffolded instructional condition in an experimental study) by creating a hierarchy of increasingly specific prompts, or forms of assistance, for a target task. Table 7.2 contains two illustrative prompt hierarchies taken from past research on scaffolding.

Hierarchies of prompts such as those included in Table 7.2 provide rough approximations of relative degrees of explicitness in the support provided during a goal-directed activity. In developing such hierarchies, researchers (or analyzers of instructional dynamics) take into consideration various issues, such as the extent to which the referents in the prompt rely on prior understanding of the task's goals, or the extent to which the prompt is exclusively verbal. There are no universally accepted guidelines for developing such prompt hierarchies. Rather, each scholar emphasizes those aspects of communication s/he views as important (e.g., verbal vs. nonverbal reference, abstract vs. concrete referring expressions). Although this situation is less than ideal, it is still possible to reach general agreement about the importance of considering the relative explicitness of the assistance provided during a task.

In the context of a specified hierarchy of prompts for a specific task, assistance is said to be contingent if (a) the level of a prompt is more specific in

TABLE 7.1
Three Essential Elements of Scaffolding

- Context
  Motivational role of participation in real activity
  Joint goal structure
- Contingency
  Responsive support
  On-line diagnosis of need
- Challenge
  Transfer of responsibility ('relinquishment')
  Performance in anticipation of understanding

TABLE 7.2
Contingency as the Adjustment of Assistance in Incremental Substeps:
Examples of Prompt Hierarchies From Two Research Projects

Tower Building (Wood et al., 1978)	Division Problems (Pratt, Green, MacVicar, & Bountrogianni, 1992)
—	No directive
General encouragement	General encouragement: ("Try this one")
—	General hints: ("How many times?")
Specific verbal information	Label substep: ("Divide them")
Select or indicate appropriate pieces	Specify step: ("How many times does 2 go into 4?")
—	Hint about step: ("That looks like too many")
Provide prepared subassembly	Give answer to step: ("It's two times")
—	Give answer & record: ("It's 2; put it here")
Demonstrate	Demonstrate

Note. Empty cells represent levels of prompts not present in the original coding system.

response to failure or less specific in response to success; and (b) the prompt provided is minimally discrepant from the previously provided prompt, that is, fewer steps away on the hierarchy of assistance. Such guidelines allow for the determination of the relative degree of contingency evident in a given instructional exchange.

The Key Role of Challenge

Context and contingency are essential to the scaffolding process, and their importance is much discussed in the literature. What is less emphasized is the importance of challenge. The notion of challenge is implicit in the often-cited need for transfer of responsibility. However, one must be challenged to take responsibility. This issue of challenging the child was evident in some early discussions of scaffolding, such as the following quote from Wood and colleagues:

> Effective instruction, thus conceived, consists in continually confronting the child with problems of *controlled* complexity, setting goals or making requests which lay *beyond* the child's current level of attainment but not so far beyond that he is unable to "unpack" or comprehend the suggestion or instruction being made. (Wood, Wood, & Middleton, 1978, p. 132)

Implicit in the aforementioned quote are issues of challenge and inference, but these issues have not received adequate attention in subsequent discussions of scaffolding. To be truly effective, scaffolded instruction must take place in a meaningful context, and instructional support must be contingent on the learner's current understanding. However, instruction containing context and contingency without challenge is not scaffolding, but skill training. Consistent with the comments of Wood et al. (1978), it is possible to argue that challenge consists of communicational tension and inference. To appreciate the importance of this issue, it is necessary to consider the pragmatics of the scaffolding situation.

The Pragmatics of Scaffolding

When, in response to a long pause or a vacant look from the child, a parent or teacher supplements an earlier question or suggestion with a more explicit one, the child is implicitly encouraged to infer a connection between the adult's two contributions to the ongoing activity. Such an inference is essential to the child's eventual mastery of the activity at hand. Without making such inferences, the child will continue to need the more explicit level of guidance; that is, there will be no increase in independent mastery. If the child engages in such inferences, she or he will be able to accomplish the task in the future in response to the less explicit suggestion.

Making such inferences is a matter of pragmatics. We owe to Grice (1989) the important insight that human communication is governed by a set of implicit conversational "rules" or maxims. The most important of these maxims is that of relation, or relevance. This maxim holds that, all other things being equal, if one party to a conversation makes a statement in response to the other party, that statement must have some relevance to the initial remark. Grice's central point was that, in situations of apparent violation of a maxim, the listener nonetheless assumes that the speaker is adhering to the maxim and is therefore motivated to work out, or infer, the initially unclear connection between the two remarks. Look, for example, at the following exchange:

Speaker A [to passer-by]: I've just run out of gasoline.

Speaker B: Oh; there's a store just around the corner.

In this example, A learns that there is a gas station around the corner, yet B never said that explicitly. Rather, by assuming that B's remark was relevant to the conversation, A has been led to infer that the "store" is a gas station.

A second Gricean maxim holds that conversational contributions must be limited in quantity to what is essential. This maxim is operative in the following example:

Speaker A: Where's Bill?

Speaker B: There's a yellow VW outside Sue's house.

Here, A learns that Bill is at Sue's house. This learning is accomplished by A's assumption that B's remark is a relevant response to the question, *and* that B's choice of the phrase "yellow VW" rather than the word "car" is important. (This example also hinges, of course, on A's prior knowledge that Bill has a yellow VW. This issue of prior knowledge will be discussed.)

A Gricean analysis helps to make sense of how conversational challenge is involved in effective scaffolding. That this is the case can be illustrated via some examples. Table 7.3 provides a hierarchy of increasingly specific prompts that mothers might implicitly "sample" from in assisting their child in a simple puzzle construction activity (note the parallel to the hierarchies of prompts depicted in Table 7.2). The arrows connecting pairs of prompts in Table 7.3 suggest possible inferences that the child might be implicitly encouraged to make during the activity by the mother's juxtaposition of prompts from different levels of the hierarchy during the ongoing exchange. For example, arrow A would apply to an exchange in which the mother began with prompt 1 ("Why don't you put your puzzle together now"), but was met with a blank stare. If she then provided prompt 2 ("Make your puzzle look like Mommy's"), thereby becoming more specific in response to the child's failure, and demonstrating "contingency," the child would be implicitly invited to assume that putting together the puzzle means making it look like the mother's copy. If the child makes such an inference, the mother's subsequent use of prompt 1 (later in the session or on a later day) might be sufficient to elicit the appropriate response.

Similarly, arrow B suggests another possible invitation to inference created by the juxtaposition of two other prompts from the hierarchy. In this case, however, the child's inference would be more indirect because the

TABLE 7.3
Potential Inferences From Successive Prompts

1. Why don't you put your puzzle together now. A
2. Make your puzzle look like Mommy's.
3. Which piece goes here? B
4. Look at mommy's puzzle to find out.
5. Which color is next to the red one in my puzzle?
6. So, what goes next to the red one in yours?
7. It's the blue one. C
8. Put the blue one next to the red one.
9. Put the blue one here [points to location].
10. Put this one [points to piece] here [points to location].
11. Like this [places piece].

mother's initial prompt was followed by a prompt with less apparent connection to the initial utterance. Thus, this hypothetical exchange might provide more challenge to the child. Yet other inferences might also be invited in alternative sequences of exchanges (e.g., the inference suggested by arrow C).

Another example of challenge and inference is provided in Table 7.4. Here, we see a sample of dialogue from a Reciprocal Teaching session (Palincsar, 1986). In this exchange, the teacher (T) is assisting one of the students in the group (S1) in constructing a summary of the reading passage. In the sequence of teacher contributions, it is possible to see a series of increasingly specific prompts analogous to those in Table 7.3, though less clear-cut. This example again demonstrates how a child is invited to infer how subsequent teacher comments relate to earlier comments. Again, via Gricean conversational maxims, the child can be led to understand what the teacher's initially general request for a summary means. This is the challenge component of scaffolded instruction.

It is important to emphasize two additional points in this context, both of which serve to point out the complexities of the dynamics involved in scaffolded instruction. First, although virtually all examples of scaffolding in the literature and all discussions of the dynamics of scaffolding emphasize the role of "dialogue," the communicational dynamics of scaffolded assistance need not be solely language based. Nonverbal exchanges also play a role, as Grice (1989) pointed out. As scholars working on gestures have demonstrated convincingly, verbal communication is continually supple-

TABLE 7.4
An Example of Scaffolding During Reciprocal Teaching

READING PASSAGE:

A cat purrs. When a cat purrs it is usually showing that it feels happy ...? Cats purr to "talk" to each other too. A kitten communicates with its mother by purring. ...

DISCUSSION ABOUT THE PASSAGE:

T: Do you remember what this paragraph is telling you S1? What did you learn? [pause] Did it move or talk in some way? Who was the cat talking to?

S1: To the mother.

T: When the cat was talking to its mother do you remember what it did? [pause] How does a cat talk to its mother? Does it make sounds? Do you remember what kind of sounds it makes? Shall we let some of the others help us out?

S2: It sometimes rubs against you on your arms.

T: What rubs against you on your arms?

S2: Cats do.

T: All right. So you would summarize that the kitten rubs against your arms. Why? Can you give us a little more information?

(Palincsar, 1986, pp. 90–91)

mented by, or sometimes replaced by, gestural messages (Alibali, Flevares, & Goldin-Meadow, 1997; McNeill, Cassell, & McCullouh, 1994). One simple example of such nonverbal contributions to a scaffolding exchange is the use of points to disambiguate an initially unclear verbal reference. Thus, if an initial request to "Bring me the remote control" is met with a blank look, a parent can readily resort to the request to "Bring me that [pointing to the desired object]." Other examples might be purely nonverbal. When, for example, in response to a child's puzzled look or hesitation, an adult follows an initially rapid, abbreviated instance of a specific modeled behavior with a slower, more deliberate or elaborated version of the behavior, the child is thereby invited to infer the connection. This is an instance of communicational inference of a nonverbal sort. The role of such exchanges in parent–child and teacher–child interaction warrants greater scrutiny (see Wood, 1990, for a related discussion).

A second point to make about the complexities of scaffolding relates to the frequency or "naturalness" of the stylized contingent exchanges described. In a thoughtful challenge to what they see as an overly optimistic picture of parent–child interactions, Becker and Goodnow (1991) argued, for example, that many parental responses to children's inappropriate behaviors or questions would be very difficult for the child to use in inferring anything about the task or situation. A similar point could presumably be made about classroom or playground exchanges. Thus, communicational challenges are not always neatly packaged, and the necessary inferences are not always clear-cut.

The Promise of Scaffolded Instruction

Despite its complexities, scaffolded instruction has the potential for meeting the online learning needs of the child and for fostering genuine learning. This is particularly true for atypical children, for whom much instruction has been limiting. Scaffolded instruction offers the potential for reinvigorating passive, skill-oriented intervention. In addition, because of the emphasis on online assessment of the child's needs and contingent assistance, there is the potential for minimizing individual differences in response to instruction (Day & Cordon, 1993). Finally, because of the crucial role of contingent assistance, scaffolded instruction highlights the importance of parent–professional communication regarding a child's needs. Parents and teachers can raise each others' awareness of the child's needs, and of opportunities for meeting those needs through challenging instructional interactions.

Although the promise of scaffolded instruction is enormous, all of the key ingredients must be in place. For example, although it is important to break down the task into sequential substeps, the adult must do more. In addition, s/he must facilitate the rebuilding or constructing of the task. In the process, the adult must empower the child (i.e., invite active investment and inference). Also, it is important to be mindful of potential impediments to the child's "uptake" of the adult's invitations to inference. Conceived in this way, effective instruction (and learning) rests on interpersonal communication and thus is social at root. Because of its social nature, and because of the pragmatic inferences involved, emphasis must be placed on the fostering of shared perspectives (on the task at hand). Equally important is the issue of interpersonal trust, trust that the other is "sincere," that is, abiding by Gricean maxims (see Stone, 1993, for an extended discussion of these points).

POTENTIAL CHALLENGES FOR CHILDREN WITH LANGUAGE LEARNING DISABILITIES

Although the promise of scaffolded instruction for children with LLD is great, effective implementation is fraught with difficulties. Table 7.5 provides a partial list of such challenges. The following contains illustrations of these challenges.

One obvious issue for children with language difficulties is the overreliance so often placed on the verbal channel of discourse exchanges to carry the instructional "force" of scaffolding. The inferences so crucial to the resolution of the communicational tensions established during scaf-

TABLE 7.5
Potential Challenges to Successful Scaffolding Exchanges
for Children With Language/Learning Disabilities

- Limited/inflexible vocabulary;
- Inflexible syntactic frames;
- Limited prerequisite content knowledge;
- Difficulties with pragmatics (nonverbal and verbal);
- Problems with attention;
- Little confidence that "it will make sense";
- Inaccurate perceptions on the adult's part of the child's needs.

folding interactions rely in multiple ways on the fluid use of language. Subtle shifts occur across teacher or parent utterances in the vocabulary used to refer to the same object or concept. A "truck" becomes a "hauler"; "shorten" becomes "cut down"; "length" becomes "distance." At times, such word shifts are the heart of what is to be learned (as when an initially confusing term is replaced in an identical syntactic frame by a simpler, more common term). At other times, the shift in terms is more stylistic. In such cases, the word shift is assumed to be "transparent," but the success of the invited inference hinges on the accuracy of an assumption about semantic transparency. Take, for example, a hypothetical discussion about "perimeter." If, in the course of that discussion, the adult uses the words "length" and "distance," it is with the assumption that the child will recognize "length" and "distance" as synonymous. Unfortunately, the vocabulary knowledge of children with language/learning disabilities is likely to be somewhat limited. This fact has obvious implications for the success of an instructional exchange that is focused not on vocabulary per se but on content knowledge, as in the aforementioned example.

Similarly, children with LLD may have limitations in the flexibility of syntactic frames. By analogy to the just cited examples of vocabulary shift, adults may make subtle changes in the syntactic frame of an utterance across two successive instances, as in the following exchange:

Parent: Can you point to the *canary?*

Child: (??)

Parent: Point to the *bird*

In such a case, the child may not make the implicitly invited inference that a canary is a kind of bird because of a failure to realize that the parent's second utterance was intended as an exact stand-in for the initial question.

Although focused specifically on linguistic knowledge, the preceding examples are closely related to the broader issue of background or content knowledge. Clearly, if the adult makes too many assumptions regarding a child's prior knowledge about a given topic, then specific references to objects or concepts may not be successfully completed. A simple example of this problem was just mentioned in the exposition of Grice's maxims, where the inference regarding Bill's whereabouts hinged on the speaker's assumption that the listener knew what kind of car Bill drove. Similar examples abound in the flow of instructional talk during a classroom lesson.

Yet another source of potential difficulty in successful scaffolding for students with LLD relates to the existence of problems with pragmatic rules themselves. Although the evidence for such difficulties is not straightforward (Craig, 1995; Leonard, 1998), there are suggestions that some children with LLD may indeed have difficulty in responding appropriately during a conversational exchange or in "reading" the pragmatic intent of the adult. Donahue (1984) pointed out, for example, that children with learning disabilities (LD) often fail to ask for clarification of inherently ambiguous statements. The repercussions of such a failure for scaffolded instruction should be obvious. More generally, several developmental psychologists have provided evidence of age-related growth in the sophistication of young children's pragmatic understandings, and of the importance of those understandings for children's interactions with adults in goal-directed task situations (Donaldson, 1978; Shatz, 1983; Siegal, 1991). Indeed, Siegal (1991) argued that the young child's failure to appreciate that adults may intentionally "suspend" Grice's maxims in explicit instructional situations may interfere with the smooth flow of learning (as when they ask a question to which they already know the answer!). Although the status of such understandings has yet to be investigated in children with LLD, it would seem important to explore this issue systematically (see Donahue & Lopez-Reyna, 1998, for a discussion).

Another potential challenge for some children with LLD in establishing meaningful participation in scaffolded instruction relates to attention. Sustained engagement in an instructional exchange requires the maintenance of attention across multiple conversational turns (with or without interruptions). Children with co-occurring attention deficit disorder, who represent by some estimates approximately 30% of the LD population (Mayes, Calhoun, & Crowell, 2000; S. E. Shaywitz & B. A. Shaywitz, 1993), may find this difficult. Another, less common problem with attention is a difficulty in the flexible shifting of cognitive set. Children with some characteristics of pervasive developmental disorders, for example, may become fixated on a recurring theme, a theme that colors many exchanges and which may therefore interfere with appropriate inferences.

An example of such a situation is evident in the exchange presented in Table 7.6. This exchange took place between a teacher and a 12-year-old girl during a lesson on superordinates. As the exchange opens, the teacher

TABLE 7.6
An Example of Inflexible Cognitive Set

Teacher's Question and Comments	Child's Answers and Comments
Teacher: What about nail, screw, glue, and tape? What do they all have in common?	*Child:* All things (that you) work, that you might find in a hardware store?
T: Yes, you could find them in a hardware store. [Writes]. But what —, what else that's alike about them?	C: The glue you might find in school supplies.
T: Right, hardware [writes] or school, supplies. But **nails**, you wouldn't find nails in the school supplies, would you?	C: You would find **those** in a hardware store.
T: You could find nails, screw, glue, and tape all in a hardware store. Right. But, what do they have in common? What else do they have in common?	C: I know I know I know what would be a good thing I know what would be a good thing to add to that.
T: Hmmm, something to add to the group, that would be interesting. What would you add?	C: Hardware supplies?
T: Well, but what do **these four** [points iteratively] particularly have in common [gestures across the four]? They **are all** found in a hardware store, but can you [gestures along list of items] think of something else that's alike about them?	[C: glances briefly at the page **after** T finishes iterative points, but looks back to T's face and doesn't seem to see any of the gesturing.]
	C: No.
T: Well, [circles word on page] let's think about how they're **used**. Maybe that would help us think about how they're, what they have in common. How do you use a nail? What do you use a **nail** for?	C: Hammering?
T: Yeah, but, would you just **hammer** [gestures hammering]? Why, why do you use a nail? What does it do? What does the nail do when you hammer it?	C: Goes into wood?
T: To do what?	C: To make something?
T: Right, to make something what? [gestures two things sticking together by slapping two palms together].	C: Big?

T: OK, you have two pieces of wood, right? When you put the nail, when you hammer the nail in, what happens?

C: It falls in.

T: It **goes** in. And then what does it do to the two pieces of wood?

C: Stick?

T: It **holds** them together, right. They stick. What about a screw? You have **two** pieces of wood [gestures with two hands] and you take a screw and you screw them together [gestures screwing]. What happens?

C: This thing? [While speaking, she simultaneously raises one hand high in air and parallel to the table].

T: Two, yeah, you take a screw and you screw two boards together. [gestures]. What happens?

C: It makes holes?

T: What does it do for them? The two pieces of wood?

C: (Cut it)?

T: If you screw, if you have two pieces of board, say you have this board and we take another board and put it here and we screw them together. [gestures]. What does the screw **do** for those two pieces of wood?

C: Screw it together?

T: It holds them **together**, right. What about glue? If I have this piece of paper and this piece of paper, [picks up paper] and I take some **glue**, [gestures adding glue and pressing down] what does the glue do?

C: Stick?

T: It, yeah, what does it do <u>to the two</u>?

C: <u>Holds it.</u>

T: Holds them **together**. And what about tape? [underlines word].

C: That holds it together?

T: [nods]. So nail, screw, glue, and tape, what do they have in common?

C: That holds them together.

T: Hold things together, right. [writes]. Can you think of something to put in this group?

C: Yeah.

T: **Another** item that **holds** things together. [writes].

C: Not a gas trimmer.

T: Something that holds **two** things together. [gestures sticking by slapping palms together].

C: That's a thing that uh that um um that trims the lawn.

T: But we're not talking about trimming the lawn now, we're talking about items that **hold** things together.

C: In a **hardware** store?

T: You could find them in a hardware store. Can you think of two things, something that **holds** things together?

Note. Utterances underlined were spoken simultaneously. Bold font indicates stress.

presents the child with a card containing the names of four objects (nail, screw, glue, and tape) and asks her to identify the commonality among the objects. The girl's initial hypothesis relates to a common location, a hardware store. During the following exchange, the teacher scaffolds the child's construction of an alternative criterion of similarity: the common function of the objects, namely to hold things together. For some time, the child appears to be following the teacher's lead, as evidenced by the following exchange:

Teacher: What do they have in common?

Child: That holds them together.

However, when the teacher further assesses the child's understanding by requesting her to suggest a new member for the category ("Can you think of something to put in this group?"), the child's suggestion of a "gas trimmer" makes it clear that she has not left behind her initial focus on "things found in a hardware store." Thus, despite the teacher's efforts and the child's superficial participation in the ongoing exchange, the child has not shifted her attention, and thus she appears to have missed an important component of the teacher's intended message about functional similarities.

Yet another challenge to effective scaffolding for the child with LLD relates to self-efficacy or self-esteem. To participate in extended instructional exchanges with full engagement requires some confidence that "it will all make sense." Unfortunately, many children with LLD suffer from negative academic self-concepts and low self-efficacy in one or more task domains (Bryan, 1998). There is some encouraging evidence that appropriately structured academic interventions can serve to build a more positive self-concept in children with LD (Elbaum & Vaughn, 2001). However, finding the crucial ingredients for such instruction is still an issue for the future.

One last issue warranting some discussion is that of the accuracy of adult perceptions of the needs of children with LLD. This issue is important in two senses. First, in capitalizing on opportunities for instruction (i.e., appropriate settings and goal-directed activities), adults must take into consideration, if only implicitly, their assumptions regarding the child's current interests and understanding. This selection of "ripe" educational opportunities relies crucially on the adult's accurate judgment of the child. At a more fine-grained level, similar microjudgments must be made on an ongoing basis during communicative exchanges. If the adult misjudges the child's uptake of new information, subsequent guidance may be inappropriate.

In this context, it is important to note that a number of studies point to low expectations for the future accomplishments of children with LD on the part of parents and teachers (Bryan, 1998). Also, although the findings are somewhat contradictory, the results of several studies suggest that parents of children with LLD tend to underestimate what their children will accomplish in a given task situation (see Stone, 1997; and Hauerwas & Stone, 2000, for reviews of this work). Finally, a number of studies of parent–child interaction in children with language impairments have reported findings suggesting that mothers of these children are significantly more directive and less challenging in their interactions (Stone & Conca, 1993).

Although it is possible that such reduced parental perceptions and directive scaffolding strategies are appropriately calibrated to the child's actual instructional needs (Marfo, 1990; Schneider & Gearhart, 1988), this may not always be the case. A study by Sammarco (Sammarco, 1984; Wertsch & Sammarco, 1985) provides one graphic example of this situation. In a comparison of the scaffolding strategies used by the mothers of children with and without diagnosed language disorders, Sammarco reported the common finding that the mothers of the atypical children were significantly more directive. Sammarco went beyond this finding, however, by comparing the mothers' estimates of their child's mastery of task-relevant vocabulary with objective evidence collected from the children. Relative to objective evidence, Sammarco found that the mothers significantly underestimated their children's vocabulary knowledge. One possible implication of such an underestimation was highlighted by Sammarco in a scaffolding pattern characteristic of several mothers, a pattern that she termed "ineffective other-regulation."

An example of such an exchange is presented in Table 7.7. In this exchange, the mother is helping the child locate a small blue helicopter to place in a specific location in the toy airport scene that they are reproducing from a model (lines 1–2). For several exchanges (lines 3–13), the mother persists in her attempts to assist the child in selecting the correct piece. However, she eventually appears to give up (line 15). At this point, she capitalizes on the fact that the child has picked up a different piece, but one that will in fact be needed eventually for another location in the toy scene. She then directs the child, using a highly directive nonverbal pointing gesture (line 16), to place that new piece where it belongs. In doing so, she has completely abandoned the original goal of the exchange (i.e., finding and placing the little blue helicopter). As Sammarco points out, it is not clear that the child has learned anything about the intent of the mother's original suggestion (line 1). Sammarco reported that such ineffective other-regulations, although common among the mothers of the children with language disorders, were rarely observed in the exchanges of the mothers of the typically developing children.

Hopefully, the examples just cited serve to make clear various ways in which scaffolded instruction can be challenging in the case of children with LLD, challenging for both the child and the instructor. In highlighting these challenges, my intent is not to suggest that scaffolded instruction is inap-

TABLE 7.7
An Example of "Ineffective Other-Regulation" During
Parent–Child Interaction

1. M: Okay now find, get the blue [mother points to the little blue helicopter in the pieces pile] helicopter [child looks to the pieces pile].
2. M: That little blue one over there.
3. M: [child picks up the little yellow airplane which is a distractor item] No
4. C: I want this one.
5. M: We don't need that one though.
6. M: We need the big yellow airplane [child looks to the pieces pile and returns the little yellow airplane to the pieces pile].
7. C: [child picks up the little blue helicopter] Yellow [child puts the little blue helicopter back down] airplane [child picks up the big blue helicopter, which is a distractor item].
8. M: Not that one, we need the little one.
9. M: That's [mother points to the big blue helicopter in the child's hand] a big one.
10. M: Find one just like that, only littler.
11. C: Okay.
12. C: This go right here [child puts the big blue helicopter back down]
13. M: Okay, find me the little one.
14. C: Little one [picks up the little red airplane], here little one.
15. M: Okay, we need that.
16. M: Here, why don't [mother points to dot on copy board where the little red airplane goes] you put that right here.
17. M: Here [mother takes the little red airplane from the child's hand and places it on the copy board].

(Sammarco, 1984, pp. 190–191)

propriate or unrealistic for such children. Rather, it is to emphasize the need for greater attention on the part of both researchers and practitioners to the dynamics of instructional activities targeted at atypical children.

MAXIMIZING THE POTENTIAL OF SCAFFOLDED INSTRUCTION FOR THE CHILD WITH LLD

Given the challenges to effective use of scaffolded instruction for children with LLD, and the assumption that such instruction is a powerful opportunity for learning, an opportunity that should be capitalized on for all children, it is crucially important to consider how to make this happen for children with LLD. The purpose of the present section is to highlight some measures that can be taken by researchers and practitioners.

Increased Parent and Teacher Awareness

One crucial implication of the enriched conception of scaffolded instruction discussed earlier is that we need to challenge children as well as support them. This issue is important for both parental and teacher instruction. Adults working with atypical children must be supportive; they must provide structure as they assist the child in new activities (see Pressley, Harris, & Marks, 1992, for a discussion of the importance of structure in constructivist teaching for children with LD). However, there is a crucial difference between structure and directiveness. Simply put, *directiveness* is structure without challenge. Unfortunately, appreciation of this distinction appears to be somewhat limited among mainstream teachers (Jordan, Lindsay, & Stanovich, 1997; Silliman, Bahr, Beasman, & Wilkinson, 2000) and among some parents (Stone & Conca, 1993). Thus, we need to raise awareness of the need to challenge as well as to support. In addition, we need a better understanding of the factors that result in directiveness versus support. To what extent are adult misperceptions of children's needs at issue? How much progress can children with LLD make under varying conditions of structure and challenge? Both researchers and practitioners need to collect systematic data about such issues as they attempt to improve instructional activities for these children.

Constructing Opportunities for Scaffolding

At this point, we know a fair amount about the crucial ingredients for the creation of scaffolded learning opportunities in the classroom. Table 7.8 contains a summary of such ingredients (adapted in part from Hogan and Pressley, 1997; and from Winn, 1994). These suggestions are the product of a good deal of instructional research over the last 10 years. Some of the suggestions come from reflection on instances of successful implementations (e.g., Rosenshine & Meister, 1992); some come from reflection on disappointing efforts to create rich learning opportunities for children with LD by modifying traditional instructional practices (e.g., O'Connor & Jenkins, 1996a, 1966b; Winn, 1994).

At a general level, good advice for how to proceed includes the clear message that teachers must be skilled and mindful of where and when to engage in scaffolded instructional activities. They must have a good understanding of the knowledge domain at issue, and of their students' collective and individual background knowledge and skills. Teachers must adjust their assistance nimbly in response to their online assessment of children's understanding, and they must challenge the children to think for themselves.

TABLE 7.8
Constructing Opportunities for Scaffolding—Some Guidelines

Prepare a Good Foundation
- Find a comfortable fit for scaffolding within preexisting personal teaching style/routines.
- Reflect on current dynamics in the classroom with an eye to opportunities for change.
- Prioritize targets for scaffolding (e.g., concepts, strategies).
- Consider appropriate grouping structures for targeted activities.
- Make participation structures predictable and comfortable.
- Foster affective engagement and enthusiasm, both in the adult and the child.

Elements of the Construction Process
- Recruit children's interest with relevant, concrete goals.
- Keep the activity meaningful (i.e., focus on end goal).
- Ask challenging questions.
- Engage in online diagnosis of the child's understanding and need for support.
- Avoid frequent provision of answers, *but* don't shy away from demonstrations and explanations.
- Embody thought processes and procedural steps in overt interchanges.
- Provide contingent assistance when necessary, *but* don't jump in too quickly.
- Respond flexibly to student errors.
- Fade intensity of support.

Maximizing the Outcomes (i.e., Maintenance, Generalization, and Ownership)
- Engage *all* students—physically *and* mentally.
- Encourage student reflection (e.g., elicit summaries of activities, self-evaluations of answers).
- Support risk taking.
- Focus students on their successes.

Specific Issues for the Child With LLD
- Ensure accurate perceptions on part of parents and teachers of the child's specific skills and readiness for challenge.
- Be alert for unnecessary "directiveness."
- Provide multiple modes of (redundant) information.
- Encourage the development and use of concrete representations of conceptual relationships and complex procedures.
- Be alert to specific impediments to inferential "uptake" of scaffolding challenges.
- Encourage/reward engagement and build self-efficacy.

Although many of these principles should apply to the child with LLD, one clear conclusion from the discussion in the previous section is that the application of the principles to the instruction of these children, at school or at home, has not necessarily been straightforward. In working to create meaningful opportunities for scaffolded exchanges involving the child with LLD, it is important to consider, for example, the reality that parents and teachers are often too directive in their interactions. In addition, teachers may not always be mindful of the extent to which classroom discourse poses linguistic challenges to the child with LLD. This may be the case even in instances in which the teacher is striving to scaffold understandings via targeted dyadic exchanges or small-group interactions. Finally, adults may overestimate the extent to which they have created learning environments in which children feel empowered to construct new understandings for themselves.

• • • • • •

The issues raised here lead to a number of suggestions for future research regarding the improvement of learning opportunities for children with LLD. We need a better understanding, for example, of the circumstances under which adults are overly directive in their interactions with atypical children. More research is needed on the connection between adult perceptions of these children's readiness for challenge and the dynamics of scaffolding exchanges. Do adults overgeneralize from isolated instances of knowledge/skills gaps to lowered expectations in other situations? Do children with LLD communicate nonverbally a sense of confusion or disinterest? We also need a better understanding of children's linguistic readiness for scaffolded instruction—both in terms of formal linguistic knowledge (vocabulary and syntax) and in terms of familiarity with pragmatic conventions.

These and other issues for future research hold the promise of leading eventually to more effective instruction for children with LLD, both at home and at school. In the meantime, it is important to use what we already know in the improvement of educational opportunities for these children. Scaffolding children's learning is hard work (Winn, 1994), and it is not always successful, perhaps for some of the reasons just discussed. However, as Wood et al. (1976) argued so well many years ago, such instruction has enormous promise to create meaningful learning, and it is crucial that we not deprive children with LLD of such opportunities (Biemiller & Meichenbaum, 1998).

REFERENCES

Alibali, M. W., Flevares, L. M., & Goldin-Meadow, S. (1997). Assessing knowledge conveyed in gesture: Do teachers have the upper hand? *Journal of Educational Psychology, 89,* 183–193.

Becker, J. A., & Goodnow, J. J. (1991). "What's the magic word?" "Were you born in a tent?"—The challenge of accounting for parents' use of indirect forms of speech with children. *The Quarterly Newsletter of the Laboratory of Comparative Human Cognition, 13,* 55–58.

Berk, L., & Winsler, A. (1995). *Scaffolding children's learning.* Washington, DC: National Association for the Education of Young Children.

Biemiller, A., & Meichenbaum, D. (1998). The consequences of negative scaffolding for students who learn slowly. *Journal of Learning Disabilities, 31,* 365–369.

Bryan, T. (1998). Social competence of students with learning disabilities. In B. Y. L. Wong (Ed.), *Learning about learning disabilities, second edition* (pp. 237–275). San Diego, CA: Academic Press.

Cazden, C. B. (1983). Peekaboo as an instructional model: Discourse development at home and at school. In B. Bain (Ed.), *The sociogenesis of language and human conduct* (pp. 33–58). New York: Plenum.

Cazden, C. (1986). Classroom discourse. In M. E. Wittrock (Ed.), *Handbook of research on teaching, third edition* (pp. 432–463). New York: Macmillan.

Cazden, C. B. (1988). *Classroom discourse: The language of teaching and learning.* Portsmouth, NH: Heineman.

Craig, H. (1995). Pragmatic impairments. In P. Fletcher & B. MacWhinney (Eds.), *The handbook of child language* (pp. 623–640). Cambridge, MA: Blackwell.

Day, J. D., & Cordon, L. A. (1993). Static and dynamic measures of ability: An experimental comparison. *Journal of Educational Psychology, 85,* 75–82.

Donahue, M. L. (1984). Learning disabled children's conversational competence: An attempt to activate the inactive listener. *Applied Psycholinguistics, 5,* 21–35.

Donahue, M. L., & Lopez-Reyna, N. A. (1998). Conversational maxims and scaffolded learning in children with learning disabilities: Is the flying buttress a better metaphor? *Journal of Learning Disabilities, 31,* 398–403.

Donaldson, M. (1978). *Children's minds.* New York: W. W. Norton.

Elbaum, B., & Vaughn, S. (2001). School-based interventions to enhance the self-concept of students with learning disabilities: A meta-analysis. *Elementary School Journal, 101,* 303–329.

Grice, P. (1989). *Studies in the way of words.* Cambridge, MA: Harvard University Press.

Hauerwas, L., & Stone, C. A. (2000). Are parents of school-age children with specific language impairments accurate estimators of their child's language skills? *Child Language Teaching & Therapy, 16,* 73–86.

Hogan, K., & Pressley, M. (1997). *Scaffolding children's learning: Instructional approaches and issues.* Cambridge, MA: Brookline Books.

Jordan, A., Lindsay, L., & Stanovich, P. J. (1997). Classroom teachers' instructional interactions with students who are exceptional, at risk, and typically achieving. *Remedial & Special Education, 18,* 82–93.

Leonard, L. (1998) *Children with specific language impairment.* Cambridge, MA: MIT Press.

Marfo, K. (1990). Maternal directiveness in interactions with mentally handicapped children: An analytical commentary. *Journal of Child Psychology & Psychiatry, 31,* 531–549.

Mayes, S. D., Calhoun, S. L., & Crowell, E. W. (2000). Learning disabilities and ADHD: Overlapping spectrum disorders. *Journal of Learning Disabilities, 33,* 417–424.

McNeill, D., Cassell, J., & McCullough, K.-E. (1994). Communicative effects of speech-mismatched gestures. *Research on Language and Social Interaction, 27,* 223–237.

Meyer, D. K. (1993). What is scaffolded instruction? Definitions, distinguishing features, and misnomers. In D. J. Lev & C. K. Kinzer (Eds.), *Examining central issues in literacy research, theory, and practice* (pp. 41–53). Chicago: National Reading Conference.

O'Connor, R. E., & Jenkins, J. R. (1996a). Cooperative learning as an inclusion strategy: A closer look. *Exceptionality, 6,* 29–51.

O'Connor, R. E., & Jenkins, J. R. (1996b). Choosing individuals as the focus to study cooperative learning. *Exceptionality, 6,* 65–68.

Palincsar, A. S. (1986). The role of dialogue in providing scaffolded instruction. *Educational Psychologist, 21,* 73–98.

Palincsar, A. S., & Brown, A. L. (1984). Reciprocal teaching of comprehension-fostering and comprehension-monitoring activities. *Cognition and instruction, 1,* 117–175.

Pratt, M. W., Green, D., MacVicar, J., & Bountrogianni, M. (1992). The mathematical parent: Parental scaffolding, parenting style, and learning outcomes in long-division mathematics homework. *Journal of Applied Developmental Psychology, 1,* 17–34.

Pressley, M., Harris, K. R., & Marks, M. B. (1992). But good strategy instructors are constructivists! *Educational Psychology Review, 4,* 3–31.

Rosenshine, B., & Meister, C. (1992). The use of scaffolds for teaching higher-level cognitive strategies. *Educational Leadership, 49,* 26–33.

Sammarco, J. (1984). *Joint problem solving activity in mother-child dyads: A comparative study of language disorder and normally achieving pre-schoolers.* Unpublished doctoral dissertation, Northwestern University, Evanston, IL.

Schneider, P., & Gearhart, M. (1988). The ecocultural niche of families with mentally retarded children: Evidence from mother–child interaction studies. *Journal of Applied Developmental Psychology, 9,* 85–106.

Shatz, M. (1983). Communication. In P. H. Mussen (Ed.), *Handbook of child psychology. Vol. 3: Cognitive development* (pp. 841–889). New York: John Wiley.

Shaywitz, S. E., & Shaywitz, B. A. (1993). Learning disabilities and attention deficits in the school setting. In L. J. Meltzer (Ed.), *Strategy assessment and instruction for students with learning disabilities: From theory to practice* (pp. 221–241). Austin, TX: Pro-Ed.

Siegal, M. (1991). *Knowing children: Experiments in conversation and cognition.* Hillsdale, NJ: Lawrence Erlbaum Associates.

Silliman, E. R., Bahr, R., Beasman, J., & Wilkinson, L. C. (2000). Scaffolds for learning to read in an inclusion classroom. *Language, Speech, and Hearing Services in Schools, 31,* 265–279.

Stone, C. A. (1993). What's missing in the metaphor of scaffolding? In E. A. Forman, N. Minick, & C. A. Stone (Eds.), *Contexts for learning: Sociocultural dynamics in children's development* (pp. 169–183). New York: Oxford University Press.

Stone, C. A. (1997). Correspondences among parent, teacher, and student perceptions of adolescent learning disabilities. *Journal of Learning Disabilities, 30,* 660–669.

Stone, C. A. (1998). The metaphor of scaffolding: Its utility for the field of learning disabilities. *Journal of Learning Disabilities, 31,* 344–364.

Stone, C. A., & Conca, L. (1993). The nature and origin of strategy deficiencies in learning-disabled children: A social constructivist perspective. In L. Meltzer (Ed.), *Strategy assessment and instruction for students with learning disabilities: From theory to practice* (pp. 23–59). Austin, TX: PRO-ED.

Wertsch, J. V., & Sammarco, J. G. (1985). Social precursors to individual cognitive functioning: The problem of units of analysis. In R. Hinde & A. N. Perret-Clermont (Eds.), *Social relationships and cognitive development* (pp. 276–293). Oxford: Clarenden Press.

Winn, J. A. (1994). Promises and challenges of scaffolded instruction. *Learning Disability Quarterly, 17*, 89–104.

Wong, B. Y. L. (Ed.). (1998). Special series on scaffolding. *Journal of Learning Disabilities, 31*, 340–414.

Wood, D. (1990). Teaching the young child: Some relationships between social interaction, language, and thought. In R. Olson (Ed.), *The social foundations of language and thought* (pp. 280–296). New York: Norton.

Wood, D., Bruner, J. S., & Ross, G. (1976). The role of tutoring in problem solving. *Journal of Child Psychiatry and Psychology, 17*, 89–100.

Wood, D., Wood, H., & Middleton, D. (1978). An experimental evaluation of four face-to-face teaching strategies. *International Journal of Behavioral Development, 1*, 131–147.

The Road Less Traveled: Prevention and Intervention in Written Language

Steve Graham
Karen R. Harris
University of Maryland

We were recently introduced to two children with special needs in an elementary school just outside Washington, DC. One of the children, Miles,[1] was a fourth-grade student with a learning disability in writing. According to his teacher, Miles avoids writing whenever possible, and it is not unusual to hear him make disparaging comments about writing and his writing capabilities. When describing his writing, the teacher characterized Miles as a "minimalist," noting that his papers are inordinately short, containing only a few ideas and very little elaboration. This description is also characteristic of his approach to writing, as he rarely does any planning in advance, preferring to "get his ideas" while writing. He further appears to use a least-effort strategy when revising, as the changes he initiates are primarily limited to minor word substitutions and unsuccessful attempts to correct errors of spelling, punctuation, and capitalization. Rarely does he make more substantive revisions, such as adding or rewriting sections of text to make them better. Finally, it takes some effort to read most of Miles's compositions, as his handwriting is difficult to read, one out of every five words is misspelled, and punctuation and capitalization are irregular. Miles's writing profile is not unusual for a child with writing and learning difficulties, as these students typically experience challenges generating content, executing the mechanical aspects of writing, and plan-

---

[1] This is not the child's real name; in all of our chapters we substitute real names with the names of fictional characters from popular science fiction or fantasy books.

ning and revising text (Englert, Raphael, Fear, & Anderson, 1988; Graham & Harris, 1994, 1997a, 1999).

The other child with a special need that we met was Cordelia, a fourth grader with a history of speech and language problems, including phonological difficulties. Like her classmate, Cordelia also had trouble with writing. An examination of the papers included in her writing portfolio supported the teacher's observations that Cordelia's language and phonological difficulties affected her written expression abilities, as her writing contained numerous grammatical, morphological, and spelling errors. Although she typically wrote as much as the other children in her class, the overall quality of her work was generally weaker; it was not as cohesive or well organized. In addition, Cordelia is very reticent about her writing, preferring not to share what she has written with others in the class.

In contrast to Miles's, it is difficult to characterize Cordelia's writing as typical for a child with speech and language difficulties. We currently know very little about the writing of these children, as the current data base is limited to a few studies (Clarke-Klein & Hodson, 1995; Gillam & Johnston, 1992; Lewis, O'Donnell, Freebairn, & Taylor, 1998) that examined a single type of writing (i.e., composing in response to a picture) by a small number of participants. If the available evidence is representative, not all children with speech and language problems have difficulties organizing their writing content (Gillam & Johnston, 1992), but errors of syntax, vocabulary, and spelling are relatively common in the writing of these students (Clarke-Klein & Hodson, 1995; Gillam & Johnston, 1992; Lewis et al., 1998).

In this chapter, we examine how schools can help children like Miles and Cordelia become skilled and engaged writers. Too often these children receive inadequate or incomplete writing instruction (Graham & Harris, 1997b, 1997c). Some are assigned to classes that focus almost exclusively on the teaching of lower level writing skills, such as conventions of usage and the mastery of handwriting and spelling, with few opportunities to actually write (Palinscar & Klenk, 1992). In contrast, others are placed in programs where frequent writing is emphasized, but little attention is directed at systematically teaching writing skills and strategies, because it is assumed that these skills can be mastered through informal and incidental methods of learning, such as capitalizing on teachable moments and providing minilessons as the need arises (see, e.g., Westby & Costlow, 1991). In our opinion, it is unlikely that children, such as Miles and Cordelia, will acquire all that they need to become skilled and engaged writers in either of these two types of programs. Instead, we contend that instruction for children with writing difficulties, including students with language learning disabilities, must take a road that is less traveled—one that (a) emphasizes both prevention and intervention; (b) responds to the specific needs of each child; (c) maintains a healthy balance between meaning, process, and form; and (d) employs both formal and informal learning methods.

The design of such a road is not an easy task, as it is not limited to a single teacher or grade. Instead, it requires a coherent, coordinated, and extended vision. The writing problems of children with language learning disabilities are not transitory difficulties that disappear quickly or easily. Our recommendations for forging this road are based on the following six principles:

1. Provide exemplary writing instruction;
2. tailor writing instruction to meet the individual needs of children who experience difficulty in learning to write;
3. intervene early, providing a coherent and sustained effort to improve the writing skills of children who experience writing difficulties;
4. expect that each child will learn to write;
5. identify and address academic and nonacademic roadblocks to writing and school success; and
6. employ technological tools that improve writing performance.

PROVIDE EXEMPLARY WRITING INSTRUCTION

In the popular cartoon series, "Calvin and Hobbes," Calvin asks his teacher, Miss Wormwood, why she isn't teaching them the genders of nouns, complaining that foreign kids know and that it's no wonder that the United States can't compete in a global market. Not stopping there, he goes on to demand sex education!

Although Calvin's concerns are clearly misplaced, the underlying issue, the importance of an exemplary education, is not. A crucial tactic in preventing writing difficulties is to provide exemplary writing instruction right from the start, beginning in kindergarten and first grade and continuing throughout the school years. Although this approach will not eradicate all writing difficulties, cases of writing failure due to poor instruction can be prevented. Exemplary writing instruction can also help to ameliorate the severity of writing difficulties experienced by other children whose primary problems are not instructional, such as children with language learning disabilities, as well as maximize the writing development of children in general.

What does exemplary writing instruction look like for children with language learning disabilities and other struggling writers? To answer this question, we drew on multiple sources to develop a list of features of effective writing instruction for these students. This included research reviews of writing instruction for students with learning disabilities and writing difficulties (e.g., Graham & Harris, 1997b; Graham, Harris, MacArthur, & Schwartz, 1991), recommendations for teaching writing to children with learning and language difficulties (Graham, 1992; Graham & Harris, 1988;

Graham, Harris, MacArthur, & Schwartz, 1998; Scott, 1989, 1994, 1999; Westby & Clauser, 1999), and studies of the instructional practices of outstanding literacy teachers (Pressley, Rankin, & Yokoi, 1996; Pressley, Yokoi, Rankin, Wharton-McDonald, & Hampston, 1997; Wharton-McDonald, Pressley, & Mistretta, in press). These features are listed in Table 8.1. They involve frequent writing in a supportive, collaborative, and motivating environment, where students are encouraged to direct and assess their own efforts, and the skills and processes underlying effective writing are modeled and directly taught by the teacher.

The impact of instruction that embodies many of the types of practices presented in Table 8.1 was illustrated in a study by Englert and colleagues (Englert et al., 1995) with first- through fourth-grade children with special needs. Most of these children were students with learning disabilities. The instructional program, entitled the Early Literacy Project (ELP), was delivered by special education teachers to small groups of students within the context of a resource room, 2 to 3 hours each day. In the ELP curriculum, a supportive writing community is created through the use of activities involving sharing and student collaboration; the teaching of writing and reading are integrated together around thematic units. Both skills (e.g., spelling) and strategy instruction for planning and revising occur within the context of these units, opportunities to engage in meaningful writing are plentiful, teaching is responsive to individual needs, and dialogue and modeling are used to demonstrate the actions and thinking involved in writing.

In addition to the spelling skills taught within the context of the ELP program, the participating students also received supplemental spelling as well as phonemic awareness instruction that is more traditional and decontextualized. Students who received ELP instruction from a veteran ELP teacher produced better organized text, wrote more words, and spelled more words correctly than students in more traditional special education classes.

Unfortunately, many students with language learning disabilities do not receive exemplary writing instruction. Christenson, Thurlow, Ysseldyke, and McVicar (1989) reported that students receiving special services spend only about 20 minutes a day writing. Over 60% of this writing time involved tasks such as writing numbers during math, handwriting and spelling practice, and filling out worksheets. This approach to instruction does not provide enough quantity or quality to ensure that children will learn all they need to know to write effectively. Although Miles and Cordelia, the two fourth graders we introduced earlier, are currently in a classroom that incorporates many of the features of exemplary writing instruction just described, this was not always the case. Their teachers in first through third grade allocated only about 15 minutes a day to writing, with most of this time devoted to the teaching of handwriting and spelling. If these two chil-

TABLE 8.1
Features of Exemplary Writing Instruction

- Establish a predictable routine where students are encouraged to think, reflect, and revise as they write.
- Develop a literate classroom environment, where students' written work is prominently displayed, word lists adorn the walls, and the room is packed with writing and reading material.
- Require that students write each day, working on a wide range of meaningful writing tasks for multiple audiences, including writing at home.
- Arrange regular conferences with each student concerning the writing topic the child is currently working on, including the establishment of goals or criteria to guide writing and revising efforts.
- Create cooperative arrangements where students help each other plan, draft, revise, edit, or publish their work.
- Encourage group or individual sharing, with students presenting their in progress work or completed papers to their peers for feedback.
- Model the process of writing as well as positive attitudes toward writing, including sharing your own writing with students.
- Provide instruction in a broad range of skills, knowledge, and strategies, including phonological awareness, handwriting and spelling, writing conventions, sentence-level skills, text structure, the functions of writing, and planning and revising;
- Insure sensitivity to individual needs through adjustments in teaching style and learning pace, minilessons responsive to current needs, and individually guided assistance with writing assignments.
- Integrate writing activities and themes across the curriculum and use reading to support writing development.
- Make writers motivated by creating a risk-free environment, and setting an exciting mood. Allow students to select their own writing topics or modify teacher assignments. Base teacher-selected topics on students' interest, reinforce children's accomplishments, specify the goal for each lesson, and promote an "I can do" attitude.
- Provide frequent opportunities for students' to self-regulate their behavior during writing, including arranging their own space, seeking help from others, or working independently.
- Establish both teacher and student assessment of writing progress, strengths, and needs.
- Hold periodic conferences and communicate frequently with parents about their child's writing progress and the goals and structure of the writing program.
- Deliver follow-up instruction to ensure mastery of targeted writing skills, knowledge, and strategies.

dren had received exemplary instruction right from the start, their writing development would most likely be more advanced.

TAILORING WRITING INSTRUCTION TO MEET THE NEEDS OF CHILDREN EXPERIENCING WRITING DIFFICULTIES

In another "Calvin and Hobbes" cartoon, Calvin is watching the news on television and yelling that this is not informative—it is a sound bite; it is entertainment; it is sensationalism! Fortunately, he notes that is all he has the patience for.

Although outstanding writing teachers do not teach "sound bites," they do recognize the importance of tailoring instruction to meet the individual needs of children experiencing difficulty learning to writing, including those with language learning disabilities. This was illustrated by teachers in a study by Dahl and Freepon (1991). They provided extensive individual and personalized help to children experiencing difficulties with writing, including scaffolding and extended guidance aimed at helping them refine and extend their writing skills. For instance, these students received additional support in mastering spelling, as their teachers spent extra time teaching them about letter–sound relationships.

Balance

One critical aspect of providing personalized and individually tailored assistance to students with language learning disabilities and other struggling writers is finding the right balance between formal and informal instruction as well as meaning, process, and form. As we noted at the beginning of this chapter, some students with language learning disabilities are assigned to classrooms that focus almost exclusively on the direct and explicit teaching of writing skills, whereas others are placed in programs where systematic and direct instruction are downplayed, as it is assumed that writing can be acquired naturally, much like learning to speak. We contend that neither of these approaches alone are adequate for teaching writing to children with language learning disabilities or other struggling writers, because an effective and complete writing program for these children involves both formal and informal methods of learning (Graham & Harris, 1994, 1997b, 1997c).

We use spelling as a touchstone to illustrate the assertion just made, drawing on the evidence presented in two recent reviews by Graham (1999, 2000). The available data indicate that poor spellers do learn new spellings as a result of frequent reading and writing, but that such gains are generally modest for this group of students. Similarly, there is a considerable body of literature that demonstrates that spelling instruction improves the spelling performance of poor spellers, but it is unlikely that such instruction is extensive or complete enough to account for all of the growth necessary to become a competent speller. For instance, adults can typically spell 10,000 or more words correctly, but are probably only directly taught 3,000 to 4,000 words at most, and some of these are not mastered when taught. Thus, neither informal or formal approaches alone appear to be powerful enough to ensure the attainment of spelling competence for students who struggle to master the intricacies of English orthography. There are, however, good reasons for using both approaches. Each approach appears to make a separate and unique impact on spelling performance; the informal approach is better at promoting some aspects of learning to spell and the formal approach, others. Children make greater gains in spelling when both approaches are used versus only one of them.

Our claim that an effective writing program for children with language learning difficulties should include both formal and informal methods of learning should not be interpreted as a recommendation that equal amounts of both are needed. Instead, the level of systematic and explicit instruction or less informal instruction needed by individual children will vary and should be adjusted accordingly. In balanced instruction, the fulcrum is the child, and balance depends on what the child needs.

This same principle applies to considerations about what children need to learn about writing. Teachers do struggling writers no favor to suggest, even implicitly, that either meaning, process, or form are unimportant, as all are essential contributors to the development of skilled writing (Graham & Harris, 1994). Likewise, the amount of emphasis placed on each of these needs to be adjusted depending on the characteristics of the individual child. Consider, for instance, the poor writers in a longitudinal study by Juel (1988). One third of these fourth grade children had difficulties with both low-level skills of form (e.g., spelling) and high-level writing processes (e.g., content generation), while the remaining students were equally divided between children experiencing problems in just one of these areas. Thus, some of these students would have benefitted from additional help with both transcription skills (see Graham, 1999) and writing strategies (see Harris & Graham, 1996), but other students needed individualized and personalized assistance in only one of these areas.

Diversity

Children who experience difficulty learning to write, including children with language learning disabilities, come from a wide variety of backgrounds and cultures. This should be taken into account when designing and adapting instruction for these students. All members of the school community, including teachers, speech–language pathologists, and learning disabilities specialists, need to be especially sensitive to cultural and background differences involving literacy experiences at home, interaction styles, discourse patterns, and views concerning the role of the teacher (Harris, Graham, & Deshler, 1998). Failure to consider these factors can undermine the effects of writing instruction. This was evident in a qualitative study by Reyes (1992). When a student misspelled a word, the teacher would write back to the child using the same word, but spelling it correctly. The Hispanic children in this classroom valued and expected direct instruction from the teacher, and they failed to realize that this approach served an instructional purpose, indicating that the teacher should have directly informed them of her intentions.

The work by Au and Mason (1983) in Hawaii provided an excellent illustration of how teachers can adapt literacy instruction to the cultural characteristics of their students. Teachers adjusted the discourse pattern in their classroom so that it was more compatible with the ones experienced by students at home. Hawaiian home events have been characterized as having a highly interactive "talk story" pattern, where individuals engage in cooperative production of responses. When conducting literacy lessons, teachers used several discourse structures that were like the talk story pattern.

The teacher of our two fourth graders, Miles and Cordelia, has made a conscious effort to be responsive to the cultural differences of the children in her classroom as well as their individual instructional needs. For instance, students in her classroom are encouraged to share and develop stories and personal narrative that relate to their cultural and personal interests. Miles, who is African American, has especially enjoyed using stories about children from Africa as a springboard for his own writing. To help him generate and organize ideas for these papers, the teacher has explicitly taught him and several other students how to plan in advance, using a semantic web. In addition, she found the funds, through a private donor, to purchase a word processor, Alpha Smart, that Miles uses when composing. Not surprisingly, Miles's stories and narratives are much longer, better organized, and more engaging.

INTERVENE EARLY

During the middle of a school day, our comic strip hero, Calvin, calls his Dad at work. Intimately familiar with Calvin's misadventures, his Dad worriedly asks if he is all right, what's the matter, and why is he calling? Checking to be sure that no one is looking, Calvin whispers into the phone that he told the teacher that he had to go the bathroom and, quick, "What is 11 + 7?"

Just as Calvin recognized the need for additional assistance, there is an increasing interest in the use of early supplementary instruction or intervention to prevent or at least partially alleviate later writing difficulties. As in the area of reading (Gaskin, 1998; Pikulski, 1994; Pressley, 1998; Slavin, Madden, & Karweit, 1989), this interest is based on the assumption that early intervention programs yield more powerful benefits than efforts to remediate writing problems in later grades. The basic goal of these programs is to help struggling writers catch up with their peers, early on in kindergarten or the primary grades before their difficulties become more intractable. Such programs typically seek to accelerate the progress of struggling students by providing them with additional quality instruction, either in a small group or one-on-one tutoring (see, e.g., Slavin, Madden, Karweit, Livermon, & Dolan, 1990).

To date, only three studies have examined the effectiveness of early intervention programs in writing. In each of these studies, the early intervention program focused on improving text-transcription skills, either handwriting or spelling. In one study by Berninger et al. (1997), first-grade children experiencing difficulty mastering handwriting were randomly assigned to five handwriting treatment groups or a phonological awareness control condition. The handwriting treatments evaluated five alternatives for teaching letter formation:

- One treatment involved the instructor modeling how to form a letter, followed by the child writing the letter the same way.
- In the second treatment, the child wrote the letter after looking at a copy of the letter that contained numbered arrows showing how to form it.
- The third treatment consisted of writing the letter from memory after looking at an unmarked copy of it.
- The fourth treatment combined treatments two and three, as the child first looked at a copy of the letter containing numbered arrows and then wrote it from memory.
- The final handwriting treatment involved writing the letter while looking at an unmarked copy of it.

Students in the control condition received phonological awareness instruction that included identifying, segmenting, deleting, and substituting syllables and sounds in words.

Specially trained tutors worked with three students in each treatment at a time, providing approximately 8 hours of instruction to each child. All of the treatment groups made greater handwriting gains than the control condition, with the combination treatment (i.e., the fourth treatment), where the child looked at a copy of the letter with numbered arrows and then wrote it from memory being the most successful. Even more importantly, the group that received the combined handwriting treatment had higher scores on a standardized writing test, the Writing Fluency Subtest from the Woodcock–Johnson Psycoeducational Battery (Woodcock & Johnson, 1990), than students in either the phonological control condition or the other handwriting groups. This finding is particularly noteworthy because it shows transfer from instruction in handwriting to composition fluency, at least for the group that made the largest handwriting gains.

In a second investigation, Jones and Christensen (1999) found that instruction aimed at improving the letter formation and handwriting fluency skills of first-grade children with poor handwriting enhanced both their handwriting and story writing performance. Over the course of an 8-week period, each of these students received handwriting instruction (individually or in a small group) from a teacher aide or a parent volunteer. Instruction concentrated on learning how to form the lower case letters of the alphabet, correcting specific errors in letter formation, and writing letters quickly and fluently. At the end of the 8-week period, the handwriting and story writing of the children who received this special instruction improved to the point that it was indistinguishable from that of their regular peers who were initially better handwriters and story writers.

In a third study by Berninger et al. (1998), second-grade children experiencing problems with spelling were randomly assigned to seven spelling treatment groups or a control condition where phonological awareness and alphabet sequence skills were taught. For the spelling treatment groups, each lesson was divided into three parts. First, students were taught common sound–letter associations. Second, they practiced the correct spelling of words that occur frequently in the writing of second-grade children. Third, a list of six key words was presented, and students were encouraged to use all six while writing a short composition. Like the practice words, these key words occur frequently in the writing of second-grade children. There was, however, no overlap between practice and key words.

The seven spelling treatment groups differed only in the methods used to learn the practice words:

- One group used a whole word approach, practicing by saying a word and its letters while looking at a copy of the word printed in black.
- A second group used a phoneme approach, sequentially saying each sound and pointing to the corresponding letter(s) while looking at a copy of the word where each phoneme/letter(s) unit was printed in a different color.
- The third group used an onset–rime approach, sequentially saying the sound and pointing to the letter(s) for the onset and rime while looking at a copy of the word where each element was printed in a different color.

- The fourth group practiced each word using both the whole word and phoneme tactics.
- The fifth group used whole word and onset–rime procedures.
- The sixth group used phoneme and onset–rime approaches.
- The seventh group used all three techniques.

Students in the control condition received phonological awareness instruction that included identifying, segmenting, deleting, and substituting syllables and sounds in words as well as instruction in identifying which letter in the alphabet come before and after other letters.

Specially trained tutors worked with two students at a time, providing approximately 8 hours of instruction to each child. As expected, the spelling performance of each of the spelling treatment groups improved over the course of instruction. In addition, one of the spelling groups evidenced improvements in writing. In comparison to children in the control condition, students who practiced words using the phoneme approach made greater gains in compositional fluency, or the amount of text produced when writing. This finding shows that it may be possible to enhance writing performance, at least for poor spellers, by improving their spelling.

The findings from these three studies provide cautious optimism that early intervention for poor handwriting or spelling can boost writing performance. Additional research is needed, however, to replicate these findings and determine if such effects are maintained over time. Some caution must also be exercised in the selection of early intervention handwriting and spelling programs, as many of the approaches employed by Berninger and colleagues (Berninger et al., 1997, 1998) did not lead to improvements in writing performance. Finally, other approaches to early intervention, such as programs to improve struggling writers' planning and revising skills, must be studied in order to provide a broader and richer range of options. Undoubtably, some of the same features that underlie effective early intervention programs in reading (see Graham & Harris, 2000), will be common to similar programs in writing. We anticipate that these will include opportunities to write and share text with others; teaching that focuses on the development of transcription as well as planning and revising skills; instruction that involves the use of explicit explanations, modeling, and scaffolded practices; and ongoing assessment to monitor progress and adjust instruction as needed. Early supplementary instruction such as this would have undoubtably benefitted our two fourth grade students, Miles and Cordelia.

EXPECT THAT EACH CHILD WILL LEARN TO WRITE

While playing with Hobbes, Calvin asks an ouija board if he will grow up to be the President? As the answer comes letter by letter, Hobbes says each letter aloud: "G ... O ... D ... F ... O ... R ... B ... I ... D." Calvin reacts by kicking over the ouija board, declaring that he did not ask for an editorial.

Like Calvin's ouija board, teachers often view children with writing difficulties negatively, setting low expectations for their performance and limiting their exchanges with them (Graham & Harris, 1997c). During literacy instruction, such negative views may take the form of less attention and praise, more criticism, briefer and less informative feedback, and fewer interactions with the teacher (Johnston & Winograd, 1985). Some teachers view these children as so challenging that a form of pedagogical paralysis can occur, as they are uncertain about what to do or lack confidence in their own capabilities to successfully teach these children (Kameenui, 1993).

As the teachers participating in the study by Englert and associates (Englert et al., 1995) cited earlier demonstrated, however, teachers are not powerless—children with severe writing difficulties, including those with learning disabilities, can be taught to write. An essential element in designing an effective writing program for these students is the recognition that they are capable and can succeed. This attitude was illustrated in an interview with an outstanding first grade teacher, who noted that she places considerable emphasis on respecting and trusting each child as a competent learner—one who can learn to work independently and productively in the classroom (Pressley, Wharton-McDonald, et al., 1996). It is also important to: (a) set high, but realistic, expectations for children's writing performance; (b) ignore negative expectations (e.g., "John is difficult and doesn't try to learn.") and perceived group expectations (e.g., "Children with language learning disabilities cannot master the regular class writing curriculum"); (c) monitor and improve the quality of classroom interactions for struggling writers; (d) help them develop an "I can do attitude"; (e) plan writing lessons so that they can accomplish tasks successfully; and (f) build a positive relationship with each child, accepting them as individuals and showing enthusiasm for their interests.

In our interactions with Miles's and Cordelia's current teacher, we have been impressed with her rapport and confidence in her students. This has been especially important for Cordelia, whose sense of efficacy, was very low at the beginning of the school year. As a result of her teacher's encouragement, interest, and high expectations, Cordelia has gradually moved from a guarded reticence, reluctant to share her work in class, to a willingness to let others hear and comment on her writing.

IDENTIFY AND ADDRESS ACADEMIC
AND NONACADEMIC ROADBLOCKS

The importance of our next principle is illustrated in a Calvin and Hobbes cartoon, where Miss Wormwood is presenting a lesson to the class, and

Calvin tunes her out by shifting his attention to his imagination. As the mysterious planet, Zartok 3, drifts closer and closer to his imagined space ship, there is a sudden break in the picture, as the face of his teacher reappears, yelling, "PAY ATTENTION." With his abrupt return to reality, Calvin sadly notes that once you change channels, the original program should not be able to change it back.

Like Calvin's problems with inattentiveness, many children, especially those with language learning disabilities, encounter obstacles that impede their success in learning to write. Children who find school challenging, for example, may exhibit one or more maladaptive behaviors, such as difficulty activating and orchestrating the elements involved in learning, a low tolerance for frustration, or attributing success to ability or luck rather than effort (Harris, 1982; Wong, 1995). For example, at Benchmark School (Gaskin, 1998), a facility that mostly serves children with learning disabilities, teachers identified 32 academic and nonacademic roadblocks to learning, including such difficulties as impulsivity, frequent absences, poor home support, disorganization, inflexibility, lack of persistence, and so forth. Only 9% of their students were viewed as having a single roadblock; the remainder had up to 10 roadblocks to learning.

Teachers need to address any roadblocks experienced by struggling writers that might interfere with their writing development. For instance, children who have difficulty activating, organizing, and maintaining cognitive and motivational resources when writing can learn how to modify this situation through the application of self-regulatory strategies, such as goal setting, self-monitoring, self-instructions, and self-reinforcement (Graham, Harris, & Reid, 1992). A study by Harris, Graham, Reid, McElroy, and Hamby (1994) illustrated how a self-regulatory strategy, such as self-monitoring, can be used to address the types of attentional problems experienced by our friend, Calvin. Fifth- and sixth-grade students with attentional difficulties were asked to count and graph daily the number of words they wrote while working on their compositions. As a result of using this simple procedure, there was a 50% increase in their on-task behavior, and their compositions became two- to three-times longer.

A second example of addressing academic roadblocks is provided in an investigation by Sexton, Harris, and Graham (1998). In this study, fifth- and sixth-grade students with learning disabilities who displayed a low level of motivation and maladaptive beliefs about the causes of success and failures were taught a planning strategy for completing persuasive essays. Instruction also included an attributional component, as students were encouraged to attribute their success to effort as well as to use the planning strategy and to use self-statements (e.g., "Good writing takes hard work"), reflecting these attributions. Following instruction, students' essays became longer and qualitatively better, and there was a positive change in their attributions for writing.

For our two fourth graders, Miles and Cordelia, their teacher also helped them overcome roadblocks that were impeding their writing performance. Miles often had trouble slowing down and thinking things through when he was planning and writing his papers. Cordelia was so anxious about misspelled words that she emphasized correct spelling more than making sense. To help Miles, his teacher taught him to say, "Whoa," silently when he needed to slow down the planning and writing process. To decrease Cordelia's anxiety about spelling, the teacher developed a personalized dictionary that included the correct spellings of words Cordelia frequently misspelled as well as words commonly used and misspelled by children in second through fifth grade. Both of these tactics had the desired effects, helping Miles become more patient and reflective when writing, and reducing Cordelia's overemphasis on spelling.

TAKE ADVANTAGE OF TECHNOLOGICAL TOOLS FOR WRITING

In a final Calvin and Hobbes cartoon, a robot doctor uses a carpenter's saw to lift up the cap of Calvin's skull and proceeds to add some additional gray matter from a jar marked "brains." The doctor informs an ecstatic Calvin that school is no longer necessary, and he can go home and have 12 years of fun. Unfortunately, Calvin's bubble bursts, as a bus arrives to pick him up for another day of school.

Although we cannot "boost the power" of children's brains yet, we can provide children with language learning disabilities with technological tools that can make the process of writing easier and more motivating and, in some instances, improve their writing performance (MacArthur, 1996). Word processing, for instance, can support struggling writers in at least three ways: (1) revising can be done without tedious recopying, (2) typing provides an inherently easier means for producing text for students with fine motor difficulties, and (3) the resulting paper is neat and can be presented in a wide range of professional looking formats (MacArthur, 1999). In addition, text production processes can be supported through the use of spell checkers, speech synthesis, word prediction, and grammar and style checkers (although this last option may be of little use to many school-aged students with language learning disabilities; see MacArthur, 1999). Planning and revising processes can be supported through outlining and semantic mapping software, prompting programs, and multimedia applications. Communication and collaboration with diverse audiences can also be promoted through the use of computer networks.

One of the most impressive accounts we have encountered of how technology can be used to support children's writing is provided by Erickson and Koppenhaver (1995). Erica, a 6-year-old with cerebral palsy who could not speak learned to use a Touch Talker, a dedicated communication device that provides speech output, using a programmable system with a keyboard composed of icons and letters. These technological adaptations allowed her to participate successfully in calendar time, a writing activity where students were directed to produce short statements about the weather, date, or anything else they thought was important.

Although technological tools provide a diverse array of options and supports, it is important to keep in mind that they do not make writing instruction superfluous (Graham & Harris, 1997b). For example, students with learning disabilities often fail to take advantage of the power of word processing when revising, as they continue to revise in the same old fashion, mostly trying to correct mechanical errors (MacArthur & Graham, 1987). Teaching students to use a revising strategy that focuses their attention on substantive changes, however, can result in a much greater use of the editing features of word processing; they are more likely to make changes involving the addition and rewriting of larger units of text (Graham & MacArthur, 1988). Likewise, a spell checker will not eliminate spelling errors, as only about one-half of them are corrected when these students use such devices (MacArthur, Graham, Haynes, & De La Paz, 1996). Consequently, the impact of technological tools will be restricted if students with language learning disabilities fail to develop the knowledge, skill, will, and self-regulation so critical to effective writing.

● ● ● ● ● ●

One of the most pressing questions in literacy instruction is what can schools do to reduce the number of children experiencing difficulties learning to write. In newspapers and other public forums, this question is often answered by suggesting that we need to do "more of this and less of that." A recommendation that is currently popular is that we need more basic skills instruction (i.e., handwriting and spelling) and less whole language or process writing (see Graham & Harris, 1997c). As the present chapter suggests, however, such simple solutions are not powerful enough, especially for children with language learning disabilities. Preventing writing difficulties and intervening successfully when writing problems do occur requires a concerted and sustained effort on the part of parents and the school community. For many of these children, writing difficulties are a chronic condition, not a temporary one. There is no easy or quick inoculation that will make their problems disappear. It is not only important to intervene early with these children, but also to provide a coherent and sustained effort over time.

In this chapter, six principles have been outlined. We believe these principles can help prevent as well as alleviate writing difficulties for children in general as well as for students with language learning disabilities. These principles focused only on what the school community can do and not on other critical constituencies, such as the family or the larger community. Thus, the principles should be viewed as necessary, but not sufficient, components of an overall response to writing disabilities. Likewise, these principles only provide a starting point for schools, as individual schools or school systems will undoubtably need to add additional principles that are responsive to their specific situations.

REFERENCES

Au, K., & Mason, J. (1983). Cultural congruence in classroom participation structures: Achieving a balance of rights. *Discourse Processes, 6*, 145–167.

Berninger, V., Vaughn, K., Abbott, R., Abbott, S., Rogan, L., Brooks, A., Reed, E., & Graham, S. (1997). Treatment of handwriting problems in beginning writers: Transfer from handwriting to composition. *Journal of Educational Psychology, 89*, 652–666.

Berninger, V., Vaughn, K., Abbott, R., Brooks, A., Abbott, S., Rogan, L., Reed, E., & Graham, S. (1998). Early intervention for spelling problems: Teaching functional spelling units of varying size with a multiple-connections framework. *Journal of Educational Psychology, 90*, 587–605.

Christenson, S., Thurlow, M., Ysseldyke, J., & McVicar, R. (1989). Written language instruction for students with mild handicaps: Is there enough quantity to ensure quality. *Learning Disability Quarterly, 12*, 219–229.

Clarke-Klein, S., & Hodson, B. (1995). A phonologically based analysis of misspellings by third graders with disordered-phonology histories. *Journal of Speech and Hearing Research, 38*, 819–849.

Dahl, K., & Freepon, P. (1991). Literacy learning in whole language classrooms: An analysis of low socioeconomic urban children learning to read and write in kindergarten. In J. Zutell & S. McCormick (Eds.), *Learner factors/teacher factors: Issues in literacy research and instruction* (pp. 149–158). Chicago, IL: National Reading Conference.

Englert, C., Garmon, A., Mariage, T., Rozendal, M., Tarrant, K., & Urba, J. (1995). The Early Literacy Project: Connecting across the literacy curriculum. *Learning Disability Quarterly, 18*, 253–275.

Englert, C., Raphael, T., Fear, K., & Anderson, L. (1988). Students' metacognitive knowledge about how to write informational texts. *Learning Disability Quarterly, 11*, 18–46.

Erickson, K., & Koppenhaver, D. (1995). Developing a literacy program for children with severe disabilities. *The Reading Teacher, 48*, 676–684.

Gaskin, I. (1998). There's more to teaching at-risk and delayed readers than good reading instruction. *The Reading Teacher, 51*, 534–547.

Gillam, R., & Johnston, J. (1992). Spoken and written language relationships in language/learning-impaired and normally achieving school-age children. *Journal of Speech and Hearing Research, 35,* 1303–1315.

Graham, S. (1992). Helping students with LD progress as writers. *Intervention in School and Clinic, 27,* 134–144.

Graham, S. (1999). Handwriting and spelling instruction for students with learning disabilities: A review. *Learning Disability Quarterly, 22,* 78–98.

Graham, S. (2000). Should the natural learning approach replace spelling instruction? *Journal of Educational Psychology, 92,* 235–247.

Graham, S., & Harris, K. R. (1988). Instructional recommendations for teaching writing to exceptional students. *Exceptional Children, 54,* 506–512.

Graham, S., & Harris, K. R. (1994). Implications of constructivism for teaching writing to students with special needs. *Journal of Special Education, 28,* 275–289.

Graham, S., & Harris, K. R. (1997a). Self-regulation and writing: Where do we go from here? *Contemporary Educational Psychology, 22,* 102–114.

Graham, S., & Harris, K. R. (1997b). It can be taught, but it does not develop naturally: Myths and realities in writing instruction. *School Psychology Review, 26,* 414–424.

Graham, S., & Harris, K. R. (1997c). Whole language and process writing: Does one approach fit all? In J. Lloyd, E. Kameenui, & D. Chard (Eds.), *Issues in educating students with disabilities* (pp. 239–258). Hillsdale, NJ: Lawrence Erlbaum Associates.

Graham, S. & Harris, K. R. (1999). Assessment and intervention in overcoming writing difficulties: An illustration from the Self-Regulated Strategy Development Model. *Language, Speech, and Hearing Services in Schools, 30,* 255–264.

Graham, S., & Harris, K. R. (2000). Helping children who experience reading difficulties: Prevention and intervention (pp. 43–67). In L. Baker, J. Dreher, & J. Guthrie (Eds.), *Teaching reading: Promoting learning and engagement.* New York: Guilford Press.

Graham, S., Harris, K. R., MacArthur, C., & Schwartz, S. (1991). Writing and writing instruction with students with learning disabilities: A review of a program of research. *Learning Disability Quarterly, 14,* 89–114.

Graham, S., Harris, K. R., MacArthur, C., & Schwartz, S. (1998). Writing instruction. In B. Wong (Ed.), *Learning about learning disabilities* (2nd ed., pp. 391–423). New York: Academic Press.

Graham, S., Harris, K. R., & Reid, R. (1992). Developing self-regulated learners. *Focus on Exceptional Children, 24,* 1–16.

Graham, S., & MacArthur, C. (1988). Improving learning disabled students' skills at revising essays produced on a word processor: Self-instructional strategy training. *Journal of Special Education, 22,* 133–152.

Harris, K. R. (1982). Cognitive-behavior modification: Application with exceptional children. *Focus on Exceptional Children, 15,* 1–16.

Harris, K. R., & Graham, S. (1996). *Making the writing process work: Strategies for composition and self-regulation.* Cambridge, MA: Brookline.

Harris, K. R., Graham, S., & Deshler, D. (Eds.). (1998). *Teaching every child everyday.* Cambridge, MA: Brookline.

Harris, K. R., Graham, S., Reid, R., McElroy, K., & Hamby, R. (1994). Self-monitoring of attention versus self-monitoring of performance: Replication and cross-task comparison studies. *Learning Disability Quarterly, 17,* 121–139.

Johnston, P., & Winograd, P. (1985). Passive failure in reading. *Journal of Reading Behavior,17,* 279–301.

Jones, D., & Christensen, C. (1999). The relationship between automaticity in handwriting and students' ability to generate written text. *Journal of Educational Psychology, 91,* 44–49.

Juel, C. (1988). Learning to read and write: A longitudinal study of 54 children from first through fourth grade. *Journal of Educational Psychology, 80,* 437–447.

Kameenui, E. (1993). Diverse learners and the tyranny of time: Don't fix blame; fix the leaky roof. *The Reading Teacher, 46,* 376–383.

Lewis, B., O'Donnel, B., Freebairn, L., & Taylor, H. (1998). Spoken language and written expression—Interplay of delays. *American Journal of Speech Language Pathology, 7*(3), 77–84.

MacArthur, C. (1996). Using technology to enhance the writing performance of students with learning disabilities. *Journal of Learning Disabilities, 29,* 344–354.

MacArthur, C. (1999). Overcoming barriers to writing: Computer support for basic writing skills. *Reading & Writing Quarterly, 15,* 169–192.

MacArthur, C., & Graham, S. (1987). Learning disabled students' composing with three methods: Handwriting, dictation, and word processing. *Journal of Special Education, 21,* 22–42.

MacArthur, C., Graham, S., Haynes, J., & De La Paz, S. (1996). Spelling checkers and students with learning disabilities: Performance comparisons and impact on spelling. *Journal of Special Education, 30,* 35–57.

Palinscar, A., Klenk, L. (1992). Fostering literacy learning in supportive contexts. *Journal of Learning Disabilities, 25,* 211–225.

Pikulski, J. (1994). Preventing reading failure: A review of five effective programs. *The Reading Teacher, 48,* 30–39.

Pressley, M. (1998). *Reading instruction that works: The case for balanced teaching.* New York: Guilford.

Pressley, M., Rankin, J., & Yokoi, L. (1996). A survey of instructional practices of primary teachers nominated as effective in promoting literacy. *Elementary School Journal, 96,* 363–384.

Pressley, M., Wharton-McDonald, R., Rankin, J., Mistretta, J., & Yokoi, L. (1996). The nature of outstanding primary-grades literacy instruction. In E. McIntyre & M. Pressley (Eds.), *Balanced instruction: Strategies and skills in whole language* (pp. 251–276). Norwood, MA: Christopher-Gordon.

Pressley, M., Yokoi, L., Rankin, J., Wharton-McDonald, R., & Hampston, J. (1997). A survey of instructional practices of grade-5 teachers nominated as effective in promoting literacy. *Scientific Studies of Reading, 1,* 145–160.

Reyes, M. (1992). Challenging venerable assumptions: Literacy instruction for linguistically different students. *Harvard Educational Review, 62,* 427–446.

Scott, C. (1989). Problem writers: Nature, assessment, and intervention. In A. Kamhi & H. Catts (Eds.), *Reading disabilities: A developmental language perspective* (pp. 303–344). Boston: Allyn & Bacon.

Scott, C. (1994). A discourse continuum for school-age students: Impact on modality and genre. In G. Wallach & K. Butler (Eds.), *Language learning disabilities in school age children and adolescents* (pp. 219–252). Needham Heights, MA: Allyn & Bacon.

Scott, C. (1999). Learning to write. In H. Catts & A. Kamhi (Eds.), *Language and reading disabilities* (pp. 224–258). Boston: Allyn & Bacon.

Sexton, M., Harris, K. R., & Graham, S. (1998). Self-regulated strategy development and the writing process: Effects on essay writing and attributions. *Exceptional Children, 64*, 295–311.

Slavin, R., Madden, N., & Karweit, N. (1989). Effective programs for students at risk: Conclusions for practice and policy. In R. Slavin, N. Karweit, & N. Madden (Eds.), *Effective programs for students at risk* (pp. 355–372). Boston: Allyn & Bacon.

Slavin, R., Madden, N., Karweit, N., Livermon, B., & Dolan, L. (1990). Success for All: First year outcomes of a comprehensive plan for reforming urban education. *American Educational Research Journal, 27*, 255–278.

Westby, C., & Clauser, P. (1999). The right stuff for writing: Assessing and facilitating written language. In H. Catts & A. Kamhi (Eds.), *Language and reading disabilities* (pp. 259–324). Boston: Allyn & Bacon.

Westby, C. & Costlow, L. (1991). Implementing a whole language program in a special education class. *Topics in Language Disorders, 11* (3), 69–84.

Wharton-McDonald, R., Pressley, M., & Mistretta, J. (in press). Outstanding literacy instruction in first grade: Teacher practices and student achievement. *Elementary School Journal.*

Woodcock, R., & Johnson, M. (1990). *Woodcock–Johnson Psycho-Educational Battery–Revised.* Circle Pines, MN: American Guidance Service.

Wong, B. (Ed.). (1995). *Learning about learning disabilities* (2nd ed.). San Diego: Academic Press.

A Fork in the Road Less Traveled: Writing Intervention Based on Language Profile

Cheryl M. Scott
Northwestern University

In "The Road Less Traveled," Graham and Harris (chap. 8, this volume) identify six principles of exemplary writing instruction. Graham and Harris are well qualified to propose such principles for two reasons. First, they have researched and summarized an extensive literature on the topic (e.g., Graham, 1999; Graham & Harris, 1993; Graham, Harris, MacArthur, & Schwartz, 1991; Harris & Graham, 1992). Second, they themselves are known as researchers of writing instruction effectiveness for children with learning disabilities (e.g., Graham, 1997; MacArthur, Graham, Schwartz, & Shaefer, 1995; Sexton, Harris, & Graham, 1998). For a behavior as complex as writing, Graham and Harris know better than most how easy it is to propose best practices and how difficult it is to demonstrate empirically that a practice or technique is truly effective. Therefore, when they condense their own and others' research on writing instruction to a small set of principles, like the E.F. Hutton commercial, we should listen. Based on my own research and clinical work with children and adolescents who have writing difficulties, all six principles ring true.

The first two principles in particular merit further attention. For the first principle, Graham and Harris list features of exemplary writing instruction often cited in the literature on writing process approaches. These features include authentic writing purpose, peer feedback, teacher conferences, teacher modeling of process, integration of writing with reading and curriculum themes, and opportunities for self-regulation of writing behaviors. The second principle makes the case against "one size fits all" in writing instruction; rather, instruction should be tailored to the needs of individual children. Here, Graham and Harris focus on finding a balance between (a) implicit and explicit instruction and (b) low-level and high-level writing objectives. *Explicit methods* provide for direct lessons on various aspects of writing whereas *implicit approaches* assume writing will develop naturally when authentic opportunities are provided. Low-level objectives are defined as form objectives, for example spelling, punctuation, and grammar; high-level objectives would target content issues, such as the organization or volume of writing. Based on a child's particular writing profile, either low- or high-level objectives would be emphasized. Graham and Harris cite the work of Juel (1988), whose research showed that one third of fourth grade problem writers had low-level difficulties, one third had high-level difficulties, and the remaining one third had problems in both areas.

Although the emphasis given to explicit or implicit methods and low- or high-level objectives is based on the needs of the child, Graham and Harris do not provide details about how such needs are determined. Presumably, finding general areas of weakness and consequent targets for intervention is not difficult. Because writing is a language medium that is easily "captured" and examined, children's texts typically provide several instructional targets. Thus, one child's writing might reveal that punctuation is a weakness but spelling is a relative strength. Another child spells poorly and never generates enough content to satisfy a particular writing assignment. This level of individualization is transparent enough.

What is more difficult is fine-tuning procedures and methods for working on those targets as well as decision making about the intensity and longevity of treatment for any particular target. For example, of the many possible ways to approach spelling, what specific techniques might work best with a particular child? Should spelling receive attention every day? Will the child be working on spelling for 6 months or will 2 years be necessary to make a real difference? Is this "deeper" level of individualization even possible? Where would we begin to look for answers to this question? Graham and Harris may have taken us along a road less traveled in their chapter, but there are many forks in the road where principled choices are not at all obvious.

One way to explore the issue of tailoring writing instruction to individual children is to examine writing difficulties within a broader framework of language impairment. It is the rare poor writer who has no other language difficulties; for instance, in listening comprehension, in reading, or in speaking. Thus, beyond the obvious way to tailor writing instruction to a particular child—examining that child's writing in some detail, is it also important to know about the broader language difficulties that the child likely has? If so, how would such knowledge affect our ability to provide exemplary writing instruction (principle 1) that is truly tailored to meet the needs of children with writing difficulties (principle 2)? In this chapter, I explore these questions by asking additional questions about the children who experience problems learning to write—questions about the nature of their writing difficulties and how those difficulties relate to other language abilities.

WRITING PROBLEMS AS LANGUAGE PROBLEMS: IMPLICATIONS FOR WRITING INTERVENTION

Graham and Harris begin their chapter with a tale of two children. The first is Miles, a fourth grade child with a learning disability in writing. We are not told whether additional learning problems such as reading or listening comprehension contribute to Miles's learning disability. Miles appears to have both high-level and low-level writing difficulties. His high-level problems include generating enough content, planning, and revising. Low-level symptoms include handwriting, spelling, punctuation, and capitalization. The second case is Cordelia, a child who has a history of speech and language difficulties (including phonological difficulties), and is now a poor writer.

The writing symptoms of Miles and Cordelia seem to overlap. Both children are poor spellers and both have difficulty in the content domain; Miles cannot produce enough content and Cordelia's content is poorly organized. The extent to which they differ is not clear because Graham and Harris highlight different problems for each, although not claiming that the other is problem-free in those areas. Unlike Miles, Cordeila is not identified as a child with a learning disability. Are the differences in the two children's language histories and their current labels (learning disabilities or speech-language impairment) important? Would such differences affect our ability to "tailor writing instruction to meet the individual needs of children [Miles and Cordelia] experiencing writing difficulties " (Graham & Harris, chap. 8, this volume)? Could we not say that both children have a language learning disability (LLD), and build an effective writing intervention program around their specific *writing* problems? Graham and Harris introduce us to Miles and Cordelia, but they do not indicate whether their instruction would be in any way similar or different.

Researchers and practitioners in the fields of regular and special education, speech–language pathology, and psychology are no strangers to debates on labels, identification and eligibility criteria, overlapping diagnostic categories, and their attendant assessment and intervention implications. An example in speech–language pathology is the ongoing debate about specific language impairment (SLI). Even though arguments about SLI as a useful clinical construct span 10 years (e.g., Aram, 1991; Friel-Patti, 1999; Kamhi, 1998; Leonard, 1991), continuing research on SLI promises to help clinicians fine-tune intervention targets and procedures.

Today, a language clinician working with a child who meets criteria for SLI knows that difficulty with morphosyntax, a signature diagnostic feature of this type of language impairment, should be a prime assessment and intervention target (Leonard, 1998). The clinician could even direct intervention more specifically to particular grammatical morphemes—those that mark verb finiteness (tense and agreement markers including past tense -*ed*, auxiliary and copula *BE, DO,* and third person singular -*s*; Rice and Wexler, 1996). Likewise, a child whose reading problems fit the category of *dyslexia* as described by Catts and Kamhi (1999; see also Kamhi & Catts, chap. 3; Westby, chap. 4, this volume) will need intense and lengthy intervention in the areas of word recognition, including sound–symbol association and in the recognition of orthographic patterns. Further, this child must become fluent in recognizing words because slow word recognition, even if accurate, still presents a major roadblock to reading comprehension (Torgesen, 1999). In the Catts and Kamhi typology, the term *dyslexia* signifies a particular type of reading disorder—one in which a child has poor word recognition but normal listening comprehension. For this child, it is poor word recognition rather than a general language comprehension problem that compromises reading. Consequently, when word recognition improves, comprehension should also improve, particularly at younger ages before "Matthew effects" become more pronounced (i.e., the poor reader falls further and further behind by virtue of reading less; Stanovich, 1986). Conversely, a poor reader who fits the Catts and Kamhi (1999) criteria for *language learning disability* (LLD) will need intervention for higher level language skills in general (e.g., listening comprehension, text structure, vocabulary, complex syntax), in addition to work on word recognition.

The reader might wonder why the examples of a language problem usually associated with spoken language (SLI) and a reading problem (dyslexia) are relevant to writing problems. The answer is that writing problems do not exist in a linguistic vacuum. A growing literature on the longitudinal course of language impairments demonstrates the inextricable ties between early spoken language impairments and later written language problems, both reading and writing (e.g., Bishop & Adams, 1990; Johnson et al., 1999; Stothard, Snowling, Bishop, Chipchase, & Kaplan, 1998). Moreover, most children with writing problems also have reading problems (Juel, 1988), as do adults who write poorly (Liberman, Rubin, Duques, & Carlisle, 1985). For many individuals with reading and spelling difficulties, both problems can be traced to the same basic underlying language deficit, namely an inability to explicitly analyze words at phonemic and morphemic levels (Liberman et al., 1985).

Given the connections between writing and other areas of language difficulty, how might that information affect writing instruction? Intuitively, knowledge about other language problems besides writing, as well as relationships among these problems, should be helpful in planning intervention. Nevertheless, the literature on writing disabilities and instruction only rarely refers to such relationships. Aspects of writing addressed in the following sections include spelling, grammar, content, and strategic writing. In each case, a review of current thinking and research tying writing to broader questions about language raises interesting and important questions about instruction.

The Language Basis of Spelling

Graham and Harris (see chap. 8, this volume) categorize spelling, along with handwriting, capitalization, punctuation, and grammar, as a low-level writing skill. It is true that spelling is clearly a means to an end; to communicate effectively in writing, one requirement is that words be spelled correctly. The designation of spelling as a low-level, or mechanical skill should not be surprising considering the status of spelling in the fields of education, learning disabilities, and cognitive psychology. Historically viewed as a visually based process, spelling only recently has been admitted into the realm of language science (Kamhi & Hinton, 2000). Compared to reading, spelling has received far less classroom attention, and is usually considered a separate and less important subject in the curriculum. Even the English lexicon, with its two seemingly dichotomous terms, *spelling* and *reading*, undermines an appreciation of relationships. If we think of spelling, not as an act of writing, but as an orthographic–linguistic system, we see that words have inherent spellings that can be read or constructed (written). Even when writing the spelling of a word, we read and review the word to determine whether it has been correctly written (Ehri, 2000). Recent emphasis on these types of relationships between spelling and reading has contributed to the increased linguistic status afforded the act of writing (spelling) words.

Within the past 10 years then, the view of spelling has changed dramatically. The view that emerges from several lines of research is that reading and spelling are closely related language-based processes. Evidence centers on the close association between spelling ability and language-based skill in phonological and morphological awareness, the developmental parallels in reading and spelling, and the relationship between reading and spelling disabilities. Additionally, a smaller group of training studies demonstrate effects of reading instruction on spelling and vice versa.

Spelling performance has been shown to be closely related to phonological awareness in young children (Liberman et al., 1985; Rivers, Lombardino, & Thompson, 1996), in older children and adolescents (MacDonald & Cornwall, 1995; Perin, 1983), and in adults (Bruck, 1993; Liberman et al., 1985). It seems obvious enough that phonological awareness would be important for spelling; one way to spell an unknown word is to say it slowly, stretching out the sounds. Once individual sounds have been isolated in this manner, the next step is to write the letter(s) for the sounds in the proper sequence. What may be less obvious is the critical mediation role played by phonological awareness and knowledge of the alphabetic principle in memorizing the spellings of words. As Ehri (2000) pointed out, committing the spelling of a word to memory is not a matter of memorizing strictly visual information. Rather, words are remembered because they "conform to the speller's knowledge of graphophonemic connections or spelling patterns" (p. 23). Knowledge of the morphological structure of words is also central in spelling. This insight accounts for the ability to apply a different sequence of letters to the end of words such as "owned" and "friend" even though both words end in the same two sounds. Likewise, morphological awareness increases the chances that the letter "c" rather than "s" is used in "medicine" if the derivation from the root word *medic* is appreciated. Performance on a range of implicit and explicit morphological tasks shows significant correlations with spelling ability (Derwing, Smith, & Wiebe, 1995; Rubin, 1991).

If both reading and spelling depend on one's facility with the alphabetic principle, it should not be surprising to find developmental parallels as children learn to read and spell and in the extent of their proficiency. In the elementary school years, not only is there consistency between developmental benchmarks of spelling and reading (Bear, Invernizzi, Templeton, & Johnston, 2000; Ehri, 1997; Kamhi & Hinton, 2000), but also between spelling and reading achievement. In the first grade, for example, children's invented spelling predicts end-of-grade reading achievement better than a standardized reading readiness test (Morris & Perney, 1984). As further evidence, researchers have looked more specifically at the consistency between children's reading and spelling of the same set of words. Gough, Juel, & Griffin (1992) found that young children had some inconsistencies in the way they read and spelled words but that more than two thirds of the words were consistent. Ehri (2000) interpreted these results as further confirmation that both reading and spelling rely on phonological knowledge. Reports comparing spelling and reading proficiency also indicate a close association. The majority of poor readers are poor spellers and, conversely, good readers are usually good spellers. The existence of a small number of good readers who are poor spellers has led some to stress the disassociations between reading and spelling (Frith, 1980). However, Bruck and Waters (1990) uncovered decoding difficulties in good readers but poor spellers and pointed out that the classification of such children as good readers was based on reading comprehension rather than decoding ability.

A final way in which associations between reading and spelling can be examined is in training studies, where effects of learning in spelling can be observed in reading and vice versa. In a carefully designed intervention experiment, Berninger et al. (1998) showed that spelling intervention sessions designed to teach explicit connections between sounds and words resulted in spelling gains (1/3 standard deviation) on national spelling tests for second grade poor spellers. Although reading was not directly trained, children also made significant gains in word recognition. A more direct demonstration of transfer of training, but in the opposite direction from reading to spelling, has also been reported. Working with second grade children, Ehri (1980) observed effects of training in reading pseudowords on spelling of the same words. In another study with second graders, children who read words containing medial flaps (e.g., "city," "huddle") were more accurate in spelling the flaps than children who only heard and spoke the words (Ehri & Wilce, 1986).

The emphasis on reading and spelling relationships and knowledge of the alphabetic principle as the basis for both has implications for instruction generally and intervention for poor spellers more specifically. Children should be taught that spoken, heard, written, or read words are composed of phonemes and morphemes, and that the ability to analyze words for these units and their associated graphemes is a key tool in spelling and reading unfamiliar words. Because spelling is a more stringent test of word knowledge than reading, requiring a perfect rendition of letter sequences, Ehri (2000) went so far as to suggest that lessons in word structure might "fall within the province of spelling instruction rather than that of reading instruction" (p. 33). This strategy would require a major pedagogical shift in some classrooms where spelling is taught mainly by distributing word lists on Monday and testing the words on Friday (Scott, 2000). Even with additional time and activities devoted to spelling, it may still be a "necessary but altogether disliked component of the school curriculum" (Allal, 1997, p. 129).

An example of integrating reading and spelling instruction with appreciation of the alphabetic principle at the core can be found in recent work by Gaskins, Ehri, Cress, O'Hara, and Donnelly (1997). These researchers and educators reported that their well-known Benchmark word identification program, which teaches children to read and spell new words by analogy to known key words (e.g., if the child knows *fair*, then *stair* can also be read or spelled) was not successful by itself for students with poor word analysis skills. To use analogies effectively as a strategy for either reading or spelling, students must have knowledge of the phonological structure of words (e.g., knowing that the word "black" has four sounds and what the sounds are). With these students, they recommended providing explicit instruction and guided practice in fully analyzing words. An instance of guided practice in word analysis would occur if a teacher said, "What did you notice when you tried to match the sounds to the letters in the word 'black'" and the child replied "the two consonant letters *ck* make only one sound" or "I didn't hear the *c*" (as one child working with Gaskins and colleagues actually said). According to Gaskins et al. (1997), the benefits of explicit letter-sound knowledge apply to the formation of word representations in memory. Children without this knowledge, the authors reasoned, were handicapped in retaining new words taught by analogy. Although exactly how much or what level of phonological awareness is truly prerequisite to the effective use of an analogy strategy (Ehri, 1998), there is little debate that phonological awareness plays an important role.

In sum, intervention for poor spellers should have the following characteristics: (a) explicit word analysis training (i.e., training in phonological awareness and the alphabetic principle) designed to address each child's specific weaknesses; (b) opportunities to apply this knowledge in activities designed to reveal similarities and differences between words and encourage appreciation of orthographic patterns (e.g., word study activities applicable to spelling, reading, and meaning as outlined by Bear et al., 2000, Zutell, 1996, and others); and (c) opportunities to apply this knowledge in text-level reading and writing (e.g., recognizing exemplars of a word pattern in written material). Instruction in explicit word analysis will be the cornerstone of the protocol. The fact that adult poor spellers retain core linguistic deficits in phonemic and morphemic awareness (Liberman et al., 1985) underscores the importance of intensive instruction in explicit word analysis— an importance that only increases with the age of the poor speller.

This integrated approach may counteract the tendency of poor spellers to see reading and writing as isolated skills, and the English spelling system as exceedingly difficult, arbitrary, and unlearnable (Scott, 2000). As spelling assumes a more central role in literacy instruction, the adjectives *low-level* and *mechanical* should be dropped as descriptors for the place of spelling in the writing process. An emphasis on spelling will contribute to the "explicit" side of the writing instruction balance advocated by Graham and Harris (chap. 8, this volume). Finally, when connections between spelling and reading are exploited, it should be easier to fine-tune instruction for individual writers who are often poor readers with specific gaps in their awareness of the alphabetic principle.

The Language Basis of Written Grammar

Grammatical difficulties in writing can be both subtle and obvious. Subtle problems occur when children fail to meet overall grammatical complexity expectations, given the nature of the writing task. For example, perhaps a student uses only simple, one-clause sentences when classmates are expressing information with embedded clauses. Another type of subtle difficulty occurs when the student continues to use grammatical varieties more typical of speaking. By age 10, most children have begun to "write like a book"; that is, they are aware at some level that certain structures are more characteristic of writing than speaking, and "written" structures begin to appear in their writing (e.g., *there stood a little tiger cub,* written by a third grade child; see Scott, 1999, for further examples). Obvious grammatical errors may also occur, as in the following examples of school-age children with language impairments (from Scott, Windsor, and Gray, 1998):

1. Yanis was a child who *grow* up on a small island in Greece (failure to mark irregular past tense).
2. He was *walk* up on the mountains (omitted present participle *-ing* marking progressive aspect).
3. They would say that it is over 60 *year* old (omitted plural *-s* marker).
4. When he went home he had * at the night time (omitted obligatory object argument, **dreams*).

As with spelling, there may be several reasons why children have grammatical difficulties when writing. As previously noted, children with SLI are known for their inability to master morphosyntactic features of language. A recent study by Scott and Windsor (2000) demonstrated that text-level writing of school-age children with SLI was particularly susceptible to grammatical error. These authors evaluated the extent to which several general language performance measures, including the amount of grammatical error, differentiated a group of 20 school-age children with SLI (*Mean* age = 11 years) from an equal number of chronological-age (CA) and language-age (LA) peers (*Mean* age = 9 years). Children produced both spoken and written summaries of two educational videotapes that provided models of either narrative or expository discourse. The children with SLI were distinguished not only from their CA peers but also their LA peers by the extent of grammatical error in writing. It was notable that grammatical error in writing was the only one of 10 general language performance measures that differentiated children with SLI from both peer groups. The interpretation was that grammatical error in writing is a differentially diagnostic feature of language impairment in older children. A diagnostic feature is one that strikes "closer to the heart of the basic problem" (Leonard, 1998, p. 28). By way of contrast, a descriptive feature characterizes the problem of language impairment but not uniquely so; a child who is typically developing but younger may also show the same feature. For example, in the Scott and Windsor research, compared to CA peers, children with SLI used shorter sentences when speaking and writing, but the same was true of LA peers.

A follow-up error analysis on the same summaries centered on finite verbs (Windsor, Scott, & Street, 2000). *Finite verbs* are those that carry obligatory tense and number marking (e.g., in the verb phrase *is walking,* present tense and singular number are both marked on *is,* the present singular form of the auxiliary verb BE). Finiteness is required in main clauses (e.g., *She is walking today because her car is in the repair shop*) and occurs in most dependent clauses as well (e.g., *Whenever it snows, she stays home; She brought a present to the teacher who helped her*). As expected, the typically developing children had mastered verb morphology in spoken and written samples. Children with language impairments were also quite accurate in speaking, but showed considerable difficulty in written samples, particularly with regular past tense, omitting the *-ed* marker in a fourth of all obligatory contexts. The picture that emerges is that school-age children with SLI continue to have difficulty with verb morphology but their problems are more apparent in written language.

Gillam and Johnston (1992) also found significant differences comparing grammatical skill in spoken and written language samples of children with language impairments. In their research, children with language impairments who were between the ages of 9 and 12 were compared to children with reading impairments as well as age and language peers on form and content measures in spoken and written narrative language. The typically developing children produced more complex sentences in writing, whereas the opposite was true of groups with language impairments and reading impairments. For these children, written sentences were grammatically simpler. The types of sentences that contributed the most to group differences were ones in which several types of complexity were combined. An example is the sentence, *The boy didn't go because he was afraid of the bats that lived in the cave.* This example contains both adverbial and relative subordinate clauses. Children with language impairments produced significantly fewer sentences of this type—sentences that had more than one subordinate clause and each one was a different type.

Gillam and Johnston (1992) were also interested in the effects of complexity and mode (whether written or spoken) on grammatical accuracy. Both factors had a substantial impact on grammatical accuracy for the children with language impairments. Whereas 12.3% of all grammatically simple spoken sentences contained errors, 78.3% of all complex written sentences contained errors. In this study, simple sentences were defined as those with only one clause; complex sentences contained two or more clauses. Gillam and Johnston did not describe the nature of the grammatical errors in either spoken or written language, but their results highlight the relationship between grammatical complexity and error for children with spoken language impairments and the dramatic way that writing increases the amount of error.

Thus, there exists a group of children and adolescents whose grammatical difficulties when writing are intransigent and unlikely to improve in an intervention program that targets only higher level aspects of writing such as organization, content, and volume. Neither can such problems be addressed in programs that consider grammar to be a lower level or mechanical skill worthy of only casual treatment. To illustrate, it is unlikely that a small amount of time spent on isolated grammar exercises (e.g., doing worksheets that require underlining regular past tense forms of verbs) will have much of an impact on the tendency of students with SLI to omit this marker in self-generated writing at the text level. Supplying obligatory past tense markers when writing is not inherently "easy." In order to write a narrative, for example, as words are called up from the lexicon, they must be recognized for grammatical class—in this case, as a verb. A judgment must be made about the tense requirements of the verb in a particular clause relative to previous clauses (and anticipating future clauses) so that text level requirements for sequences of events are met. In spoken language, these decisions take place largely at an implicit level. When writing, however, explicit knowledge is required during an activity (writing) that is inherently more difficult than speaking. Furthermore, the verb must be spelled and, in this case, the difference between rule-governed but variable pronunciation of regular past tense as /t/, /d/, or /əd/ and the invariant spelling –ed may confuse the issue.

Rather than decontextualized exercises at the word or sentence level, it would seem more appropriate to begin working on this problem where it occurs—in self-generated, text-level writing, exploring what the student knows about each of these types of requirements. Instances of correct use of regular past tense should be pointed out as well. It may become obvious that it is necessary to build awareness of this marker in isolated lists of words or sentences, but this should not be the first or only activity used to treat the problem.

If two thirds of all poor writers have difficulty generating appropriate content and organization (Juel, 1988), it is highly likely that many of these students show a more subtle type of grammatical difficulty. Rather than (or perhaps in addition to) making ostensible grammatical errors, these students fail to generate the quantity and variety of complex grammar expected for their age or grade. Recalling that many poor writers are poor readers and that many poor readers have generalized higher level language difficulties, including grammar (Catts & Kamhi, 1999), this characterization of the poor writer becomes even more probable. Because grammar is the carrier of complex content, it is difficult to separate higher level grammatical structures from their meaning contexts.

Capitalizing on the form–meaning connections in writing, Scott (1995a, 1995b) described discourse-based approaches to teaching grammar. Written language is a medium that facilitates this type of instruction because the language is "captured" and available for purposes of awareness, analysis, practice, and application activities. The core principles involved are not inherently complicated. Basically, higher level grammatical structures are made more salient for students and their *raison d'être* (their meaning function) is explained. For example, a student whose writing rarely includes relative clauses is taught to identify such clauses in written materials and to appreciate that they are devices that "pack" information about nouns into the text. In narratives, such clauses develop characterization of protagonists (... *her mother who was always in a hurry*), and in informational texts they narrow and define (... *policies that relate more specifically to international trade*). In historical writing, nonrestrictive relative clauses are used to provide relevant background (... *Harold, whose army had just marched across England, was* ...). The next step would be for the language specialist to model the use of such structures in writing. Eventually, students practice constructing such forms in their own writing under guidance, and with time, more independently. A key is to find texts that interest students. Instances of target structures in their own writing, the writing of peers, and writing about topics of high interest facilitate the learning process. Students usually produce at least a few target structures before any instruction has begun; the goal of intervention is to make students aware of these forms when they do occur, and increase their frequency. A similar regimen could be used for any type of grammatical structure of interest. Higher level forms in addition to relative clauses might include adverbial conjuncts, complex verb phrases marked for tense, aspect, and mood (*he could have danced* ...), nominal clauses functioning as subjects, and subordinate clauses with later developing conjunctions (e.g., *whenever, provided that, although* ...). Inventories of higher level structures important in writing for older children can be found in several places (e.g., Nippold, 1998; Perera, 1984; Scott, 1988).

The Language Basis of Written Content

According to Juel (1988), two thirds of children with writing problems have high-level difficulties with content. Either they do not generate enough of it, what they do generate is poorly organized, and or they fail in other ways to produce adequate, relevant content geared to real or imagined readers of their writing. Here again, knowledge of a child's performance in reading, speaking, and listening would contribute to a writing intervention program. In a recent longitudinal study of second grade poor readers, 57% of these children had shown measurable receptive oral language deficits and 50% had shown expressive language problems 2 years previously as kindergartners (Catts, Fey, Zhang, & Tomblin, 1999). Oral language behaviors measured included standardized lexical and grammatical tasks at the word and sentence levels as well as a narrative generation task. An important feature in the design of the Catts et al. (1999) study was that oral language difficulties were measured 2 years prior to the measurement of reading. The longitudinal as opposed to concurrent measurement of oral language and reading, and in particular the measurement of oral language at the very beginning of any formal training in reading, greatly diminished the possibility that reading influenced oral language skills. Because many poor readers are poor writers, extrapolation of these results to writing would underscore the importance of examining receptive and expressive spoken language abilities in poor writers, or at the very least, knowing their language histories. When working with a poor writer who shows a more generalized language impairment, it is unrealistic to expect that writing will be better than language functioning generally. Teachers and clinicians must find ways to address the generalized language weaknesses of this group of poor writers, and to integrate writing instruction with speaking and or listening and reading work.

One example of a text-level content objective that could be expected to have an impact on all modalities in a positive way is the area of text structure. Teaching a child to recognize examples of a particular text structure template (e.g., compare–contrast) in material heard or read should have a positive impact on texts the child produces, whether spoken or written. From the early elementary grades onward, narrative text structure can be explicitly taught; from the mid elementary grades, expository and persuasive text structures should receive attention as well (Nippold, 1998; Scott, 1994, 1999; Westby, 1994, 1999). Research has shown that explicit instruction in text structure results in improved narrative as well as expository reading comprehension and writing composition (Armbruster, Anderson, & Ostertag, 1987; Griffin, Malone, & Kameenui, 1995; Raphael, Kirschner, & Englert, 1988). Although less is known about the effects of text structure instruction on speaking and listening, the expectation would be for a positive impact in these areas as well. There are numerous sources currently available that detail methods for teaching a variety of text structures (e.g., Culatta, Horn, & Merritt, 1998; Culatta & Merritt, 1998; Westby, 1999; Westby & Clauser, 1999). The key element is that the children and adolescents recognize the relevance of these lessons for all language applications—as an aid to listening comprehension, reading comprehension, and content organization in both speaking and writing.

The Language Basis of Strategic Writing

A final area to explore individualization in writing instruction is at the "meta" level of strategic writing. Since the advent of the process approach to writing instruction (Graves, 1983), writing teachers and researchers have promoted the direct teaching and modeling of task-specific strategies (e.g., planning , revising) and more general strategies (e.g., goal-setting and self-reinforcement). An example of a comprehensive strategy approach is the Self-Regulated Strategy Development (SRSD), a model developed by Harris and Graham (1996). According to Graham and Harris (1999), a series of studies point to the effectiveness of SRSD in improving writing quality, knowledge about writing, the approach to writing, and self-efficacy.

Graham and Harris (1999) addressed the topic of tailoring intervention as it relates to strategy instruction in a case study of an adolescent with a learning disability. Alvin (age 12) had a severe writing problem, as confirmed by his writing achievement scores on the Woodcock-Johnson Psychoeducational Battery (Woodcock & Johnson, 1990). Interestingly, Alvin's writing scores contrasted with oral language and reading scores on the WJPB, which were within normal ranges. (The authors acknowledged that a more in-depth examination of oral language would be in order.) Graham and Harris (1999) argued that a child with difficulties in writing (like Alvin) and listening comprehension (unlike Alvin) would be an unlikely candidate for SRSD because the listening comprehension problem would complicate understanding of the motivation for and use of cognitive strategies. Graham and Harris do not offer any research that would support this caveat, however. Although an adolescent with general language comprehension problems might need more intensive instruction in the nature and use of writing strategies, it seems premature to conclude that this approach would be inappropriate. To the contrary, in the area of reading, the teaching of strategic comprehension monitoring skills has been a staple of reading intervention (Westby, 1999). If we assume that many older poor readers have more generalized language comprehension problems, but nevertheless learn to be better strategic readers, then perhaps the Graham and Harris (1999) suggestion about poor writers should be re-examined. Here again, true tailoring of writing instruction to individual children awaits intervention research in which results are described in relation to participants' broader language profiles.

• • • • • •

Graham and Harris have provided six valuable principles for our consideration when designing writing instruction programs. They remind us that "there is no easy or quick inoculation that will make their [poor writers'] problems disappear" (chap. 8, this volume). Graham and Harris have looked long and hard at these children and observed the chronic nature of their problems for which quick fixes (e.g., "back to basics" movements) are likely to disappoint. As even more is learned about the language basis of reading and writing difficulties and as subtypes of this large number of children are identified more reliably, true tailoring of exemplary writing instruction practices will be more commonplace. The argument presented here is that instruction and intervention for writing disabilities awaits a deeper level of individualization based on a child's unique profile of language abilities in speaking, listening, reading, and writing domains and hypotheses about the relationships among these abilities. It is essential that more is known about relationships across domains (e.g., writing and speaking), and relationships within writing (e.g., spelling and composition). Graham and Harris have been at the forefront of a series of recent investigations into the later type of relationships (De La Paz & Graham, 1997; Graham, 1990; Graham, Berninger, R. Abbott, S. Abbott, & Whitaker, 1997).

Almost all of us, adults as well as children, spend more time speaking and listening than reading (Catts, 1996), and more time reading than writing. There is a parallel in the scope and history of the scientific investigation of speaking and listening, reading, and writing difficulties in children. Research into spoken language impairments in children has intensified in the last 20 years and continues to this day (e.g., Leonard, 1998). The past 10 years have been a particularly productive time for researchers in reading disabilities, prompting the appointment of a national committee of reading experts to summarize and critique the recent body of research and suggest implications for prevention and treatment of reading disabilities (Report of the National Reading Panel: Teaching Children to Read, 2000; Snow, Burns, & Griffin, 1998). Summarizing a large body of research on reading intervention, Lyon and Moats (1997) noted that the critical question is which children can benefit from which reading intervention approaches at which stages of their development. The question is equally applicable for writing intervention. Perhaps the intensity of research in other language modalities can now be extended to writing, and we will come to better understand that there are different types of poor writers who deserve different types of intervention. The visibility of poor writing coupled with the necessity to write well in academic and eventual employment settings makes this effort all the more important.

REFERENCES

Allal, L. (1997). Learning to spell in the classroom. In C. Perfetti, L. Rieben, & M. Fayol (Eds.), *Learning to spell: Research theory, and practice across languages* (pp. 129–150). Mahwah, NJ: Lawrence Erlbaum Associates.

Aram, D. (1991). Comments on specific language impairment as a clinical category. *Language, Speech, and Hearing Services in Schools, 22*, 84–87.

Armbruster, B., Anderson, T., & Ostertag, J. (1987). Does text structure/summarization instruction facilitate learning from expository text? *Reading Research Quarterly, 22*, 331–346.

Bear, D., Invernizzi, M., Templeton, S., & Johnston, F. (2000). *Words their way* (2nd ed.). Upper Saddle River, NJ: Prentice-Hall.

Berninger,V., Vaughan, K., Abbott, R., Brooks, A., Abbott, S., Rogan, L., Reed, E., & Graham, S. (1998). Early intervention for spelling problems: Teaching functional spelling units of varying size with a multiple-connections framework. *Journal of Educational Psychology, 90,* 587–605.

Bishop, D., & Adams, C. (1990). A prospective study of the relationship between specific language impairment, phonological disorders and reading retardation. *Journal of Child Psychology and Psychiatry, 31,* 1027–1050.

Bruck, M. (1993). Component spelling skills of college students with childhood diagnoses of dyslexia. *Learning Disability Quarterly, 16,* 171–184.

Bruck, M., & Waters, G. (1990). An analysis of the component spelling and reading skills of good readers–good spellers, good readers–poor spellers, and poor readers–poor spellers. In T. Carr & B. Levy (Eds.) *Reading and its development* (pp. 161–206). San Diego, CA: Academic Press.

Catts, H. (1996). Defining dyslexia as a developmental language disorder: An expanded view. *Topics in Language Disorders, 16,* 14–29.

Catts, H., Fey, M., Zhang, X., & Tomblin, B. (1999). Language basis of reading and reading disabilities: Evidence from a longitudinal investigation. *Scientific Studies of Reading, 3,* 331–361.

Catts, H., & Kamhi, A. (1999). Defining reading disabilities. In H. Catts, & A. Kamhi (Eds.), *Language and reading disabilities* (pp. 50–72). Boston, MA: Allyn & Bacon.

Culatta, B., Horn, D., & Merritt, D. (1998). Expository text: Facilitating comprehension. In D. Merritt, & B. Culatta (Eds.), *Language intervention in the classroom* (pp. 215–276). San Diego, CA: Singular.

Culatta, B., & Merritt, D. (1998). Enhancing comprehension of discourse. In D. Merritt, & B. Culatta (Eds.), *Language intervention in the classroom* (pp. 175–214). San Diego, CA: Singular.

De La Paz, S., & Graham, S. (1997). Effects of dictation and advanced planning instruction on the composing abilities of students with writing and learning problems. *Journal of Educational Psychology, 89,* 203–222.

Derwing, B., Smith, M., & Wiebe, G. (1995). On the role of spelling in morpheme recognition; Experimental studies with children and adults. In L. B. Feldman (Ed.), *Morphological aspects of language processing* (pp. 189–209). Hillsdale, NJ: Lawrence Erlbaum Associates.

Ehri, L. (1980). The development of orthographic images. In U. Frith (Ed.), *Cognitive processes in spelling* (pp. 311–338). London: Academic Press.

Ehri, L. (1997). Learning to read and learning to spell are one and the same, almost. In C. A. Perfetti, L. Rieban, & M. Fayol (Eds.), *Learning to spell: Research, theory, and practice across languages* (pp. 237–269). Mahwah, NJ: Lawrence Erlbaum Associates.

Ehri, L. (1998). Word reading by sight and by analogy in beginning readers. In C. Hulme & R. M. Joshi (Eds.), *Reading and spelling: Development and disorders* (pp. 87–112). Mahwah, NJ: Lawrence Erlbaum Associates.

Ehri, L. (2000). Leaning to read and learning to spell: Two sides of a coin. *Topics in Language Disorders, 20*(3), 19–36.

Ehri, L., & Wilce, L. (1986). The influence of spellings on speech: Are alveolar flaps /d/ or /t/? In D. Yaden & S. Templeton (Eds.), *Metalinguistic awareness and beginning literacy* (pp. 101–114). Portsmouth, NH: Heinemann.

Friel-Patti, S. (1999). Specific language impairment: Continuing clinical concerns. *Topics in Language Disorders, 20*(1), 1–13.

Frith, U. (1980). Unexpected spelling problems. In U. Frith (Ed.). *Cognitive processes in spelling* (pp. 495–515). London: Academic Press.

Gaskins, I., Ehri, L., Cress, C., O'Hara, C., & Donnelly, K. (1997). Analyzing words and making discoveries about the alphabetic system: Activities for beginning readers. *Language Arts, 74,* 172–184.

Gillam, R., & Johnston, J. (1992). Spoken and written language relationships in language/learning-impaired and normally achieving school-age children. *Journal of Speech and Hearing Research, 35,* 1303–1315.

Gough, P., Juel, C., & Griffin, P. (1992). Reading, spelling, and the orthographic cipher. In P. Gough, L. Ehri, & R. Treiman (Eds.), *Reading acquisition* (pp. 35–48). Hillsdale, NJ: Lawrence Erlbaum Associates.

Graham, S. (1990). The role of production factors in learning disabled student's compositions. *Journal of Educational Psychology, 82,* 781–791.

Graham, S. (1997). Executive control in the revising of students with learning and writing difficulties. *Journal of Educational Psychology, 89,* 223–234.

Graham, S. (1999). Handwriting and spelling instruction for students with learning disabilities: A review. *Learning Disabilities Quarterly, 22,* 78–98.

Graham, S., Berninger, V., Abbott, R., Abbott, S., & Whitaker, D. (1997). Role of mechanics in composing of elementary school students: A new methodological approach. *Journal of Educational Psychology, 89,* 171–182.

Graham, S., & Harris, K. (1993). Teaching writing strategies to students with learning disabilities: Issues and recommendations. In L. Meltzer (Ed.), *Strategy assessment and instruction for students with learning disabilities: From theory to practice* (pp. 271–292). Austin, TX: Pro-Ed.

Graham, S., & Harris, K. (1999). Assessment and intervention in overcoming writing difficulties: An illustration from the self-regulated strategy development model. *Language, Speech, and Hearing Services in Schools, 30,* 255–264.

Graham, S., Harris, K., MacArthur, C., & Schwartz, S. (1991). Writing and writing instruction for students with learning disabilities: Review of a research program. *Learning Disability Quarterly, 14,* 89–114.

Graves, D. (1983). *Writing: Teachers and children at work.* Portsmouth, NH: Heinemann.

Griffin, C., Malone, L., & Kameenui, E. (1995). Effects of graphic organizer instruction on fifth-grade students. *Journal of Educational Research, 89,* 93–107.

Harris, K., & Graham, S. (1992). Self-regulated strategy development: A part of the writing practice. In M. Pressley, K. Harris, & J. Guthrie (Eds.), *Promoting academic competence and literacy in school* (pp. 277–309). San Diego, CA: Academic Press.

Harris, K., & Graham, S. (1996). *Making the writing process work: Strategies for composition and self-regulation.* Cambridge, MA: Brookline Books.

Johnson, C., Beitchman, J., Young, A., Escobar, M., Atkinson, L., Wilson, B., Brownlie, E., Douglas, L., Taback, N., Lam, I., & Wang, M. (1999). Fourteen-year follow-up of children with and without speech/language impairments:

Speech/language stability and outcomes. *Journal of Speech, Language, and Hearing Research, 42,* 744–760.

Juel, C. (1988). Learning to read and write: A longitudinal study of 54 children from first through fourth grades. *Journal of Educational Psychology, 80,* 437–447.

Kamhi, A. (1998). Trying to make sense of developmental language disorders. *Language, Speech, and Hearing Services in Schools, 29,* 35–44.

Kamhi, A., & Hinton, L. (2000). Explaining individual differences in spelling ability. *Topics in Language Disorders, 20*(3), 37–49.

Leonard, L. (1991). Specific language impairment as a clinical category. *Language, Speech, and Hearing Services in Schools, 22,* 66–68.

Leonard, L. (1998). *Children with specific language impairment.* Cambridge, MA: The MIT Press.

Liberman, I., Rubin, H., Duques, S., & Carlisle, J. (1985). Linguistic abilities and spelling proficiency in kindergarteners and adult poor spellers. In D. Gray & J. Kavanaugh (Eds.), *Biobehavioral measures of dyslexia* (pp. 163–176). Parkton, MD: York Press.

Lyon, G. R., & Moats, L. (1997). Critical conceptual and methodological considerations in reading intervention research. *Journal of Learning Disabilities, 30,* 578–588.

MacArthur, C., Graham, S., Schwartz, S., & Schafer, W. (1995). Evaluation of a writing instruction model that integrated a process approach, strategy instruction, and word processing. *Learning Disability Quarterly, 18,* 278–291.

MacDonald, G. W., & Cornwall, A. (1995). The relationship between phonological awareness and reading and spelling achievement eleven years later. *Journal of Learning Disabilities, 28,* 523–527.

Morris, D., & Perney, J. (1984). Developmental spelling as a predictor of first-grade reading achievement. *The Elementary School Journal, 96,* 145–162.

Nippold, M. (1998). *Later language development.* Austin, TX: Pro-Ed.

Perera, K. (1984). *Children's writing and reading.* London: Blackwell.

Perin, D. (1983). Phonemic segmentation and spelling. *British Journal of Psychology, 74,* 129–144.

Raphael, T., Kirschner, B., & Englert, C. (1988). Expository writing program: Making connections between reading and writing. *The Reading Teacher, 40,* 838–847.

Report of the National Reading Panel: Teaching Children to Read. (2000). Available: NICHDClearinghouse@mail.nih.gov

Rice, M., & Wexler, K. (1996). Toward tense as a clinical marker of specific language impairment in English-speaking children. *Journal of Speech and Hearing Research, 39,* 1239–1257.

Rivers, K., Lombardino, L., & Thompson, C. (1996). Effects of phonological decoding training on children's word recognition of CVC, CV, and VC structures. *American Journal of Speech-Language Pathology, 5*(1), 67–78.

Rubin, H. (1991). Morphological knowledge and writing ability. In R. Joshi (Ed.), *Written language disorders* (pp. 43–69). Boston, MA: Kluwer Academic Publishers.

Scott, C. (1988). Spoken and written syntax. In M. Nippold (Ed.), *Later language development: Ages nine through nineteen* (pp. 49–95). San Diego, CA: College-Hill.

Scott, C. (1994). A discourse continuum for school-age students: Impact of genre and modality. In G. Wallach & K. Butler (Eds.). *Language and learning disabilities in school-age children and adolescents: Some underlying principles and applications* (pp. 219–252). Needham Heights, MA: Allyn & Bacon.

Scott, C. (1995a). Syntax for school-age children: A discourse perspective. In M. Fey, J. Windsor, & S. Warren (Eds.), *Language intervention: Preschool through the elementary years* (pp. 107–143). Baltimore, MD: Paul H. Brookes.

Scott, C. (1995b). A syntax approach to discourse teaching. In D. Tibbets (Ed)., *Language intervention beyond the primary grades*. Austin, Tx: Pro-Ed.

Scott, C. (1999). Learning to write. In H. Catts & A. Kamhi (Eds.), *Language and reading disabilities* (pp. 224–258). Needham Heights, MA: Allyn & Bacon.

Scott, C. (2000). Principles and methods of spelling instruction: Applications for poor spellers. *Topics in Language Disorders, 20*(3), 66–82.

Scott, C., & Windsor, J. (2000). General language performance measures in spoken and written narrative and expository discourse of school-age children with language learning disabilities. *Journal of Speech, Language, and Hearing Research, 43,* 324–339.

Scott, C., Windsor, J., & Gray, T. (1998, November). *A typology of grammatical error in older children with language learning disorders*. Paper presented at the annual meeting of the American Speech-Language-Hearing Association, San Antonio, TX.

Sexton, M., Harris, K., & Graham, S. (1998). Self-regulated strategy development and the writing process: Effects on essay writing and attributions. *Exceptional Children, 64,* 295–311.

Snow, C., Burns, S., & Griffin, P. (1998). *Preventing reading difficulties in young children*. Washington, DC: National Academy Press.

Stanovich, K. (1986). Matthew effects in reading: Some consequences of individual differences in the acquisition of literacy. *Reading Research Quarterly, 86,* 360–406.

Stothard, W., Snowling, M., Bishop, D., Chipchase, B., & Kaplan, C. (1998). Language-impaired preschoolers: A follow-up into adolescence. *Journal of Speech, Language, and Hearing Research, 40,* 407–418.

Torgesen, J. K. (1999). Assessment and instruction for phonemic awareness and word recognition abilities. In H. Catts & A. Kamhi (Eds.), *Language and reading disabilities* (pp. 128–153). Needham Heights, MA: Allyn & Bacon.

Westby, C. (1994). The effects of culture on genre, structure, and style on oral and written texts. In G. Wallach & K. Butler (Eds.). *Language and learning disabilities in school-age children and adolescents: Some underlying principles and applications* (pp. 180–218). Needham Heights, MA: Allyn & Bacon.

Westby, C. (1999). Assessing and facilitating text comprehension problems. In H. Catts & A. Kamhi (Eds.), *Language and reading disabilities* (pp. 154–219). Needham Heights, MA: Allyn & Bacon.

Westby, C., & Clauser, P. (1999). The right stuff for writing: Assessing and facilitating written language. Assessing and facilitating text comprehension problems. In H. Catts & A. Kamhi (Eds.), *Language and reading disabilities* (pp. 259–324). Needham Heights, MA: Allyn & Bacon.

Windsor, J., Scott, C., & Street, C. (2000). Finite verb use in spoken and written language by school-age children with language impairments. *Journal of Speech, Language, and Hearing Research, 43,* 1322–1336.

Woodcock, R., & Johnson, M. (1990). *Woodcock-Johnson Psychoeducational Battery: Tests of Achievement*. Chicago, IL: Riverside.

Zutell, J. (1996). The directed spelling thinking activity (DSTA): Providing an effective balance in word study instruction. *The Reading Teacher, 50,* 98–108.

"Hanging with Friends": Making Sense of Research on Peer Discourse in Children With Language and Learning Disabilities

Mavis L. Donahue
University of Illinois at Chicago

Zachary is a 9-year-old with significant language and learning disabilities who is fully included in a third grade classroom. He is withdrawn and rarely makes eye contact with peers. When he occasionally attempts to start a conversation, articulation problems make him difficult to understand. At the beginning of the year, he is mostly ignored by typical peers. One day these students discover that Zachary can make surprisingly realistic animal sounds. Whenever there is a lull in the classroom activity or on the playground, a child often requests "Zachary, do your bear (monkey, parrot ...)!" When other adults visit the classroom, his classmates invite them to "Listen to what Zachary can do!" Zachary enjoys the attention and eagerly complies. The general education teacher is tolerant of these episodes, but the learning disabilities teacher and speech–language pathologist are concerned that encouraging this age-inappropriate behavior may not be helpful for Zachary's social and language development. In their view, Zachary is becoming the "class mascot," and this patronizing behavior marks him as "weird" and "different."

On the other hand, for the first time, Zachary has a "ticket" for entry into social interactions with typical peers. Occasionally the "making animal sounds" game is extended to making rude noises that most teachers would censor, but that Zachary and the other boys find hilarious. Yet he also has the opportunity to model more positive social behavior. As the year goes by, he becomes part of a network of three or four boys who hang out with him on the playground, at lunch, and in cooperative groups. When his mother asks Zachary about the events of his school day, he tells her "I hanged with my friends." His academic skills show significant gains. His friends cheer when Zachary wins the classroom award for "Most Improvement" at the end of the year.

Perhaps at no time in history have so many diverse theoretical perspectives converged on the importance of positive peer interaction to human development. Even medical models now acknowledge the benefits of peer support to physical and emotional well-being. One recent media frenzy centered on a book (Harris, 1998) that convincingly reinterpreted decades of research to support the claim that peers significantly outweigh parents in their influence on child development. Of course, it is no news that poor peer relations in childhood are well-documented "red flags" for a variety of later academic, emotional, and vocational problems (see Bukowski, Newcomb, & Hartup, 1996; Crick & Dodge, 1994; Gresham & Macmillan, 1997, for reviews). Conversely, close peer relations can be a powerful buffer for the life stressors that children face (e.g., Juvonen & Wentzel, 1996). For example, talking with friends seems to be an important source of social support and affiliation (e.g., Denton & Zarbatany, 1996). Yet, surprisingly little is known about the social worlds of children for whom positive communication with peers may be most essential, that is, those with significant language learning difficulties.

The goal of this chapter is to highlight some recurring themes in the somewhat fragmented database on peer communicative interactions of school-age children with language and learning disabilities. The challenge is to create a mosaic from a patchwork quilt of research literature on peer interaction on students identified as having learning disabilities (LD) or specific language impairment (SLI). Comprehensive reviews of peer interaction for each of these groups are available (cf., Brinton & Fujiki, 1999; Donahue, 1994; Gallagher, 1993; Lapadat, 1991; Nippold, 1994; Rice, 1993), but the two lines of research are surprisingly separate. For example, although the two groups of researchers often use the same developmental theories, research, and methodologies to inform their investigations, they often fail to even cite the research of the other field.

This lack of cross-fertilization is unfortunate, as there is increasing evidence that school-age children identified as having SLI and those identified with LD are samples drawn from the same population. Of course, these groups are not homogeneous on any language, cognitive, or social variables. On the contrary, there is great heterogeneity within both groups, but there may be nearly 100% overlap in that heterogeneity across the two groups. In fact, some would argue that inadvertent variations in referral, assessment, and service delivery models influence the assignment of diagnostic categories as much as actual child characteristics (e.g., Gartner & Lipsky, 1987.)

On the positive side, however, a closer look reveals that the two databases can complement each other. Research on children with SLI focuses more on the preschool years, when literacy disabilities cannot be reliably identified. As students with SLI seem to disappear as adolescence approaches, research on students with LD can be used to fill the gap. Samples of participants with SLI tend to be very small, but more carefully defined. The learning disabilities research base typically uses larger samples and, therefore, has access to more powerful statistical procedures, including the ability to examine individual and development differences. Viewed together, a more complete picture emerges.

BRIEF HISTORY

Teachers and parents have undoubtedly always recognized the central role of peer interaction in the development of children with language and learning disabilities. Forefathers and foremothers of both fields also acknowledged social development (e.g., Johnson & Myklebust, 1967; Kirk, 1963; Orton, 1937) as a significant challenge for many of these students. Yet, as the emerging fields struggled to identify and address the cognitive processes that underlie language and literacy disabilities, social development was given little attention. In fact, most definitions of LD or SLI specifically exclude students whose academic or language difficulties are primarily caused by problems in social interaction.

In 1974, two articles were published that made the quality of these children's social lives impossible to ignore. Bryan (1974a) reported that mainstreamed children identified as LD were not only less popular than other children, but also that their communicative environment with typical peers was more hostile (Bryan, 1974b). These startling findings ignited an explosion of research on the social development of students with LD (Bryan, 1999). More than 200 studies in the past 25 years have replicated, extended, refined, and clarified these findings. More recently, research on SLI has echoed the findings that peer acceptance and interactions are challenging for many of these children as well (e.g., Gertner, Rice, & Hadley, 1994; Rice, 1993). According to parent reports about their children who are "late talkers" (Paul & James, 1990; Paul, Spangle-Looney, & Dahm, 1991), these social problems may emerge as early as 2 years of age.

These studies have varied widely in theoretical perspectives, methodological techniques, and their participants' individual and demographic characteristics and histories of educational placements (see Gresham & MacMillan 1997; Nippold, 1994; and Pearl & Bay, 1999, for reviews). Despite this variation, a meta-analysis of 152 of these studies (Kavale & Forness, 1996) showed that about 75% of students with LD had social skills characteristics that were significantly different from those of typical peers. This proportion held true across teacher, peer, and self- ratings, and across most aspects of social competence. (Of course, these children do not fall into one profile of social skills deficits, but may comprise several subtypes; e.g., Donahue, Hartas, & Cole, 1999; McKinney & Speece, 1986).

The stability of these findings is particularly compelling given the context of the measures that are used to actually identify language learning disabilities. It is likely that no single cognitive, language, or academic measure is sufficiently powerful to differentiate students with LD from typical peers. Even the dozens of recent studies confirming phonological processing as an important predictor of literacy development (see Keogh, chap. 2, this volume; Kamhi & Catts, chap. 3, this volume) are not likely to claim that as many as 3 out of 4 students with reading disabilities show deficits in phonological awareness tasks.

Despite this unprecedented amount and rate of research productivity and the stunning consistency of the findings on social correlates of LD and SLI, the mystery remains unsolved. Why are children identified as having specific problems in language and literacy development so vulnerable to difficulties in social interaction? Even more puzzling is the finding that these social difficulties seem remarkably resistant to intervention. Social skills interventions that focus on teaching children specific interactional skills do not have a promising record (Forness & Kavale, 1996; Mathur, Kavale, Quinn, Forness, & Rutherford, 1998). In a meta-analysis of 53 studies of the effectiveness of teaching social skills to students with learning disabilities, Forness and Kavale (1996) found disappointingly small gains, even in short-term assessments. This suggests that atypical social interactions reflect multiple and interactive characteristics of children and their social environments, and that intervention models that do not acknowledge such complexity will not succeed.

MODEL BUILDING

Efforts to understand the complexity of peer interaction have addressed a fundamental dilemma in the interpretation of communicative difficulties of students with language learning disabilities (e.g., Brinton & Fujiki, 1993; Craig, 1993; Donahue, 1994; Hummel & Prizant, 1993; Redmond & Rice, 1998). Are their atypical interactional styles due to limitations in language comprehension and production? Or are their styles in fact adaptive and strategic responses to their history of communicative difficulties and concomitant social environments (e.g., Donahue, Szymanski, & Flores, 1999)? One lens for this inquiry (Donahue, 1994) emerged from a review of research on children with LD, identifying key variables as the child's language proficiency, discourse environments, and beliefs about social status. Three profiles were proposed: children participate in talk as if they are "newcomers," "immigrants," or "imposters" to the peer culture. Depending on the conversational context, all three styles may be used by the same child.

In the most obvious profile, some children appear to communicate in classrooms in a style similar to that of a naive participant or "newcomer" to the classroom. Despite experiencing the same discourse input as classmates, language and social information processing deficits within the child may lead to an incomplete or inaccurate derivation of the classroom's discourse rules. Other children participate in classroom talk as if they are not only new to a particular classroom culture, but also are recent "immigrants" from an unfamiliar culture. This different set of discourse rules has at least two sources. First, due to their academic and interactional difficulties within the regular classroom, some children with LD are actually provided quantitatively and qualitatively different data for deriving discourse norms. For example, in conversation with a child who rarely talks, teachers and classmates may acknowledge and even encourage any verbal turns, even if they stray from the topic or flow of the discourse. Second, "interference" from the communicative norms of the special education setting may complicate the child's efforts to overcome his or her newcomer status.

Unlike the first two profiles, the "imposter" profile does not assume that children with LD have constructed a deficient or different repertoire of discourse rules. Instead it suggests that some children are well aware of the appropriate rules for social interaction, but feel like imposters among their peers. Due to awareness of their own social, linguistic and communicative limitations, they may purposefully select different discourse strategies to save face. In other words, children with LD who perceive themselves to be low-status classroom participants may evolve a model for discourse behaviors that accommodate goals for social interaction that differ from those of achieving and well-accepted classmates. One overriding goal is to make sure that their imposter status is not discovered. For example, Emily, a high school student with a long history of language and learning disabilities and peer isolation, evolved rather skillful conversational strategies to take her turn without taking social or linguistic risks by using stock phrases, repetitions of her partner's comments, and formulaic "slang" (Donahue et al., 1999).

In a converging search for interpretive frameworks, Redmond and Rice (1998) used the database on younger children with SLI to formulate two explanations for their co-occurring social and emotional difficulties. Like the "newcomer" profile, their "social deviance model" assumes that atypical social behaviors are due to underlying social–emotional disabilities of the child, which in turn may result from, cause, interact with, or co-occur with language disabilities. In contrast, their "social adaptation model" resembles the imposter and immigrant profiles in its assumptions that social interactions of children with SLI are compensatory behaviors, reflecting the natural consequences of language difficulties. Social responses can be explained by the interactions of the communicative demands of the environment, limited verbal resources, and biases and behaviors of others, but filtered through an "intact psychosocial system." For example, Zachary seemed to recognize that his "animal noises trick" served as his single strategy for peer access, and he willingly recruited it to earn a place in a social group.

Both the Donahue (1994) and Redmond and Rice (1998) schemas point out the futility of a search for one-directional, causal relationships among social and language disabilities. However, before new research can be planned that tests hypotheses about the interactions of these factors, a much more comprehensive and detailed model is needed. Fortunately, Crick and Dodge (1994) reformulated an elegant and data-based model of social information processing aspects that underlie social behaviors and social adjustment. Capturing the multiplicity of factors that may contribute to individual differences in social behaviors, their model holds great potential for reinterpreting existing research on peer interactions in students with language and learning disabilities, for informing intervention, and for generating new research directions.

MODEL OF SOCIAL INFORMATION PROCESSING

As shown in Fig. 10.1, the Crick and Dodge (1994) framework defines and validates six steps that have been found to be related to children's actual social behaviors and adjustment. In their theory, children approach any social situation with a database of memories of past social experiences and schemas, and then receive a particular set of social cues as input. Children's behavioral responses (Step 6) are an outcome of the ways in which these cues are processed through five steps:

1. Encoding, through perceiving, and attending to both internal and external cues;
2. representing and interpreting the cues;
3. selecting a goal for the situation;
4. retrieving possible responses from long-term memory;
5. evaluating these responses and their outcomes and then selecting one response;
6. the behavioral enactment of that response.

Most important, although presented as a sequential model, feedback loops connect all previous steps, filtered through the database of stored social experiences and knowledge. (Crick & Dodge, 1994, are careful to make clear that this model is not intended to represent actual brain processes, but represents one schema for enabling researchers and practitioners to think systematically about what specific aspects of social cognition may underlie specific social behaviors.)

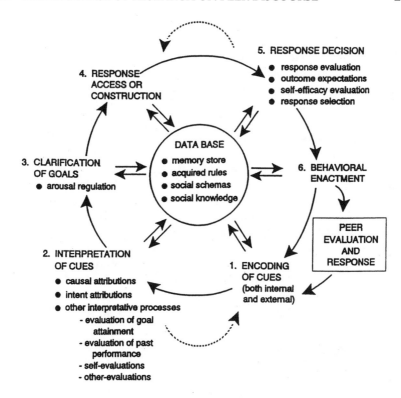

FIG. 10.1.   Social information-processing model of children's social adjustment. From Crick & Dodge (1994). Copyright © 1994 by the American Psychological Association. Reprinted with permission.

Steps 1 and 2 are particularly intricate phases. Based on prior experiences with peers, children perceive and assign meaning to their cues, analyze the possible causes, make inferences about the other persons' perspective and intent, and evaluate previous and current social goals for themselves and their peers. For example, suppose Marco brings cupcakes to celebrate his birthday, and his teacher suggests that he pass one out to each child. Marco goes by Kevin's desk without giving him a cupcake. How will Kevin respond? If he has been bullied or treated rudely by Marco in the past, he is likely to attend to those cues that signal a hostile intent rather than an accident, and to then interpret the causes and Marco's intent as intentionally "mean." During Steps 3 and 4, Kevin selects a goal or desired prosocial or antisocial outcome (e.g., getting a cupcake, making a friend, avoiding conflict or embarrassment, retaliating), and then accesses from memory possible responses to meet that goal (e.g., grabbing a cupcake, trying to get Marco's attention, giving up, telling the teacher). Step 5 allows Kevin to evaluate his repertoire of possible responses, a process that involves analyzing the appropriateness and the possible consequences of each response, as well as his self-efficacy (beliefs that he has the ability to enact the response). The final decision leads to Kevin's social behavior and Marco's response, which then provides input to start the cycle again.

In the actual incident on which this example is based, Kevin was a child with a history of language delay, and persisting word retrieval problems. His reputation for angry outbursts and impulsive behavior caused most peers to avoid him. Probably in light of these experiences, Kevin incorrectly interpreted the situation as a deliberate omission on Marco's part. Choosing the goal of getting a cupcake, Kevin may have accessed an appropriate set of solutions, but then rejected verbal responses due to his lack of self-efficacy that he could skillfully attract Marco's attention. So Kevin chose the nonverbal strategy of sticking his foot out to trip Marco as he came down the other side of the aisle. Startled, Marco looked down at Kevin's desk, said "Oh, sorry," hurriedly gave him a cupcake, and backed off.

METHODS FOR STUDYING PEER TALK

Research on communicative interactions has used a wide range of methods for eliciting talk among peers. These methods can be organized along a continuum of "How natural/authentic is the interaction?" They range from observations of children's interactions during free play, to "scripted" tasks, in which children enact a discourse genre with a real peer, to role-playing tasks with tight constraints on topic, communicative goals and context, imaginary listeners, and no feedback. Not surprisingly, findings have varied according to the nature of the tasks. Regardless of the methodological differences, however, children with LD or SLI generally show communicative styles with peers that differ significantly from those of comparison children.

One way of making sense of the wide array of findings is to compare and reflect on the social information processing demands of the different tasks, using the Crick and Dodge (1994) model. In the remainder of this chapter, the Crick and Dodge (1994) lens will be applied to the findings of a representative study from four paradigms for collecting data on peer talk: peer access, joint decision making, scripted discourse, and role playing. These paradigms vary according to the number of social information processing steps that the task requires.

Peer Access

In general, the peer interaction difficulties of children with LD or SLI are most glaring in studies with more naturalistic ways of collecting talk, in which most or all of the social information processing steps are obligatory, interactive, and recursive. For example, many observational studies have found that children with LD seem to be interactionally "out-of-sync," even in familiar settings with their classmates and teachers (see Donahue, 1994, and Pearl & Bay, 1999, for reviews).

One sensitive measure of children's social development is their ability to enter ongoing peer interactions (e.g., Asher & Coie, 1990), a skill obviously essential to initiating and maintaining peer relationships. In order to control for peer reputation and history, unacquainted pairs of children are introduced and invited to play a model building game together. After about 10 minutes of interaction, a target child (also unacquainted) is brought into the room and introduced, and the triad is left alone. Craig and Washington (1993) used this methodology to compare the peer access abilities of five 7-year-old children with SLI and two comparison groups with typical language development: younger children matched on MLU, and age-matched children. Although there was wide variation in access strategies, startling group differences were found. All of the typical children gained peer access quickly and easily. Of the five children with SLI, three were never successful in joining the interaction, and two gained access using only nonverbal means, that is, without speaking.

Although it is difficult to isolate the social–cognitive deficiencies that may underlie failure to gain peer access, the authors convincingly rule out insufficient expressive language skills, emotional–behavioral disorders, and lack of motivation. Interestingly, the two students with SLI who gained peer access (albeit nonverbally) had higher receptive language scores than the three who remained excluded. This finding implicates difficulties in Steps 1 and 2 (encoding and interpretation of cues) as possible explanations. The power of the central core of the Crick and Dodge (1994) model is also illustrated, that is, how children's previous history of unsuccessful social experiences filters their perceptions of new encounters. Even with peers with whom they had a "clean slate" of social experiences, the children with SLI used ineffectual discourse strategies, reflecting their lack of self-efficacy that they would be successful in being accepted as playmates. In a replication and extension of this study with six older children with SLI (between 8 and 12 years old), Brinton, Fujiki, Spencer, and Robinson (1997) showed that, even after four children with SLI managed to gain peer access, they were not equal partners in the subsequent discourse.

Joint Decision Making

Several studies have used joint decision making tasks to assess the intersection of children's conversational and social problem-solving styles. Although not as unconstrained as peer access tasks, these negotiations are still interactionally complex; turn-taking must be coordinated through perceiving and interpreting rapid social cues among three partners, while simultaneously producing and evaluating persuasive tactics that sway the partners' opinions. The findings of three studies suggested that students with LD differed from their partners in their goals for the interaction (Step 3 of the Crick and Dodge, 1994, model). Their overriding agenda seemed to be camouflaging their social–cognitive and communicative limitations although appearing to be equal partners in the interaction. They were remarkably successful at accessing and selecting responses that accomplished this goal.

Triads of children in grade 3 through grade 8 were asked to reach a consensus on the ranking of 15 potential gifts for their classroom (Bryan, Donahue & Pearl, 1981). Triads composed of one student with LD and two same-sex classmates were compared with triads of typical achievers. Students with LD talked as much as their partners and were more eager to agree with their classmates' opinions and to respond to requests for information. However, they avoided those strategies that may have demanded linguistic fluency or conflict-resolution skills; that is, they were less likely to disagree or to attempt to negate their partners' opinions, to bid for the conversational floor, or to make comments that kept the group on task. Not surprisingly, students with LD had little impact on their groups' final decisions. Interestingly, this strategically passive conversational style was found in students even during interactions with their mothers (Bryan, Donahue, Pearl, & Herzog, 1984) and in young (grade 1 and grade 2) poor readers who had not yet been labeled as having reading disabilities (Donahue & Prescott, 1988).

In a similar triadic decision-making task, Brinton, Fujiki, and McKee (1998) examined the negotiation strategies of six children with SLI in both receptive and expressive language domains. Comparison groups of children of the same age (between ages 8 and 12) or language level were created. These target children were placed in triads with two partners of the same age and from the same schools. In an effort to control for familiarity, only partners who had not played with the target children at home were included. Triads were asked to work together in choosing and sharing a snack.

In contrast to the Bryan et al. (1981) study, the Brinton et al. (1998) findings suggested that the children with SLI selected the same goal (Step 3 of the Crick and Dodge, 1994, model) as other children. Compared to their partners, children with SLI contributed a similar proportion of talk, and seemed motivated to have an impact on the final snack decision. Perhaps because they were not interacting with familiar peers with whom they shared a social history, these students may have had a greater sense of self-efficacy. However, their repertoire of persuasive strategies (Step 4) was less sophisticated. Children with SLI used fewer and less sophisticated persuasive tactics to support their opinions. No such imbalances were evident with the age- or language-matched triads. A similar task with the same participants actually measured the degree to which children changed their partners' decisions (Fujiki, Brinton, Robinson, & Watson, 1997). Like the findings of studies by Bryan et al. (1981) and Donahue and Prescott (1988), children with SLI had less influence on their partners' decisions than their age-matched comparison group.

Scripted Discourse

Another approach for collecting peer talk evaluates children's knowledge of a particular discourse script. This constrains the first 3 steps of the social information processing load by assigning children a script useful for interpreting social cues, a goal to fulfill, and a role to play. For example, on less constrained tasks with a familiar peer, the conversation is embedded within a history of social interaction in which social roles and rules may be well established. A scripted task may give children "permission" to try out novel strategies that do not usually fit their own and others' perceptions of their social status.

   "Having an argument" is one interesting example of a scripted discourse task, used by Stevens and Bliss (1995). Children with SLI in grade 3 through grade 7 were categorized as having expressive language deficits only (SLI-E) or combined receptive-expressive deficits (SLI:R-E), and then matched to classmates without language impairments of the same age and gender. Dyads of children of the same age and language ability were encouraged to start a dispute, for example, "Have an argument about who is the strongest." This task has the advantage of tapping children's online encoding and interpretation of social cues, as well as Steps 4, 5, and 6 in the Crick and Dodge (1994) model. Unexpectedly, the arguments of dyads with and without SLI were much more similar than different. Children with SLI:R-E produced slightly fewer argument strategies than children with SLI-E, but no differences were found between those with SLI and their typical classmates on this measure. Note that the children with SLI were all enrolled in self-contained settings, and that their "opponent" was also a child with SLI. The combination of familiarity and similar language abilities may have mitigated the social–information processing demands of the task, and enhanced the children's self-efficacy.

In another example of evaluating peer discourse skills in a more supportive script, Hartas and Donahue (1997) asked junior high-school students to participate in a simulated telephone "hot line" conversation. This is a role that few students with LD may be invited to play, yet sharing problems has been found to be an important aspect of maintaining friendships (e.g., Vaughn & Haager, 1994). Interestingly, students with LD were as skilled as other students at managing the conversational turn-taking, and playing the role of "caller," which entailed describing a social problem (i.e., keeping friends, sibling conflicts) and asking for and evaluating advice. In fact, students with LD who first played the role of "advisor" and then played the role of "caller" were actually more active in evaluating the quality of advice given. In the advisor role, however, students with LD offered fewer advice statements, confirming previous findings of persistent deficits in their social–cognitive repertoire (Step 4).

One scripted discourse method shed some light on the "Peer Evaluation and Response" phase after Step 6 in the Crick and Dodge (1994) model. What happens when students with language learning disabilities are given a script that compels them to take an unaccustomed social role, that is, the active and dominant conversational partner? When students with LD (grade 2 and grade 4) played the role of a "talk show host," interviewing nondisabled classmates, they had difficulty maintaining the flow of the dialogue. In particular, they asked fewer open-ended questions and their "guests" produced fewer elaborated responses (Bryan, Donahue, Pearl, & Sturm, 1981). Another kind of data confirmed a more subtle peer response. Using the same videotapes, J. Bryan, T. Bryan, and Sonnefeld (1982) showed adult raters (unaware of children's group status or the purpose of the task) the nonverbal behavior of the talk show guests only. Guests interviewed by talk show hosts with LD were rated as more hostile and less relaxed than guests of hosts without LD.

A second study of boys in grade 3 through grade 8 illustrated the social "cost" of changing one's conversational style, suggesting that even subtle conversational norms are enacted in delicately balanced social relationships (Donahue & Bryan, 1983). After listening to a brief audiotaped dialogue modeling conversation initiating and maintaining strategies, boys with LD then produced more open-ended questions and contingent comments during their talk show (relative to a control group of boys with LD who did not hear the dialogue model). This suggests that the model induced the boys with LD to rethink their social goals (Step 3), to access these strategies more readily (Step 4), and/or increase their self-efficacy in using more assertive conversational tactics (Step 5).

Unexpectedly, however, the guests of talk show hosts with LD in the modeling condition actually offered fewer elaborated responses and more requests for clarification than did guests of control hosts with LD. This supports that the "low-profile" social goals of students with LD may reflect their accurate awareness that efforts to change their conversational style will be met by subtle resistance from their classmates. This explanation suggests an awareness of conversational norms that is more sophisticated than most students with LD are given credit for having.

Fortunately, this hypothesis could be tested directly, as this was one of the very few studies that included direct assessments of children's beliefs about the communicative task. Each child was asked "Now that you've been a host on a talk show, suppose you were giving advice to another kid to help him be a good talk show host (guest?) What things would you tell him?" Children's responses were surprisingly sophisticated. Most telling, the responses of the boys with LD who had heard the dialogue model indicated greater awareness of their own conversational skills and of the verbal and nonverbal performance of their guests. This provides even more compelling evidence for the importance of understanding children's database of prior social experiences, their self-perceptions, and the feedback peers provide.

Role Playing

Role playing has been used to pinpoint a wide variety of children's pragmatic and social skills, including each step of the Crick and Dodge (1994) social information-processing model. Children are asked to imagine a particular social context and communicative partner, and then to formulate an appropriate communicative intention, for example, requests, tactful messages, conflict resolutions. However, given that the social cues and context are imaginary, the children's social goals are not their own, and there is no listener feedback, these tasks' resemblance to naturally occurring interactions is problematic. However, role-playing tasks have been shown to be predictive of many social development outcomes (e.g., Asher & Coie, 1990; Crick & Dodge, 1994).

In one of the few studies that assessed multiple aspects of knowledge underlying role playing of responses to peer conflict, Tur-Kaspa and Bryan (1994) compared children with LD in grades 3 and 4 and grades 7 and 8 with their low-achieving and average-achieving classmates. Participants were told five brief vignettes about children in a social conflict, for example, *One free period Bill has nothing to do. He walks outside and sees two of his classmates playing a game. Bill really wants to play with them. He walks up to them, but they just keep on playing.* Students were then asked to retell and interpret the incident (Step 1 and Step 2). Next they were asked to generate some solutions for the main character (Step 4). Students with LD performed more poorly than typically developing students on these phases. However, when asked to evaluate strategies proposed by the experimenter (Step 5), students with

LD were as capable as other students of differentiating competent from incompetent solutions. This pattern suggested that students with LD had an adequate knowledge base of social norms and tactics. Yet when asked to put themselves into the vignette ("Which of these solutions would you choose?"), thereby activating their own database of social experiences, as well as their self-evaluation (Step 2) and self-efficacy (Step 4), students with LD preferred less competent strategies than typically developing peers. The final task held constant all the previous knowledge steps; a socially skillful response was suggested and students were asked only to role play, that is, *Could you show me how you would go about saying it to your classmates?* Adult judges who listened to audiotapes of the role-playing episodes (with students' group status not identified) perceived the enactments of the students with LD to be less effective than those of other students, including the responses of low-achieving peers.

This apparent "disconnect" between knowledge of appropriate social responses and actual social behavior is a familiar theme in research on students with LD. These findings highlight the importance of students' self-perceptions of their own status in peer social networks and their self-efficacy in using strategies that they realize may only be successful for typically developing children. Together, these beliefs may lead to atypical personal goals for social interaction. On a similar social problem-solving task involving hypothetical peer conflict scenarios (Carlson, 1987), boys with LD knew the socially appropriate strategy (Step 4 and Step 5) when the goal of the interaction was specified by the experimenter (eliminating Step 3); however, when the goal was unspecified, boys with LD were more likely to select the less assertive goals of accommodating the partner or avoiding the conflict rather than compromising.

The Tur-Kaspa and Bryan (1994) study also represented one of the first attempts to explore the contributions of expressive and receptive vocabulary to this role-playing task. Across groups, scores on the Expressive One-Word Picture Vocabulary Test (Gardner, 1990) and the Peabody Picture Vocabulary Test-Revised (Dunn & Dunn, 1981) were moderately correlated with performance in encoding, number of solutions, preference for competent solutions, and role playing (correlations between .34 and .48). Interestingly, receptive vocabulary appeared to be a somewhat stronger correlate than expressive vocabulary with these variables, even with those that seemed most likely to require expressive language proficiency (number of solutions and role playing).

The role of expressive and receptive language abilities in role-playing about peer conflict was also explored by Stevens and Bliss (1995) in the study described previously. Like the Tur-Kaspa and Bryan (1994) methodology, students listened to brief vignettes about peer conflicts and then retold each story to assess their encoding and interpretation of the social cues

(Step 1). In contrast to the Tur-Kaspa and Bryan (1994) findings, all students could convey the essential meaning of each vignette. However, when asked to generate solutions for the imaginary protagonists, children with both types of SLI proposed fewer types of solutions and less developmentally sophisticated solutions (Step 4). In particular, persuasive tactics and requests for explanation and/or information were suggested less frequently by the children with SLI. Unexpectedly, children with receptive language impairments (SLI:R-E) performed similarly to the SLI:E group.

• • • • • •

Viewed together, these studies provide convincing evidence that children with LD or SLI are at high risk for difficulties in peer discourse. The skillful use of comparison groups of language-matched children or low achievers suggests that these problems are not simply a correlate of language proficiency, academic achievement, or developmental lag. Clearly, we do not need any more studies that use the group design "deficit" model, for example, concluding "students with LD or SLI are less skilled than (a comparison group) at (fill-in-the-blank) social domain." The Crick and Dodge (1994) model not only highlights the intricate intertwining of various social cognitive aspects that underlie peer discourse, but also helps to explain the large individual differences that most researchers report, both within and between samples.

These analyses also underline the futility of identifying isolated target behaviors for intervention. It is not enough to recognize that children with language and learning disabilities differ from peers in encoding and/or interpreting social cues and have less access to appropriate social responses. Clearly, interventions will not be effective until we have a deeper understanding of the interactive contributions of individuals' database of experiences, social goals, and self-efficacy, and the feedback they receive from peers. With these insights, social responses that seem inappropriate (e.g., Zachary's animal noises) may actually serve strategic social purposes, and, therefore, are likely to be resistant to even the most well-designed interventions.

To inform meaningful interventions, it is now time to expand our research base by designing studies that ask the difficult questions. First, children's voices about their beliefs and goals for communication are curiously silent (Donahue, 1997). Although there is a large literature on self-perceptions of social and academic status for students with LD (e.g., Pearl & Bay, 1999), there are virtually no data on their beliefs about their own language and discourse abilities. However, some recent data suggest a mismatch between the communication skills that adults consider to be important and those valued by adolescents (Reed, McLeod, & McAllister,

1999). Future studies of peer discourse will derive richer interpretations of the data if a "debriefing" phase is included, in which children's understandings of the purpose of the interaction and their perceptions of their own performance are assessed. Children's beliefs and goals for a particular conversation within a particular context are a rich source of data about their understanding of how discourse enacts social affiliations and hierarchies (Donahue, 2000).

Another way of going beyond the "deficit model" is to identify and study socially "resilient" children, that is, those with language and learning disabilities who have been successful in peer interaction. Are their discourse strategies similar to those of typical children, or have they evolved different ways to interact with peers that accommodate their language limitations? One explanation for the lack of efficacy of social skills interventions (e.g., Kavale & Forness, 1996) may be their focus on teaching social skills that are endorsed by adults, and used by typically developing and socially accepted children. If these behaviors do not fit the social niche that children with language learning disabilities and their peers have negotiated, it is not likely that intervention will have an impact. Case studies of the discourse styles of resilient children with LLD are needed to shed light on effective strategies that may not be readily apparent to adults (e.g., Donahue et al., 1999).

A related research direction is to identify social contexts that foster peer interaction for students with LLD. One approach may be to shift the focus from general peer rejection and neglect to a closer look at mutual friendship. Despite well-documented evidence of peer difficulties, students with LD have been found to have as many mutual friends as other students, although perhaps not of the same quality (Wiener & Sunohara, 1998). Further, most had mutual friends who did not have learning disabilities (e.g., Vaughn & Haager, 1994). As having even one mutual friend can be an important protective factor for social and classroom adjustment problems, it is essential that we know more about the nature and development of these friendships. Understanding how children with language and learning disabilities engage in discourse with their mutual friends may be useful for language assessment, by providing an optimal site for eliciting children's peer discourse knowledge. Language intervention models may then build on these strategies for enhancing communication skills with other peers who are not close friends.

Many critical questions that focus on broader social contexts remain unanswered. As practitioners in LD and speech–language pathology meet each other in typically constructivistic general education classrooms, they are coming to the same realization: Access to the academic curriculum depends on skills for engaging in cooperative social interaction with peers. What are the characteristics of professionals who are particularly adept at creating classroom communities that scaffold positive peer relationships? How can we enhance the role of parents in fostering peer friendships for their children (e.g., Wiener & Sunohara, 1998)? Finally, how can professionals collaborate in the shared mission of improving children's peer interactions in multiple contexts? Practitioners are making university faculty aware that we can no longer afford to prepare professionals who do not share understandings of theoretical frameworks, research findings, and approaches to assessment and intervention. Clearly, the ability to "hang with friends" is the ultimate outcome measure not only for children, but also for the adults who care about them.

REFERENCES

Asher, S., & Coie, J. (Eds.). (1990). *Peer rejection in childhood*. New York: Cambridge University Press.

Brinton, B., & Fujiki, M. (1993). Language, social skills, and socioemotional behavior. *Language, Speech and Hearing Services in the Schools, 24*, 194–198.

Brinton, B., Fujiki, M., & McKee, L. (1998). Negotiation skills of children with specific language impairment. *Journal of Speech, Language, and Hearing Research, 41*, 927–940.

Brinton, B., Fujiki, M., Spencer, J., & Robinson, L. (1997). The ability of children with specific language impairment to access and participate in an ongoing interaction. *Journal of Speech, Language, and Hearing Research, 40*, 1011–1025.

Brinton, B., & Fujiki, M. (1999). Social interactional behaviors of children with specific language impairment. *Topics in Language Disorders, 19*(2), 49–69.

Bryan, J., Bryan, T., & Sonnefeld, J. (1982). Being known by the company one keeps: The contagion of first impressions. *Learning Disability Quarterly, 5*, 288–294.

Bryan, T. (1974a). Peer popularity of learning disabled children. *Journal of Learning Disabilities, 7*, 621–625.

Bryan, T. (1974b). An observational analysis of classroom behaviors of children with learning disabilities. *Journal of Learning Disabilities, 7*, 26–34.

Bryan, T. (1999). Reflections on a research career: It ain't over till it's over. *Exceptional Children, 65*, 438–447.

Bryan, T., Donahue, M., & Pearl, R. (1981). Learning disabled children's peer interactions during a small-group problem-solving task. *Learning Disability Quarterly, 4*, 13–22.

Bryan, T., Donahue, M., Pearl, R., & Herzog, A. (1984). Conversational interactions between mothers and learning disabled or nondisabled children during a problem-solving task. *Journal of Speech and Hearing Disorders, 49*, 64–71.

Bryan, T., Donahue, M., Pearl, R., & Sturm, C. (1981). Learning disabled children's conversational skills: The television talk show. *Learning Disability Quarterly, 4*, 250–259.

Bukowski, W., Newcomb, A., & Hartup, W. (1996). *The company they keep: Friendship in childhood and adolescence*. New York: Cambridge University Press.

Carlson, C. (1987). Social interaction goals and strategies of children with learning disabilities. *Journal of Learning Disabilities, 20*, 306–311.

Craig, H. (1993). Social skills of children with specific language impairments: Peer relationships. *Language, Speech and Hearing Services in the Schools, 24,* 206–215.

Craig, H., & Washington, J. (1993). Access behaviors of children with specific language impairment. *Journal of Speech and Hearing Research, 36,* 322–337.

Crick, N., & Dodge, K. (1994). A review and reformulation of social information-processing mechanisms in children's social adjustment. *Psychological Bulletin, 115,* 74–101.

Denton, K., & Zarbatany, L. (1996). Age differences in support processes in conversations between friends. *Child Development, 67,* 1360–1373.

Donahue, M. (1994). Differences in classroom discourse styles of students with learning disabilities. In D. Ripich & N. Creaghead (Eds.), *School discourse* (pp. 229–261). San Diego, CA: Singular Press.

Donahue, M. (1997). Beliefs about listening in students with learning disabilities: "Is the speaker always right?" *Topics in Language Disorders, 17*(3), 41–61.

Donahue, M. (2000). Influences of beliefs and goals on school-aged children's pragmatic performance: Lessons learned from kissing the Blarney Stone. In L. Menn & N. Bernstein-Ratner (Eds.), *Methods for the study of language production* (pp. 353–368). Mahwah, NJ: Lawrence Erlbaum Associates.

Donahue, M., & Bryan, T. (1983). Conversational skills and modeling in learning disabled boys. *Applied Psycholinguistics, 44,* 251–278.

Donahue, M., Hartas, D., & Cole, D. (1999). Research on interactions among oral language and emotional/behavioral disorders. In D. Rogers-Adkinson & P. Griffith (Eds.), *Communication and psychiatric disorders in children: Theory and intervention* (pp. 69–97). San Diego: Singular Press.

Donahue, M., & Prescott, B. (1988). Reading disabled children's conversational participation in dispute episodes with peers. *First Language, 8,* 247–258.

Donahue, M., Szymanski, C., & Flores, C. (1999). "When Emily Dickinson met Steven Spielberg": Assessing social information processing in literacy contexts. *Language, Speech, and Hearing Services in Schools, 30,* 274–284.

Dunn, L., & Dunn, L. (1981). *Peabody picture vocabulary test-revised.* Circle Pines, MN: American Guidance Services.

Forness, S., & Kavale, K. (1996). Treating social skill deficits in children with learning disabilities: A meta-analysis of the research. *Learning Disability Quarterly, 19,* 2–13.

Fujiki, M., Brinton, B., Robinson, L., & Watson, V. (1997). The ability of children with specific language impairment to participate in a group decision task. *Journal of Children's Communication Development, 18*(2), 1–10.

Gallagher, T. (1993). Language skills and the development of social competence in school-age children. *Language, Speech, and Hearing Services in Schools, 24,* 199–205.

Gardner, M. (1990). *Expressive one-word picture vocabulary test–revised.* Novato, CA: Academic Therapy Publications.

Gartner, A., & Lipsky, D. (1987). Beyond special education: Toward a quality system for all students. *Harvard Educational Review, 57,* 367–390.

Gertner, B., Rice, M., & Hadley, P. (1994). Influence of communicative competence on peer preferences in a preschool classroom. *Journal of Speech and Hearing Research, 37,* 913–923.

Gresham, F., & MacMillan, D. (1997). Social competence and affective characteristics of students with mild disabilities. *Review of Educational Research, 67,* 377–415.

Harris, J. R. (1998). *The nurture assumption: Why children turn out the way they do.* New York: Free Press.

Hartas, D., & Donahue, M. (1997). Conversational and social problem-solving skills in adolescents with learning disabilities. *Learning Disabilities Research and Practice, 12,* 213–220.

Hummel, L., & Prizant, B. (1993). A socioemotional perspective for understanding social difficulties of school-age children with language disorders. *Language, Speech, and Hearing Services in Schools, 24,* 216–224.

Johnson, D., & Myklebust, H. (1967). *Learning disabilities: Educational principles and practices.* New York: Grune & Stratton.

Juvonen, J., & Wentzel, K. (Eds.). (1996). *Social motivation: Understanding children's school adjustment.* New York: Cambridge University Press.

Kavale, K., & Forness, S. (1996). Social skill deficits and learning disabilities: A meta-analysis. *Journal of Learning Disabilities, 29,* 226–237.

Kirk, S. (1963). Behavioral diagnosis and remediation of learning disabilities. In *Conference on exploration into the problems of the perceptually handicapped child* (pp. 1–7). Evanston, IL: Fund for Perceptually Handicapped Children.

Lapadat, J. (1991). Pragmatic language skills of students with language and/or learning disabilities: A quantitative synthesis. *Journal of Learning Disabilities, 24,* 147–158.

Mathur, S., Kavale, K., Quinn, M., Forness, S., & Rutherford, R. (1998). Social skills interventions with students with emotional and behavioral problems: A quantitative synthesis of single-subject research. *Behavioral Disorders, 23,* 193–201.

McKinney, J., & Speece, D. (1986). Academic consequences and longitudinal stability of behavioral subtypes of learning disabled children. *Journal of Educational Psychology, 78,* 365–372.

Nippold, M. (Ed.). (1994). Pragmatics and social skills in school-age children and adolescents. *Topics in Language Disorders, 14*(3).

Orton, S. (1937). *Reading, writing, and speech problems in children.* New York: Norton & Company.

Paul, R., & James, D. (1990). Language delay and parental perceptions. *Journal of the American Academy of Child and Adolescent Psychiatry, 29,* 669–670.

Paul, R., Spangle-Looney, S., & Dahm, P. (1991). Communication and socialization skills at ages 2 and 3 in late-talking young children. *Journal of Speech and Hearing Research, 34,* 858–865.

Pearl, R., & Bay, M. (1999). Psychosocial correlates of learning disabilities. In V. L. Schwean & D. H. Saklofske (Eds.), *Handbook of psychosocial characteristics of exceptional children* (pp. 443–470). New York: Kluwer Academic/Plenum Press.

Redmond, S., & Rice, M. (1998). The socioemotional behaviors of children with SLI: Social adaptation or social deviance? *Journal of Speech, Language, and Hearing Research, 41,* 688–700.

Reed, V., McLeod, K., & McAllister, L. (1999). Importance of selected communication skills for talking with peers and teachers: Adolescents' opinions. *Language, Speech and Hearing Services in Schools, 30,* 32–49.

Rice, M. (1993). Don't talk to him; He's weird: A social consequences account of language and social interactions. In A. P. Kaiser & D. B. Gray (Eds.), *Enhancing children's communication: Research foundations for intervention* (pp. 139–158). Baltimore, MD: Brookes.

Stevens, L., & Bliss, L. (1995). Conflict resolution abilities of children with specific language impairment and children with normal language. *Journal of Speech and Hearing Research, 38,* 599–611.

Tur-Kaspa, H., & Bryan, T. (1994). Social information processing skills of students with learning disabilities. *Learning Disabilities Research and Practice, 9,* 12–23.

Vaughn, S., & Haager, D. (1994). Social competence as a multi-faceted construct: How do children with learning disabilities fare? *Learning Disability Quarterly, 17,* 253–266.

Wiener, J., & Sunohara, G. (1998). Parents' perceptions of the quality of friendship of their children with learning disabilities. *Learning Disabilities Research and Practice, 13,* 242–257.

11

Communicating With Peers in the Classroom Context: The Next Steps

Patricia A. Prelock
University of Vermont

In her discussion of the research on peer discourse, Donahue (chap. 10, this volume) presents a number of themes that have evolved over the course of the last 30 years. She identifies a current challenge for those interested in understanding research related to specific populations. That challenge is making sense of two separate lines of research, one for students with learning disabilities (LD) and the other for students with specific language impairment (SLI). Donahue provides the reader with an opportunity to consider the interrelationship between these two lines of research, suggesting that children with learning disabilities and specific language impairment are being discussed from the same population.

Donahue begins her discussion with an examination of the early history of peer interaction and its relationship to language and LD. This brief historical review highlights two concerns that have implications for those educators interested in the language, learning, and social interactions of children. There is an apparent vulnerability in social interactions for children identified with language and LD (Gertner, Rice, & Hadley, 1994; Johnson & Myklebust, 1967; Kavale & Forness, 1996; Orton, 1937; Rice, 1993). Further, interventions for supporting children with social problems have had limited success (Forness & Kavale, 1996; Mathur, Kavale, Quinn, Forness, & Rutherford, 1998).

In an effort to understand social interactional complexities as they relate to children with language and LD, Donahue reviews social development models that have been used to explain the profiles of children with language learning disabilities (LLD) and problems in their peer interaction. She highlights the Crick and Dodge (1994) framework as a model of social information processing and defines six steps that could be used to explain how children take known or familiar information from past social experiences and integrate this memory with the input gained through novel experiences. Donahue proposes that readers reexamine the available literature on the social interaction behaviors of children with LD and SLI using the Crick and Dodge (1994) lens. She suggests that one way to enhance our understanding of the social interaction problems experienced by these children is to consider the processing demands of various social tasks, such as peer access, joint decision making, scripted discourse, and role playing.

Two critical themes were evident from Donahue's review. The first theme relates to the pervasive use of a deficit model in the literature to explain the social behavior of children with language learning disabilities. For example, the language problems experienced by these students might include an inability to initiate and maintain conversation, negotiate, or problem solve with peers that can then lead to peer rejection and social withdrawal (Brinton, Fujiki, Montague, & Hanton, 2000). The second theme is a lack of recognition of the potential roles that the environment and the context of the community might have on the social interaction opportunities of children with LLD. There is value in reconsidering the interpretation of children's unsuccessful peer interactions using an information-processing model, such as the one initially proposed by Dodge (1986) and then reformulated by Crick and Dodge (1994). However, the Crick and Dodge (1994) model gives little consideration to the potential influence of language function in social discourse. That is, how do children use the language that they have in verbal exchanges with peers? For example, children impaired in their ability to comment or provide clarification during conversational discourse may have fewer and less successful social exchanges than children impaired in their ability to formulate grammatically appropriate sentences, but use the language they do have to offer information or repair misunderstood messages. Further, as children are given fewer opportunities to engage in social discourse with peers when teacher-directed instruction typically characterizes classroom experiences (see Stone, chap. 7, this volume), a consequence may be limited opportunities for observation of and practice in using language in meaningful social contexts like peer interaction.

The purpose of this chapter is to describe the social interaction difficulties of children with LLD as a framework for addressing two practice questions particularly relevant to school settings. The first practice question concerns how peer discourse or social interaction problems should be assessed for children with LLD; the second question considers how opportunities for successful peer experiences in the school community might be created. An expanded view of the Crick and Dodge (1994) model is used to address these questions with applications made to the assessment and intervention considerations that Donahue (chap. 10, this volume) raised. The relevance of these questions to school practice lies in the need for better ways to ensure successful inclusion and integration of students in their school community.

SOCIAL INTERACTION DIFFICULTIES OF CHILDREN WITH LLD

Many studies have described the problems experienced by children with LLD when engaging in peer interactions (e.g., Brinton, Fujiki, & McKee, 1998; Brinton, Fujiki, Spencer, & Robinson, 1997; Forness & Kavale, 1996; Fujiki, Brinton, Morgan, & Hart, 1999; Fujiki, Brinton, Robinson, & Watson, 1997; Gertner et al., 1994; Rice, 1993). Withdrawal, a frequently cited characteristic of children with LLD, is seen as a probable limitation for the successful access of peers in social interactions (Brinton et al., 1997). For example, children who have been excluded by their peers because of previous unsuccessful attempts to initiate and sustain meaningful interactions (e.g., aggressively interrupting a small group of students playing a game) may be limited in their ability to attract the interest of these peers in future interactions. Further, children who prefer to be alone or who are fearful of engaging in interactions with other children will have limited experience with the social conventions that often define successful interactions (e.g., initiating a conversation of interest, maintaining a topic, listening to the other speaker, waiting for turns, etc.). Past failures in social interactions could lead to social isolation because of the limited opportunities to learn from and adjust to those social behaviors that work versus those that do not work in a particular setting.

Children with LLD have been shown to demonstrate three different types of withdrawal: solitary–active, solitary–passive, and reticent behavior (Fujiki et al., 1999; Rubin & Asendorpf, 1993). Those children described as solitary–active are seen as being actively excluded by their peers, whereas children described as solitary–passive are considered as unsociable and enjoying solitude. Children with reticent behavior are viewed as wanting to interact with their peers but exhibit fears around doing so. Understanding the type of children's withdrawal behavior is important because of the consequences that withdrawal has on their sociability or their ability to cooperate, share, and work with others. In school contexts, sociability has a positive impact on both peer and teacher perceptions. Children who are cooperative play partners are perceived positively by their teachers and peers whereas more aggressive children who have frequent negative exchanges with their peers are often rejected by those peers and are seen negatively by their teachers (Ladd & Price, 1987).

Fujiki and colleagues (1999) more closely examined the withdrawal and sociable behaviors of children with language impairment in comparison to their typically developing age-matched peers. They found that, although children's language difficulties made them vulnerable for social problems, their language deficits were not sufficient to explain the range of social difficulties they exhibited. Further, Fujiki et al. (1999) noted that social problems persisted for some children with language impairment.

Some studies also report that children who are unable to adapt to the discourse rules of the classroom experience academic failure, partly due to their inability to access the learning that occurs through teacher–peer dialogues (Donahue, 1994; Morine-Dershimer, 1985). Further, children who are ineffective in their use of "talk" in the classroom are often perceived as less valuable participants by both their peers and teachers (Donahue, 1994; Morine-Dershimer, 1985; Peterson, Wilkinson, & Hallinan, 1984).

The Crick and Dodge (1994) information processing model offers a more integrated view of what might be occurring in the actual social problems experienced by children in classroom settings. This model proposes that children have within their repertoire a schema of previous social experiences, and when they are confronted with a specific social event they appear to respond to certain social cues, often dependent on their past memories of similar experiences. Previous research implicated the language deficits of children with LLD in explaining their unsuccessful peer interactions (e.g., Brinton et al., 1997; Fujiki, Brinton, & Todd, 1996; Gertner et al., 1994; Rice, 1993). In contrast, the Crick and Dodge (1994) model recognizes the influence of past experience, the social context, and the unique processing approach of individual children or how children perceive the stated or implied intent of a teacher or peer message, the importance of a particular message, and or the response requirements in a novel or familiar situation. If we consider that children with LLD often spend less time engaged with their classmates in learning tasks (Bryan, 1974) and that their specific language deficits make it difficult for them to attend to and participate in difficult academic tasks (Donahue, 1994), it is not unreasonable to assume that the integrity of their social schemas would be at risk. This may be one explanation for the findings by Fujiki et al. (1996) that language deficits themselves are insufficient to explain the social interactional problems reported for children with language impairments. Further, Crick and Dodge (1994) suggested that, as children process the responses they receive from peers, they identify how they "feel" about the responses, which then influences their self-perceptions and subsequent responses to peers. An added challenge for children with LLD might be an inability to "name" a specific feeling and effectively express the feeling that most appropriately matches the situation.

As a result of the alternate perspective offered by Crick and Dodge (1994), teachers, speech–language pathologists and others interested in the social communication and social behavior of children may need to reconsider their approaches to assessment and instruction. Reconsideration appears indicated if the social interactions of students with LD or language impairment are to be understood and supported. These considerations are highlighted in the discussion that follows.

STRATEGIES FOR ASSESSMENT OF SOCIAL COMMUNICATION IN CHILDREN

Understanding the social communication problems experienced by children with LLD requires a re-examination of how these difficulties are assessed. There are at least six strategies that teachers and speech–language pathologists, among others, might employ to assess a student's social experiences and social schemas or scripts. First, it is important to identify the context of previous social experiences for children with LLD. These experiences include the social roles they have taken on, the success or failure they have had in particular social roles, and their understanding of the social schemas and scripts they currently use to engage in social contexts. Teachers and speech–language pathologists might consider combining a number of these strategies, depending on a specific child's age and ability level. The information obtained could expand an understanding of the potential impact social contexts and scripted events have on the ability of a child with LLD to perform in school.

- Interview family members and past and present school staff regarding relevant social events experienced by an individual child. The purpose is to identify the child's ability to use and respond to social cues to initiate and sustain an interaction. For example, parents of young children might be asked if their child has gone to a birthday party, if they have visited the library, if they have eaten out at a restaurant, if they have gone to the post office, or if they have been invited to another child's house to play. These are often familiar events for young children, requiring some knowledge of the social context, including (a) the roles of the participants, (b) the relevant language that is associated with the context, and (c) the affective signaling of the participants that provides information about the communicative success or failure of the interaction.
- For older children, teachers might be asked about the child's experiences at lunch or recess with peers, what games with rules the child understands and participates in, or how the child selects a partner or partners for cooperative group work and the communicative success or failure within the group. These are common experiences for school children that require an ability to recognize their varying roles

as a speaker and listener. This includes when and how children initiate a relevant topic, take turns in conversation to maintain the topic, identify confusion and ask for clarification, end the conversational exchange, and respond to the nonverbal cues of their communicative partner.

• Observe the classroom and talk with the classroom teacher about the social learning contexts that are used to implement the curriculum. Important information to obtain would include teacher and peer expectations for cooperative group work, collaborative projects, small group activities, or choice time.

• Interview the child to gain an understanding of his or her own social intentions and those of the child's peers in social events. For example, for young children, a key question is how they might approach a group of peers engaged in play or initiate a new play scheme. Older children might be asked how they become a part of a team of students playing soccer or baseball at recess.

• Interview the child to gain an understanding of the child's knowledge of classroom scripts. For example, for young children, one question might ask how they would describe the arrival and departure script in school. Older children might be asked what the preparation is for taking a spelling test or taking attendance and delivering it to the office secretary.

• Interview the child about their understanding of how to regulate classroom "talk." For example, for young children, a question might be how they know when talking is permitted versus when listening is expected in the classroom. Older children might be asked to explain how they ask for help during independent work.

Second, it is critical to examine the purposes served by the social responses that children with LLD exhibit. Therefore, teachers and speech–language pathologists might collaborate to re-evaluate inappropriate responses provided by students with LD to determine the purpose(s) each serves. For example, if a student provides what initially appears to be an irrelevant or "off-topic" comment in a conversational exchange or in response to a question asked, the teacher or speech–language pathologist might do the following:

• Ask the student how the response related to the current content (e.g., *How does your comment relate to what was just said?*).
• Explore why the student felt the response was relevant (e.g., *Why do you think this information is important?*).
• Assess whether or not the student understood the previous utterance (e.g., *When Carla said _____, what do you think she meant?*)

Third, the expectations for peer interaction and social responsiveness in the context of the school curriculum must be known. It would be important for the speech–language pathologist and teacher to collaborate on designing a way to analyze the individual components of a curricular task, and specify the social discourse role a student might take on to complete the task successfully. For example, if a teacher assigns a group project, the teacher and speech–language pathologist may need to define what it means to collaborate and identify particular roles students might take on to complete the task in a specified time with the participation of all members of the group. The teacher might suggest there be a timekeeper to track the progress and time needed for each task, a recorder to write down the group's ideas, and a facilitator to ensure that group members participate and all questions or required tasks are addressed. The teacher might also define the rules for brainstorming within the group and identify the responsibility for participation of each group member.

Fourth, children's ability to perceive their own intentions and the intention of others must be assessed. For example, a videotape could be made of a child in both successful and unsuccessful social events based on appropriately interpreted or misinterpreted communicative intentions. The child's ability to differentiate between successful and unsuccessful social experiences based on accurately perceived or misunderstood intentions could be probed. The teacher and speech–language pathologist could also probe the child's ability to explain why a message was misunderstood.

Fifth, the child's ability to identify and explain successful and unsuccessful social experiences should be investigated. Therefore, it might be useful to ask students how they responded in a social encounter as well as why they reacted in a particular way. Further, it would be important to determine if students could accurately evaluate the success of a social interaction both from their perspective and those of their social communication partner. The use of this strategy might occur more often for older children and would require that the teacher and speech–language pathologist have a clear understanding of the individual student's ability to describe a range of social experiences. For example, if a student was not selected as a peer partner for a particular activity, the student may perceive intentional rejection, whereas the peer making the selection may have felt the student did not want to join in because previous attempts to engage the student had failed.

Finally, because social problems have been reported to persist in children with LLD, a child's social competence should be considered in language assessment (Brinton & Fujiki, 1999; Fujiki et al., 1996, 1999). The following activities might be useful in both planning and implementing a comprehensive assessment of a student's social competence:

- Consider the influence of withdrawal and sociable behaviors on spontaneous language sampling as well as the language requirements on social–behavioral scales that are often used by psychologists to assess a child's social behavior (Fujiki et al., 1999). It could be that many of the behaviors psychologists are examining are influenced by the language behaviors students may or may not possess.

- Validate reported and observed difficulties in social–communication contexts by utilizing child behavior rating scales that teachers can complete and self-perception surveys that individual children can complete. For example, children can be given the *Friendship Quality Scale* (Bukowski, Hoza & Boivin, 1994), while teachers might be asked to use the *Social Skills Rating System—Teacher Form* (Gresham & Elliott, 1990) or the *Teacher Behavioral Rating Scale* (Hart & Robinson, 1996).

- Collaborate with families, educational staff, and children with LLD to ensure a comprehensive view of the children's social–communication strengths and challenges in a variety of tasks and learning contexts.

To summarize, six strategies were described that have implications for assessing social competence in children. Teacher and student interactions were suggested to identify those social contexts that children have some experiences with versus little experience. Learning about the purposes served in communication exchanges as well as what expectations there are for communication are critically important for school success. Students must be able to relay their own intentions and perceive and expand on those of others in conversational exchanges, while at the same time determine the success or failure of a particular exchange. Finally, teachers and speech–language pathologists must be familiar with the persistent language problems characteristic of children with LLD that impact on the ability of these students to be successful communicative partners.

ENHANCING SOCIAL COMMUNICATION IN CHILDREN: INSTRUCTIONAL STRATEGIES

Both the structural and conversational aspects of language difficulties present in children with LLD place them at risk for social communication problems (Goldstein & Gallagher, 1992). The success or failure of individual children's social experiences and peer interactions is highly variable, however (Brinton, et al., 2000). Creating opportunities for positive social experiences is critical to support a child's ability to engage successfully in peer interactions in the school community. Educational staff who utilize assessment strategies, such as those just outlined, to determine the social, cognitive, and linguistic components that might be impacting on a child's ability to communicate in social contexts are more likely to create meaningful opportunities for social engagement.

Donahue, Szymanski, and Flores (1999) recognized the importance of re-interpreting the social responses of children with LLD in light of the Crick and Dodge (1994) information-processing model. Donahue et al. (1999) proposed that the classroom was a natural context in which to integrate a child's social and communication needs, and that literacy activities, in particular, could be effective in expanding a child's perceptions of the intentions of others in a variety of social contexts.

In the following discussion, three specific intervention strategies are described: capitalizing on classroom literacy activities, utilizing classroom scripts in role play, and facilitating problem solving. Teachers and speech–language pathologists must consider, however, the developmental age and ability level of individual students to determine the utility of particular literacy based or social reasoning strategies.

Capitalizing on Classroom Literacy Activities

The use of books with social communication themes has potential for modeling successful social interactions; for example, commercially available books that tell a story about making friends. Other choices include self-made books designed to tell a story about working cooperatively in groups in the classroom, being a good listener, or introducing yourself to a new friend. These books could be reviewed with students, identifying the relevant social behavior of the characters in the story and "teasing out" alternative behaviors. Such an activity provides another practical experience from which students can learn about particular social expectations.

Utilizing Classroom Scripts in Role Play

Generating written scripts and engaging in role play around those scripts would also support an information-processing view of social events, highlighting opportunities for children to generate a social context, evaluate social intentions in a specific context, and enact potential responses to a social event (Donahue et al., 1999). For example, teachers and speech–language pathologists might collaborate to develop a script for working cooperatively in a peer group on a classroom project, and defining group roles and the specific responsibilities for speaking and listening.

Other scripts might be considered that have social relevance for particular students and require attention to the roles, intentions, and social behaviors of other students. These might include participating in a team sport, making phone calls to friends, going to a movie, playing a board game, eating lunch together, entering a group of peers already engaged in an activity, or problem solving a disagreement with a peer.

To increase the value of learning through scripts, teachers or speech–language pathologists might meet with students to debrief their understanding of the role-played social experience. Debriefing may be effective in expanding students' social repertoire. Ultimately, some students are provided with a way to initiate problem solving and to determine strategies they could access should they encounter an event similar to the scripted role play.

Facilitating Problem Solving

Fostering an ability to solve the problems so often encountered in social interactions is a critical skill to teach and support in school-age students. Crick and Dodge (1994) indicated that, with age, children often increased their ability to detect subtle features of social events and were more able to attend to relevant versus irrelevant details.

However, another component of children's developing information-processing capacity is a tendency toward rigidity in their use of previously established response patterns (see also Stone, chap. 7, this volume). It is important to utilize intervention or instructional strategies that capitalize on children's developmental strengths in social information processing while bridging their weaknesses with meaningful support. Initially, Crick and Dodge recommend creating hypothetical situations through interviews, questionnaires, or videotapes. There is a real opportunity here to create a literacy context in which to pursue the development of social information-processing mechanisms. Children might be required to "read" a social situation, which is illustrated through pictures, a story in a book, or a videotape using accomplices. Following the use of a hypothetical situation, it would be important to have children engage in discussions around real social experiences that they have faced, requiring them to interpret social cues related to the problems they may have encountered.

To read a social encounter effectively, it may be useful for children with LLD to be videotaped in actual social communication exchanges with peers. Reviewing videotapes with support may be most effective in helping children to develop their self-evaluation abilities. Speech–language pathologists and teachers can use videotapes to discuss with students relevant social cues that were attended to or missed and social responses that were successful or unsuccessful. Social behaviors that interfered with success can be highlighted and alternative strategies brainstormed. Further, engaging peers in this dialogue may help to share the responsibility for achieving satisfaction in social encounters.

As part of the intervention process, it would be important to document the effectiveness of the strategies that were incorporated to support the social communication of children with LLD in their social encounters with peers. This could be done through pre- and post-assessments of observed social behaviors, teacher perceptions of sociability, and student perceptions of successful versus unsuccessful peer communication. Portfolios describing students' role play and self evaluations of successful and unsuccessful peer encounters should be collected to look for growth over time and the implementation of strategies learned.

Conclusions. Instructional strategies that may benefit students with LLD the most would be those that facilitate problem solving. For younger students, it may be useful to use books with social scripts or themes. Older students might benefit from participating in role play, which requires reading social situations and determining the adjustments needed to support the success of future social encounters.

· · · · · ·

Limited information is available regarding the acceptance of differences in social interaction styles among peers or the opportunities for scaffolding peer interactions in academic environments (see also Stone, chap. 7, this volume). It is unclear what types of friendships are sought by students with LLD, or the effects of students' challenges in social interactions on their school performance related to the cooperative group activities often used in literacy instruction (see Donahue, chap. 10, this volume). As classrooms continue to employ cooperative learning as a method for peers to collaborate in their academic learning (Slavin, 1995), the skill disparity among peers must be considered (Brinton et al., 2000). Just as children come to school with their own ideas about the academic content they are learning (Nelson, 1999), they also arrive with a set of social experiences that will influence their success within social–communication events.

Speech-language pathologists, special educators, general educators, and others interested in peer communication need to reconsider their role in intervention as one of creating positive peer experiences within the school community. Educational staff need to collaborate in both designing and implementing cooperative group work and other social dialogues that include children with LLD. Donahue (chap. 10, this volume) points out that children's access to the academic curriculum is dependent on their ability to engage in cooperative peer group activities; this ability will be partially determined by the opportunities they are given to experience and problem solve both successful and unsuccessful social interactions and the strategies that teachers, speech-language pathologists, and others use to scaffold their experiences across a variety of contexts.

REFERENCES

Brinton, B., & Fujiki, M. (1999). Social interactional behaviors of children with specific language impairment. *Topics in Language Disorders, 19*(2) 49–69.

Brinton, B., Fujiki, M., & McKee, L. (1998). Negotiation skills of children with specific language impairment. *Journal of Speech and Hearing Research, 41,* 927–940.

Brinton, B., Fujiki, M., Montague, E. C., & Hanton, J. L. (2000). Children with language impairment in cooperative work groups: A pilot study. *Language, Speech, and Hearing Services in Schools, 31,* 252–264.

Brinton, B., Fujiki, M., Spencer, J., & Robinson, L. (1997). The ability of children with specific language impairment to access and participate in an ongoing interaction. *Journal of Speech, Language, and Hearing Research, 40,* 1011–1025.

Bryan, T. H. (1974). An observational analysis of classroom behaviors of children with learning disabilities. *Journal of Learning Disabilities, 7,* 26–34.

Bukowski, W. M., Hoza, B., & Boivin, M. (1994). Measuring friendship quality during pre- and early adolescence: The development and psychometric properties of the friendship quality scale. *Journal of Social and Personal Relationships, 11,* 471–484.

Crick, N., & Dodge, K. A. (1994). A review and reformulation of social information-processing mechanisms in children's social adjustment. *Psychological Bulletin, 115,* 74–101.

Dodge, K. A. (1986). A social information processing model of social competence in children. In M. Perlmutter (Ed.), *The Minnesota symposium on child psychology* (Vol. 18, pp. 77–125). Hillsdale, NJ: Lawrence Erlbaum Associates.

Donahue, M. L. (1994). Differences in classroom discourse styles of students with learning disabilities. In D. N. Ripich & N. A. Creaghead (Eds.), *School discourse problems* (2nd ed., pp. 229–261). San Diego, CA: Singular Publishing Group, Inc.

Donahue, M. L., Szymanski, C. M., & Flores, C. W. (1999). When "Emily Dickinson" meets "Steven Spielberg": Assessing social information processing in literacy contexts. *Language, Speech, & Hearing Services in Schools, 30,* 274–284.

Forness, S., & Kavale, K. (1996). Treating social skill deficits in children with learning disabilities: A meta-analysis of the research. *Learning Disability Quarterly, 19,* 2–13.

Fujiki, M., Brinton, B., Morgan, M., & Hart, C. H. (1999). Withdrawn and sociable behavior of children with language impairment. *Language, Speech, and Hearing Services in Schools, 30,* 183–195.

Fujiki, M., Brinton, B., Robinson, L., & Watson, V. (1997). The ability of children with specific language impairment to participate in a group decision task. *Journal of Children's Communication Development, 18,* 1–10.

Fujiki, M., Brinton, B., & Todd, C. (1996). Social skills of children with specific language impairment. *Language, Speech, and Hearing Services in Schools, 27,* 195–202.

Gertner, B. L., Rice, M. L., & Hadley, P. A. (1994). Influence of communicative competence on peer preferences in a preschool classroom. *Journal of Speech and Hearing Research, 37,* 913–923.

Goldstein, H., & Gallagher, T. M. (1992). Strategies for promoting the social-communicative competence of young children with specific language impairment. In S. L. Odom, S. R. McConnell, & M. A. McEvoy (Eds.), *Social competence of young children with disabilities: Issues and strategies for intervention* (pp. 189–213). Baltimore, MD: Paul H. Brookes Publishing.

Gresham, F. M., & Elliott, S. N. (1990). *Social skills rating system-teacher form.* Circle Pines, MN: American Guidance Service.

Hart, C. H., & Robinson, C. C. (1996). *Teacher behavioral rating scale.* Unpublished teacher questionnaire, Brigham Young University, Provo, UT.

Johnson, D., & Myklebust, H. (1967). *Learning disabilities: Educational principles and practices.* New York: Grune & Stratton.

Kavale, K., & Forness, S. (1996). Social skill deficits and learning disabilities: A meta-analysis. *Journal of Learning Disabilities, 29,* 226–237.

Ladd, G. W., & Price, J. M. (1987). Predicting children's social and school adjustment following the transition from preschool to kindergarten. *Child Development, 58,* 1168–1189.

Mathur, S., Kavale, K., Quinn, M., Forness, S., & Rutherford, R. (1998). Social skills interventions with students with emotional and behavioral problems: A quantitative synthesis of single-subject research. *Behavioral Disorders, 23,* 193–201.

Morine-Dershimer, G. (1985). *Talking, listening and learning in elementary school classrooms.* New York: Longman.

Nelson, G. D. (1999). Science literacy for all in the 21st century. *Educational Leadership, 57*(2), 14–17.

Orton, S. (1937). *Reading, writing, and speech problems in children.* New York: Norton & Company.

Peterson, P., Wilkinson, L., & Hallinan, M. (1984). *The social context of instruction: Group organization and group processes.* Orlando, FL: Academic Press.

Rice, M. L. (1993). Don't talk to him; he's weird: A social consequences account of language and social interactions. In A. P. Kaiser & D. B. Gray (Eds.), *Enhancing children's communication: Research foundations for intervention* (pp. 139–158). Baltimore, MD: Paul H. Brookes.

Rubin, K. H., & Asendorpf, J. B. (1993). Social withdrawal, inhibition, and shyness in childhood: Conceptual and definitional issues. In K. H. Rubin & J. B. Asendorpf (Eds.), *Social withdrawal, inhibition, and shyness in childhood* (pp. 3–28). Hillsdale, NJ: Lawrence Erlbaum Associates.

Slavin, R. E. (1995). *Cooperative learning* (2nd ed.). Boston, MA: Allyn & Bacon.

Technology and Literacy: Decisions for the New Millennium

Julie J. Masterson
Southwest Missouri State University

Kenn Apel
Western Washington University

Lisa A. Wood
Southwest Missouri State University

Technology is a way of organizing the universe so that man doesn't have to experience it.

—Frisch (n.d.)

Our technology has already outstripped our ability to control it.

—Bradley (n.d.)

It has become appallingly obvious that our technology has exceeded our humanity.

—Einstein (n.d.)

For a chapter on the use of technology to facilitate literacy skills, these three quotes may appear out of place and somewhat peculiar as an introduction. However, it is precisely for their somewhat ominous tone and their rather familiar ring that they are included. These thoughts reflect the concerns often expressed by language specialists who feel pressed to use technology in their instructional practices with students with language literacy disabilities (LLD). Feelings of loss of control, fears that computers will take over the role of the language specialist, and images of students lined up in front of computers like automatons are real to some language specialists. Indeed, the devaluation and dehumanization of students with literacy disabilities whom language specialists serve has the potential to occur more frequently in this age of technology (Locke, 1998).

New technologies and computer programs are abundant, readily available, and attractive to the consumer. The allure of these well-packaged products may encourage their use without regard for the needs of the individual or the skills required to benefit from their use. Such easy access may result in use of products that are not consistent with the language specialist's knowledge of literacy development (Commission on Physical Sciences, Mathematics, and Applications, 1999). However, these concerns need not deter the language specialist from using technology to develop and accommodate students' literacy skills. Indeed, it is the potential of technology, coupled with the language specialist's knowledge of literacy development and the prerequisite skills needed for the use of technology, that can lead to new and innovative instructional practices and more inclusive practices for students' literacy disabilities.

Traditionally, services for students with literacy disabilities have focused on both developing new literacy skills and providing accommodations for such students' disabilities. Often, accommodations focused on changing the requirements for a student, such as altering or reducing the need to write papers and read class materials that were required for students with typical literacy skills. For students with literacy disabilities, these accommodations frequently resulted in limited access to the curriculum compared to their typically developing peers. With the advent of technology, services still focus on improving skills and providing accommodations. However, the manner in which these goals can be implemented has changed, with the results having highly significant effects on the lives of students with literacy disabilities (Wood & Masterson, 1999). With new technologies, students have additional, effective means for learning literacy skills. In addition, accommodation no longer necessarily means limited opportunities or experiences for students. Rather, accommodations through the use of technology may allow students greater access to the curriculum than they have experienced before.

This chapter considers the factors that influence the decision to use technology to develop students' literacy skills. First, the role of technology in literacy development is contemplated. Within this discussion, the skills language specialists and students need to benefit from technology are described as are the advantages that accompany the use of technology in literacy development. Second, the research regarding technology applications for literacy development is reviewed and suggestions for current practice and future research are offered.

THE ROLE OF TECHNOLOGY IN LITERACY DEVELOPMENT

Technology plays a substantial role in the lives of all students, including students with literacy disabilities. These students are part of the digital world, a new world created through sophisticated computer based technologies that rely on data transmission and management in the form of numerical digits. Presently, it is difficult to ignore or be unaffected by the digital world. Indeed, today's students are no longer part of an industrial-based economy; rather, they already are participants in a rapidly growing, information-based economy (Carvin, 2000). As language specialists help prepare today's students for their futures, they should be aware that over two thirds of the careers available to students will require some knowledge of computers or other technologies (Carvin, 2000). This fact is real, and it has profound and significant implications for language specialists who are not fluent in their ability to use technology and for their students who may not have the prerequisite skills to fully embrace and profit from technology. However, when knowledgeable specialists observe the prerequisite skills needed to use technology, students with literacy disabilities may indeed benefit from technology as a learning tool for literacy development.

Prerequisite Skills for Students

For students with literacy disabilities, and for those language specialists who serve them, there are several skills required for the effective use of technology for literacy development. To be optimal facilitators of change, language specialists must have a thorough understanding of technology, literacy development, and the learning process. To fully benefit from technology as a tool for literacy development, students must have a basic proficiency in language and literacy, sufficient world knowledge, and the ability to think through strategies that assist them with their own unique needs. When these factors are addressed, the specific advantages of technology can lead to successful development and accommodation of literacy skills.

Prerequisites for Language Specialists. Technology has become both a tool for learning as well as a medium for communication (Commission on Physical Sciences, Mathematics, and Applications, 1999). Language specialists and students are expected to use information technology every day for academic, recreational, and social reasons. Both the specialist and the student must become skilled in their use and understanding of technology to best appreciate and reap the benefits it can provide for their lives. With this in mind, the language specialist should use technology to advance students' literacy skills while also helping to bolster their knowledge of technology itself. To do this, the specialist must know about technology, view technology as a tool to be used for literacy development, and integrate the use of technology based on a deep understanding of literacy development.

The Commission on Physical Sciences, Mathematics, and Applications (1999), representing professionals from a wide variety of disciplines, was convened to examine the skills and knowledge base needed to help students meet the demands of the digital world. A basic and powerful finding of this commission was that all professionals who work with students must be "fluent" in technology (Commission on Physical Sciences, Mathematics, and Applications, 1999). Fluency in technology necessarily involves thoroughly understanding the conceptual underpinnings of technology, possessing the problem-solving heuristics to trouble-shoot difficulties, and demonstrating the basic computer skills to implement a variety of technologies (Commission on Physical Sciences, Mathematics, and Applications, 1999). Being technologically fluent allows the specialist to deal with current and future technology situations, while also implementing creative and self-generated ideas to meet the needs of the students served. With a well-grounded knowledge of technology, language specialists can provide opportunities for students to learn about a variety of topics while also becoming active learners of the technology itself. In this way, the specialist is facilitating the student's knowledge and use of literate language while simultaneously preparing the student to meet the technological demands of the future. In addition, when language specialists become fluent in their understanding and use of technology, they then gain control of technology, and technology becomes for them a tool for facilitating learning.

It is important that language specialists should view technology as a tool, rather than as an approach (Apel, 1999). An *approach* represents a process or set of procedures that have as their basis a definition of the skill being learned and a theory for how learning occurs. A *tool*, whether technological or psychological, is a mediational device that can be used to support how students recognize and develop contexts for learning (Wertsch, 1991). Just as language specialists modify and manipulate other nontechnology tools (e.g., toys, school texts, and materials) to best facilitate their students' literacy development, so too should they be able to alter or select specific features of technology tools to meet students' individual needs.

Some technology tools may not permit language specialists to individualize and modify the technology to meet the specific needs of their students. For example, some computer programs may provide little flexibility in how the program can be utilized, or which components of the program can be maximized for instruction. In this case, the technology, and not the language specialist, is dictating what students experience and learn. Language specialists are wise to abandon the use of these particular tools. When intervention procedures are determined by technology tools and not the specialist, there is a greater chance that literacy development will be impeded (Apel, 1999). To guard against this occurrence, language specialists must fully integrate their knowledge of literacy development and their appreciation for differences among learners with their understanding of technology.

The key to facilitating literacy development, regardless of whether technology is involved, is an approach based on the language specialist's knowledge of literacy and a theory of learning consistent with that knowledge (Apel, 1999). Knowledge of literacy development is best gained from a thorough reading of developmental literature in this area. *Literacy development* includes not only skills such as reading, writing, and spelling, but also those skills that contribute to literacy development, such as oral language development, metalinguistic skills, including phonemic and morphological awareness, and metacognitive skills (Apel & Masterson, 2000; Catts & Kamhi, 1999; Ehri, 2000; Graham & Harris, 1999; Nelson, 1998).

Literacy learning best occurs when viewed as a mutually constructed process between two or more individuals (e.g., Duchan, 1995; Hewitt, 2000; Nelson, 1998). In this social–constructivist viewpoint, an experienced individual, in this case, the language specialist, scaffolds information within real world contexts to optimize the learning process for the student. Students are provided opportunities to learn that encourage them to use the skills they already possess to gain additional skills and knowledge, while the language specialist provides physical, linguistic, and emotional support to aid that learning. Following this theory of learning, technology can be used to facilitate literacy learning, but only when the specialist is the primary agent of change. Technology does not have the capability to solve the learning problems of the students with literacy disabilities. Rather, it is the specialist, armed with knowledge of literacy development and an understanding of the learning process, who can make a difference in individual students' lives.

Without an understanding of literacy and a theory for how students develop literacy skills, language specialists are ill-prepared to explain how or why progress may be occurring. In the worst case scenario, they may fail to facilitate their students' literacy skills. When language specialists are knowledgeable in literacy development and how students learn, they are well prepared to develop or modify technology tools to best meet the literacy needs of their students. We advocate the social–constructivist viewpoint for literacy learning because of evidence from effective intervention practices that supports this theory (e.g., Apel & Swank, 1999; Masterson & Crede, 1999; Silliman, Wilkinson, & Hoffman, 1993). However, the main point is that language specialists should identify a theory of learning that they judge to best represent empirical and clinical evidence for literacy learning and then use this theory as the foundation for their intervention practices.

Prerequisites for Students. Students with literacy disabilities must be able to balance the literacy skills to be learned with the procedures needed to perform the tool's functions. Students with literacy disabilities often have poor language skills, insufficient world knowledge, and difficulty using metacognitive and self-regulation strategies to perform tasks (Catts & Kamhi, 1999; Singer & Bashir, 1999). Without these prerequisite skills and capabilities, these students are poorly prepared to use technology as a means for developing or accommodating their literacy skills.

Students with literacy disabilities are likely to struggle with certain technologies because of their language deficits. For example, students who have difficulties comprehending text may explore options or "levels" within certain computer programs less frequently than their peers with typical comprehension skills (Wissick & Gardner, 2000). Additionally, due to confusions in the purpose and meaning of instructional feedback provided by computer programs, some students with literacy deficits ignore the feedback or treat it as if it is the focus of the program, rather than a means to encourage the student's learning of the content (Wissick & Gardner, 2000). Finally, some of the problem solving skills needed to use technology tools require verbal mediation skills (Commission on Physical Sciences, Mathematics, and Applications, 1999). When students are less able or less likely to use language to solve problems, either verbally or conceptually, they benefit less from programs that encourage active participation and decision making (Wissick & Gardner, 2000). Without these prerequisite language skills, then, success with technology as a tool for literacy development may be diminished.

The poor language skills of students with literacy disabilities also may lead to deficits in their general world knowledge, when compared to peers with typical language and literacy skills. Students with literacy deficits read less and engage in fact-finding exercises less frequently than their typically developing peers (Graham & Harris, 1999). Because of inadequate world knowledge, students with literacy disabilities demonstrate less accuracy and a slower pace when using technology than their peers with more developed literacy skills (Wissick & Gardner, 2000). This, then, may lead to a *Matthew effect* (Stanovich, 1986), such that students with better world knowledge increase their knowledge base at a faster rate than those students with less world knowledge. Thus, students with literacy disabilities may require other nontechnological opportunities to acquire world knowledge, such as experienced-based, real-world activities, to benefit from technology.

Finally, poor language skills and insufficient world knowledge may result in decreased use of metacognitive and self-regulation strategies. Students with literacy disabilities have been shown to experience confusion and frustration on computer programs that require movement through multiple levels or links (Wissick & Gardner, 2000). These students are less likely to utilize navigational tools or help options because these devices require actively thinking about the processing required to perform the tasks.

Thus, their use of metacognitive strategies, in this case, their ability to reflect on how to solve a navigational problem, is reduced compared to their typically developing peers. Additionally, students with literacy disabilities take less frequent advantage of computer options that allow more user control, often viewing screens within a program without a goal or purpose (Wissick & Gardner, 2000). These latter behaviors suggest that students with literacy disabilities demonstrate less self-regulation strategies than students with typical learning abilities. Unlike their typically developing counterparts, students with literacy disabilities use fewer strategies to help them manage the demands of the task, such as management of time and the self-talk that motivates learning (e.g., De La Paz & Graham, 1997; De La Paz, Swanson, & Graham, 1998; Graham, 1997). Without support and facilitation of self-regulation strategies (Singer & Bashir, 1999), students with literacy disabilities are more likely to demonstrate a "learned helplessness" when interacting with certain technologies.

The prerequisite skills required of the specialist and the student must be observed to take full advantage of technology as a learning tool. When these skills are addressed, successful development and accommodation of literacy skills is more likely to occur. In addition, the advantages that accompany technology tool use are likely to be realized.

Advantages of Technology for Literacy Development and Accommodation

Technology offers many advantages for promoting literacy development and accommodations. For example, language specialists can use computer programs as conversational resources while they model desired skills and strategies. They can use technology to directly instruct the skills to be learned (e.g., phonemic awareness or spelling), while also providing the student with prompts and cues that encourage thinking, problem-solving, and manipulation of new ideas. Just like other nontechnological products, a particular computer program can be a means to facilitate literacy skills. However, technology may offer certain advantages not available with other types of nontechnological tools.

Multimedia computer programs designed to target literacy potentially can evoke the rich oral language traditions and expressions. This link between oral and literate forms of language may be missing in other print media, such as books and other written materials (Lanham, 1995). Multimedia programs often allow individuals to hear the fine-tuned nuances of voice and inflection and see the delicate facial expressions that provide additional information and relate the subtle meanings of the speaker. With such technology, students who have struggled with the decontextualized nature of language in traditional text may be able to benefit from this particular medium, which can serve as a bridge between conversational and the more literate styles of language.

Technology also can be used to accommodate ongoing difficulties that students with literacy disabilities may experience in ways not possible before the advent of technology (Wood & Masterson, 1999). Students with literacy disabilities may continue to have literacy deficits, yet the handicap associated with the deficits can be decreased by continued use of a technology tool. Common examples include the use of spell checkers or speech recognition software to decrease the negative effects of poor spelling and writing skills. Use of tools such as these may be beneficial for a number of reasons. First, these tools reduce the linguistic demands placed on the student, freeing up needed memory and attentional resources to deal with content of writing. Additionally, it may be that these tools decrease students' feelings of helplessness as they begin to appreciate their usefulness to aid them in their writing. Thus, with some technology tools, greater participation in the curriculum of their peers may be possible.

Technology tools will never become "miracle cures" for students with literacy disabilities. Language specialists must continue to use these tools wisely and knowledgeably while guiding their students in their learning with instructional cues that develop and build on prerequisite literacy and technology skills (Wissick & Gardner, 2000; Wood & Masterson, 1999). They also must consider the needs of their students within their current environments (e.g., school and home contexts) and possible future environments (e.g., work settings), so that the technology tools serve to enhance their literacy skills rather than limit them (Raskind, 1998). The remaining section(s) of this chapter highlight technology that may be used to facilitate literacy development. The focus of the chapter will be on writing skills and spelling primarily because we feel that the applications in these areas are the best representatives of the potential for technology. Underlying this discussion is the assumption that language specialists will continue to consider the match between the tool used, their understanding of technology, and their knowledge of literacy skills and learning. Only by creating a match between knowledge and practices can language specialists hope to facilitate literacy development while simultaneously maintaining a focus on the individual.

GENERAL WRITING SKILLS

In this section, the effects of technology, specifically microcomputers, on both the process and products of writing are discussed. Before beginning, it is important to describe how writing is defined and evaluated in the microcomputer literature. *Writing* is a complex process that develops over time, so research regarding microcomputer effects on writing skills ranges from a focus on early skills (e.g. print awareness) to later abilities (e.g., narrative structure) (Shilling, 1997). In the development of later conventional writing, variables used to evaluate the effects of technology on writing performance are both *quantitative* and *qualitative.* Quantitative changes may include number of words produced, number of sentences produced, or number of drafts produced (Borgh & Dickson, 1992; Morton, Lindsay & Roche, 1989a, 1989b; Nichols, 1996; Owston & Wideman, 1997). Qualitative changes may include grammatical accuracy and overall quality of writing sample (Borgh & Dickson, 1992; Mavrogenes, 1989; Nichols, 1996; Owston & Wideman, 1997). The changes in the classroom context resulting from the use of a word processor also have been studied to determine the impact of microcomputers on writing (Snyder, 1993). Finally, researchers have evaluated the effectiveness of computers on writing through exploration of student attitudes toward writing (Moore & Karabenick, 1992) and teachers' methods for implementing technology into their classrooms (Snyder, 1995).

In addition to defining how writing is evaluated, it is important to consider the characteristics of the learners included in the studies of interest. The benefits of technology might vary depending on factors, such as the writer's age or the presence of a disability. Consequently, the conclusions offered by authors should always be taken within the context of the specific software and/or hardware studied as well as the characteristics of the students included in the research.

Keyboarding

Before children can use software for writing purposes, they must have a method of computer access. Wood and Masterson (1999) provided information about methods for accessing the computer. Their discussion ranges from alternative input options for individuals with physical disabilities to programs for improving keyboarding skills. Although there are a variety of options for the input of text, the most common one is certainly keyboarding. For young children, learning the purpose of function keys, letter locations, and mouse operations are initial steps in using computers. These methods for letter production and drawing are different than early drawing and letter formation with pencil and paper. For example, when using keyboards, children must alternate their attention between the input modality and the text as it is displayed on the computer screen, whereas use of pencil and paper does not involve such shifts in attention (Olson & Sulzby, 1991). Understanding the differences between production of text via pencil and paper versus the computer may be helpful in developing successful methods for teaching mouse and early keyboarding skills.

In early literacy activities, children may hunt and peck or use a mouse to activate letters (Olson & Sulzby, 1991); however, they still need to learn the various keyboard functions. Kajs, Alaniz, Willman, and Sifuentes (1998) described a teacher's use of color-coded primary keyboard functions to facilitate kindergarten children's use of computers. In this case study, the space key, return key, and shift key were color coded to provide an association between the color and key function. Students were reported to benefit from the color-coding method for teaching keyboard functions. Moore and Karabenick (1992) reported successful use of color-coded keyboards to facilitate use of function keys with fifth-grade students.

As children develop the ability to produce more conventional writing, automated input and/or keyboarding skills may become increasingly important. Snyder (1993) pointed out that it is difficult to determine the effectiveness of word processing if students are not familiar with keyboarding. Many of the studies examining the effectiveness of word processing on writing included information regarding keyboard instruction as well as criteria for keyboarding skills that were met in order to participate in the projects (Langone, Levine, Clees, Malone, & Koorland, 1996; Moore & Karabenick, 1992; Nichols, 1996: Snyder, 1995). These data suggest that keyboarding can indeed be taught and improved and that the benefits of word processing must be considered relative to an individual's keyboarding proficiency if keyboarding is the primary method of text entry.

Word Processing

As stated previously, determining the effectiveness of word processing is difficult due to the many variables surrounding this area of research, such as the features and sophistication of the specific word processing program used as well as the characteristics of the users. Research has indicated positive effects of word processing programs during the earliest stages of writing in kindergarten and first-grade students (Mavrogenes, 1989; McBee, 1994; Olson & Sulzby, 1991). However, researchers have cautioned that the manner in which a word processing program is implemented may be the key factor for successful use. As a result, the unique contributions of technology to early literacy instruction need examination (Mavrogenes, 1989; McBee, 1994).

Other researchers have investigated the effects of word processing on the conventional literacy skills of children ranging from the third to eighth grade (Nichols, 1996; Owston & Wideman, 1997; Snyder, 1993). Preliminary findings suggest that greater access to computers may result in higher writing scores (Owston & Widerman, 1997), more sentences and words produced (Nichols, 1996), and better quality of argument and expository report genres (Snyder, 1993). However, some of these same studies report measures of writing (e.g., grammatical accuracy) that did not differ significantly when word processing was compared to pencil and paper methods of writing.

Some studies have included special features such as text to speech translation software (i.e., "talking word processors") when investigating the effects of word processors on writing skill (Borgh & Dickson, 1992; Shilling, 1997). Shilling (1997) noted that computers, both with and without speech synthesis, appeared to be beneficial in helping children to understand the functions of print. Borgh and Dickson (1992) compared the use of a "talking word processor" to a conventional word processing program with 24 second- and 24 fifth-grade students. The authors concluded that students preferred to write and edit more in the condition with spoken output; however, they did not find a significant difference in the length, quality, or audience awareness measures of stories produced in the two conditions. With the advances in text to speech translation, the effect of this and other specialized features will need to be explored further.

Moore and Karabenick (1992) examined the effects of producing and delivering pen-pal letters via the computer on both the writing performance and attitudes of fifth-grade students. Twenty-six students wrote pen-pal letters via the Internet and a comparison group of 24 students participated in journal writing and computer software activities characterized as drill and practice. Students who participated in letter and delivery via the computer did exhibit more positive attitudes toward the computer. These students did not, however, demonstrate more positive attitudes toward reading and writing than the comparison group.

Like most tools, the benefits of word processing software are influenced by the instructional methods employed by the classroom teacher while using the computer (Snyder, 1995). After presenting a series of case studies of grade 6 and grade 7 classrooms, Snyder concluded that outcomes were influenced by the teachers' approach to writing in general and, specifically, the use of computers in writing. Further, the technology provided to the teachers as well as their own experience with computers were influential in the implementation of computers into writing instruction.

There are still many unanswered questions concerning the use of computers for the development of some emergent literacy skills and later conventional writing. It seems that the approach to writing instruction, whether on the computer or with pencil and paper, is as important as the writing tool itself. However, it would appear that comparison of the reasons students were more or less successful when using computers is difficult at best. Different programs were used in each of the studies, and the underlying instructional philosophy seemed to vary with the microcomputer applications used in each study. As mentioned, it is likely that the researchers' definition of language and their theory of learning influenced how the technology tool was used. Additionally, it should be pointed out that both the computers and programs already discussed have been replaced by better, easier, and faster technology.

Word Prompt Programs

Word prompt programs are *word prediction tools* that provide a list of words after a particular letter has been keyed into the computer. For example, if the user types a *T* at the beginning of a sentence, the software might list, *The, This, That, Those, There.* The user chooses the desired word that is then inserted into the text. Word prompt programs were originally designed for individuals with severe disabilities. Newell et al. (1992) provided summary information on 17 case studies that focused on the use of word prompt programs with children of varying literacy levels and a range of disabilities. The participants included children with cerebral palsy, muscular dystrophy, a chromosomal disorder, Down syndrome and a hearing impairment, a visual impairment, and specific learning disabilities. Literacy skills for all of the participants in the case studies were below or equivalent to a third-grade level. Use of the word prompt program was incorporated into their regular school work. Initially, use of the program was demonstrated by a teacher and then made available during the school day or in some instances for homework. Specific intervention techniques were based on the individual needs of the participants, and varying degrees of prompts were provided with the use of the word prediction program. The effects of word prompt programs on the length of writing was primarily analyzed through writing samples produced in the education environment. The authors noted that the word prediction program could facilitate both qualitative changes (e.g., increased length of writing samples) and quantitative changes (e.g., better spelling).

Because word prompt programs decrease the demands in keyboarding, spelling, and lexical selection placed on the user, it seems reasonable to expect increases in general writing skills. There is a trade-off, however, in that some students may find it tedious to wait for the computer to display the list of selections before moving on with sentence construction. Further research on the effects of word prompt programs on writing skills in students with and without disabilities is needed.

Speech Recognition Software

One of the most promising new technologies for facilitating writing skills is speech recognition technology (SR). The technology is attractive because it makes it easier to convert language into digital form. That is, for many students, the demands of keyboarding make the establishment of a digital form of their story, report, or letter overwhelming. It seems reasonable to hope a student would be more amenable to editing and revising drafts of text if the original entry were less demanding.

When using speech recognition software, the user speaks into a microphone and the words appear on a computer screen in word processing format. Of course, the software system does not actually understand what is being spoken, but rather matches the input to stored templates, which consist of sound patterns (Lange, 1991). SR systems vary according to the type of input they allow. Most of the earlier systems required that the user speak in single words. Such systems were categorized as *discrete.* Most of the current systems allow continuous speech and do not require the user to pause between words or phrases. In fact, accuracy is usually better when users speak in phrases than when in single words.

SR systems also can be defined according to the degree of flexibility involved in recognition (Mathy-Laikko & Bilyeu, 1994; Thomas-Stonell, Kotler, Leeper, & Doyle, 1998). An SR system can be user independent, as is the case for corporate applications such as telephone recognition programs that must recognize certain input phrases from any potential customer. SR can also be user dependent or user adaptable, and each user is required to "train" the system on selected passages of text in order for the system to develop the appropriate recognition templates for that user. In user adaptable programs, the system continues to modify the templates as a result of both the matches and mismatches between its word selections and the speaker's intended words.

The affordability of speech recognition systems has improved dramatically during recent years. Olshan (1999) recently reviewed seven packages widely available on the market. He rated factors such as comprehension level, accuracy, speed, and editing commands. Olshan's report, although somewhat subjective, illustrates the fact that users can find SR systems that are both powerful and affordable. Other descriptions and reviews of SR technology can be found in Flatley (1998), Highland (1997), Lange (1993), and Milheim (1993). However, readers should be cautioned that such reviews are based on technology that may have changed by the time this chapter is published, and the findings may no longer be applicable. Consequently, the strengths and weaknesses of specific SR programs currently available are not addressed. However, interested readers may consult Olshan's (1999) article in *Home Office Computing* or visit the associated website to seek an evaluation that is even more up-to-date.

It is beneficial to distinguish between the use of SR technology as an optional versus necessary input tool. For many individuals with severe disabilities, such as those involved in the reports reviewed by Cavalier and Ferretti (1996), access via a traditional keyboard is not possible. Consequently, the benefits of SR systems can be evaluated and compared to other adaptive access options, such as touch screens and special keyboards. For other users, SR technology is an option for input. That is, users are able to use a traditional keyboard; however, due to constraints in linguistic abilities, keyboarding skills, or other factors, they might prefer and perform better when using SR as the input device. Mathy-Laikko and Bilyeu (1994) raised the possibility of using SR technology with students with literacy disabilities. They suggested that although the technology might be promising, several obstacles would need to be overcome. For example, students would have to have the necessary reading skills to complete the training component. Each individual user must train the system to his or her own speech patterns. This is accomplished by reading aloud several screens of text. Most of the text included in the training modules requires a fairly sophisticated level of reading proficiency.

Wetzel (1996, 1997) discussed the use of SR as a method for accommodating the written language skills of students with literacy disabilities. He reported on the use of VoiceType with one student who was classified as learning disabled. This program requires fairly extensive training and the use of discreet speech. According to the software manual, the program can be trained to recognize 90% of a user's input; however, it only recognized 74% of the words used by Wetzel's student. Wetzel indicated that the student was often frustrated by the program's identification of nonspeech noises (e.g., breaths, coughs) as words.

Research regarding the effects of SR technology on writing skills is just beginning. We need to know whether benefits of bypassing keyboarding outweigh the efforts and frustration that often accompany a student's use of SR. Data as to whether this method of initial text entry results in increases in editing and revising need to be collected. Most important, comparisons of the final writing products produced via traditional keyboard entry to those produced via speech recognition need to be made.

SPELLING

Dedicated Programs

Wood and Masterson (1999) discuss four types of software that can potentially impact spelling performance. *Dedicated programs* are those that have been developed specifically to provide direct instruction for spelling. Often, dedicated programs center around word lists that share a common orthographic pattern (e.g., short vowels, r-controlled vowels) or morphological feature (e.g., derivations, suffixes). Some lists are simply labeled, *Spelling Demons*. Most programs include a variety of activities for each list such as dictation games, puzzles, and letter-scramble games. Wood and Masterson (1999) suggested that such programs can be useful, particularly when they include a feature that allows the clinician or teacher to adapt the list and training materials to the specific needs of the student. For example, some programs allow the teacher to create personalized spelling lessons that contain not only the words to be targeted, but also the foils (i.e., wrong answers) to which the correct spellings will be contrasted.

Like many spelling curriculums, computer software that is organized around word patterns may be beneficial in facilitating students' knowledge of orthographic principles, and such knowledge should help both in decoding as well as spelling (Bear, Invernizzi, Templeton, & Johnson, 2000; Ehri, 2000). The challenge, however, is to get the students to use this knowledge in their every day writing experiences. Without conscious efforts to bridge the skills targeted in software activities to classroom (and personal) writing experiences, the language specialist might be disappointed in the outcomes of the time spent by the student with the programs.

Spell Check and Text-to-Speech Translation

Wood and Masterson (1999) also discussed the use of the spell check function of typical word processing software as a means to accommodate, as well as facilitate, spelling skills. Spell checkers might best be used in conjunction with text-to-speech translators (i.e., "talking word processors"). The language specialist should provide specific training for students in the optimal use of these tools, including information regarding their strengths and limitations. For example, students might be told that spell checkers are based on a "dictionary" methodology. They compare every word encountered to the stored forms in the dictionary. When there is no match, the word is returned as a potential spelling error. This method has two ramifications. First, correct words, such as proper nouns or unusual words, may be highlighted as potential mistakes, and students should not automatically assume that the "computer is right—there is an error." Second, accurate spellings of words other than the intended form will not be identified by the software (e.g., spelling *cute* as *cut*). Explanation of the dictionary methodology might help the student understand why this happens; however, the student will still need another strategy to identify such errors. The text-to-speech translators can be helpful in meeting this need. The student can be encouraged to listen carefully as the computer "reads" a passage and identifies any erroneous words. Hopefully, they would recognize the mistake if they heard a sentence such as, *There in the window was a* cut *little puppy.* Of course the usefulness of text-to-speech translators is contingent on the quality of the synthesized speech. Further, a misspelled word might be pronounced as though it were correct (e.g., *rane* for *rain*) because many of the algorithms are based on common phonetic conversions. Combining feedback from spell checkers and text-to-speech translators should increase the power of the student to monitor his or her own spelling; however, it, too, has some vulnerabilities. Identification of errors such as, *I red the book last night* remains problematic for most software.

We know of no published studies that have systematically evaluated the unique contributions of spell checkers or talking word processors to spelling skills. Masterson and Crede (1999) reported data from a single subject who had a specific spelling disability. Dedicated programs, spell checkers, and talking word processors were used as central components of a multi-faceted intervention approach. After a relatively short training program (i.e., twice per week for 6 weeks), the student showed increases in both standardized and performance-based measures of spelling. The intervention method stressed the use of problem solving and a variety of strategies to formulate optimal hypotheses regarding spelling, such as word sort and proofing activities (Bear et al., 2000). The researchers then encouraged the student to use these spellings in several types of activities, such as spelling to dictation and engaging in authentic writing experiences. The technology tools, in this case, commercial computer games and word processors, provided optimal opportunities for both hypothesis formulation and use of spelling skills (e.g., proofing a word processing document containing misspellings that represented the student's initial spelling errors).

Word Prompt Programs

The final tool to address spelling skills discussed by Wood and Masterson (1999) is word prompt software. As previously discussed, Newell and colleagues (1992) reported on several case studies in which the effects of word prompt programs on various measures of written language were explored. Spelling accuracy was included, and the authors reported that the average spelling scores for all children showed a reduction of misspelled words from 25% to 8% when assisted by the predictive program compared to use of a word processor alone.

Sturm, Rankin, and Beukelman (1994) investigated the effect of word prompt programs on the written language performance of students with literacy and behavioral disabilities in the intermediate elementary grades. Students composed stories through handwriting, word processing, and word processing with a word prompt feature. The results from Sturm and colleagues (1994) indicated that the word prompt program improved spelling skills.

Like the other technology tools for spelling, word prompt programs hold significant promise. Language specialists should be aware that such programs have associated metalinguistic, metacognitive, and attitudinal demands. Metalinguistic demands include requiring students to search and locate words on the word lists. The keyboard input, whether a single letter or more, must be close enough to the intended form for the software to access the appropriate list of choices. The closer the input is to the intended form, the less the metacognitive demands. Finally, students who have fairly good keyboarding skills may have to decrease their typing speed to use a word prediction/prompt program. Some students may find that such an adjustment is not worth the proposed benefits.

Technology tools have significant potential for individuals with spelling disabilities. They can be used both to facilitate improvement in one's skills as well as to compensate for weaknesses. Future research is needed to systematically explore the influence of technology use on spelling performance.

• • • • • •

A review of the literature presented in this chapter illustrates the fact that although the use of technology with students with literacy disabilities is promising, it remains a fruitful area for additional research. It is interesting that both the promise of microcomputer software as well as the need for research in the area have been highlighted for almost 20 years (e.g., Masterson, 1995; Staples, Erickson, & Koppenhaver; 1994; Torgesen & Young, 1983; Volin, 1989). In addition, unlike studies that have examined the effects of specific approaches to literacy instruction, studies of the usefulness of technology will be dependent on the practices underlying the delivery of the instruction (National Institute of Child Health and Human Development, 2000). The need to capitalize on the uniqueness of the computer and the ability to accomplish tasks that would otherwise be impossible should be emphasized.

Although the call to examine the effective use of technology in literacy intervention was made over 15 years ago, the paucity of empirical research in this area suggests that the call remains unanswered. It is quite possible that new technologies will allow individuals, both with and without literacy disabilities, to achieve literacy levels higher than previously possible. However, systematic studies of sufficient subject size, conducted with the appropriate experimental controls, are necessary to determine whether the possibilities will become realities.

As language specialists increase their use of technology to serve students with literacy disabilities, they may experience firsthand the thoughts and feelings expressed in the quotes used at the beginning of this chapter. However, our hope is that language specialists will carefully consider the factors that may affect successful use of technology to develop students' literacy skills along with the research regarding technology applications for literacy development. With these considerations, we believe that language specialists will hold a similar view of technology as did Ralph Waldo Emerson (n.d.) over a century ago: "All tools and engines on earth are only extensions of man's limbs and senses" (page number unknown). Technology should always be viewed as an extension of the language specialist's limbs, senses, and most importantly, creative and theoretical mind. Only then will students truly benefit from our interventions.

REFERENCES

Apel, K. (1999). Checks and balances: Keeping the science in our profession. *Language, Speech, and Hearing Services in the Schools, 30,* 98–107.

Apel, K., & Masterson, J. (2000). Spelling assessment: Charting a path to optimal instruction. *Topics in Language Disorders, 20*(3), 50–65.

Apel, K., & Swank, L. K. (1999). Second chances: Improving decoding skills in the older student. *Language, Speech, and Hearing Services in Schools, 30,* 231–242.

Bear, D. R., Invernizzi, M., Templeton, S., & Johnson, F. (2000). *Words their way* (2nd ed.). Upper Saddle River, NJ: Merrill.

Borgh, K., & Dickson, W. P. (1992). The effects on children's writing of adding speech synthesis to a word processor. *Journal of Research on Computing in Education, 24*(4), 533–544.

Bradley, O. (n.d.). In *Creative Quotations* [Online]. Available: http://www.creativequotations.com

Carvin, A. (2000). Mending the breach: Overcoming the digital divide [Online]. Available: http://www.glef.org/edutopia/newsletters/spring2000/carvin.html

Catts, H., & Kamhi, A. (1999). *Language and reading disabilities.* Neeham Heights, MA: Allyn & Bacon.

Cavalier, A., & Ferretti, R. (1996). Talking instead of typing: Alternate access to computers via speech recognition technology. *Focus on Autism and Other Developmental Disabilities, 11*(2), 79–85.

Commission on Physical Sciences, Mathematics, and Applications. (1999). *Being fluent with information technology.* Washington, DC: National Academy Press.

De La Paz, S., & Graham, S. (1997). Effects of dictation and advanced planning instruction on the composing of students with writing and learning problems. *Journal of Educational Psychology, 89,* 203–222.

De La Paz, S., Swanson, P., & Graham, S. (1998). The contribution of executive control to the revising of students with writing and learning difficulties. *Journal of Educational Psychology, 90,* 448–460.

Duchan, J. (1995). *Supporting language learning in everyday life.* San Diego, CA: Singular.

Ehri, L. (2000). Learning to read and learning to spell: Two sides of a coin. *Topics in Language Disorders, 20*(3), 19–36.

Einstein, A. (n.d.). In *Creative Quotations* [Online]. Available: http://www.creativequotations.com

Emerson, R. W. (n.d.). In *Creative Quotations* [Online]. Available: http://www.creativequotations.com

Flatley, M. (1998, December). Voice recognition software. *Business Education Forum, 44*–45.

Frisch, M. (n.d.). In *Creative Quotations* [Online]. Available: http://www.creativequotations.com

Graham, S. (1997). Executive control in the revising of students with learning and writing difficulties. *Journal of Educational Psychology, 89,* 223–234.

Graham, S., & Harris, K. (1999). Assessment and intervention in overcoming writing difficulties: An illustration from the self-regulated strategy development model. *Language, Speech, and Hearing Services in the Schools, 30,* 255–264.

Hewitt, L. (2000). Does it matter what your client thinks? The Role of theory in intervention: Response to Kamhi. *Language, Speech, and Hearing Services in the Schools, 31,* 186–193.

Highland, P. (1997, October). Voice recognition technology. *Business Education Forum, 30*–32.

Kajs, L. T., Alaniz, R., Willman, E., & Sifuentes, E. (1998). Color-coding keyboard functions to develop kindergartners' computer literacy. *Journal of Computing in Childhood Education, 9*(2), 107–111.

Lange, H. (1991). Voice technologies in libraries: A look into the future. *Library Hi Tech, 35,* 87–96.

Lange, H. (1993). Speech synthesis and speech recognition: Tomorrow's human-computer interfaces? *Annual Review of Information Science and Technology, 28,* 153–185.

Langone, J., Levine, B., Clees, T. J., Malone, M., & Koorland, M. (1996). The differential effects of a typing tutor and microcomputer-based word processing on the writing samples of elementary students with behavior disorders. *Journal of Research on Computing in Education, 29,* 14–58.

Lanham, R. A. (1995, September). Digital literacy: Multimedia will require equal facility in word, image, and sound. *Scientific American, 273,* 198–200.

Locke, J. L. (1998). Where did all the gossip go? Casual conversation in the information age. *Asha, 40*(3), 26–31.

Masterson, J. (1995). Future directions for microcomputer use by speech-language pathologists and audiologists. *Language, Speech, and Hearing Services in Schools, 26,* 212–222.

Masterson, J., & Crede, L. (1999). Learning to spell: Implications for assessment and intervention. *Language, Speech, and Hearing Services in Schools, 30,* 243–254.

Mathy-Laikko, P., & Bilyeu, D. (1994, July.). *Voice input technology: The myth and the (current) reality.* Seminar presented to the Nebraska Augmentative Communication Conference, Mahoney State Park.

Mavrogenes, N. (1989). *A comparative study of three methods of promoting literacy in kindergarten and first grade 1987–88.* Chicago, IL: Chicago Public School. (Eric Document Reproduction Service No. 339 025)

McBee, D. (1994). *The effect of technology on emergent writing.* Nikiski, AK: University of Alaska Southeast. (Eric Document Reproduction Service No. 372 390)

Milheim, W. (1993). Computer-based voice recognition: Characteristics, applications, and guidelines for use. *Performance Improvement Quarterly, 6,* 14–25.

Moore, M. A., & Karabenick, S. A. (1992). The effects of computer communications on the reading and writing performance of fifth-grade students. *Computers in Human Behavior, 8,* 27–38.

Morton, L. L., Lindsay, P. H., & Roche, W. M. (1989a). Word processing effects on writing productivity and revision at elementary and junior high school levels. *The Alberta Journal of Educational Research, 35*(2), 145–163.

Morton, L. L., Lindsay, P. H., & Roche, W. M. (1989b). A report on learning disabled children's use of lab-based word processing versus pencil-and-paper for creative writing. *The Alberta Journal of Educational Research, 35*(4), 283–291.

National Institute of Child Health and Human Development (2000). *Report of the national reading panel: An evidence-based assessment of the scientific research literature on reading and its implications for reading instruction.* Bethesda, MD: National Institute of Child Health and Human Development.

Nelson, N. M. (1998). *Childhood language disorders in context: Infancy through adolescence.* Boston, MA: Allyn & Bacon.

Newell, A. F., Arnott, J. L., Booth, L., Beattie, W., Brophy, B., & Ricketts, I. W. (1992). Effect of the "PAL" word prediction system on the quality and quantity of text generation. *Augmentative and Alternative Communication, 8*, 304–311.

Nichols, L. M. (1996). Pencil and paper versus word processing: A comparative study of creative writing in the elementary school. *Journal of Research on Computing in Education, 29*(2), 159–166.

Olshan, J. (1999, February). Speech recognition programs. *Home Office Computing,* 81–88. Available: http://www.smalloffice.com

Olson, K., & Sulzby, E. (1991). Computer as a social/physical environment in emergent literacy. In J. Zutell & S. McCormick (Eds.), *Learner factors/teacher factors: Issues in literacy research and instruction* (pp. 111–118). Chicago, IL: The National Reading Conference, Inc.

Owston, R. D., & Wideman, H. H. (1997). Word processors and children's writing in a high-computer-access setting. *Journal of Research on Computing in Education, 30*(2), 202–220.

Raskind, M. A. (1998). Selecting the right assistive technology. *National Council on Learning Disabilities News, Fall,* 3–4.

Shilling, W. (1997). Young children using computers to make discoveries about written language. *Early Childhood Education Journal, 24,* 253–259.

Silliman, E. R., Wilkinson, L. C., & Hoffman, L. P. (1993). Documenting authentic progress in language and literacy learning: Collaborative assessment in classrooms. *Topics in Language Disorders, 14*(1), 58–72.

Singer, B. D., & Bashir, A. S. (1999). What are executive functions and self-regulation and what do they have to do with language learning disorders? *Language, Speech, and Hearing Services in the Schools, 30,* 265–273.

Snyder, I. (1993). The impact of computers on students' writing: A comparative study of the effects of pens and word processors on writing context, process and product. *Australian Journal of Education, 37*(1), 5–25.

Snyder, I. (1995). Toward electronic writing classrooms: The challenge for teachers. *Journal of Information Technology for Teacher Education, 4*(1), 51–65.

Stanovich, K. E. (1986). Matthew effects in reading: Some consequences of individual differences in the acquisition of literacy. *Reading Research Quarterly, 21,* 360–401.

Staples, A., Erickson, K., & Koppenhaver, D. (1994, December). *Uses of technology and educational media in literacy instruction for children with developmental disabilities.* Paper presented at the annual convention for The Association for Persons with Severe Disabilities, Atlanta, GA.

Sturm, J. M., Rankin, J. L., & Beukelman, D. R., (1994, November). Using word-prompt computer programs with LD student writers. Poster session presented at the American Speech–Language-Hearing Association Convention, New Orleans, LA.

Thomas-Stonell, N., Kotler, A., Leeper, H., & Doyle, P. (1988). Computerized speech recognition: Influence of intelligibility and perceptual consistency on recognition accuracy. *Augmentative and Alternative Communication, 14*, 51–56.

Torgesen, J., & Young, K. (1983). Priorities for the use of microcomputers with learning disabled children. *Journal of Learning Disabilities, 16*(4), 234–237.

Volin, R. (1989). The computer as an integral component in the clinic. *Journal for Computer Users in Speech and Hearing, 5*, 89–92.

Wertsch, J. V. (1991) *Voices of the mind: A sociocultural approach to mediated action*. Cambridge, MA: Harvard University Press.

Wetzel, K. (1996). Speech-recognizing computers: A written-communication tool for students with learning disabilities? *Journal of Learning Disabilities, 29*, 371–380.

Wetzel, K. (1997). Speech-recognizing computers: A written-communication tool for students with learning disabilities? In R. Higgins, & R. Boone (Eds.), *Technology for students with learning disabilities* (pp. 55–74). Austin: Pro-Ed, Inc.

Wissick, C. A., & Gardner, J. E. (2000). Multimedia or not to multimedia: That is the question for students with learning disabilities. *Teaching Exceptional Children, 32*(4), 34–43.

Wood, L., & Masterson, J. (1999). Use of technology to facilitate language skills in school-age children. *Seminars in Speech and Language, 20*(3), 219–232.

Part III

Legal and Policy Issues
in Special Education
and Postsecondary Education

Legal, Administrative, and Policy Issues in Special Education

Allan G. Osborne, Jr
Snug Harbor Community School

Legal disputes between parents and school officials can be very costly. The cost is not just in dollars. It also involves costs in terms of the diversion of resources, the toll on school personnel, and, most importantly, the breakdown in the relationship between the parents and the school. The best way to deal with a legal dispute is to prevent it from occurring in the first place.

A careful analysis of the thousands of lawsuits that have arisen since the passage of the Individuals with Disabilities Education Act (IDEA) would show that many could have been avoided. In many situations, the disputes arose as a result of poor communication between school personnel and the parents. However, many of the cases, particularly those in which the school district has been the losing party, could have been prevented if school officials and special education practitioners simply had more knowledge of special education law. Preventive school law seeks to find permanent solutions to the situations that give rise to conflicts between parents and school districts. This chapter presents information on legal issues that are relevant for special education and related services providers. It is impossible to cover all of the myriad provisions of the IDEA, Section 504 of the Rehabilitation Act of 1973, and the Americans with Disabilities Act (ADA; see Battle, chap. 14, this volume). Thus, only the major procedural and substantive provisions of these laws are discussed. Issues that have been selected for discussion are those that are most related to the day-to-day provision of special education and related services.

In 1975 Congress passed landmark legislation designed to provide the nation's students with disabilities with unprecedented access to educational services. Originally known as the Education for All Handicapped Children Act (1975), that legislation is now known by its new title, the Individuals with Disabilities Education Act (1997). The statute, as amended, calls for school districts to provide students with disabilities with an appropriate education in the least restrictive environment. The law also provides students with disabilities and their parents with due process rights, including the right to contest school district decisions regarding the provision of a free appropriate public education. Consequently, since the enactment of the law in 1975, literally thousands of lawsuits have been filed challenging school district decisions.

The IDEA is not the only law governing special education in the schools. In addition, section 504 of the Rehabilitation Act and the ADA provide students with disabilities with additional protections. Section 504 prohibits discrimination against individuals with disabilities by recipients of federal funds. The ADA expands section 504's discrimination prohibition to the private sector, but includes provisions applicable to public entities. In addition, all states currently have laws governing the provision of special education. However, a discussion of state statutes is beyond the scope of this chapter.

PROCEDURAL ISSUES

Evaluation and Classification

The IDEA requires states, and consequently school districts, to establish procedures to assure that all students with disabilities are properly identified and evaluated (IDEA, § 1412, a, 2, 1997). Those procedures, along with the test instruments chosen, may not be culturally or racially biased. In fact, students whose language or mode of communication is not English, must be evaluated in their native language or usual mode of communication (IDEA, § 1414, b, 3, 1997). The IDEA stipulates that all assessments are to be administered by trained personnel in conformance with the instructions provided by the test producer (IDEA, § 1414, b, 2, 1997). If a student is found to be eligible for special education, the school district is required to develop an individualized education program (IEP) for that child, but the IEP can be invalidated if it is based on a flawed evaluation of the child (*Bonadonna v. Cooperman*, 1985).

The student is entitled to an independent evaluation if the parents disagree with the school district's evaluation. However, the school district is required to pay for the independent evaluation only if the parents can show that the district's evaluation was not appropriate. If the parents do obtain an independent evaluation, the school district must consider the results of that evaluation (Assistance to the States, § 300.503, 1999). However, that does not mean that the school district must adopt the recommendations of the independent evaluator (*G.D. v. Westmoreland School District*, 1991).

Rights of Parents and Guardians

Parents are given considerable due process rights on behalf of their children in the special education process. The intent of the IDEA is for them to become partners with school district personnel in the development of IEPs. The school district must provide the parents with proper notice before it proposes to take any action regarding the child's identification or placement (IDEA, § 1415, b, 3, 1997). The parents must be invited to participate in all meetings in which the student's evaluation or placement will be considered (Assistance to the States, § 300.345, 1999). If the parents disagree with any decisions made by school district personnel, they may seek resolution either through voluntary mediation or an administrative due process hearing. If the parents disagree with the final result of the administrative hearing process, they may appeal to the federal or state courts (IDEA, § 1415, 1997). Failure to provide parents with the rights outlined in the IDEA can invalidate an otherwise appropriate IEP (Osborne, 1996).

Change in Placement Procedures

Once a child has been placed in special education, that placement may not be arbitrarily changed. Again, before any change in placement may occur, the parents must be given proper notification. The child's placement also may not be changed while any administrative due process or judicial proceedings are pending absent parental consent or a court order (IDEA, § 1415, j, 1997).

The actual determination of what constitutes a change in placement can be tricky. For example, if a special education classroom was physically moved from one school to another as part of a school district reorganization, that would not be considered a change in placement as long as the student's IEP could be fully implemented in the new location. By the same token, the usual movement of a student from one level to another (i.e., elementary to middle school) is not a change in placement if the student's IEP can be fully implemented after the change (Osborne, 1996).

However, any move that would affect the IEP or its implementation would be considered a change in placement. Obviously, changing a child from a resource room situation to a substantially separate class for students with behavioral disorders would be a change in placement. The elimination of a component of the student's educational program would also constitute a change in placement (*Abney v. District of Columbia*, 1988). Minor changes are allowable, however. The key to determining whether or not the change is acceptable is how the modification will affect the student's learning (*DeLeon v. Susquehanna Community School District*, 1984).

SERVICE DELIVERY ISSUES

Determining an Appropriate Educational Placement

Although the IDEA mandates that school districts provide students with disabilities with an appropriate education, it provides little guidance in terms of what constitutes appropriate. The IDEA's regulations indicate that an appropriate education consists of special education and related services and is provided in conformance with an IEP (Assistance to the States, § 300.13, 1999). However, a precise definition of the term *appropriate* cannot be found in either the statute itself or its implementing regulations. Thus, we must turn to court decisions for further guidance as to what constitutes an appropriate education.

In *Board of Education of the Hendrick Hudson Central School District v. Rowley* (1982), the U.S. Supreme Court gave us a minimal definition of an appropriate education. This case arose when the parents of a kindergarten student with a hearing impairment protested the school district's refusal to provide the child with a sign-language interpreter. Lower courts had ordered the school district to provide the requested interpreter, holding that an appropriate education was one that allowed the student with a severe hearing impairment to achieve at a level commensurate with that of peers without hearing impairments. However, the Supreme Court, finding that the student was achieving passing marks and advancing from grade to grade without the sign-language interpreter, reversed. The high Court held that an appropriate education was one that was formulated in accordance with all of the IDEA's procedures and was designed to provide the student with some educational benefit. Whereas the student in the *Rowley* case was receiving some educational benefit without the sign-language interpreter, the Court held that the school district was not required to provide the interpreter even though the student might achieve at a higher level with those services.

The *Rowley* decision established a minimum standard for what constitutes an appropriate education. However, individual states may set higher standards. Courts in North Carolina, New Jersey, Massachusetts, Michigan, and California have held that those states have higher standards of appropriateness (Osborne, 1996). For example, in Massachusetts, the state statute requires school districts to develop an educational program that will provide the student with maximum feasible benefit (*David D. v. Dartmouth School Committee*, 1985). In some of these decisions the courts also specifically ruled that the higher state standard replaced the federal standard because one of the requirements of the IDEA is that special education programs must meet the standards of the state educational agency (IDEA, § 1401, 8, B, 1997).

In recent years, the *Rowley* standard has been further refined. Courts have indicated that the *some educational benefit* criteria require more than just minimal or trivial benefits (*Carter v. Florence County School District Four*, 1991; *Hall v. Vance County Board of Education*, 1985). Other courts have expanded the criteria by stating that the educational benefit must be meaningful (*Board of Education of East Windsor Regional School District v. Diamond*, 1986; *Polk v. Susquehanna Intermediate Unit 16*, 1988) or appreciable (*Chris C. v. Gwinnett County School District*, 1991). One court stated that the gains made by a student must be measurable to meet the *Rowley* criteria (*J.S.K. v. Hendry County School Board*, 1991).

It is impossible to provide an exact definition of an appropriate education because special education and related services must be provided on an individualized basis. Thus, what is appropriate for one child may not be appropriate for another. The courts have given school practitioners, parents, and attorneys some guidelines. The program must provide the student with meaningful educational benefit. A program would be meaningful if it was reasonably expected to result in progress toward the goals and objectives of the student's IEP.

Least Restrictive Environment

The IDEA states that a student with disabilities must be educated in the least restrictive environment. The law specifically states that removal of students with disabilities from the regular educational environment may occur only when the nature or severity of the disability is such that education in regular classes with the use of supplementary aids and services cannot be achieved satisfactorily (IDEA, § 1412, a, 5, 1997). In recent years this provision has generated a fair amount of controversy as a result of the inclusion movement. Inclusion is a philosophy whereby students with disabilities are educated in general education classrooms alongside their peers without disabilities.

The terms *least restrictive environment, mainstreaming,* and *inclusion* are frequently confused. *Least restrictive environment* is a legal term that refers to the mandate that students with disabilities are to be educated as close to the general education setting as possible. *Mainstreaming* is an educational term that refers to the practice of placing students with disabilities in the general education environment for a portion of the school day. *Inclusion* is the practice of educating students with disabilities within the general education environment. Inclusion may be full or partial. Students may be removed from the general education environment, if necessary, to provide specialized services.

In two high profile cases appeals courts have ordered school districts to place students with moderate to severe cognitive disabilities in regular education classes as opposed to segregated special education classrooms

(*Oberti v. Board of Education of the Borough of Clementon School District*, 1993; *Sacramento City Unified School District v. Rachel H.*, 1994). In these and other decisions, the courts have held that there are several factors that school districts must consider when determining the least restrictive environment for a given student. Factors, as summarized by the Ninth Circuit Court of Appeals, address: (a) the educational benefits of placement in a regular classroom, (b) the nonacademic benefits of such a placement, (c) the effect the student would have on the teacher and other students in the class, and (d) the costs of an inclusionary placement (*Sacramento City Unified School District v. Rachel H.*, 1994). In applying these factors, courts have been required to perform a balancing act. In fact courts often will rule that it is appropriate to sacrifice a degree of academic benefit for the sake of increased social benefit (Osborne & DiMattia, 1994).

Inherent in these decisions is the principle that school districts must make all reasonable efforts to place students with disabilities in an inclusionary setting by providing them with supplementary aids and services to ensure success. This does not mean, however, that all students with disabilities must be placed in regular education classes. Courts have approved segregated settings where the school district was able to show that the students could not function in a regular education setting, or would not benefit from placement in such a setting, even with supplementary aids and services. For example, in *Clyde K. v. Puyallup School District* (1994), the court held that an off-campus alternative program was the least restrictive environment for a disruptive and assaultive student whose own behavior prevented him from learning. The court further found that the student's behavior had significantly impaired the education of the other students in the regular education setting. In *Capistrano Unified School District v. Wartenberg* (1995) the court approved a private school placement after stating that mainstreaming, which had resulted in total failure, was not appropriate for a student who had a history of not doing well in regular education programs. The bottom line is that an inclusionary placement should be the placement of choice. A segregated placement should be contemplated only when an inclusionary placement has failed in spite of the school district's best efforts or there is overwhelming evidence that it is not feasible.

Private and Residential School Placements

In spite of the IDEA's preference for placing students in the least restrictive environment, it is recognized that such a placement is not feasible for all students. Thus, the IDEA requires school districts to offer a continuum of placement alternatives to meet the special education needs of students with disabilities (Assistance to the States, § 300.551, a, 1997).

A private school placement may be required when the school system simply does not have an appropriate placement available. This may occur in situations where the student has a low incidence type of disability and there are not enough students with the same type of disability within the district to warrant development of a program (*Colin K. v. Schmidt*, 1983). Courts have consistently recognized that school districts, particularly smaller districts, cannot afford to develop specialized programs for a small number of students and, thus, must look outside the district for placements.

Residential placements are ordered by the courts when it can be shown that the student's disabilities require 24 hour per day programming or consistency between the school and home environments. Generally, students in this situation are those with severe, profound, or multiple disabilities (*Gladys J. v. Pearland Independent School District*, 1981). Residential placements may also be necessary for students with significant behavior disorders (*Chris D. v. Montgomery County Board of Education*, 1990) or those who require total immersion in an educational environment in order to progress (*Abrahamson v. Hershman*, 1983).

If a residential placement is required for purely educational reasons, the costs of such a placement must be fully borne by the school district. School districts cannot require parents to contribute toward the cost of a residential placement (*Parks v. Pavkovic*, 1985). However, if the placement is made for other than educational reasons, such as medical or social reasons, the school district is required to only pay for the educational component of the residential placement (*McKenzie v. Jefferson*, 1983). In these instances, the school district may enter into a cost-share agreement with other agencies. One caveat, however: One court held that the school district was responsible for all costs associated with a residential placement when the student's educational, medical, social, and emotional needs were so intimately intertwined that they could not be treated separately (*North v. District of Columbia Board of Education*, 1979).

Extended School Year Programs. If students with disabilities require an educational program that extends beyond the traditional school year, it must be provided. In several early decisions, federal appeals courts held that extended school year programs must be an available option and that a school district's refusal to consider such programs violated the IDEA (Osborne, 1996). An extended school year program is generally required when a student's regression and the time it takes to recoup lost skills interferes with overall progress toward the attainment of the goals and objectives of the student's IEP (*Armstrong v. Kline*, 1979). The regression the student suffers must be greater than the regression that normally occurs during a school vacation. If the regression is minimal, an extended school year program is not required (*Anderson v. Thompson*, 1981).

Related Services

Under the IDEA school districts must provide related, or supportive, services to students with disabilities if those services are needed to assist the students in benefitting from their special education programs (IDEA, § 1401, 22, 1997). The IDEA specifically lists developmental, supportive, or corrective services, such as transportation, speech–language pathology, audiology, psychological services, physical therapy, occupational therapy, recreation (including therapeutic recreation), social work services, counseling services (including rehabilitative counseling), medical services (for diagnostic or evaluative purposes only), and early identification and assessment as related services (IDEA, § 1401, 22, 1997).

The only limitation placed on what could be a related service is that medical services are exempted unless they are specifically for diagnostic or evaluative purposes. Thus, the list of related services is not exhaustive but could include other services that may be required to assist a student with disabilities to benefit from special education. For example, services such as artistic and cultural programs or art, music, and dance therapy could be related services. Related services may be provided by persons of varying professional backgrounds with a variety of occupational titles.

Although related services are often considered to be auxiliary services, their importance cannot be minimized. By their very definition, related services are provided to ensure that the student with disabilities benefits from his or her total special education program. Thus, related services can often be the critical element that determines whether or not the child will receive a free appropriate public education from a proposed IEP.

Related services must be provided only to students who are receiving special education services. Under the IDEA's definitions, a child is disabled only if the child requires special education *and* related services (emphasis added; IDEA § 1401, 3, A, ii, 1997). Because related services are required to be provided only when necessary for a child to benefit from special education, a school district is not required to provide related services when the child is not receiving special education (*Irving Independent School District v. Tatro*, 1984).

One of the most controversial topics under the rubric of related services involves the distinction between medical and school health services. In 1984, the U.S. Supreme Court held that a service, such as catheterization, that can be performed by a school nurse or trained layperson, is a required related service under the IDEA (*Irving Independent School District v. Tatro*, 1984). Obviously, any procedures that, by law, must be performed by a licensed physician would be exempted medical services. Thus, psychiatric therapy would not be a related service because a psychiatrist is a licensed physician. Many students with significant medical needs require round-the-clock nursing services. This type of service falls somewhere in the continuum between school health services and medical services. However, the U.S. Supreme Court recently held that full-time nursing services are a required related service, not an exempted medical service (*Cedar Rapids Community School District v. Garret F.*, 1999; Osborne, 1999).

Another potentially costly related service is the provision of assistive technology devices or services. In 1990, the IDEA was amended to add definitions of assistive technology devices and services. An *assistive technology device* is any item or piece of equipment that is used to increase, maintain, or improve the functional capabilities of individuals with disabilities (IDEA, § 1401, 1, 1997). These devices may include commercially available, modified, or customized equipment. An assistive technology service is designed to assist an individual in the selection, acquisition, or use of an assistive technology device (IDEA, § 1401, 2, 1997). It includes an evaluation of the individual's needs, provision of the assistive technology device, training in its use, coordination of other services with assistive technology, and maintenance and repair of the device. These services will be required when it is necessary for a child to receive an appropriate education under the *Rowley* standard. They also may allow many students with disabilities to benefit from education in less restrictive settings.

State law may govern whether a particular service is considered to be a related service or a special education service. For example, although speech–language service is a related service under the IDEA, in some states, it is a special education service. In those states, speech–language intervention could be provided as a stand-alone service.

Discipline

Probably the most controversial legal issue in special education concerns the imposition of disciplinary sanctions on students with disabilities. Although the IDEA makes no direct reference to discipline, many of its provisions have implications for the application of disciplinary sanctions on special education students. This is a very sensitive issue as it pits the duty of school administrators to maintain order, discipline, and a safe school environment against the rights of special education students to receive a free appropriate public education in the least restrictive environment. Although most will agree that the power of school officials to maintain discipline should not be frustrated, it must be understood that a student should not be denied the rights accorded by the IDEA if the student's misconduct is caused by the student's disability.

School officials may impose disciplinary sanctions on special education students as long as they follow procedures that do not deprive the students of their rights. School administrators may use normal disciplinary sanctions, including suspensions, with special education students by following usual procedures and providing customary due process (*Goss v. Lopez*, 1975). School administrators do face some restrictions when they intend to impose more drastic punishments, such as an expulsion, or wish to change the student's placement for disciplinary reasons. Basically, in these situations, the due process procedures in the IDEA replace the normal due process protections.

A long line of case law held that students with disabilities could not be expelled for misconduct that was related to the student's disability but could be expelled if there was no relationship between the misconduct and disability (Osborne, 1997). Although the U.S. Supreme Court has supported the prohibition of expelling students for disability related misconduct, it has stated that special education students may be suspended for up to 10 days (*Honig v. Doe*, 1988). During that cooling-off period, school personnel may attempt to negotiate an alternative placement with the student's parents. If they are unsuccessful, and can show that the student is truly dangerous, they may obtain a court injunction or administrative order allowing them to exclude the student from school (*Honig v. Doe*, 1988; IDEA, § 1415, k, 2, 1997). The IDEA requires school officials to conduct a functional behavioral assessment and take action to address the student's misconduct within 10 days of taking disciplinary action (IDEA, § 1415, k, 1, B, 1997).

The IDEA, as amended in 1997, allows school officials to transfer a student who is found in possession of a weapon or drugs to an alternative educational setting for a period of up to 45 days (IDEA, § 1415, k, 1, A, 1997). This may be done even over the objections of the student's parents.

The IDEA stipulates that school districts must continue to provide educational services to special education students who have been properly expelled for conduct unrelated to their disabilities (§ 1412, a, 1, A, 1997). This provision codified existing U.S. Department of Education policy stating that educational services must be provided in this situation (Osborne, 1997) and reversed a controversial decision of the Fourth Circuit Court of Appeals, which held that no such requirement existed under the IDEA (*Commonwealth of Virginia v. Riley*, 1997).

In reviewing a situation involving the discipline of a student with disabilities, courts must balance the right of the student to receive a free appropriate public education against the duty of school officials to maintain a safe and orderly environment for all students. The Eighth Circuit Court of Appeals had to do just that in *Light v. Parkway C-2 School District* (1994). The case involved a student who was prone to impulsive, unpredictable, and aggressive behavior that included biting, hitting, kicking, poking, throwing objects, and overturning furniture. In approving the student's removal from the current educational placement, the court stated that removal could occur when the school district was able to show that the student presented a danger and all reasonable efforts had been made to minimize the likelihood that the student would injure herself or others.

REMEDIES FOR A FAILURE TO PROVIDE APPROPRIATE SERVICES

Damages

Lawsuits for educational malpractice in special education have not been successful. In the past, the courts generally have not imposed punitive damages on school authorities for failing to provide a free appropriate public education. Similarly, general damages awards for pain and suffering have not been prevalent (Osborne, 1996). However, recent litigation indicates that this may be changing (*W.B. v. Matula*, 1995). In several recent lawsuits, courts have indicated that monetary damages may be available under other statutes, such as Section 504, if the parents can show that school officials intentionally discriminated against the student or egregiously disregarded the student's rights (*Whitehead v. School Board for Hillsborough County*, 1996; *Walker v. District of Columbia*, 1997). The operative word here is *intentional.* If school officials act in good faith, but their efforts fall short of the statutory requirements, generally they will be immune from damages.

Tuition Reimbursement

Sometimes parents, dissatisfied with the school district's educational placement, unilaterally enroll their disabled child in a private school and later seek to recover tuition expenses. The U.S. Supreme Court has held that parents are entitled to tuition reimbursement if they succeed in showing that the school district failed to offer an appropriate placement and that their chosen placement is appropriate (*Burlington School Committee v. Department of Education, Commonwealth of Massachusetts*, 1985). The Court reasoned that awarding reimbursement simply requires the school district to retroactively pay the costs it should have been paying all along. In a later decision, the Court held that parents are also entitled to tuition reimbursement, even if their chosen placement was not in a state approved facility, as long as it provided an otherwise appropriate education (*Florence County School District Four v. Carter*, 1993). However, when parents make unilateral placements, they do so at their own financial risk because they are not entitled to be reimbursed if the school district can show that it offered, and could provide, an appropriate educational placement.

Parents are also entitled to be reimbursed for unilaterally obtained related services if they can show that the school district failed to provide the needed services. For example, courts have frequently ordered school districts to reimburse parents for the costs of counseling or psychotherapy after the parents succeeded in showing that these services were necessary for the child to benefit from special education (*Gary A. v. New Trier High School District No. 203*, 1986; *Straube v. Florida Union Free School District*, 1992).

Compensatory Services

An award of tuition reimbursement is of little use to parents who are unable to make a unilateral placement in a private school because they cannot afford to pay the tuition costs up front. When parents cannot afford to take the financial risk of making a unilateral placement, their child may remain in an inappropriate placement for some time while the dispute winds its way through administrative due process hearings and judicial proceedings. In a situation such as this, the court may award additional educational services along with prospective relief to compensate the child for the loss of appropriate educational services. Compensatory services would be provided during a time period when the student would not normally receive services, such as during the summer months or after the student's eligibility for services has ended.

   In determining whether an award of compensatory educational services is justified, most courts have applied a rationale similar to that used in tuition reimbursement cases. These courts have ruled that compensatory services, like reimbursement, simply compensate the student for the school district's failure to provide an appropriate placement. The reasoning behind compensatory educational services awards is that an appropriate remedy should not be available only to those students whose parents could afford to provide them with an alternate educational placement while litigation was pending (*Lester H. v. Gilhool*, 1990; *Manchester School District v. Christopher B.*, 1992; *Todd D. v. Andrews*, 1991). Generally, compensatory services are provided for a time period equal to the time the student was denied services (*Valerie J. v. Derry Cooperative School District*, 1991). They may be granted even after the student has passed the ceiling age for eligibility under the IDEA (*Pihl v. Massachusetts Department of Education*, 1993). As is the case with tuition reimbursement, awards of compensatory educational services are granted only when it has been determined that the school district failed to provide an appropriate placement.

Attorney Fees

The costs of litigation can be very high, for parents as well as school districts. Many parents, after successfully bringing a lawsuit against the school district, believed that they should be reimbursed for their legal expenses. These parents felt that they achieved a hollow victory when they prevailed in their dispute with the school district but were left with burdensome legal bills.

In 1984, the U.S. Supreme Court held that recovery of legal expenses was not available under the IDEA (*Smith v. Robinson*, 1984); but 2 years later, Congress responded by amending the IDEA with the Handicapped Children's Protection Act (HCPA; 1986). The HCPA gave courts the power to grant an award of reasonable attorney fees to parents who prevailed against the school district in any action or proceeding brought pursuant to the IDEA. The award is to be based on the prevailing rates in the community in which the case arises. Under the HCPA, the courts may determine what is a reasonable amount of time to have spent preparing and arguing the case in terms of the issues litigated. The award may be limited if the school district made a settlement offer more than 10 days before the proceedings began that was equal to or more favorable than the final relief obtained. A court may reduce a fee award if it finds that the parents unreasonably protracted the dispute (*Howie v. Tippecanoe School Corporation*, 1990), the attorney's hourly rate was excessive (*Beard v. Teska*, 1994), or the time spent and legal services furnished were excessive in light of the issues litigated (*Hall v. Detroit Public Schools*, 1993).

ANTI-DISCRIMINATION LAWS

In addition to the IDEA, students with disabilities have rights under, and are protected by, two other significant pieces of federal legislation. The first, Section 504 of the Rehabilitation Act of 1973, provides that "a[n] otherwise qualified individual with a disability … shall, solely by reason of her or his disability, be excluded from participation in, be denied the benefits of, or be subjected to discrimination under any program or activity receiving Federal financial assistance" (Rehabilitation Act, § 794, 1973). The second law, the Americans with Disabilities Act (ADA), was passed in 1990 to provide a comprehensive national mandate for the elimination of discrimination against individuals with disabilities (ADA, § 12101, b, 2, 1990). It effectively extends the protections of Section 504 to the private sector but has implications for public entities, such as schools.

Although most students with disabilities are covered by the IDEA, Section 504, and the ADA, only the latter two statutes may protect some students. Inasmuch as a student must require special education services to fall under the auspices of the IDEA, a student with disabilities who does not need special education services would be protected only by Section 504 and the ADA. One court has held that Section 504 does not require affirmative efforts to overcome the student's disability but only prohibits discrimination on the basis of the disability (*Lyons v. Smith*, 1993).

Section 504 and the ADA both require school districts to provide reason-able accommodations to a student with disabilities. This may involve mod-est accommodations, such as allowing the student to be accompanied in school by a service dog (*Sullivan v. Vallejo City Unified School District*, 1990) or providing basic health services that would allow a medically fragile stu-dent to be present in the classroom (*Irving Independent School District v. Tatro*, 1984). Accommodations that are unduly costly, create an excessive monitoring burden, expose others to excessive risk, or fundamentally alter the nature of a program generally are not required (*Eva N. v. Brock*, 1990; *Kohl v. Woodhaven Learning Center*, 1989).

MANAGING THE LEGAL SYSTEM

Preventing Legal Disputes

Over the past 10 years, there has been an interest in a field known as *preven-tive law* (Bednar, 1989). The main purpose of preventive law is to prevent a legal dispute from arising. If one inevitably does arise, a secondary pur-pose of preventive law is to put the school district in a favorable position. Preventive school law seeks to find permanent solutions to the situations that give rise to conflicts between parents and school districts.

A careful analysis of the thousands of lawsuits that have arisen since the passage of the IDEA would show that many could have been avoided. In many situations, the disputes arose as a result of poor communication be-tween school personnel and the parents. However, many of the cases, par-ticularly those in which the school district has been the losing party, could have been prevented if school officials and special education practitioners had simply had more knowledge of special education law.

Thus, a first step in preventing legal disputes is to provide those who are involved in the special education process with ongoing training around the legal issues in special education. The training must be ongoing because the law is constantly evolving. A second, but equally important step, is to de-velop and implement appropriate and legally correct policies and proce-dures. These policies and procedures must be implemented consistently; staff training is essential to assure that this occurs.

Mediation

In spite of a school district's best efforts, legal conflicts arise. Mediation is an excellent means of resolving those conflicts in an a nonadversarial man-ner. The IDEA mandates that states establish procedures to allow parties to resolve disputes via a mediation process (IDEA, § 1415, e, 1997). Mediation is voluntary on the part of those involved in the dispute and cannot be used to delay or deny an administrative due-process hearing.

The most important benefit of mediation is that it can help to salvage the relationship between the parent and school officials because the process is basically nonadversarial. However, for mediation to be successful, each party must be willing to compromise. School officials must be willing to listen to any reasonable proposals advanced by the parents and should be prepared to make counterproposals.

Administrative Due Process Hearings

Under the IDEA, states are required to establish a mechanism for an impartial due process hearing for the resolution of disputes between the parents and the school district (IDEA, § 1415, f, 1997). States are free to establish either a one or two-tiered system of administrative due process hearings. In a one-tiered system, the hearing is provided by the state. In a two-tiered system, the initial hearing is provided at the local level with provision for an appeal at the state level. A hearing may be held for any matter related to the provision of a free appropriate public education.

Court Action

The IDEA gives the losing party in an administrative hearing the right to bring a civil action in any federal or state court of competent jurisdiction (IDEA, § 1415, i, 2, 1997). The courts are empowered to grant whatever relief they determine is appropriate. When a dispute reaches the court level, the court will receive and review the administrative record; however, the parties are entitled to present additional evidence. The courts have placed some limitation on what additional evidence is acceptable. Generally, courts will not hear evidence that could have been introduced at the administrative level, but was not; new evidence, or evidence that was not available previously, will be admitted.

Which party bears the burden of proof varies according to jurisdiction and the particular circumstances of the case (Osborne, 1996). A full analysis of those circumstances is beyond the scope of this chapter. However, in many situations, the burden may be on the school district to prove, by a preponderance of the evidence, that its proposed IEP is appropriate.

● ● ● ● ● ●

Federal laws guaranteeing students with disabilities a free appropriate public education and prohibiting discrimination on the basis of the disability have provided these students with unprecedented access to the public schools. Implementing these laws has not been without controversy, however. As a result of disputes between parents and school district officials, thousands of lawsuits have been filed in the past 20 years, making this one of the most explosive areas of school law.

Litigation is costly, not only in terms of dollars but in the expenditure of human capital as well. It is far better to devote available resources to the education of children than to litigation. School officials who understand the law are in a much better position to make legally correct decisions and thus avoid costly litigation. In this respect, there is no substitute for adequate legal and procedural training of those involved in the special education process. In the long run, the cost of this training will result in much greater savings.

REFERENCES

Abney v. District of Columbia, 849 F.2d 1491, 47 Educ. L. Rep., 460 (D.C. Cir. 1988).

Abrahamson v. Hershman, 701 F.2d F.2d F.2d 223, 9 Educ. L. Rep., 837 (1st Cir. 1983).

Americans With Disabilities Act, 42 U.S.C. § 12101 *et seq.* (1990).

Anderson v. Thompson, 658 F.2d 1205 (7th Cir. 1981).

Armstrong v. Kline, 476 F. Supp. 583 (E.D. Pa. 1979), *rem'd. sub nom.* Battle v. Commonwealth of Pennsylvania, 629 F.2d 269 (3d Cir. 1980), *on rem'd.* 513 F. Supp. 425 (E.D. Pa. 1981).

Assistance to the States for the Education of Children With Disabilities (1999), codified at 34 C.F.R. § 300 *et seq.,* originally published in the *Federal Register,* March 12, 1999.

Beard v. Teska, 31 F.3d 942, 93 Educ. L. Rep., 530 (10th Cir. 1994).

Bednar, W.C. (1989). Preventive school law. In W. E. Camp, J. K. Underwood, & M. J. Connelly (Eds.), *Current Issues in School Law* (pp. 281-284). Topeka, KS: National Organization on Legal Problems of Education.

Board of Education of East Windsor Regional School District v. Diamond, 808 F.2d 987, 36 Educ. L. Rep., 1136 (3d Cir. 1986).

Board of Education of the Hendrick Hudson Central School District v. Rowley, 458 U.S. 176, 102 S. Ct. 3034, 73 L. Ed. 2d 690, 5 Educ. L. Rep., 34 (1982).

Bonadonna v. Cooperman, 619 F. Supp. 401, 28 Educ. L. Rep., 430 (D.N.J. 1985).

Burlington School Committee v. Department of Education, Commonwealth of Massachusetts, 471 U.S. 359, 105 S. Ct. 1996, 85 L. Ed. 2d 385, 23 Educ. L. Rep., 1189 (1985).

Capistrano Unified School District v. Wartenberg, 59 F.3d 884, 101 Educ. L. Rep., 640 (9th Cir. 1995).

Carter v. Florence County School District Four, 950 F.2d 156, 71 Educ. L. Rep., 633 (4th Cir. 1991), *aff'd. on other grounds sub nom.* Florence County School District Four v. Carter, 510 U.S. 7, 114 S. Ct. 361, 126 L. Ed. 2d 284, 86 Educ. L. Rep., 41 (1993).

Cedar Rapids Community School District v. Garret F., ___ U.S. ___, 119 S. Ct. 992, 143 L. Ed.2d 154, 132 Educ. L. Rep., 40 (1999).

Chris C. v. Gwinnett County School District, 780 F. Supp. 804, 72 Educ. L. Rep., 146 (N.D. Ga. 1991).

Chris D. v. Montgomery County Board of Education, 743 F. Supp. 1524, 62 Educ. L. Rep., 1001 (M.D. Ala. 1990).

Clyde K. v. Puyallup School District No. 3, 35 F.3d 1396, 94 Educ. L. Rep., 707 (9th Cir. 1994).

Colin K. v. Schmidt, 715 F.2d 1, 13 Educ. L. Rep., 221 (1st Cir. 1983).

Commonwealth of Virginia v. Riley, 106 F.3d 559, 116 Educ. L. Rep., 40 (4th Cir. 1997).

David D. v. Dartmouth School Committee, 775 F.2d 411, 28 Educ. L. Rep., 70 (1st Cir. 1985).

DeLeon v. Susquehanna Community School District, 747 F.2d 149, 21 Educ. L. Rep., 24 (3d Cir. 1984).

Education for All Handicapped Children Act, 20 U.S.C. ' 1400 *et seq.* (1975).

Eva N. v. Brock, 741 F. Supp. 626, 62 Educ. L. Rep., 112 (E.D. Ky. 1990).

Florence County School District Four v. Carter, 510 U.S. 7, 114 S. Ct. 361, 126 L. Ed. 2d 284, 86 Educ. L. Rep., 41 (1993).

Gary A. v. New Trier High School District No. 203, 796 F.2d 940, 33 Educ. L. Rep., 1052 (7th Cir. 1986).

G.D. v. Westmoreland School District, 930 F.2d 942, 67 Educ. L. Rep., 103 (1st Cir. 1991).

Gladys J. v. Pearland Independent School District, 520 F. Supp. 869 (S.D. Tex. 1981).

Goss v. Lopez, 419 U.S. 565, 95 S. Ct. 729, 42 L. Ed. 2d 725 (1975).

Hall v. Vance County Board of Education, 774 F.2d 629, 27 Educ. L. Rep., 1107 (4th Cir. 1985).

Hall v. Detroit Public Schools, 823 F. Supp. 1377, 84 Educ. L. Rep., 205 (E.D. Mich. 1993).

Handicapped Children's Protection Act, 20 U.S.C. ' 1415(*i*)(3) (1986).

Honig v. Doe, 484 U.S. 305, 108 S. Ct. 592, 98 L. Ed. 2d 686, 43 Educ. L. Rep., 857 (1988).

Howie v. Tippecanoe School Corporation, F. Supp. 1485, 60 Educ. L. Rep., 457 (N.D. Ind. 1990).

Individuals with Disabilities Education Act, 20 U.S.C. § 1400 *et seq.* (1997).

Irving Independent School District v. Tatro, 468 U.S. 883, 104 S. Ct. 3371, 82 L. Ed. 2d 664, 18 Educ. L. Rep., 138 (1984).

J.S.K. v. Hendry County School Board, 941 F.2d 1563, 69 Educ. L. Rep., 689 (11th Cir. 1991).

Kohl v. Woodhaven Learning Center, 865 F.2d 930, 51 Educ. L. Rep., 383 (8th Cir. 1989).

Lester H. v. Gilhool, 916 F.2d 865, 63 Educ. L. Rep., 458 (3d Cir. 1990).

Light v. Parkway C-2 School District, 41 F.3d 1223, 96 Educ. L. Rep., 98 (8th Cir. 1994).

Lyons v. Smith, 829 F. Supp. 414, 85 Educ. L. Rep., 803 (D.D.C. 1993).

Manchester School District v. Christopher B., 807 F. Supp. 860, 79 Educ. L. Rep., 865 (D.N.H. 1992).

McKenzie v. Jefferson, EHLR 554:338 (D.D.C. 1983).

North v. District of Columbia Board of Education, 471 F. Supp. 136 (D.D.C. 1979).

Oberti v. Board of Education of the Borough of Clementon School District, 995 F.2d 1204, 83 Educ. L. Rep., 1009 (3d Cir. 1993).

Osborne, A. G. (1996). *Legal issues in special education.* Needham Heights, MA: Allyn & Bacon.

Osborne, A. G. (1997). *Disciplinary options for students with disabilities.* Dayton, OH: Education Law Association.

Osborne, A. G. (1999). Supreme court rules that schools must provide full-time nursing services for medically fragile students. *Education Law Reporter, 136,* 1–14.

Osborne, A. G., & DiMattia, P. (1994). The IDEA's least restrictive environment mandate: legal implications. *Exceptional Children, 61,* 6–14.

Parks v. Pavkovic, 753 F.2d 1397, 22 Educ. L. Rep., 1128 (7th Cir.1985).

Pihl v. Massachusetts Department of Education, 9 F.3d 184, 87 Educ. L. Rep., 341 (1st Cir. 1993)

Polk v. Susquehanna Intermediate Unit 16, 853 F.2d 171, 48 Educ. L. Rep., 336 (3d Cir. 1988).

Rehabilitation Act, Section 504, 29 U.S.C. § 794 (1973).

Sacramento City Unified School District Board of Education v. Rachel H., 14 F.3d 1398, 89 Educ. L. Rep., 57 (9th Cir. 1994).

Smith v. Robinson, 468 U.S. 992, 104 S. Ct. 3457, 82 L. Ed. 2d 746, 18 Educ. L. Rep., 148 (1984).

Straube v. Florida Union Free School District, 801 F. Supp. 1164, 78 Educ. L. Rep., 390 (S.D.N.Y. 1992).

Sullivan v. Vallejo City Unified School District, 731 F. Supp. 947, 59 Educ. L. Rep., 73 (E.D. Cal. 1990).

Todd D. v. Andrews, 933 F.2d 1576, 67 Educ. L. Rep., 1065 (11th Cir. 1991).

Valerie J. v. Derry Cooperative School District, 771 F. Supp. 483, 69 Educ. L. Rep., 1067 (D.N.H. 1991)

Walker v. District of Columbia, 969 F. Supp. 794, 120 Educ. L. Rep., 447 (D.D.C. 1997).

W.B. v. Matula, 67 F.3d 484, 104 Educ. L. Rep., 28 (3d Cir. 1995).

Whitehead v. School Board for Hillsborough County, 918 F. Supp. 1515, 108 Educ. L. Rep., 239 (M.D. Fla. 1996).

Legal Issues in Serving Postsecondary Students With Disabilities

Dolores E. Battle
Buffalo State College

The increases in the number of students with learning disabilities on college and university campuses present challenges for faculty and staff. Although most faculty are able to understand that they need to make special accommodations and academic adjustments for students with "visible" disabilities, such as blindness and motor difficulties, they commonly question whether the accommodations given to students with learning disabilities give these students an unfair advantage over students with no disability. Moreover, faculty are being challenged to alter the ways they instruct, advise, and counsel students. Because of these challenges, faculty and staff must understand the nature of learning disabilities and the type of appropriate accommodations and academic adjustments necessary to provide students access to the academic and nonacademic programs and services of the institution.

Given federal legal requirements, colleges and universities are required to review their policies and philosophies as they strive to make postsecondary education available to all students. These include admission policies to both the institution and to programs within the university, provision of reasonable accommodations and academic adjustments in both course delivery and course evaluation, and the need to provide access to nonacademic programs and services. Because of the newness of these laws, their impact on postsecondary institutions is being defined and clarified by the legal system on an ongoing basis. This chapter addresses the emerging issues relative to students with disabilities in postsecondary institutions. Special emphasis is given to (a) those laws that have an impact on students with learning disabilities, (b) important comparisons among provisions of these laws, (c) definitions of disability in the pertinent laws, (d) accommodations and academic course adjustments, and (e) effective instruction for college and university students with disabilities.

LAWS IMPACTING ON HIGHER EDUCATION

Overview

In 1964, the Civil Rights Law was passed by the federal government to prohibit discrimination in employment on the basis of race, color, sex, religion and national origin. The law did not provide persons with disabilities with specific protection as had been granted to other groups. In response to this void, Congress passed three statutes to provide protection from discrimination to persons with disabilities—the Rehabilitation Act (1973), the Education For All of the Handicapped Children Act of 1975 and its amendments (amended as the Individuals with Disabilities Education Act [IDEA; 1997]), and the Americans with Disabilities Act (ADA; 1990). IDEA had the effect of increasing the number of students with disabilities who complete elementary and secondary education with the knowledge and skill necessary for postsecondary education. Together, these laws have resulted in significant increases in the number of persons with disabilities seeking postsecondary education.

In 1978, slightly less than 3% of first-year college students reported having a disability. By 1998, the percentage had more than tripled to 9.4% or more than 140,000 first-year college students. This means that nearly one in every 10 full-time first-year students in colleges and universities reports having at least one disability (HEATH Resource Center, 1999). In a survey of college students with disabilities conducted in 1998 (as shown in Table 14.1), students identified themselves as having disabilities in the following categories: learning disabilities, health-related impairment, vision impairment, hearing impairment, orthopedic impairment, speech impairment, and other impairments. Not included as separate categories are emotional and psychological impairments, which may be represented in the category of *other*.

Although increases occurred in all areas of disabilities, the most significant increase pertained to students with learning disabilities, the largest single group of students with disabilities. Table 14.1 shows that the percentage of college freshmen reporting a learning disability increased between 1988 and 1998 from 1.2% to 3.5%. This increase represents nearly 41% of all disabilities reported by college freshmen, an increase from 15.7% reported in 1988 (HEATH Resource Center, 1999; Henderson, 1999).

TABLE 14.1

Percentage of Full-Time College Freshmen Reporting Disabilities, Selected Years (1988–1998)

Disability	1988	1991	1994	1996	1998
Speech	.3%	.5%	.3%	.3%	.5%
Orthopedic	1.0%	1.2%	.9%	.9%	.8%
Learning Disability	1.2%	2.2%	3.0%	3.1%	3.5%
Health-Related	1.2%	1.3%	1.5%	1.6%	1.7%
Partially sighted/blind	1.9%	2.2%	2.0%	2.0%	1.1%
Hearing	.8%	.9%	.9%	.9%	.9%
Other	1.4%	1.6%	1.7%	1.8%	1.9%
TOTAL	7.0%	8.8%	9.2%	9.2%	9.4%

Sources: HEATH Resource Center (1999), American Council on Education. Based on unpublished data from the Cooperative Institutional Research Program, UCLA, selected years; College Freshmen with Disabilities: A Biennial Statistical Profile. American Council of Education, Washington, DC. (1999, p. 3).

Individuals with Disabilities Education Act (1990)

With the passing of the Rehabilitation Act of 1973, interest emerged to provide assurance that children with disabilities would be provided an equal opportunity to receive an education. The Education for All Handicapped Children Act became law in 1975 (P.L. 94–142). It was amended and renamed the Individuals with Disabilities Education Act (IDEA, 1990; PL 101–476). The purpose of IDEA is to ensure access to education for individuals with disabilities from birth through age 21 years (for further discussion, see Osborne, chap. 13, this volume). The law provides equal protection and equal access to education for person with disabilities in preschool, elementary, and secondary education programs. It does not extend to persons in colleges and universities.

IDEA guaranteed a free and appropriate public education to students with disabilities. As a result, the number of students with disabilities completing secondary school has increased dramatically with subsequent increases in the number of students with disabilities enrolling in 2- and 4-year postsecondary education institutions (Leyser, Vogel, Wyland & Bruille, 1998).

The Rehabilitation Act of 1973

The Rehabilitation Act of 1973 emerged from the civil rights legislation of 1964. It is often regarded as the first national "civil rights" legislation for persons with disabilities. Like the Civil Rights Act of 1964, the intent of the law was to ensure that individuals with a disability would have equal employment opportunity. The law prohibits discrimination against otherwise qualified individuals on the basis of a disability and applies only to public and private recipients of federal aid. However, because most public and private colleges are the recipients of federal assistance, even if only in the form of student financial aid, the statute applies to all postsecondary institutions.

Included in the various sections of the act are provisions that call for nondiscrimination in institutions receiving federal financial assistance. Section 503 and Section 504 are of direct importance to postsecondary education institutions. Section 503 mandates nondiscrimination on the basis of disability in institutions and entities that receive federal financial assistance. Section 504 is a nondiscrimination and program access statute. It requires that "no otherwise qualified person with a disability be denied access to, or the benefits of, or be subjected to discrimination by any program or activity provided by an institution or entity receiving federal financial assistance" (29 U. S. C. § 794, a).

Subpart E of Section 504 deals specifically with postsecondary institutions. It requires that institutions make appropriate academic adjustments and reasonable modifications to policies and practices to ensure that persons with disabilities have access to all academic and nonacademic programs and services offered by the institution.

Of significance in this definition is the notion of "no otherwise qualified person." It becomes the institution's responsibility to describe the essential qualifications of a position and to justify any qualification that may have a discriminatory effect. Under the law, public agencies, including colleges and universities receiving federal assistance, may not "exclude an otherwise qualified student from any part of its program or services, or otherwise discriminate against an applicant or a student with a disability" (Tucker, 1996, p. 3).

The Americans with Disabilities Act

In 1990, Congress held hearings to determine the extent to which discrimination continued against persons with disabilities in spite of the Rehabilitation Act of 1973. It concluded that discrimination against persons with disabilities continued to be pervasive in such critical areas as employment, public accommodations, public services, transportation, and telecommunications. Congress also found that discrimination against persons with disabilities denied them the opportunity to compete on an equal basis with others, causing the public unnecessary expenses resulting from dependency and nonproductivity. As a result, Congress passed the Americans With Disabilities Act (ADA) in 1990.

The Rehabilitation Act of 1973 and the ADA are similar with respect to higher education. Generally, a postsecondary institution governed by Section 504 of the Rehabilitation Act or the ADA may not exclude an otherwise qualified student from any part of its programs and services, or otherwise discriminate against an applicant or student with a disability. Both laws refer to "qualified handicapped students." Both laws require that institutions covered by Section 504 or the ADA provide students with disabilities reasonable accommodations or academic adjustments where required to meet the nondiscrimination mandate and ensure that students with disabilities are informed about how to access appropriate services.

The ADA (1990) extends the policies of the Rehabilitation Act (1973) to prohibit public entities, (e.g., state governments, public schools, and public colleges) from denying qualified individuals with disabilities the right to participate in or benefit from the services, programs, or activities they provide, and from subjecting such individuals to discrimination solely on the basis of their disability (42 U. S. C. § 12102). The five titles of the ADA prohibit discrimination in employment, public services, public accommodations, and services operated by private entities, telecommunications, and others, such as insurance carriers. Of particular interest are Title II and Title III. Title II covers "public entities," including any state or local government and any of its departments, agencies or other instrumentalities, whether or not they receive federal funds. Title III covers the accessibility of all programs, goods, and services by both public and private entities that provide public accommodation. Because private colleges operate places of public accommodation, they must also comply with the provisions of the ADA.

Although postsecondary institutions had been subject to nondiscrimination statutes since 1973, the full impact of the laws did not reach postsecondary institutions until the passage of the ADA in 1990. By 1990, a full generation of children educated under IDEA was ready for college.

SOME CRITICAL COMPARISONS

IDEA Versus ADA and Section 504

As mentioned earlier, once students reach postsecondary education, the IDEA does not apply. IDEA applies to children ages 0 to 21 years who have not completed secondary school. The ADA and Section 504 become the legal entities assuring nondiscrimination for students in postsecondary education. Identifying the needs of postsecondary students with learning disabilities is a significant challenge. This is partly due to several of the differences among IDEA, the ADA, and Section 504.

Students in elementary and secondary education are identified as having a disability through an established process whereby the institution takes responsibility for identification, assessment, diagnosis of the disability, and developing the individualized educational programs. All costs are provided by the local educational agency with federal and state assistance. Parents fully participate in decision making involving the educational program of their child (see Osborne, chap. 13, this volume, for discussion). Under the ADA, students have the responsibility to disclose to the institution or to the properly designated person within the institution that they have a disability, which requires accommodations and academic adjustments.

Confidentiality.   One major difference between secondary and postsecondary policies for students with disabilities involves confidentiality. In developing Section 504, Congress did not specifically detail rules related to the confidentiality of disability related information. However, information regarding disability gained from medical examinations or other postadmission information is considered confidential and should be shared with others in the institution on a need-to-know basis only. Disability related information is treated as medical information and is not subject to the Family Educational Rights and Privacy Act (FERPA; 1974), also known as the Buckley amendment. Faculty members do not have the right or need to access diagnostic information regarding the student's disability. They only need to know what accommodations are necessary to meet the students needs and then only with the permission of the student.

Parents are also excluded from a role in disclosure and decision making because of FERPA. The amendment gives students access to their records, but it also prohibits disclosure of those records and information to parents or other persons not specifically authorized by the student and those without a specific educational need to know. Whereas parents were involved as shared decision makers in the education of their children in elementary and secondary education, they are excluded from that participation when the young adult enters college or university. This transition is often difficult for students unless they are prepared in advance to understand their responsibility and the skills necessary for advocating their own educational needs.

Costs of Identifying Educational Needs.   A second difference between elementary–secondary education for students with disabilities and education in postsecondary education is the cost for identification of disability. In elementary and secondary education, the cost of identification and evaluation to determine educational needs of a student with a disability is at the expense of the local educational agency with federal and state support. In postsecondary education, the cost for identification becomes the responsibility of the student. This often presents problems for those students who do not have sufficient financial resources or insurance coverage to bear the cost of assessment and documentation.

ADA Versus Section 504

As applied to higher education, the ADA and Section 504 have few differences. Both prohibit postsecondary institutions from discriminating on the basis of disability. One difference between the two laws relates to notice and analogous procedural requirements. Under Section 504, the institution must post notices that it does not discriminate with respect to admission, or access to, or treatment of employment in its programs or activities and must fully identify its Section 504 coordinator (Tucker & Goldstein, 1991). The ADA Title II requires the institution to post notices stating that the ADA applies to its programs, services, and activities. Under both entities, institutions must post their procedures for filing complaints.

The ADA Title II has a more expansive definition of "auxiliary aids and services" to make aurally and visually delivered information available to persons with hearing, speech, and vision impairments. The services include, but are not limited to, qualified interpreters, assistive listening devices, videotext displays, and telecommunication devices for the deaf (TDDs). Public institutions are not required to use the newest or most advanced technology as long as the auxiliary aid that is selected affords effective communication.

In addition, Title II imposes an additional requirement that public entities give primary consideration to the requests of individuals with disabilities in determining what auxiliary aid and other service is necessary (28 CFR § 35.160, b, 92). A public entity must honor the request unless the entity can demonstrate that another effective means of communication exists, or that the use of the means chosen would impose an undue financial burden on the institution (Kincaid, 1994).

Finally, public entities must have available TDDs, or equally effective communication systems, for communicating by telephone with applicants or students. Institutions that operate telephone emergency services must provide access to individuals who use TDDs and computer modems. They must place signs at all entrances to each of its facilities, directing users to an accessible entrance or to a location where information about accessible facilities can be obtained.

WHO IS DISABLED UNDER SECTION 504 AND THE ADA?

Under IDEA, persons with disabilities are defined by specific categorical definitions, such as mental retardation, visual impairment, learning disability, hearing impairment, speech impairment, or other health impairment. The ADA and the Rehabilitation Act do not provide specific disorder or disability diagnoses to satisfy the eligibility for protection under the acts. Instead, the definition of who has a disability is defined by the ability to perform daily life functions.

Under the Rehabilitation Act of 1973, a person with a disability is one who "has a physical or mental impairment which substantially limits one or more major life functions; has a record of such an impairment; or is regarded as having such impairment" (29 U.S. C. Section 706, 8, B). The ADA provides comprehensive civil rights protections for "qualified individuals with disabilities." According to the ADA, an individual with a disability is an *otherwise qualified* individual who has *a physical or mental impairment* that *substantially limits* one or more of the *major life activities,* has a record of such impairment, or is regarded as having such an impairment (42 U. S. C. A. § 12102, 2; note the similarity of this definition to Section 504). An individual with a disability is one who, with or without reasonable accommodations, can perform the essential functions of the employment position that this individual holds or desires.

With respect to postsecondary education, a qualified person with a disability is one who meets the admission, academic, and technical standards of the program with or without accommodation. However, the laws require that institutions make *reasonable accommodations* to allow persons with disabilities access to the academic and nonacademic programs and services offered by the institution.

It should be noted that the definitions of the central components in the definition have become controversial as the courts have been called in to help define the scope of the law. In order to be protected under the ADA, students must meet all four components of the definition: (1) otherwise qualified, (2) impairment, (3) substantially limits, and (4) major life activity. It is also necessary to understand a fifth component, reasonable accommodation. Each of these components is now discussed.

Otherwise Qualified

Only Section 504 uses the term *otherwise qualified* (29 U. S. C § 794, a). The ADA specifies only that the persons with a disability be "qualified" (42 U. S. C. § 12112). The terms both mean that the individual must meet the eligibility requirements of the program, with or without reasonable accommodations, in spite of the limitations imposed by the disability.

In a case heard by the United States Supreme Court (*Southeastern Community College v. Davis,* 1979), college officials determined that a student with hearing impairment was not qualified for admission to the program in nursing because of her dependence on lip reading. The institution said that she did not meet the standards for admission and that there were no reasonable accommodations that they could make to permit her to receive the benefit of the program. In deciding for the institution, the courts ruled that the applicant was not otherwise qualified for the program. The ruling stated that permitting the student to enroll in the program with the assistance of a full time supervisor for her clinical training would result in a substantial lowering of its standards and a subsequent alteration in the fundamental standards of its program. In 1985, the Court provided additional, yet inconclusive, direction on the qualified individual issue. It said that reasonable accommodations would allow persons with a disability to have meaningful access to a program but would not require "substantial" changes, adjustments, or modifications to an existing program (*Alexander v. Choate*, 1985).

Thus, essential eligibility requirements depend on the type of service or activity involved. For some activities, such as licensing programs, the ability to meet specific skill and performance requirements may be "essential." For other activities, such as where the public entity provides information to anyone who requests it, the "essential eligibility requirements" may be minimal.

Impairment

A *physical or mental impairment* is defined as any physiological disorder or condition, cosmetic configuration, or anatomical loss affecting one or more of the bodily systems. These include neurological, musculoskeletal, special sense organs, respiratory (including speech organs), cardiovascular, reproductive, digestive, genito–urinary, hemic and lymphatic, skin, and endocrine systems. A second component refers to any mental or psychological disorder, such as mental retardation, organic brain syndrome, emotional illness, and specific learning disabilities. Examples of physical of mental impairments include, but are not limited to, such contagious and noncontagious diseases and conditions as orthopedic, visual, speech, and hearing impairments, as well as cerebral palsy, epilepsy, muscular dystrophy, multiple sclerosis, cancer, heart disease, diabetes, mental retardation, emotional illness, specific learning disabilities, HIV disease (whether symptomatic or asymptomatic), tuberculosis, drug addiction, and alcoholism. Homosexuality and bisexuality are not physical or mental impairments under the ADA. This list is not meant to be all inclusive, but rather is given as exemplars of the types of disorders or conditions that may result in an impairment.

The regulations promulgated by the ADA and Section 504 specifically include a learning disability as a covered physical or mental impairment. The ability to learn is held to constitute a major life activity. However, neither the ADA nor Section 504 define the term, *learning disability*. In the absence of a definition of learning disability in ADA or Section 504, the courts rely on the definition stated in the IDEA. IDEA defines a *specific learning disability* as "a disorder in one or more of the basic psychological processes involved in understanding or in using language, spoken or written, which disorder may manifest itself in imperfect ability to listen, think, read, write, spell, or do mathematical calculations" (20 U. S. C. A. § 1401, a, 15; West Supp., 1991).

Substantially Limits

Substantial limitation means that the person is unable to perform a major life activity or is *significantly* restricted in the performance of a major life activity as compared to the condition, manner, or duration under which the average person in the general population can perform the same major life activity. The issue of how significant a disability must be to be eligible for protection has become an issue in itself. As found in case law, at least four options exist in defining "substantial"—(a) in comparison to most people in the general population, (b) in comparison to the average person having comparable skills and training, (c) in comparison to the average student without an impairment, and (d) in consideration of a disparity between inherent capacity and performance. Five case law examples are now presented.

In *Price v. National Board of Medical Examiners* (1997), three medical students with attention deficit disorder failed to qualify as students with a disability because their individual skills exceeded those of the general population and the students had been able to achieve their status as medical students without prior supports or identification as students with disabilities. The medical students were denied the right to special accommodation in taking the medical examination because the judge ruled that they were able to perform at a higher level than the general population without accommodation as witnessed by their lack of need for accommodations throughout postsecondary education and medical school.

In *Bartlett v. New York State Board of Law Examiners* (1997), a bar applicant with a learning disability alleged that the Board of Law Examiners violated the ADA and Section 504 by denying her requests for accommodations on a state bar examination. In the ruling by the court, Bartlett was considered to have a disability because she required significant accommodations in order to perform the major life activity of work in the profession for which she had studied. The judge viewed her to be substantially limited in relation to other law students with similar education and training who were taking the bar examination. In the *Bartlett* case, the substantial limitation was compared to those with equal training for the career of her choice; in the *Price* case, the substantial limitation was defined in terms of the general public.

In *Gonzales v. National Board of Medical Examiners* (1999), the student did not provide documentation that his learning disabilities substantially impaired the major life function of reading and learning. Gonzales had petitioned for extra time from the Board of Medical Examinations. The Board refused his documentation that he had a learning disability, stating that he had done well in high school and in college without receiving accommodations. The courts thus ruled that he did not have a learning disability because he had self-accommodated to his disability. This case has ramifications for deciding whether a person who uses accommodations, such as a computer, and thus obtains good grades, can be considered to have a disability. This case will likely be heard by the United States Supreme Court.

Interestingly, in another case, *Pazer v. New York State Board of Law Examiners* (1994), the courts proposed that, in some instances, the disparity between inherent capacity and performance permits the inference that a person has a learning disability, even though an individual's performance may meet or exceed that of the ordinary person. However, the court did recognize that each case had to be decided on its own merit and that every low achiever would not necessarily qualify as disabled. In the *Bartlett* case, the substantial limitation was compared to those with equal training for the career of her choice; in the *Price* case, the substantial limitation was defined in terms of the general public. In *Pazer v. New York Board of Law Examiners* (1994), the courts proposed that, in some instances, the disparity between inherent capacity and performance permits the inference that a person has a learning disability.

The courts have continued to deal with cases that attempt to define the "substantially limits" section of the definition. In another case, *Bowers v. NCAA* (1998), a special education student was declared to be ineligible to play football because of his academic performance. Bower claimed that he had a disability and therefore his special education courses should be used to determine his eligibility to play NCAA football rather than regular education core courses. The NCAA agreed that it would change its eligibility requirements for student athletes with learning disabilities. Given these conflicting and inconsistent interpretations of the threshold of "substantially limits" by the lower courts, the issue may eventually be decided by the higher courts so that the definition of persons with a disability can be consistently applied.

Major Life Activity

The definition of *major life activity* under Section 504 was clarified in *Alexander v. Choate* (1985). A major life activity or function was defined as "caring for one's self, performing manual tasks, walking, seeing, hearing, speaking, breathing, learning, and working."

These functions are not exhaustive and have been interpreted by the United States Supreme Court as examples. To illustrate, in a recent case, *Abbott v. Bragdon* (1997), a person with asymptotic HIV was declared to be disabled because he was substantially limited in the major life function of procreation.

Reasonable Accommodation

Under Section 504 and the ADA, a reasonable accommodation is any modification or adjustment to a job or work environment that will enable a qualified person with a disability to perform essential job functions. In higher education, it is any modification or adjustment in the academic or nonacademic programs or services that will allow the person with a disability access to the program. An accommodation is reasonable if it will enable a person with a disability to perform the required functions without undue financial or administrative burden on the institution.

Section 504 regulations suggest three types of accommodations that may be made to assist a student with a disability in obtaining a postsecondary education: (a) academic adjustments, (b) modifications or alterations of course requirements, and (c) the provision of auxiliary aids (Tucker & Goldstein, 1991). Under the ADA, reasonable accommodations may include a number of different vehicles. These include: (a) making existing facilities used by employees or students readily accessible and usable by individuals with disabilities; (b) restructuring or modifying work schedules; (c) the acquisition or modification of equipment or devices; (d) appropriate adjustment or modifications of examinations, training materials, or policies; (e) the provision of qualified readers or interpreters; and (f) other similar accommodation for persons with disabilities. Accommodations do not require the elimination of essential job functions, the creation of new positions, or the lowering of performance standards.

Undue Hardship. In determining whether an accommodation would impose an undue hardship on an institution, several factors must be considered. These include the nature and cost of the accommodation, the overall financial resources of the institution or the facilities involved in the provision of the reasonable accommodation, and the effect of the expenses on the operation of the facility. Typical accommodations that are considered non- or low-cost accommodations are:

- Providing physical access to individuals who use wheelchairs or who have motor disabilities by providing ramps, handrails, widening doorways, and rearranging shelves and furniture that would otherwise block access;
- raising, lowering, or adapting equipment to heights or positions required by persons with disabilities;

- voice-activated tape recorders and computer software, books on tape, text enlargers, text readers, and other technological equipment that provides access to print materials for persons with disabilities.

Reasonable Accommodations in Higher Education. Claims against post-secondary institutions most commonly arise in three areas: those involving admission, those involving access to nonacademic programs and services, and those involving the provision of reasonable accommodations for students with disabilities (Tucker & Goldstein, 1991). Providing reasonable accommodations for students with disabilities without compromising the integrity or content of an academic program offers challenges for postsecondary institutions. To be considered reasonable, an accommodation must not result in a (a) fundamental alteration in an essential component of the program, (b) threat to the health or safety of others, (c) substantial change in the manner in which education or instructional services are provided. Also, the accommodation may not cause undue financial burden or hardship to the institution (Jarrow, 1997).

Section 504 regulations combined with agreement from the United States Department of Education indicate that three types of accommodations may be made to ensure that a student with a disability receives a postsecondary education. These include academic adjustments, modifications or alteration of course examinations, and the provision of auxiliary services and aids (Tucker, 1996). Examples of modifications in these areas include:

- Modifications in academic requirements that do not result in a fundamental alteration in the standards or technical requirements of the program;
- changes in the length of time allotted to complete a course or degree program;
- alternative testing formats, textbooks on tape or other accommodations as indicated on a case-by-case basis.

Institutions are not required to make alterations or adjustments if the adjustment would result in a *fundamental alteration* to the standards of the program. This requirement has been the focus of much attention in the application of ADA and Section 504 to postsecondary education.

For example, in *Wynne v. Tufts University Medical School* (1991), a medical student with dyslexia requested an oral examination rather than a multiple-choice examination in a biochemistry course. The medical school investigated alternative testing formats and decided that the multiple-choice examination not only tested the fundamental knowledge base, but also tested the student's ability to make informed choices that were deemed necessary and fundamental to the medical training offered. The courts supported the school's denial of the alternative testing format.

In a similar case, *Ohio Civil Rights Commission v. Case Western Reserve University* (1996) a nursing student requested an accommodation that would allow her to complete a nursing program on a part-time basis and do much of her work from home using case studies rather than having direct experience in the clinical setting. The request was denied for two reasons: First, it was the opinion that making clinical judgments at the bedside was fundamental to the program. Second, any alteration in the time for completion of the program would result in hardship to the program as it rotated other students through the clinical sequence.

Like the other components of the law, the issue of reasonable accommodation was undefined in the initial legislation and thus is being determined by case law. The courts have argued that, if a college student is able to establish that he or she is disabled and qualified for admission to the program, the institution has the responsibility to explore accommodations or academic adjustments that will allow the student to participate in its academic and nonacademic programs on a nondiscriminatory basis. Court decisions contend that the college must review the qualifications of the student on a case-by-case basis to determine the student's ability to succeed given appropriate learning strategies, effective academic adjustments, and effective use of technology. Institutions are not required to make fundamental alterations in the standards of the program in the accommodations. However, they are required to investigate all reasonable alternatives, including their feasibility, cost, and effect on the academic program, when a suggested academic adjustment cannot be provided.

Not all courts agree on the extent to which an institution must demonstrate that it is not reasonable to provide suggested academic modifications. For example, a student who is blind was denied admission to medical school because, in the opinion of the medical school, she was not qualified to observe or perform fundamental activities of the medical program, such as the reading of EKGs and X-rays in a reasonably independent manner (*Ohio Civil Rights Commission v. Case Western Reserve University*, 1996). However, a student at Temple University Medical School was provided accommodations, such as books on tape, readers, modified lectures, and an aide who described tables, charts, EKGs, and X-rays, and provided descriptions of conditions so that she could meet the program requirements. The independent ability to perform the tasks was not considered to be germane for the Temple University medical program. But, the court held that Case Western Reserve University had no obligation to investigate or to provide the same level of accommodations provided at another institution.

ACCOMMODATIONS AND ACADEMIC ADJUSTMENTS

A learning disability is the most frequently occurring disability among college students with disabilities (Henderson, 1999). However, as mentioned earlier, neither the ADA nor Section 504 define *learning disability*. The issue is that students with learning disabilities have a variety of needs for accommodations. For example, the disability may affect the student's ability to learn effectively in a specific subject area, affect the student's perceptual or processing abilities, or have an impact on the ability to recall or reproduce information. Furthermore, the student may excel in one area and yet be unable to deal with information in another.

Because different types of learning disabilities can manifest themselves in different ways, a range of accommodations must be made available to students. However, an institution is not required to provide personal attendants, individually prescribed devices, or readers for personal use or study or other devices of a personal nature. It is only obligated to provide tutorial services to students with disabilities in the same manner as it does to students without disabilities. An important point is that an institution may not charge for necessary accommodations. Table 14.2 summarizes types of accommodations that may be offered.

In spite of the number of students with learning disabilities and the number of accommodations that are provided, a serious problem continues to exist. There is an absence of empirical research on the educational outcomes that would support the types of accommodations most appropriate and effective for students with learning disabilities (Finn, 1998).

Course Waivers and Substitutions

A frequent accommodation that students request is for waiver of a course, a course requirement, or the substitution of a required course for another. Although curriculum waivers are expressly cited in the regulations governing Section 504 and Title II of the ADA, there is no absolute requirement that they be granted. The decision of whether a course waiver for a student with a disability should be granted begins with the question of whether the student is "otherwise qualified" for the program as defined by the ADA and Section 504. Section 504 defines "otherwise qualified" as an individual who, although disabled, "meets the academic and technical standards requisite to admission or participation in the program or activity" (34 CFR § 104.3, k, 3). The institution must make such reasonable accommodations that may be available to assist the student in meeting the program standards unless such accommodations "would fundamentally alter the nature of the program or activity" (28 CFR § 35.130, b, 7).

TABLE 14.2
Types of Accommodations for Certain Students With Learning Disabilities

> Extend time allowed to complete a course or a program.
> Adapt the method of instruction.
> Substitute one course for another required course.
> Modify or waive foreign language requirements.
> Allow extended time on examinations.
> Provide essay rather than objective exams (or otherwise modifying test formats).
> Allow the student to take an examination in a quiet distraction-free room.
> Substitute oral, typed, or written exams for written exams.
> Allow a student to clarify or rephrase questions in his or her own words before answering.
> Provide an alternative to optical scanning score sheets.
> Allow the use of calculators, secretary's desk reference, or dictionary during examinations.
> Allow a student to tape lectures.
> Provide tutors.
> Provide note takers.
> Provide taped textbooks or e-books on-line.
> Provide readers for examinations.

Source: Tucker & Goldstein (1991). Reprinted with permission from the Legal Rights of Persons with Disabilities: An Analysis of Federal Law. Copyright © 1992 by L.P.R. Productions, 747 Dresher Road, Horsham, PA 19044-0980. All rights reserved. For more information on Legal Rights of Persons with Disabilities: An Analysis of Federal Law, please call 1-800-341-7874, ext. 347.

Academic requirements that are fundamental to a program of instruction or to a particular degree program of an educational institution need not be waived. However, an institution must make a reasoned deliberation to determine whether the course at issue is fundamental to its educational program. The institution must also demonstrate that it considered alternative means of accommodating students with disabilities and the cost and feasibility of the accommodation. If the institution declines to grant a waiver, it must demonstrate that it came to this decision after full consideration that available alternatives would lower academic standards or require fundamental alteration in the program requirements.

For example, as mentioned earlier, in *Wynne v. Tufts University School of Medicine* (1991, 1992), a student with dyslexia claimed that his medical school violated the Rehabilitation Act of 1973. The violation was based on refusal of his requested accommodation that an oral examination replace a multiple-choice examination in biochemistry. After several appeals, the university was able to satisfy the court on three counts. First, it had considered alternative means. Second, the alternatives would have resulted in lowering the academic standards of the program, and, finally, the alternatives would substantially devalue the medical degree from the university.

Waiver of Foreign Language and Mathematics Requirements

Mathematics Requirements. The most frequently requested course waivers or substitutions are in areas of mathematics and foreign language. Requests for course substitutions or waivers are made on the basis of their impact on program standards. For example, it would not be reasonable for a student majoring in accounting to request a waiver of coursework in mathematics because the ability to perform mathematical operations is fundamental to accounting functions. However, it may be reasonable to allow a substitution of a course in logic for a mathematics requirement for a student who is majoring in history.

In *City University of New York* (1992), the college refused to waive a general mathematics requirement for a student with a learning disability, but offered to provide other accommodations to the student, including substitution of the particular mathematics course for another course, use of a calculator, and allowing extended time during tests. The student refused the accommodations offered, insisting on the waiver. The U.S. Office of Civil Rights (OCR) ruled that the college had not violated Section 504 by refusing to waive the general mathematics requirement, because the college considered the requirement to be essential, and all students graduating from the institution were required to demonstrate competency in mathematics. The university had offered reasonable alternative to the requirement without fundamentally altering its requirement.

In a similar case, in *Southwest Texas State University* (1991), the OCR found that the university violated Section 504 when it refused to allow a student with a learning disability to substitute another course for a required algebra course. In this case, the university did not show that the algebra requirement was essential to the program. The student's advisors believed that there were two other courses that could have been substituted for the algebra course without a fundamental alteration in the program.

Foreign Language Requirements. Nearly 52% of adult students with learning disabilities have difficulty learning a foreign language (Vogel, 1998). In addition to difficulty learning their native spoken language, adult students often have continued language problems that compromise their ability to listen to, speak, write, and spell in a second language (Downey & Snyder, 2000; Hill, Downey, Sheppard, & Williamson, 1995). As a consequence, students with learning disabilities frequently make requests for waiver of foreign language requirements in both secondary and postsecondary education.

Many institutions permit students with documented difficulty in learning a second language to substitute a course in literature or culture in place of studying a foreign language. However, *Indiana University Northwest* (1992) refused to waive a foreign language requirement for a student with a learning disability because it considered foreign language to be essential to the degree that the student sought. The institution offered to accommodate the student's needs by offering extended time on the examinations, giving permission to take the course through correspondence school, and the provision of foreign language tutors.

In another much publicized and important case, Boston University was successful in demonstrating that the study of foreign language is fundamental to its century-old standards in the College of Arts and Sciences. It did not permit waiver or substitution of foreign language study requested by a group of students with learning disabilities (*Guckenberger v. Boston University*, 1998). After being challenged by the courts to provide deliberative justification of its foreign language standard, the university was able to provide sufficient justification that the study of foreign language was central to its philosophy of a liberal arts education. It provided the courts with the steps that it would take to provide assistance to students with learning disabilities to meet the standard successfully. After a hotly contested series of court actions, the court sided with the university and decided that it would not interfere with the standard that the university established. Thus, the students' request to be exempted from foreign language study was denied.

Other academic institutions have sought alternative pathways. At the University of Colorado at Boulder, the Foreign Language Modification Program demonstrated that students with difficulty learning a foreign language were able to achieve foreign language proficiency when provided appropriate instruction modified to accommodate their individual needs (Downey & Hill, 1992; Downey & Snyder, 2000; Hill et al., 1995). This special program illustrates that, as the requests for waiver of foreign language requirements increase, colleges and universities will be required to develop policies to maintain the fundamental standards established for their academic program if these standards include the study of foreign language. If necessary, academic institutions will be expected to establish appropriate modifications and accommodations to support those students with learning disabilities who are required to study foreign language.

A final issue is that, when accommodations are required, they must be provided in a timely manner. These include adjustment to the timelines for the completion of the degree, substitution of course requirements, adaptation in the way courses are delivered, and use of tape recorders in classrooms (*San Francisco State University,* 1997). As noted earlier, colleges and universities are not required to provide personal health care attendants, readers for personal use or study, or other personal devices or services.

Documentation

The provision of reasonable accommodation and academic adjustments is based on the impact of the disability in relation to the student's ability to perform the essential functions of the academic program or course. Documentation of disability and its impact on the student's ability to function has been an important issue in postsecondary education.

To receive the accommodations provided to persons with disability, a student must first provide documentation that he or she is eligible to be identified as a person with a disability. Second, the documentation must indicate how the disability affects the student's ability to perform the essential functions of the course or program. Institutions are not required to provide accommodations or academic adjustments until the student provides documentation of disability and has expressed the need for accommodation. A further point is that the documentation provided must be sufficiently comprehensive to specify the nature of the disorder or impairment, describe how the abilities and limitations of the student relate to the particular program at issue, and make recommendations that describe how the student's difficulties can be compensated. The documentation must establish the need for a particular accommodation or adjustment. An example comes from Columbia University (*Pell v. Trustees of Columbia University,* 1998). A student with dyslexia alleged that the university violated Section 504 by refusing to exempt her from the foreign language requirement. In support of her request, she provided two letters from her physician. The letters did not specifically recommend that the student be exempted from foreign language. In spite of the university's repeated requests to provide the necessary documentation, the student declined, saying that the physician's documentation of disability was sufficient. The court disagreed with the student and rejected her claim.

However, all students with a disability do not require accommodations and the accommodations may differ depending on the particular situation or course being taken. For example, a student with a missing finger may be impaired in a course that requires manual dexterity, but may not need accommodation in a course that relies on lecture and demonstration. Once the student has provided sufficient documentation from a properly licensed or certified professional, the college or university is responsible for providing reasonable accommodations that meet four standards. Accommodations must not result in an unfair advantage to the student, not require significant alteration to the fundamental standards of the program or activity, not result in lowering academic standards, or not cause undue financial hardship or burden to the institution.

Recency of Documentation.   Two important issues related to documentation are the recency of the documentation and the qualifications of the person providing the documentation. The first issue is how recent the documentation must be to support the eligibility for services as a person with a disability. *Portland State University* (1992) instituted a 3-year rule for documentation. In other words, documentation of a disability needed to be completed within 3 years of the request for accommodations and academic adjustments. This meant that students who had been identified with a disability while in secondary school would need to be recertified as a junior or senior in postsecondary education.

In 1997, several students with a learning disability at Boston University challenged a similar rule saying that the University improperly implemented a 3-year retesting requirement. (*Guckenberger v. Boston University,* 1997). The argument was made that, once an individual reached 18 years of age, there was no demonstrated change in a specific learning disability, such as dyslexia. However, because the symptoms of attention deficit hyperactivity disorder (ADHD) can change in different environments, are often treated with medication, and often remit from adolescence to adulthood, persons with ADHD can be required to be retested before being identified as a qualified person with a disability.

It is important to recognize that the specific accommodations needed for a particular course or program can change over time or can vary with the situation. Documentation of need for an accommodation in one setting may be inappropriate for the accommodation in another setting. Accommodations necessary for a course in English literature, for example, may be very different from those needed for a course in art history. Any documentation should provide evidence of the impact of the disability on the particular course or program being considered, as well as the specific accommodation necessary for that situation.

Qualification of the Evaluator.   The documentation of persons with disabilities and the recommendations for appropriate accommodations must come from an appropriately licensed or certified professional. At *California State University–Long Beach* (1992), a student was denied eligibility as a student with a disability because, in spite of repeated requests from the institution, she did not provide documentation of the disability from an appropriately licensed physician. She provided a statement of learning disability from an optometrist. The courts ruled that an optometrist was able to provide documentation of an ocular dysfunction, but could not provide documentation of a learning disability.

In *Guckenberger v. Boston University* (1997) the institution did not want to accept documentation provided by a school psychologist because the school psychologist did not hold a doctorate. The courts ruled that an appropriately licensed school psychologist had tested the student and required the university to accept the documentation of the disability provided by the appropriately licensed professional. In contrast, in *Bartlett v. New York State Board of Law Examiners* (1997), it was determined that members of the New York State Bar were not qualified to determine whether or not the candidate for the bar examination was not eligible for accommodations as a person with a disability. The basis for this ruling was that the examiners did not hold the credentials for making the determination of the presence or absence of a learning disability and, thus, were unable to determine the relevance of the requested accommodations.

INSTRUCTION OF COLLEGE AND UNIVERSITY STUDENTS WITH DISABILITIES

Instructional Modifications

Raising awareness among faculty at postsecondary institutions is essential to meeting the needs of postsecondary students with disabilities. Because the number of students with disabilities has increased so dramatically in recent years, it is unlikely that many instructors have had the opportunity to learn how to provide instruction to students with disabilities. It may also be the case that some faculty are primarily interested in their research and scholarship and place a secondary interest on pedagogy. Furthermore, their interest in developing pedagogy for students with disabilities may be compromised by their belief that these students are not eligible or qualified for postsecondary education in the first place. They may not be aware of their legal responsibilities, the limitations of reasonable accommodations, and the various techniques that may be effective with students with disabilities.

In a survey conducted by Leyser, Vogel, Wyland, and Bruille (1998), it was determined that many faculty had limited training in working with students with disabilities and limited knowledge of the types of accommodations that may be necessary to meet students' needs. Although most faculty indicated support for integration of students with disabilities into their courses, they also recognized that they had little information about university resources and supports. Hill (1996) reported that faculty were most willing to allow tape recordings or lectures, provide a list of readings, and provide detailed syllabi. They were less willing to read material presented on overheads, provide lecture notes, or use a variety of media to present course content. As faculty move to include course materials into online and distance education formats, the need for accessibility of course materials for persons with disabilities will increase.

Universal Design

A recent trend in the education of postsecondary students with disabilities involves the use of *universal curriculum design.* This concept is based on the principles of universal environmental design, which increases physical access to buildings, transportation systems, and other environmental systems. This type of universal design benefits not only those with disabilities, but also makes the lives of many easier.

Universal curriculum design is grounded in the principle that learning can and should be made accessible to all students regardless of their learning abilities and needs. It involves multimode teaching and multimode assessment to enhance the learning of all students, including those with disabilities. Universal design uses instructional strategies that address various learning modalities of all learners in order to benefit the diverse student body. Principles of universal design are incorporated into the planning and delivery of instruction rather than being offered as separate accommodations, much as architectural designs are included in the planning of new construction, such as elevators and special lifts.

The goal of universal design in to be as inclusive as possible, thus meeting the needs of more of the student body and reducing the need for academic accommodations for students with learning disabilities (Silver, Bourke, & Strehorn, 1998) According to the Center of Applied Special Technology (CAST; Orkwis, 1999), three principles of universal design allow the curriculum to provide (1) multiple representations of the information being presented, (2) multiple or modified means of expression, and (3) multiple or modified means of motivating and engaging students. Faculty use strategies and materials that are flexible and adaptable for all students and thus maximize the potential to meet the needs of students with disabilities in a positive and efficient manner. A premise is that universal design has the potential to offer various methods of representation, engagement, and expression. However, the efficacy of universal design in instruction still remains a matter for rigorous research documentation.

• • • • •

Research in the area of postsecondary students with disabilities continues to emerge. Issues related to distance learning, the use of classroom technology, and universal design as primary means of delivering instruction present challenges to students with disabilities. The number of students with disabilities in colleges and universities will continue to grow in the foreseeable future. Developing policies and programs is critical to ensure that all students with disabilities have equal access to academic and nonacademic programs and services provided by postsecondary institutions. The U. S. Department of Education has begun to support the development of model demonstration projects to improve the quality of postsecondary education for students with disabilities. These programs should provide insight in the strategies that produce effective results in meeting the needs of college and university students with disabilities.

Thomas (2000) provided three guidelines that may offer help to institutions dedicated to offering a quality education to students with disabilities:

1. Establish and publish guidelines for students to follow in providing documentation of disability.
2. Maintain awareness of and access to new technology and instructional techniques that facilitate the learning of students with disabilities.
3. Promote ongoing training of administrators, faculty, and staff regarding the needs of students with disabilities.

The solution to the challenges of meeting the needs of postsecondary students with disabilities must be determined through collaboration and teamwork among all those involved in the educational process.

REFERENCES

Abbott v. Bragdon, 107 F.3d .934, 2 0A .D. D. 616 §1.03,10.01 (1st Cir. 1997).

Alexander v. Choate, 469 U.S. 287 (1985).

Americans with Disabilities Act of 1990, 42 U. S. C. § 12102 *et seq.* (1998); Title II, §12131 *et seq.* (1998) ; 28 C.F. R §§ 35.101-35.191 (1998); Title III, §12181 *et seq* 1998); 28 C.F. R. § 36.101-36.608.

Bartlett v. New York State Board of Law Examiners, 970 Suppl. 1094 (S. D. N. Y. 1997).

Bowers v. NCAA, 9. F. Supp. 2nd 460 (D. N. J., 1998).

California State University–Long Beach. Complaint No 09-92-211-1. (OCR. Region IX, 1992).

City University of New York 3 NDLR ¶ 104 (OCR Region II, 1992).

Downey, D., & Hill, B. (1992, April). *Accommodating the foreign language learning disabled student.* Paper delivered at the Foreign Language Learning and Learning Disabilities Conference, American University, Washington, DC.

Downey, D. M., & Snyder, L. (2000). College students with LLD: The phonological core as risk for failure in foreign language classes. *Topics in Language Disorders,* 21(1), 82–92.

The Family Educational Rights and Privacy Act (FERPA) (1990), 20 USCA § 1232 1232(g); 34C. D. R. Part 99 (1989).

Finn, L. L. (1998). Student's perceptions of beneficial learning disability accommodations and services at the postsecondary level. *Journal of Postsecondary Education and Disability, 13*(1), 46–67.

Gonzales v. National Board of Medical Examiners, 60 F. Supp. 2d 703, 138 Ed. Law Reporter 403. 16 NDLR P 56 E. (D. Michigan 1999).

Guckenberger v. Boston University, 957 F. Supp. 306, 327 (D. Mass., 1997).

Guckenberger v. Boston University, 8 F. Supp. 2d 82, 91, 128 Ed. Law Rep. 181 (D. Mass., 1998).

HEATH Resource Center (1999). Profile of 1998 college freshmen with disabilities. Washington DC: American Council of Education.

Henderson, C. (1999). *Update on college students with disabilities.* Washington, DC: HEATH Resource Center.

Hill, J. L. (1996). Speaking out: Perceptions of students with disabilities regarding adequacy of services and willingness of faculty to make accommodations. *Journal of Postsecondary Education and Disability, 12*(1), 22–43.

Hill, B., Downey, D., Sheppard, M., & Williamson, V. (1995). *Accommodating the needs of students with severe language learning difficulties in modified foreign language classes. Broadening the Frontiers of Foreign Language Education.* Lincoln, IL: National Textbook.

Indiana University Northwest. 3 NDLR ¶ 150 (OCR Region V, 1992).

Individuals with Disabilities Education Act (1990). 20 U. S. C. § 1400 *et seq.*

Individuals With Disabilities Education Act (IDEA) (1997), 20 USCA § 1401.

Jarrow, J. E. (1997). *The ADA's impact on postsecondary education.* Columbus, OH: Association of Higher Education and Disability.

Kincaid, J. E. (1994). *Issues in higher education and disability law.* Columbus, OH: Association of Higher Education and Disability.

Leyser, Y., Vogel, S., Wyland, S., & Bruille, A. (1998). Faculty attitudes and practices regarding students with learning disabilities: Two decades after implementation. *Journal of Postsecondary Education and Disability, 13*(3), 5–19.

Ohio Civil Rights Commission v. Case Western Reserve University, 666 N. E. 2d. 1376 (Ohio, 1996).

Orkwis, R. (1999). *Curriculum access and universal design for living.* (ERIC Digest: E586, EDO-99-14). Reston, VA: The Council for Exceptional Education.

Pazer v. New York State Board of Law Examiners, 849 F. Supp 284 (S. D. N. Y. 1994).

Pell v. Trustees of Columbia University 11 NDLR ¶ 322 (S. D. N. Y. 1998)

Portland State University 4. NDLR 212. OCR Region X (1992).

Price v. National Board of Medical Examiners, 966 F. Supp. 419 (S. D. W. Va. 1997).

Public Law 94–142 (1995). Education For All Handicapped Chilcren Act (EAHCA) 20 USCA § 1400.

Rehabilitation Act of 1973, as amended by the Rehabilitation Act Amendments of 1974, 29 U. S. C. § 794 (1998); 34 C. F. R. §§ 104.1-104.7 (1998).

San Francisco State University, 11 National Disability Law Reporter 722 (OCR 1997).

Silver, P., Bourke, A. & Strehorn, K. C. (1998). Universal instructional design in higher education: An approach for inclusion. *Equity & Excellence in Education, 31*(1), 47–51.

Southeastern Community College v. Davis, 442 U. S. 397 (1979).

Southwest Texas State University Complaint No. 06-90-2084 (OCR Region VI, 1991).

Thomas, S. B. (2000). College students and disability law. *Journal of Special Education,* *33*(4), 248–257.

Tucker, B. (1996). Application of the Americans with Disabilities Act (ADA) and Sect. 504 to colleges and universities: An overview and discussion of special issues relating to students. *Journal of College and University Law, 23 Journal of College and University Law, 1,* 1–41.

Tucker, B. P., & Goldstein, B. A. (1991). *Legal rights of persons with disabilities: an analysis of federal law. Vol. 1.* Hornsham, PA: LRP Publications.

Vogel, S. (1998). Adults with learning disabilities. In S. Vogel & S. Reder (Eds.), *Learning disabilities and adult education* (pp. 5–28). Baltimore, MD: Paul H. Brookes.

Wynne v. Tufts University School of Medicine, 932 F. 2d 19 (1st Cir. 1991).

Wynne v. Tufts University School of Medicine, 976 F. 2d 791 (1st Cir. 1992).

Author Index

Subject Index

A

African American Vernacular English (AAVE)
age-referenced approach, 120–127
auxiliary verbs, 116, 123, 129–130, 140, 141
AAVE and SAE features, overlap between, 115, 118, 125, 127, 130–131
clause length measures, 123
code switching, 124
complex syntax, 123, 124, 125
contrastive dialect analysis approach, 129–133
contrastive features, 128
cultural identification, 119
culturally less biased measures of language processing, 110, 126–127
dialect density measure (DDM), 124, 125, 126, 129–130
ebonics controversy, 113
factors in learning to read and spell
cultural conflict hypothesis, 113
instructional hypothesis, 114
moderator variable hypothesis, 114
phonological sensitivity hypothesis, 115, 119, 125, 134, 138, 140
linguistic markers of spoken language impairment, 125, 129, 133, 141
linguistic zeros, 116, 123
morphosyntactic development, 118, 120, 125–126
noncontrastive analysis approach, 127–129
noncontrastive features, 128
obligatory linguistic contexts, 129, 133, 141
phonological features, 117
regional variations, 117, 120, 127
Southern African American Vernacular English (SAAVE), 129, 130, 133
reading, 140
type and frequency of feature use, 119
variables affecting, 124, 126
variable inclusions, 116, 117, 119, 123, 126, 128, 129, 141
co-occurrence relations, 126
zero copula, 116, 130, 133
Americans with Disabilities Act (ADA) (1990), 297, 298, 309–310, 316, 318, 324
comparison of provisions
with IDEA, 319, 320, 321
with Rehabilitation Act (1973), 319, 321, 322
with Section 504, 319, 320, 321, 322, 323, 324
impairment, definition of, 323
reasonable accommodations, 310
in post-secondary education, 322, 326–327, 329–333
Ascendancy hypothesis, 14
illusory recovery, 14
Attention deficit-hyperactivity disorder (ADHD), 100–101

C

Causes of reading disability
causal chain model, 7
cause and consequence, 13, 20, 58
distributed causality perspective, 10, 13, 14
unitary perspective, 8, 13, 14
phonological core deficit, 7
phonological skills, 33
Classroom discourse, 152, 157, 159, 161, 170–171

355